PLACES

ENERGY, ECOLOGY, AND THE ENVIRONMENT SERIES

ISSN 1919-7144

This new series will explore how we live and work with each other on the planet, how we use its resources, and the issues and events that shape our thinking on energy, ecology and the environment. The Alberta experience in a global arena will be showcased.

PLACES
LINKING NATURE, CULTURE AND PLANNING

J. GORDON NELSON AND
PATRICK L. LAWRENCE

UNIVERSITY OF
CALGARY
PRESS

University of Calgary Press
2500 University Drive NW
Calgary, Alberta
Canada T2N 1N4
www.uofcpress.com

LIBRARY AND ARCHIVES CANADA CATALOGUING IN PUBLICATION

Nelson, J. G. (James Gordon), 1932-
         Places : linking nature, culture and planning / J. Gordon Nelson and
Patrick L. Lawrence.

(Energy, ecology, and the environment, ISSN 1919-7144 ; 1)
Includes bibliographical references and index.
ISBN 978-1-55238-254-7

         1. Environmental protection–Planning. 2. Ecological assessment
(Biology). 3. Human ecology. 4. Sustainable development. 5. Land use.
I. Lawrence, Patrick Lloyd, 1965- II. Title. III. Series: Energy,
ecology, and the environment series ; 1

HC79.E5N445 2009   333.7   C2009-902707-0

The University of Calgary Press acknowledges the support of the Alberta Foundation for the Arts for our publications. We acknowledge the financial support of the Government of Canada through the Book Publishing Industry Development Program (BPIDP) for our publishing activities. We acknowledge the financial support of the Canada Council for the Arts for our publishing program.

   Canada Council Conseil des Arts
for the Arts du Canada

Printed and bound in Canada by Marquis
∞ This book is printed on FSC Silva & Flo Dull paper

Cover design by Melina Cusano
Page design and typesetting by Melina Cusano

CONTENTS

LIST OF FIGURES

LIST OF TABLES

Dedicated to the University of Waterloo
with thanks for the many challenges and opportunities.

PREFACE

Climatologists warn us of the threat of global warming. Geologists talk of rising risks from hazards such as earthquakes and volcanic eruptions. Economists focus on growing inflation or unemployment. Biologists express alarm about the increasing number of species at risk. But rarely do we hear about how all these changes come together to affect the character of a place. Yet the places that we live in, visit, or hear about have been changing in numerous interacting ways for centuries.

Changes have been especially pronounced since World War II, when large-scale chemical, plastic, and other goods, and new machinery and other technology began to transform cities, countryside, and wilderness in Canada and around the globe. Much of the change was due to widespread enthusiasm for development, particularly the progressive stages of the economic development model introduced by Walter Rostow in the 1950s and quickly adopted by new post-WWII institutions such as the World Bank. Investment of financial, technical, and other capital was seen as the means of moving places from a low-income rural and underdeveloped way of life to an industrial, urban, and advanced one.

Unfortunately the extent and profundity of changes in places that we and other life inhabit is frequently poorly understood. People see, sense, or are partially informed about changes but do not comprehend their interactions and extent. They do not know how to think about places in a comprehensive way. They are not taught or encouraged to gain a full sense of place.

This book is intended for all those concerned about the history and future of places everywhere and particularly students, professionals, and civic decision-makers who aspire to better things in the future. The book aims to move beyond the specialized view of places given to us through disciplines or fields of study such as geology, biology, economics, sociology, and land use. These specialized approaches have their values. But limited descriptions of places carry big costs. They do not paint the big picture needed to understanding the complexity of places. And when specialized information is emphasized in planning and decision-making, groups and people with other interests and values tend to be neglected or left out. Their contributions to and needs in shaping environments, communities, and places are not adequately addressed in decision- making.

The approach put forward in this book to link various specialities into a fuller and more meaningful understanding of places is the ABC method. This was developed in numerous studies in Canada, Europe, and Asia in the last three decades. The ABC method links geology and the earth sciences (Abiotic), plant and animal communities (Biotic), and land use, institutions, and other human (Cultural) information in a systematic, interactive, dynamic, and comprehensive portrayal of places. To understand places you need to know your ABC's!

While the book is intended to offer something to all those concerned with places, some parts will be of greater interest to some readers than others. The organization of the book illustrates the flexibility of the method. It can be used at various scales for many different kinds of places. It can also be applied quickly or over a longer time using a variety of information and resources, including computer and other new technology. Part I contains chapters illustrating Detailed Analytical Applications of the method. These should be of particular interest to professionals and others aiming to achieve the wider and deeper understanding of places needed in planning, management, education, and decision-making. Citizens working to become more fully informed and involved in the future of places would benefit from these more detailed and complex chapters as well. Understanding places in these terms would assist citizens wishing to participate more effectively in the formal aspects of planning, management, and decision-making.

Subsequent parts of the book include chapters that are less technical and of more general interest. The chapters in Part II are examples of Focused Summaries of Detailed Analytical Studies. They are intended to highlight and focus detailed study findings for particular planning or other purposes. These chapters are easier for most people to understand and should be of particular value to busy decision-makers. The chapters in Part III, on Comprehensive Overviews and Assessments, aim at achieving a broad understanding of places by using the ABC method as an organizational framework for information needed to get a general sense of a place for planning or other purposes. The chapters in Part IV, on Rapid Reconnaissance Studies, use the ABC method in a similar way to gain a quick understanding of places in a limited time. The chapters in Parts II, III, and IV should be useful to the general reader and are relevant to the specialist and professional as well. Part V includes chapters on use of the ABC in education and the preparation of landscape guides as well as discussion of progress and future prospects for the ABC method.

The reader should begin by reviewing Chapters 1 and 2 on the ABC concept and its origins. He or she can then proceed to either Part I, II, III, IV, or V, depending on personal background and intentions. In other words, the various parts of the book are valuable in their own right as well as providing entry points to the reading and use of the whole.

Overall, this book responds directly to recent calls for a stronger sense of place among professionals, decision-makers, and citizens. These calls arise largely because economic and other proposals for change do not take sufficient advance account of the environmental, social, and other effects of proposals. These effects are consequently inadequately understood and dealt with, leading frequently to protracted conflicts. If the effects are anticipated at all, they tend to be seen imperfectly as side effects or externalities which can be dealt with as the proposed project unfolds. Many of the ensuing difficulties could be anticipated and more effectively planned for in advance. This could be done by using an ABC approach to build a broad or comprehensive sense of place for proposals in all their geologic, biotic, land use, social, and institutional dimensions.

Gordon Nelson, Waterloo, April 2009
Patrick Lawrence, Toledo, April 2009

ACKNOWLEDGMENTS

A book embracing roughly four decades of research obviously reflects the contribution of many organizations and people. Funding and other support for research on various chapters was provided by the Social Science and Humanities Research Council of Canada, Parks Canada, and other agencies of the Canadian government, the Ontario Ministry of Natural Resources and other agencies of the Ontario provincial government, the Canadian International Development Agency (CIDA), Canadian Arctic Resources Committee, the Donner Foundation, the Ontario Ministry of Culture, the Royal Canadian Geographical Society, the Grand River Conservation Authority, Saugeen Valley Conservation Authority, Long Point Biosphere Foundation, Carpathian Ecoregion Project, World Wildlife Fund (WWF), Heritage Resources Centre, and the University of Waterloo.

The work could not have been done without their assistance, nor that of many interested people. A number of these individuals are co-authors of certain chapters. Many professional colleagues, students, and people interested in the study areas also provided advice, assistance, and other support. To mention even most of them is beyond the space available here. Indeed, in many cases, their names lie at the edge of possible recall. We are in debt to all those people and thank them very much for their help.

The first author is especially grateful to Patrick Lawrence, the principal co-author of this book, who gave much aid in the editing and preparation of the manuscript. He is also most grateful to John Theberge, who was an early partner in the development of the ABC method in the Yukon. Jamie Bastedo was a principal force in the work. Paul Smith and Paul Grigoriew made substantial contributions at that time as well. Caron Olive and Ellsworth LeDrew were fine collaborators in the Indonesian and Asian studies. Andy Skibicki did much good work on studies in Ontario. Special thanks go to Lucy Sportza and Graham Whitelaw for their invaluable comments on a late draft of this manuscript. Thanks are offered to Barry Levely for assistance with the preparation of the maps, Ashleigh Beyer for her work on the manuscript, and Mila Kaufman for administrative support. The final preparation of the manuscript owes much to the initial editing and design skills of Beth Dempster and the final editing and design by Peter Enman, Melina Cusano, and others at the University of Calgary Press. Whatever strengths this book has are due to these supportive organizations and friends, and I am greatly in their debt.

Gordon Nelson, Waterloo, April 2009

I

INTRODUCING THE ABC METHOD: TOWARDS COMPREHENSIVE AND ACCESSIBLE INFORMATION SYSTEMS FOR CONSERVATION AND DEVELOPMENT[1]

J.G. Nelson, J. Theberge, and J. Bastedo

INTRODUCTION

The way people understand and value places strongly influences decisions they make about their conservation and development. Places are more than mere locations. They consist of a broad set of natural and human processes and features, whose interactions and characteristics change through time. Bedrock, weather and climate, plants, animals, soils, human land uses, technology, institutions and social learning, or culture, vary among and define places as we know them.

Yet people tend to understand places primarily from a narrow economic, social, or natural perspective, depending on their knowledge, experience, and special interests. They tend to plan and make decisions about the conservation and development of places in terms of these more limited views. Their plans and decisions reflect the focused information that is generally provided by influential agencies and organizations as a basis for understanding places and the effects of impending change.

The nature of the available information is a critical factor in understanding and making decisions about places, their conservation, and development. Information is important in several ways, including its character, scope, and level of detail. Some information can be said to be more objective or descriptive than other information, for example, numerical data on areas covered by forests, by crops, or by other types of land use. Other information is more interpretive. It involves assessment of, or judgment about, the significance of certain features or processes. Such assessments often differ among individuals and groups involved in making a decision. Thus, woodlots consisting of diverse, relatively undisturbed forest will generally be seen as more significant by naturalists than by farmers. Historic buildings are more likely to be seen as worthy of protection by a historian than a developer. Such differences in assessments about the significance of forests, soil types, historic structures, or other features or processes often are related to the goals, values, and preferences of the different groups involved in a decision.

To be equitable in the sense of being open to all concerned groups and persons, the information field should be as comprehensive as possible. It should be pluralist in the sense that the available information is accessible and significant from the standpoint of many different values, perspectives, and interests. Without a wide range of information, some groups could be disadvantaged in decision-making. The type of information they need may not be in the information pool made available for a decision. Furthermore the information should be presented in language and format that is understandable to a wide range of groups and individuals. This is a major challenge to specialists and to thinkers who work to bring diverse technical and local knowledge together in ways accessible to as many concerned parties as possible.

A comprehensive and accessible information system is, therefore, fundamental to effective and equitable planning and decision-making for conservation and development. The foregoing argument may seem obvious, but it is constantly violated in information systems that have been developed to make decisions. For example, some resource and environmental inventory systems include geologic and biological information but not information on land use or land tenure, population distribution, or other socio-economic or cultural topics of value in deciding on new projects or programs. As another example, even when the information systems are slanted toward natural or biophysical information, certain data of interest to recreational or conservation groups may be missing, for example, on animals or wildlife. A lot of this unevenness arises from the fact that information systems are generally prepared by professionals and reflect their disciplinary expertise and language rather than those of members of other disciplines or of most citizens. Access to comprehensive and accessible information is therefore a major cross-disciplinary, professional and civic concern.

THEORY AND METHOD

Thoughts about the need for access to wide-ranging and diverse information on places for planning by many different people led a number of colleagues at the University of Waterloo to begin working, in the 1970s, on a flexible and comprehensive system known as the ABC resource survey method. The method provides for the collection of a wide range of information of Abiotic (geologic, geomorphologic, hydrologic), Biotic (plants, wildlife), and Cultural (demographic, land-use, educational, institutional) kinds.

The method also provides for collecting, evaluating, and interpreting such information in terms of its significance and constraints for certain programs, projects, and purposes in accordance with the values, preferences, and goals of different people. When applied in a more scientific sense, the method can be quite technical. When applied in a more conceptual or guiding way, it can be used in a general manner. Details on the method are available in various publications (Bastedo et al., 1984; Grigoriew et al., 1985; Nelson et al., 1988). Here we discuss fundamentals underlying the method to provide an introductory understanding of its goals and character and set the stage for the illustrative case studies in the rest of this book.

General Overview of the ABC Method

Please note that the ultimate aim of the ABC method is to get the user to think consistently about bringing Abiotic, Biotic, and human or Cultural information together in understanding and planning for places. This is done in four broad stages or levels. The first is in assembling the information needed to map and describe a place. The second and third involve selecting, mapping, and describing what is significant and what is challenging or constraining about understanding and planning for a place. The fourth level focuses on preparing a plan in response to an impending proposal or change for a place.

Figure 1.1 lays out these four stages schematically. This diagram was created to illustrate the framework of the ABC method as it developed in the 1980s. At that time the intention was to create a relatively precise method of assembling and integrating diverse kinds of information for use in planning for conservation and sustainable land use in Yukon and northern Canada. The method was seen as a technical and scientific approach to providing the kind of information demanded by environmental assessment tribunals and other formal planning and decision-making procedures in the North.

Figure 1.1 also reflects a conservation and sustainable land-use perspective in response to oil and gas, pipeline, mining, and other land-use proposals likely to have major impacts on the environment and ways of life in the North. The following section on Details of the ABC method reflects this background, as do the chapters in Part I on Detailed Analytical Studies.

Use of the method widened later when more emphasis was put on creating a better general understanding of places. This broader use is apparent in Parts II, III, IV, and V, which include Focused Summaries of Detailed Studies, Comprehensive Overviews and Assessments, Rapid Reconnaissance Studies, and Communication and Education, respectively. With this general overview as background, some readers are now in a position to understand many chapters in Parts II, III, and IV. Readers with more technical interest should read the following section on Details of the ABC method.

Details of the ABC Method

Figure 1.1 outlines the key elements in the ABC method, showing its detailed development through four levels, although the third one has

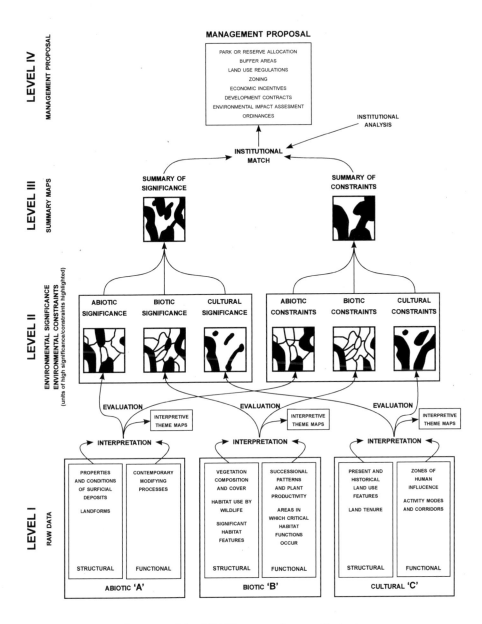

Figure 1.1   Key elements of the ABC Resource Survey Method

often not been used. The procedures of the method are rather complex and initially challenging to master. In this respect some readers with a more practical or professional bent may prefer to begin with the detailed example of the use of the method in Chapter 4 on Planning for Presqu'ile Provincial Park, Ontario, before reading the following abstract description of the procedures involved in its use.

FIRST LEVEL: THEME MAPS

At the first level, what is called "raw" or basic data are usually collected in the form of a series of theme maps. These maps can be used to give information on many Abiotic, Biotic, and Cultural topics. Although these theme or Level I maps are prepared separately and may seem to fragment the information field, they are intended collectively to help understand the whole. One way this can be achieved is by overlaying the different maps in order to understand the patterns and interactions that give a place or landscape its character and distinctiveness.

At the start of a study, it is useful to try to focus on the preparation of a number of key theme maps in the interests of economy and as a way of searching for basic patterns and guides as to what to do next. The choice of these initial maps is very important and should be done on the basis of widespread scoping or consultation in order to make sure that information of value to concerned groups and persons is not left out at this or a later stage; otherwise, their vital interests could be neglected by lack of needed information. A preliminary historical or contextual study of the settlement, land use, and human and natural history of a place can help to identify vital themes of long-time importance which can be selected for mapping at the start.

FIRST LEVEL: STRUCTURAL AND FUNCTIONAL MAPS

In the early version of the ABC method developed for use in northern Canada, each theme is covered by both a structural and a functional map. One set of maps illustrates structures or features, for example relief and slope, or vegetation patterns. These feature or structural maps are accompanied by a second set of maps showing functions or processes, for example soil erosion or forest succession. However, structural and functional data can be combined on one Abiotic or Biotic map if cost or other circumstances seem to make that efficient and effective.

One of the important innovations of the ABC method is the development of Cultural theme maps to parallel and be overlaid or compared with the Abiotic and Biotic maps. From a form or structural standpoint, many Cultural theme maps can be prepared, for example on villages and settlements, roads, railroads, airports and other communications, historic sites or place names.

A Cultural functional map also can be prepared which shows spatial patterns and interactions among settlements, roads, population distribution, and other human themes. These can often be very important in guiding planners to identify issues and challenges. The Cultural functional map brings together or integrates the Cultural themes spatially into nodes, corridors, and hinterland areas. Nodes and corridors are areas where villages, roads, industry, population, and other activities concentrate and tend to grow or decline in space and time in ways that cause us to want to plan and manage them. Hinterland or outlying areas are those where economic, social, and other themes or activities are less focused and do not generally pose planning issues in the same way as the nodes and corridors. For the foregoing reasons, the Cultural functional or process map is a key map in the ABC method. Its use is shown in Chapters 4 and 5 on Presqu'ile Provincial Park and Bruce Peninsula National Parks, Canada.

SECOND LEVEL: SIGNIFICANCE AND CONSTRAINTS MAPS

At the second level of the ABC method, other maps are prepared which integrate and evaluate the significance and constraints of information shown in the first level theme maps. Thinking about significance and constraints involves more than the essentially descriptive work typical of Level I in the ABC method. Identifying significance and constraints involves judgments and must be done in relation to the goals or objectives of governments, businesses, universities, or others interested in understanding and planning for conservation and development challenges. For example, if information from Level I is being overlaid and evaluated in order to identify and plan for important wildlife or other environmentally significant areas, then Abiotic and Biotic (or natural) information will usually be selected and ranked preferentially. In other words, unique plant or animal species, breeding areas, migratory routes, and old growth forests are all likely to be of high interest and significance. In this context also, lumbering, residential development, and other Cultural themes or patterns are likely to be identified and ranked highly as potentially important stresses or constraints that could damage or destroy significant natural areas like those just referred to.

If interest at the significance and constraints level is focused on historic, archaeological, and other aspects of cultural or human rather than natural heritage, then clearly historic sites, old cemeteries, ancient native villages, and other features will be identified and ranked highly or preferentially. In sum, differences in significance and constraints can reflect the different purposes, values, and preferences of interested persons and organizations.

It follows from the foregoing that careful scoping and consultation are very important in deciding on what is to be identified and mapped for significance and constraints. If a technical or specialist group – a consultant or government agency – is preparing a set of significance and constraints maps, then this group should consult widely to identify goals, values, and preferences and select an appropriate system. In this context, it must be recognized that no one set of maps can be considered as correct, because groups with different training, backgrounds, interests, and values could produce different sets of significance and constraints maps themselves if they wished to do so. These could be put into the public participation or decision-making arena for consideration by the agencies or groups working towards a decision.

It is important to note that the constraints map in the Cultural part of the ABC method can be prepared basically as a potential conflict-resolution map. This constraints map can be used to organize the theme maps or Level I data spatially into three general types of areas:

conflict zones, tension zones, and compatibility zones. The decisions on whether conflict, tension, or compatibility zones exist are made by studying various interacting Abiotic, Biotic, and Cultural themes or patterns in terms of criteria such as: the magnitude of effects that they have on one another or on the resources or environment on which each depends, the type of technology and disturbance associated with them, and settlement or other changes that they bring. The identification of conflict, tension, and compatibility zones can be very helpful to planners and citizens in thinking about and designing responses or solutions through negotiations and other means. Examples are given in chapters 5 and 9. Identification of conflicts and tensions can lead to negotiations, adjustments, compromises, and other resolutions.

THIRD LEVEL MAPS: INTEGRATION

The third level in the ABC method involves attempts to integrate the Abiotic, Biotic, and Cultural information in a combined map. This level has not been used consistently in work to date, although the case study of Presqu'ile Provincial Park planning in Ontario (Chapter 4) does involve Level III mapping. One basic reason for neglecting Level III is that this integration involves a mixing of different Abiotic, Biotic, and Cultural themes, concerns, and values — apples and oranges — a very difficult challenge. The tendency, therefore, has been to consider and correlate the information as it is mapped Abiotically, Biotically, and Culturally at the second level in the method. The second- and the first-level data have then been linked to the results of the analysis of institutional and planning arrangements called for in the fourth level of the method.

In some cases Abiotic, Biotic, and Cultural data are already integrated in the general manner envisioned for Level III in the ABC method. An example arises in the use of satellite imagery or aerial photography to map land cover or landscape patterns. The results of this mapping often incorporate landforms, vegetation, land uses, human settlement, and other diverse information into different land cover types or landscape mosaics (Nelson et al., 1992). Chapter 9 illustrates such an application of the ABC method in Indonesia. Similar application of the method will be made as use of satellite images increases.

FOURTH LEVEL MAPS: INSTITUTIONAL ANALYSIS

By institutional analysis is meant identifying and understanding the role and potential of the laws, regulations, guidelines, zoning, economic incentives, environmental impact assessments, or other social rules and tools that can be applied to a planning challenge. These are then assessed in terms of their strengths and weaknesses in offering promising responses. For example, in dealing with the conservation and use of natural areas in the Oak Ridges Moraine north of Toronto, Ontario, we would be interested in the strengths and weaknesses of the provincial Municipal Planning Act, the Mining Act, and other policies of the Ontario Ministry of Natural Resources, the watershed management role of Ontario Conservation Authorities, private land owner stewardship programs, and so forth. The next step would be to try to analyze the strengths and weaknesses of these in terms of important planning and management criteria such as agency track record, agency zoning, and other regulatory and co-ordination powers. In the end, the aim would be to try and match the Abiotic, Biotic, and Cultural patterns with laws, agencies, programs, and organizations likely to have the capacity to resolve challenges and to plan and manage in accordance with the natural and cultural characteristics of the different areas. Chapters 6 and 7 are very important illustrations of the use of institutional analysis as part of the Cultural component of the ABC method. The chapters are studies of the Aishihik region, Yukon, and the Eastern Beaufort Sea in the Northwest Territories of Canada in the late 1970s and early 1980s, respectively.

Early identification of planning challenges or goals to be addressed in research are of fundamental importance because they steer the organization and use of the theme or first-level mapping in the ABC method. The planning challenges or goals also steer the selection of the criteria to be used in deciding upon significance and constraints at Level II in the method. These same principles apply to the criteria selected for evaluation or assessment of land cover or landscape mosaics produced from satellite images and air photos as shown in Chapter 9 on a study in Indonesia.

For planning, it is also important to recognize that every effort should be made to identify, understand, and build on existing institutional arrangements, which often are neglected and not fully used. More innovative responses should be considered only after reaching as full an understanding as possible of current institutions and their potential application to the challenges. Another significant point is that the application of the ABC method may not lead to a planning or management response, but rather to recognition of the need for more research to provide for greater understanding, communication, or educational activities. Furthermore, while readers may think primarily of government programs, the ABC method definitely applies to the private domain. Private landowners are seen as having a strong interest in the use and conservation of their land in their own and society's interest. Institutional arrangements, which apply to private owners, are therefore of major concern as, for example, in cases involving First Nations or other cultural groups (see Chapter 5).

In summary, several key points have been stressed in regard to contemporary land-use, resource, and environmental decision-making for places. First, a wide-ranging information base, upon which various interest groups can build their cases, is essential to equity and to effective long-term planning, management, and decision-making. Second, information varies in its technical detail and character but should be presented in ways understandable and useful to various disciplinary and professional groups and to citizens. Third, information, as well as the planning and management system, should be in the pluralist spirit, providing for recognition of all interested groups and individuals. Information should also be presented in language and images that encourage their participation in decisions. Fourth, information and planning systems should provide for both the public and private sectors and the interaction among them. This provides the wide range of information needed for the co-operative and adaptive planning, management, and decision-making called for in the frequently complex and uncertain circumstances facing us today. And finally, planning is a progressive and multi-layered process, which generally proceeds through increasing levels of detail. The ABC method is useful at all stages but seems especially valuable at the early strategic planning stage in assessing the natural and cultural context or circumstances for possible change and determining likely courses of action or alternatives in addressing the challenges.

Survey and information systems are, however, only part of a long-term solution, which must involve basic guiding concepts or values such as sustainable development. A basic purpose of Chapter 3 is to briefly introduce such key concepts. Information systems should also be linked to a wider range of tools than in the past, including environmental and other assessments, monitoring, mitigation, rehabilitation, and other aspects of the neglected "back end" of the overall management process. A system such as the ABC method can provide the framework for many of these important considerations. Before proceeding to the chapters in this book, which are intended to illustrate the ABC method, the reader's appreciation of its purpose and contributions will be enhanced by a brief history of its origins.

NOTES

1   Adapted from J.G. Nelson, "A Step toward More Comprehensive and Equitable Information Systems: The ABC Resource Survey Method," In *Greenways and Green Space on the Oak Ridges Moraine: Towards Cooperative Planning*. Occasional Paper #14. Department of Geography, Trent University, Peterborough, Ontario, 1990.

REFERENCES

Bastedo, J.D., J.G. Nelson, and J.B. Theberge. 1984. "An ecological approach to resource survey and planning for environmentally significant areas: The ABC method." *Environmental Management* 8(2): 125–134.

Grigoriew, P., J.B. Theberge, and J.G. Nelson. 1985. *Park Boundary Delineation Manual: The ABC Resource Survey Approach*. Occasional Paper 4. Waterloo: University of Waterloo.

Nelson, J.G., P. Grigoriew, P.G.R. Smith, J.B. Theberge, and J.D. Bastedo. 1988. "The ABC resource survey method: The ESA concept and comprehensive land use planning and management." In *Proceedings of the First Symposium of the Canadian Society for Landscape Ecology and Management*, ed. M. Moss, 143–175. Montreal: Polyscience Publications.

Nelson, J.G., E. LeDrew, Dulbahri, J. Harris, and C. Oliver. 1992. *Land Use Change and Sustainable Development in the Segara Anakan Area of Java, Indonesia: Relevant Information from Remote Sensing, On-ground Survey and the ABC Method*. Technical Paper 7. A joint publication of the Earth-Observations Laboratory of the Institute of Space and Terrestrial Science and the Waterloo: Heritage Resources Centre, University of Waterloo.

2

ORIGINS OF THE ABC METHOD

J.G. Nelson

EARLY DAYS

Original work on the ABC method was undertaken in the 1960s and 1970s primarily for subdivision development and land-use planning. One of the theoretical stems for this early effort was applied ecology. The approach was led by biologists and earth scientists. Their focus was on building ecosystem thinking into improved landscape and environmental planning for urban development (Dorney and Hoffman, 1979). In this respect the ABC method was primarily an attempt to organize and integrate wide ranging natural information on geology, hydrology, plants and animals with land-use, social and human information in more comprehensive urban planning. At that time, this was seen largely as a matter of engineering and economics.

In the 1960s and 1970s, rapid growth in human population, technology, resource consumption, and economic development were having growing impacts on water and air quality, plant and animal species and habitats, scenery, traditional land uses, communities, landscapes, and other valued elements of the world around us. Indeed, about a decade earlier in the mid-1950s, a major international symposium on Man's Role in Changing the Face of the Earth was held in New York to draw scientific, scholarly, and civic attention to the post-World War II unleashing of these changes and their accelerating impacts on the environment – where this term was used in the broad natural and social sense, the *milieu* in the French sense of the term (Thomas, 1956). This interest in the human role in changing the face of the earth was the second major body of thought that led to the development of the ABC method. Changes in environment and landscape were foci of concern here, but as much or more from a human or cultural as a natural perspective.

Among those scientists, scholars, and professionals most heavily involved in the man's role approach were geographers, anthropologists, sociologists, conservationists, and social planners. They saw interactions between humans and the environment principally in terms of the evolution of technology, architectural and landscape design, consumption preferences, economic policies, and other influences of cultural origin. This contrasted with the biological and ecological perspective. The focus here was processes such as: long-term evolution of plant and animal species, associations and processes, bedrock and landform characteristics, cycles of flood and drought, and other fluctuations in the natural world. As a result of these differences in perspective the scientists, scholars, and professionals of a cultural persuasion and those of a natural one tended – and still tend – to look past one another in their perceptions of environmental and development challenges – and the kinds of information needed to deal with them.

HUMAN ECOLOGY

Increasing damage and destruction to places, the environment, and human heritage in the 1960s and 1970s did, however, lead to a growing interest in more closely linking the biological or ecological and the cultural or human approaches to these challenges. Initially this was reflected in calls for closer links between environmental and economic planning. The need for linkages was greater than this, however, and slowly led to a growing interest in more fully integrating geologic, biologic, land-use, social, and other learning into a comprehensive understanding of the complex we label the environment. This, in turn, caused an increasing number of researchers and practitioners to see promise in human or cultural ecology, or the interaction among human technological, socio-economic, and other learning or culture and the hydrological, biological, and other processes at work in natural systems. The human ecological approach had been known for many years, notably since its blossoming among geographers, sociologists and other scholars, scientists and professionals at the University of Chicago in the 1920s (Barrows, 1923). This approach to a more comprehensive and integrated understanding of human-environment interactions was also employed in practice, if not in name, by philosophically oriented planners such as Lewis Mumford (1932). Such thinking is reflected in their large-scale designs for New York City and surrounding regions in the early decades of the twentieth century.

Human ecological ideas were picked up by some leading landscape architects and planners in the 1960s. A very prominent example is the work of Ian McHarg (1969). He developed a system in which maps of water regimes, forests, soils, and other natural features and processes were overlaid with alternative highway, subdivision, or other human proposals in order to seek the best fit, minimize environmental disturbance, and find an aesthetically pleasing and functional design.

Another example of the rising interest in human ecology during the 1960s was the work of Gilbert White, a geographer who had completed his Ph.D. with Harlan Barrows and other proponents of this approach in the 1930s at the University of Chicago (Barrows, 1923). After serving in government and university administration, White turned his attention to research in human ecology upon returning to Chicago as a professor in the 1950s. He began to do research with his students on floods, droughts, and other hazards which had long been of concern to him (White, 1942).

White and his students gained greater understanding of floods and other hazards through studies that focused on human dimensions such as peoples' perceptions and attitudes toward flood events (Burton et al., 1968). Through field research and interviews, they found that people did not, for example, remember floods well and tended to underestimate or deny prospects for their reoccurrence. These researchers pointed out that damage and destruction of property by floods were not hazards arising solely from acts of god or from natural processes. They were also a result of consistent human movement and settlement in high-risk areas. One consequence was the placing of greater emphasis on zoning and other regulation of flood-plain occupance as an alternative to the increasingly costly breakwalls and other engineering or "technical fixes" dominant in hazard-response policy and practice. As a result of their work, White and his colleagues developed human ecological frameworks or models that built perceptual, economic, land-use, insurance, and other cultural approaches into what had previously been a predominantly engineering response to hazards.

Another example of a human ecological approach is manifest in historical research on wilderness, national parks, and other aspects of nature conservation. Land-use history and landscape-change studies in Banff and other Canadian National Parks in the 1960s and 1970s revealed that, in contrast with official pronouncements, these areas were not pristine wilderness untrammelled by humans. These landscapes had been changed through centuries of interaction between nature and early First Nations hunting and other activities, and later by European or Caucasian lumbering, mining, railroad, and other developments (Nelson, 1969).

Initially these early Canadian landscape-change studies were undertaken more or less independently. Each focused on a particular theme such as changing forests and wildlife (Nelson and Byrne, 1966), the growth and impact of Banff townsite (Scace, 1967), human interaction with the grizzly bear (Noble, 1972), and the impact of the snowmobile (Masyk, 1972). The realization grew that what was needed was an analytical framework or model that would bring together and guide such studies in future. The framework that arose was four-part, consisting of perceptions, attitudes and values, strategies and institutional arrangements, technology, and ecology. The ecological component of the framework was a general one. It embraced the geologic, hydrologic, biotic, climatic, and other biophysical processes and features that interacted with human activities to shape the landscape of places. The framework was used, for example, as an organizational tool in an international workshop on national parks and related reserves in the USSR in 1976 (Nelson et al., 1978).

In this human ecological framework, myriad and diverse human activities were seen as being influenced by and generally organizable and understandable in terms of: perceptions, attitudes and values; policies and institutional arrangements; and technology. These three fundamental components represented distinct yet interrelated aspects of human learning. They shaped the kind, intensity, and extent of human land and resource use and its effects on what some called *landscape*, some *environment*, and others *nature*. This kind of thinking had considerable influence on the development of the ABC method.

The development of the method in the 1970s, 1980s, and 1990s grew from efforts to link together more effectively the applied ecology thrust driven mainly by biologists and the human ecological thrust driven mainly by geographers, anthropologists, and other students of human culture and society. Much of the early work on the method, as it appears in this volume, was done through collaboration between an ecologist, John Theberge, myself, a geographer, and Jamie Bastedo and other graduate students in planning who were doing research in the Yukon (Bastedo et al., 1984).

SPECIALIZATION AND THE NEED FOR INTEGRATION

A major motivation for the development of the method was the growing need to provide specialists, professionals, planners, decision-makers, and citizens with a generally understandable way of bringing diverse scientific, scholarly, professional, and local or traditional knowledge together to address environmental and development challenges arising in many places or regions on earth. The need for a comprehensive yet integrated approach grew with the trend to greater and greater specialization in learning generally, particularly after World War II. This specialization is very apparent, for example, in molecular, micro-, or other biology, or in various types of chemistry or economics. It is also apparent in traditionally more general disciplines such as geography and anthropology. Specialists and professionals require cross-disciplinary or cross-sectoral frameworks to understand how their work links with others. And what has been said of the specialists certainly applies to professionals, citizens, politicians, and other decision-makers.

The ABC method is aimed at meeting this need, albeit imperfectly because of the frequently turbulent and uncertain circumstances applying to environment and development problems. A key attribute of the method is the preparation of maps that can fit together to portray the suite of Abiotic, Biotic, and Cultural elements of a land-use or environmental-planning challenge. The ABC method basically involves the mapping of human ecology as a foundation for greater overall understanding of places and more equitable, efficient, and effective planning and decision-making.

IN SUMMARY

The principal purpose of this book is to describe a systematic approach to the collection, organization, interpretation, and application of the diverse information needed to understand and plan for places. The approach is through the presentation of case studies of the use of the method in different parts of the world over the last several decades.

The case studies or chapters are organized and highlighted under four broad headings: Detailed Analytical Studies (Part I), Focused Summaries of Detailed Studies (Part II), Comprehensive Overviews and Assessments (Part III), Rapid Reconnaissance Studies (Part IV), and Communication and Education (Part V). Readers with technical and professional interests may wish to start with Part I. Readers with more general interests may wish to begin with Parts II, III, IV, or V. The simplest or most basic applications are in Part IV on Rapid Reconnaissance Studies.

The studies in this book were prepared at different times for different places as the method evolved over the last twenty-five years. They have been edited for inclusion as chapters in this book, generally without changing or updating the findings made at the time of the study. The reader will see that, while the ABC method was put forward initially as a resource survey method, its use has broadened with experience. Over the span of its development, the method has also widened from its original relatively technical basis to one that is more civic in character, reflecting an ongoing search for effective ways of bringing different scientific and scholarly disciplines and professions together with concerned citizens. In this respect, the book shows the flexibility of the method in terms of different kinds of places, scales, time, resources and technology, and different users and purposes. In these respects also, the method addresses one of the major social challenges of our time, the need for more equitable, participatory, and effective understanding and planning of places.

REFERENCES

Barrows, Harlan. 1923. "Geography as human ecology." *Annals Association of American Geographers* xii: 1–14.

Bastedo, J.D., J.G. Nelson, and J.B. Theberge. 1984. "An ecological approach to resource survey and planning for environmentally significant areas: The ABC method." *Environmental Management* 8(2): 125–134.

Burton, I., R.W. Kates, and G.F. White. 1968. *The Human Ecology of Extreme Geophysical Events.* Institute of Behavioural Science Working Paper No. I. University of Colorado, Boulder.

Dorney, R.S., and D.W. Hoffman. 1979. "Development of landscape planning concepts and management strategies for an urbanizing agricultural region." *Landscape Planning* 6: 151–177.

MacKaye, Benton. 1962. *The New Exploration: A Philosophy of Regional Planning.* Urbana: University of Illinois Press.

Masyk, J. 1972. *The Snowmobile in Banff National Park.* MA thesis. Geography. University of Calgary, Calgary.

McHarg, Ian. 1969. *Design with Nature.* Garden City, NJ: Natural History Press.

Mumford, Lewis. 1932. "The plan of New York." *New Republic* 71 (15 June): 121–126; (19 June): 146–154.

Nelson, J.G. 1969. *Land Use History, Landscape Change and Planning Problems in Banff National Park.* IUCN Bulletin. International Union for Conservation of Nature. New Series 2: 80–82.

Nelson, J.G., and A.R. Byrne. 1966. "Man as an instrument of landscape change: fires, floods and national parks in the Bow Valley, Alberta."*Geographical Review* 56(2): 226–258.

Nelson, J.G., R.D. Needham, and D.L. Mann. 1978. *International Experience with National Parks and Protected Reserves.* Department of Geography Publication Series No. 12. Waterloo: University of Waterloo.

Noble, B. 1972. Man and Grizzly Bear: Banff National Park. MA thesis. Geography. University of Calgary, Calgary.

Scace, R.C. 1967. *Banff, Alberta, Historical Geography and Planning Problems.* MA thesis. Geography. University of Calgary, Calgary.

Thomas, W.L., ed. 1956. *Man's Role in Changing the Face of the Earth.* Chicago: University of Chicago Press.

White, G.F. 1942. Human Adjustment to Floods. In *Geography, Resources and Environment.* Vol. I. *Selected Writings of Gilbert F. White, 1986,* ed. R.U. Kates and I. Burton. Chicago: University of Chicago Press.

QUESTIONS FOR THE READER

The following questions and projects are provided as guides to help the reader to think through and understand the ABC method. Additional questions and projects may be contrived for those with a keen interest in the method and its use in analyzing, synthesizing, and interpreting a wide range of information for decision-making purposes. All the questions and projects are general and can be applied to all chapters in this book.

1) When was this study completed? Why was it undertaken? In your view, did it achieve its objectives?

2) How did the ABC method contribute to the study, and what were the advantages and disadvantages in using it? Is there another method that you think would have been more effective, and why?

3) In what ways did the use of the method bring about information that might otherwise not have been available to various users?

4) What theory was used in applying the ABC method and was the method amenable to the use of this theory in addressing the challenges addressed in the study? Do you think another theory could have been used to greater advantage, and why?

5) Discuss the use of the ABC method in terms of its effectiveness, efficiency, and equitability, being sure to

consider a range of economic, social, land-use, and environmental criteria.

6) Do you think that the use of the method provided a wider or more comprehensive understanding of the situation being addressed, and do you think this understanding was more useful than a more specialized approach? What are some examples of more specialized approaches that might have been used and what do you think would have been the advantages and disadvantages in relation to the ABC method?

7) Do you think the application of the method could have been improved? How, and with what results?

8) Do you think that the ABC method provided the information needed to understand and address a matter of public interest in an effective, efficient, and equitable manner? Please give reasons for your answer.

Sample Research Projects

1) As many of our applications of the ABC method were completed some years ago, please undertake research to determine how the situation under study has changed in the intervening years. In doing so, consider the economic, social, land-use, and environmental aspects, and their interactions and effects on the landscape. Please evaluate the significance of the ABC application to these changes and associated planning challenges, now and in the future.

2) Select a major challenge to a community or place familiar to you. Design a study using the ABC method which would address this challenge and apply the method based on available documentary information.

3) Select a plan or a planning proposal and evaluate it in terms of the ABC method. The plan could be for a

communication or transportation route, a new housing development, a park, or comparable project.

4) Analyze and assess the location or proposed location of a waste disposal or other major pollution risk in terms of the ABC method and prepare a report in a format appropriate for a public hearing or a responsible decision-making body.

5) Analyze and assess the information needed to plan for a flood or other hazard in a river valley, shoreline, or comparable situation in terms of the ABC method and draw some guidelines or conclusions for planning.

6) Undertake a rapid reconnaissance survey of a local area in terms of the ABC method and prepare the report in a form advantageous to a potential developer.

7) Undertake a heritage landscape guide for an area of interest to you and prepare the report in a form useful for educational and/or tourism purposes.

Definitions

Some general definitions of key criteria referred to in the foregoing assignments are provided for the reader to consider.

Effective: the use of the method provides the information needed by a proponent(s) and the wider affected public to understand and address the challenge at hand.

Efficient: parsimonious in terms of the funding, time, and other resources needed to gain relevant information.

Equitable: the information is brought together and presented in a manner accessible to the concerned parties.

SOME HINTS ON BEGINNING AN ABC STUDY

1. Establish the purposes or goals of the study as these will guide the collection, organization, and analysis of the information. The scope, intensity, and complexity of information collection, organization, and analysis will be much greater for a technical study aiming at the preparation of a formal park management plan as in Chapter 3 on Presqui'le Provincial Park than in Chapter 19 on preparing a landscape guide for the Grand River, Ontario.

2. Carefully plan the study, including setting time and resource limits for its completion and identifying individual roles if it is a team project, recognizing it is a cross-disciplinary effort with broad knowledge requirements. This guidance applies to a team effort such as Chapter 5 on Bruce Peninsula National Park planning as well as an individual effort such as Chapter 12 on the San Pedro Valley of Arizona.

3. Carefully organize or design the information collection, the description, analysis, and assessment and the writing/reporting phases of the study. Initial information collection should involve about one third of the time, although this process tends to continue throughout the study. In this phase, themes, topics, or issues need to be initially defined as well the features, processes, or indicators for which information is required. Description, analysis, and assessment of the information needed to complete levels 1, 2, 3, and 4 should also involve about one third of the time. In this phase regular efforts should be made, especially in a group or team project to compare work on the abiotic, biotic, and cultural dimensions and seek connections and directions going forward. In some cases, this will require careful collection, analysis, and interpretation of institutional information such as laws, policies, and plans, as for example in Chapter 6 on planning for Aishihik, Yukon. In other cases, linking the four levels of the ABC system may not be particularly

arduous, especially if the aim is to better understand a place such as the Mai Po marshes in Chapter 16, or Fairy and Peninsula Lakes in Chapter 13, rather than preparing detailed plans as in Chapter 6 or in Chapter 3 on Presqui'le Provincial Park. Writing and preparing the report should also involve about one third of the time. However, in complex projects, this can be a relatively time-consuming phase, which might require up to 40 per cent of the project time and resources. It is helpful to write up results as work proceeds, lessening the load at the end.

4. Identify information sources such as scientific or scholarly journals, books and technical reports, local histories and stories, newspapers, photograph archives, map collections, government files, and 'grey literature,' while seeking leads through informal discussions and consultations. In many cases, much of the information needed to complete a study is already available in published or public sources. Some projects will, however, be based on available documents and field mapping as in Chapter 4 on Presqui'le Provincial Park.

5. Consider holding open houses or workshops, especially in more complex team projects. Here you can announce your study, its purposes, and motivations, explain its relevance to people, and ask for sources of information or other assistance. Meetings with officials and technical people can be very useful in selecting themes and gaining access to relevant information. But the purpose of the meeting should be clear in advance, as should expected outcomes, with some stress on their value to attendees or the community.

6. Prepare a project bibliography, organizing the references and sources of information in terms of the ABC, relevant themes, and other useful categories. In preparing such a bibliography, the display of previous research and available information may reveal an unrecognized

or insufficiently understood issue that could change the orientation of the study and its outcome.

7. Stay focused and do not consume too much time on what may turn out to be interesting, but not highly relevant, information. Consider terminating searches for certain blocks of information if they are difficult to secure or their salience is elusive. Keep checking against the purpose or goals of the study. Do review and assessment regularly individually or as a team. Examples of the need to do this can be seen in Chapter 7 on the East Beaufort Sea, or Chapter 8 on the Grand as a Heritage River.

8. Watch for opportunities to be innovative in completing the project. For example, in the Long Point work recorded in Chapter 10, the impetus for an ABC study came from the local Biosphere Reserve Committee, a group of citizens who had limited science background but were faced with using numerous technical reports involving concepts and language unfamiliar to them. The decision was made to prepare an Environment Folio, a set of sixteen chapters on the abiotic, biotic, and cultural dimensions of the Long Point area written in generally understandable language with numerous maps and illustrations appealing to a wide audience and currently available online for school use.

At this point the reader can proceed to the case studies, keeping these highlights and other introductory comments in mind as you think through and assess the results and their usefulness in terms of the study goals or your educational purpose.

PART I

PART I:
DETAILED ANALYTICAL STUDIES

INTRODUCTION

Our work on the ABC method began with research on planning national parks, territorial parks, wildlife reserves, and other types of protected areas in northern Canada in the 1980s. Yukon and Northwest Territories were then under heavy pressure for exploitation of petroleum and other mineral resources. Threats to wildlife, the natural environment, and way of life of native people – First Nations – were rising rapidly. With support from the Canadian Arctic Resources Committee (CARC), a non-government conservation organization, and the Canadian Donner Foundation, a philanthropic agency, we undertook surveys to map key mountain sheep, grizzly, waterfowl, wetland, and other habitat that we labelled as environmentally significant areas or ESAs. These surveys evolved into the ABC method, which included mapping, description, analysis, and assessment of geologic, plant, animal, land-use, and other features as well as laws, policies, regulations, parks and protected areas, and other means of conserving and sustainably developing places in the Yukon. We also began to apply the ABC method to similar challenges in other parts of Canada, Europe, and Asia in the later 1980s and 1990s. Part I contains detailed examples of this work.

Part I begins with the relatively general Chapter 3. It sets the stage for subsequent chapters by introducing sustainable development, landscape ecology, ecotourism, rational planning, and other concepts fundamental to the creation and management of national parks and other protected areas, as well as land use and conservation generally. In addition to these key concepts, Chapter 3 highlights historical mapping and analysis of land-use and landscape change from the 1930s to the 1990s to show the great extent and intensity of recent recreational and other developments in Banff National Park. This study underlines the value of the historical perspective taken in many of the ensuing chapters in this book. The chapter concludes with a summary of a detailed analysis of Georgian Bay Islands National Park, this being used as a vehicle for introducing some institutional and planning theory and methods that are pertinent to national parks and other land-use and conservation challenges discussed later in the book.

Chapter 4 is a detailed study of small southern Presqu'ile Provincial Park, on Lake Ontario's north shore, about a hundred kilometres east of the Toronto metropolis. This chapter is intended to give a full and detailed illustration of the application of the ABC method, in this case as a basis for zoning the park in order to separate conflicting land uses and protect the natural environment. The chapter is basic reading for those interested in learning how to use the ABC method. It is an edited version of a fourth-year university student report prepared for a field course on the ABC method. The chapter demonstrates that, in spite of its apparent complexity, the method can be effectively applied by beginning researchers under general direction, after about a week of careful instruction.

Chapter 5 is a detailed application of the ABC method to the Bruce Peninsula National Park and environs. It was also prepared by a team of graduate students and professors in a seminar at the University of Waterloo. The study was completed on a part-time basis in 1987. The work is based mainly on secondary sources and involved limited fieldwork and consultations by the students. Both professors were familiar with the study area for the proposed new national park in the Bruce Peninsula and contributed this knowledge to the research. The results include a wide range of Abiotic, Biotic, and Cultural maps and text intended for use in delimiting national park boundaries, zoning, land use, planning, and management within and around the park. The results also were intended for interpretation, education, and research purposes. In the end, the study was hindered by data limitations. The time and resources available also did not allow for a detailed institutional and planning analysis of the government agencies and other organizations involved in and affected by the establishment of the park. The study is, therefore, not as complete as originally planned but still presents much information of value to the understanding of the national park and its environs as well as providing a preliminary basis for planning, management, and decision-making generally.

Chapter 6, a study of the Aishihik environmentally significant area (ESA), south-central Yukon, is a report on about six months of detailed field research and eighteen months of part-time analysis, assessment, and writing during the 1980s. The Aishihik area was one of six recognized as of high geologic, plant, animal, scenic, recreational, and other interest in a preliminary study aimed at preparing a conservation strategy for the Yukon. The detailed study involved helicopter surveys, unstructured satellite image, and air photo analysis and extensive on-the-ground surveys by an interdisciplinary faculty and graduate student team of geomorphologists, biologists, geographers, and planners. The literature on Aishihik was also thoroughly reviewed in government archives and libraries in Whitehorse and later at the University of Waterloo and other libraries in the south. The Aishihik study was an early application of the ABC method and included comprehensive structural and functional mapping of the Abiotic, Biotic, and Cultural dimensions of the area. Space limitations prevent inclusion of all the mapping and text in this chapter. A number of the maps are presented, including one of a proposed land management plan. The preparation of this plan shows how the ABC method can be extended beyond mapping, analysis, and assessment of landform, plant, animal, land-use, and other features and processes to include detailed analysis and selection of protected areas and related planning arrangements for an area.

3

1997

EMERGING THEORY AND METHODS FOR LAND USE AND CONSERVATION PLANNING AND DECISION-MAKING FOR NATIONAL PARKS AND PROTECTED AREAS[1]

J.G. Nelson, R. Serafin, A. Skibicki, and P.L. Lawrence

INTRODUCTION

Sustainable development, ecotourism, landscape ecology, and other new concepts and approaches have been advanced to help deal with the growing land-use pressures threatening the ecological and social services that national parks and protected areas offer to society. Yet, relatively little research is being done on the nature and character of these pressures. Serious historical and evaluative research is also lacking on the kinds and effectiveness of planning, management, and decision-making undertaken in response to these land-use changes. Without such information we are in a poor position to make informed choices about how land-use changes should be planned, managed, and decided upon in future.

Remote sensing, Geographical Information Systems (GIS), and other methods are available to carry out land-use studies more effectively and efficiently than in the past. Comprehensive ecologically based land-use mapping and analysis systems such as the ABC Resource Survey Method have been developed. New concepts and methods for analyzing and assessing experience with planning, management, and decision-making systems also have been introduced in recent years. These ideas have mainly been generated for other than national parks and protected areas but are applicable to them. They deal with such relevant topics as environmental justice and civic science (Funtowicz and Ravetz, 1993; Dempster and Nelson, 2001).

NATIONAL PARKS AND PROTECTED AREAS

The many important contributions – or ecological and social services – that national parks and protected areas offer to local, national, and global societies are being increasingly recognized by more and more people (Nelson, 1991). These services include: conservation of water, forest, and other resources, wildlife habitats, ecosystems, and biodiversity; protection of archaeological, cultural, and historic resources; education; research; tourism and other economic activities. National parks and protected areas offer support not only to human kind, but also to all life on Earth. Yet at the same time that awareness of their contributions is rising, national parks and protected areas are under growing and often damaging pressure from accelerating tourism, recreation, forestry, mining, and other land-use activities (Ross and Saunders, 1992).

Sustainable Development

The idea of sustainable development is seen by many people as one important response to the land-use pressures upon parks and protected areas (IUCN, 1980; World Commission on Environment and Development, 1987). Sustainable development is planned in such a way as to: 1) preserve essential ecological processes such as animal migration routes or staging areas for birds; 2) protect the range or diversity of plants, animals, and natural communities; and, 3) maintain productivity of soil, wetland, and other resources. According to the World Commission on Environment and Development, or Brundtland Commission (1987), sustainable development also provides for equity or for comparable access to environmental opportunities for present and future generations.

The application of the concept of sustainable development to national parks and protected areas seems highly promising. On the other hand, some observers believe that the concept will open the way for more environmentally damaging growth in the longer run. A basic challenge with the concept of sustainable development is to determine what it actually means in terms of land-use changes and their effects 'on the ground.' Assessments of the land-use, economic, social, and environmental effects of proposed changes are therefore needed to help decide whether they are compatible with ideas on sustainable development.

Ecotourism

The concept of ecotourism is seen as another basic way of responding to growing recreation and tourism pressures upon national parks and protected areas (Nelson et al., 1993). Various definitions of ecotourism have been put forward. These definitions are generally similar in stressing that ecotourism builds on the ecological qualities of an area and is conducted in such a way as not to damage or destroy these valued qualities. Ecotourism also conveys the idea that tourism activities are, to a considerable degree, under local control and provide a high level of local benefits. Some observers have noted that the idea of ecotourism is still largely perceptual. Much lies in the eye of the beholder. The meaning of the term can vary from person to person, place to place, and group to group. An understanding of the kinds of land uses involved in ecotourism and an assessment of their ecological, social, and economic effects is therefore necessary for sound decision-making.

Theory and Method

Advances in theory and method are also seen as a way of reducing economic and land-use pressures on national parks and protected areas. These advances in theory seem to be particularly important in North America, where for many decades notions of pristine environments and wilderness have been fundamental guiding concepts in planning and managing national parks and protected areas (Nash, 1967; McKibben, 1990).

Among the more important new fields of thought are landscape ecology and conservation biology (Forman and Godron, 1986; Woodley, 1996; Nelson and Serafin, 1992). In general, these fields include concepts such as maintaining viable wildlife populations, biodiversity, ecological integrity, and corridors and connectivity among parks and protected areas and surrounding greater park ecosystems.

It is from the lands and waters around national parks and protected areas that many, if not most, of the stresses on them generally arise. Interest is growing, therefore, in identifying and delimiting the greater park ecosystems that are tied by river flow, watershed, or other processes to the national parks and protected areas, and vice versa. The ecological integrity or health of the national parks and protected areas is seen as mainly being a function of the ways in which the lands, waters, and atmosphere in the greater park ecosystem are used, planned, managed, and decided upon. The ecological health and sustainable development of the greater park ecosystem are, in turn, seen as dependent upon the range and intensity of human uses and impacts occurring in national parks and protected areas and the ecological and social services they offer to places located within the system's boundaries. In this basic way, ecosystems, land and resource uses, and protected areas are intimately intertwined.

The basic problem is that, while new concepts such as sustainable development, ecotourism, and landscape ecology can be helpful, they are not in themselves sufficiently precise to provide specific guidance for land-use planning, management, and decision-making. Any proposed land uses and their social and environmental effects need to be described, analyzed, and assessed before we can decide whether they represent ecotourism or sustainable development.

Land Use

In spite of the obvious importance of land-use processes, patterns, and changes to planning, management, and decision-making for national parks and protected areas, the topic has not received attention commensurate with its ecological and social significance (Turner et al., 1990). This statement is especially applicable to North America, although it also is relevant in Europe and other parts of the world. This is not to say that illustrative examples of the value of land-use studies and information have not long been available to us. Tubbs (1968) examined the natural history of the New Forest in southern England, providing a detailed account of the more than a thousand-year role of domestic stock-grazing in maintaining the character and distribution of the ancient forests, the heath, and other communities.

Rackham (1986) used historic land-use studies to explain the character and distribution of trees and woodland in British landscapes. Boyd and Boyd (1990) have interwoven historic land and resource use with natural changes to explain the evolving character of the remote western islands of Scotland. In the United States and Canada, some work has also been done on land-use changes in national parks and protected areas, for example, in the Everglades (Tebeau, 1986).

Various approaches to land-use studies on protected areas can be made, depending on the situation and the available resources. Simple historical mapping of changes in recreational land use and technology can be quite instructive for planning, managing, and decision-making, and for education and interpretation. Figure 3.1 consists of a series of maps estimating increases in the kind and extent of recreational facilities and technology in Banff National Park from 1930 to 1992 (Nelson, 1994). The maps show that recreational land use has intensified and spread cumulatively over the years and undoubtedly produced many associated changes in the vegetation, wildlife, and other aspects of the park environment. From a planning standpoint, it is important to prepare simple historical land-use and recreational change maps and analyses for all major national parks in order to chart the extent of land-use changes and obtain indicators of their environmental and socio-economic effects. This basic mapping can be used strategically to decide whether more detailed research is needed on any ongoing or proposed changes and their effects.

A fundamental reason for preparing such maps and studies is that people are generally unaware of the growth in intensity and extent of recreation, tourism, and related land uses over the years. They are, therefore, not as concerned as they might be about further recreational

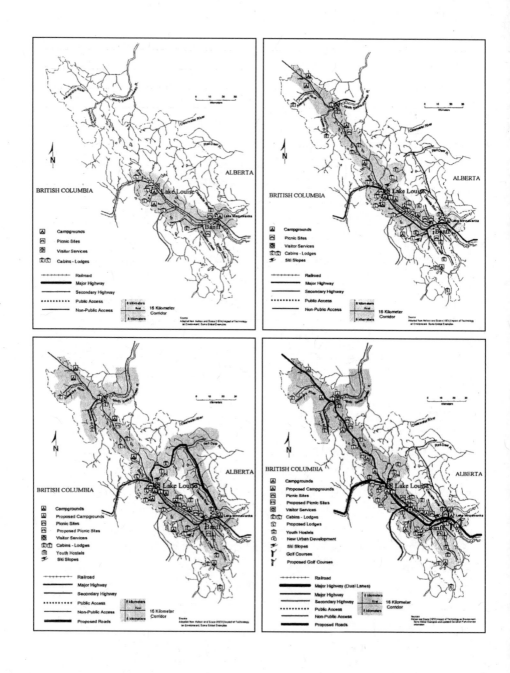

Figure 3.1   Recreational Facilities Development in Banff National Park, 1930, 1960, 1971, 1992

or other land-use changes and their effects on forests, animal habitat, and other aspects of park and protected area ecosystems. This lack of awareness extends not just to visitors but also to planners, managers, and decision-makers, including politicians. Information on changes in land use in and around national parks and protected areas is something that people of varied backgrounds, experience, and interests can understand. Appreciation of these changes can promote interest in and concern about the effects of land-use changes on economy, society, and environment. For this fundamental reason, land-use changes should be mapped, monitored, and reported upon regularly in national parks and protected areas.

THE ABC RESOURCE SURVEY METHOD

A comprehensive, dynamic, and interactive approach to land-use mapping and research is ultimately desirable and useful for learning and general understanding, as well as for planning, management, and decision-making. The land-use, resource and environmental survey and assessment system known as the ABC Resource Survey Method has been developed with these desired characteristics of comprehensiveness, dynamism, and interaction in mind (Bastedo et al., 1984; Nelson et al., 1988). The method is basically one of applied human ecology. The ultimate goal is to map, analyze, and assess human relations with the environment. Working toward this goal requires studies, not only of geologic and biological aspects of the environment, but also the values, ideas, technology, policies, and land-use activities that humans use to adapt to and change the world around them.

The ABC method is comprehensive in that it covers: Abiotic, including geologic, landform, and hydrologic information; Biotic, including plant, animal, and soils information; and Cultural, including land-use, economic, human heritage, land management, institutional, and other human information. The method is dynamic in that it can be used to prepare historic maps and analyses and to link Abiotic, Biotic, and Cultural (or human) patterns, processes, and changes. It is also dynamic in that it provides for both historic and current mapping and analyses. The method is interactive in that it can be used in a cross-disciplinary way to link scientists, scholars, planners, and managers of different training, backgrounds, and interests. It can also be used to involve businessmen and concerned citizens and gain information from them for mapping, research, and planning. In particular, people in a study area can be consulted about what is important to them and the results can be used in selecting topics for theme, significance, and constraint mapping.

For the purposes of this chapter, the important thing is that the method can be used to undertake land-use mapping as part of the Cultural component of the ABC system. This land-use mapping can then be linked to land tenure and management, to commercial and economic activity, to bird-watching and other recreational activities, to forest and wildlife patterns, and to other processes and effects of concern in planning, management, and decision-making. The ABC method is flexible in terms of the topics, issues, or themes to be mapped, as well as in terms of scale and research detail. Decisions on selection of information and mapping ultimately depend on the purposes of the study. The criteria for deciding on significance and constraints mapping (Level II) can be selected in terms of the goals and objectives of the study, as specified at the fourth level in the method.

In this chapter we are using 'land use' in the general sense that is often understood for this term, i.e., human activities that are revealed on the surface of the Earth as residential areas, croplands, forests, and other patterns. However, these patterns have been referred to by some professionals as *land cover* or landscape patterns with the term *land use*, then, referring to the human activities that occur within and are reflected to various degrees in such land cover types (Meyer and Turner, 1994). Mapping cultivated areas or forest cover types does not, for example, normally reveal what logging, recreational, or other uses are actually occurring within the land cover types. In this context, what we have mapped in our use of the method has often been land cover changes.

At the first stage of mapping (Level I) information can be mapped in two basic ways. The first way is by preparing a set of theme maps on topics or issues of concern to planners, managers, and citizens. The use of theme maps is especially appropriate where a considerable amount of information is already available in government files, scientific reports, and other sources and the theme maps can be prepared primarily on the basis of this existing information.

The second way is by preparing land cover maps from air photos or satellite images. These land cover maps are especially useful where existing information is sparse, although the land cover maps can also be used to supplement or augment theme maps of existing information in cases where this seems desirable or important. Both the theme and land cover mapping approaches are usually supplemented by field studies 'on the ground.'

LAND-USE AND CONSERVATION PLANNING AND DECISION-MAKING

A brief summary of a detailed application of the ABC method will be given here to illustrate its usefulness in organizing, evaluating, and interpreting diverse information for land-use and conservation planning and decision-making. This discussion will introduce the reader to some of the fundamental products of the method, notably as they arise from a better understanding of the spatial dimension of land-use planning and decision-making aimed at protection of important geologic, biological, and other features of a landscape or place. This brief illustrative example will help ease the reader into the detailed studies in the following chapters of Part I. It will also allow for a short discussion on some of the basic concepts or types of planning referred to in ensuing chapters of Part I, as well as other chapters later in this book.

The brief summary highlights a detailed application of the ABC method to the development of an Ecosystem Conservation Plan (ECP) for Georgian Bay Islands National Park in Ontario, Canada (Figure 3.2) (Nelson and Skibicki, 1997). The purpose of an ECP has been identified by Parks Canada as reducing the undesirable effects of human activities in the region around a national park and ultimately within the park itself. The region around the park is defined as the Greater Park Ecosystem. The ECP identifies ecosystem problems, issues, and concerns. It proposes a series of strategies, co-operative arrangements, reports, and other activities needed to maintain the ecological health and integrity of the park and surrounding areas. Georgian Bay Islands National Park is situated along the southeastern shore of Georgian Bay on fifty-nine dispersed islands and shoals of varying size. The total area of the park is 25 km^2 with the largest island – Beausoleil Island – extending over 10.9 km^2. Many smaller islands and shoals make up the land holdings in the park. The national park has many significant natural and cultural values.

A comprehensive set of theme, significance, and constraint maps was prepared outlining the Abiotic, Biotic, and Cultural information on the national park. Selected examples of these maps are shown in Figures 3.3 and 3.4. A proposed spatial framework for the ECP was also identified, which consists of a Core Area and an Area of Cooperation and Communication (Figure 3.5). Both of these areas have fuzzy rather than hard boundaries.

Within the Area of Cooperation and Communication, a transition area close to Georgian Bay Islands National Park was recognized as deserving special attention – this is referred to as the Near-core Area. A system of Key Ecological Areas (KEAs) – places with rare plants and animals, old-growth forest, wildlife habitat, and other features and processes ecologically supportive of this small fragmented national park – was also identified, based largely on provincial parks and wildlife areas, municipal environmentally significant areas, and other sites recognized by governments and NGOs for their natural values and services. Several sites with significant natural and cultural features and interpretive and other facilities that could encourage collaboration among concerned government agencies and NGOs were identified as Cooperative Heritage Areas (CHAs). Our final report advanced a set of ideas or concepts – the Core, the Near-core Area, and the Area of Cooperation and Communication – and a set of organizational arrangements or institutions – Parks Canada, a Consultative Committee, and a Greater Park Ecosystem Forum – which could be used to carry out the co-operative activities needed to implement the ECP (Nelson and Skibicki, 1997). Subsequent to our study, government planners, NGOs, researchers, and local people began working toward a Biosphere Reserve, which has since been established.

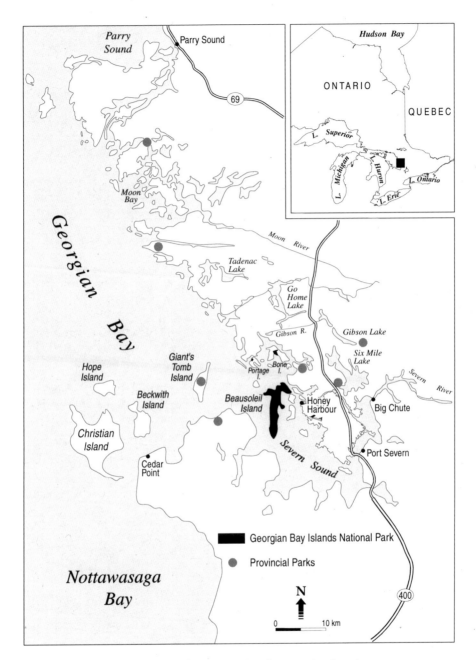

Figure 3.2   Georgian Bay Islands National Park, Ontario, Canada

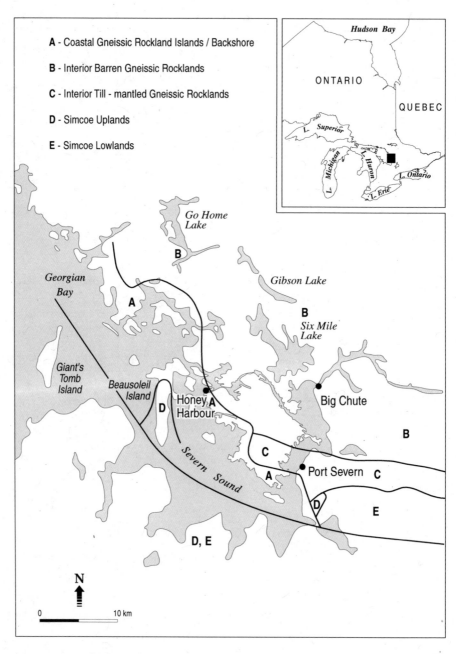

A - Coastal Gneissic Rockland Islands / Backshore

B - Interior Barren Gneissic Rocklands

C - Interior Till - mantled Gneissic Rocklands

D - Simcoe Uplands

E - Simcoe Lowlands

Figure 3.3   Physiographic Regions of Georgian Bay Islands National Park

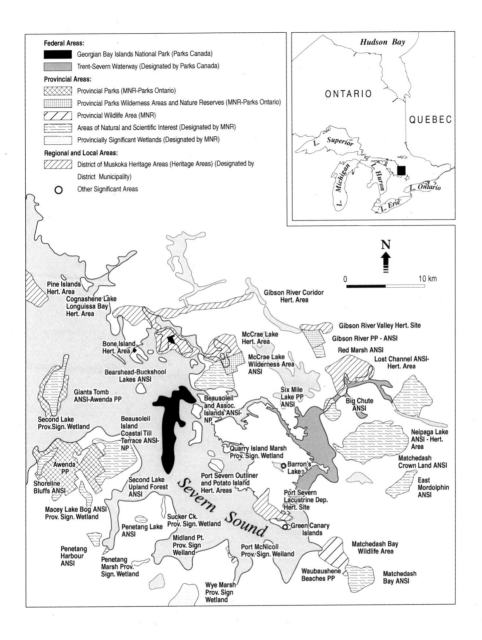

Figure 3.4   Protected Areas and Naturally Significant Areas of Georgian Bay
Islands National Park

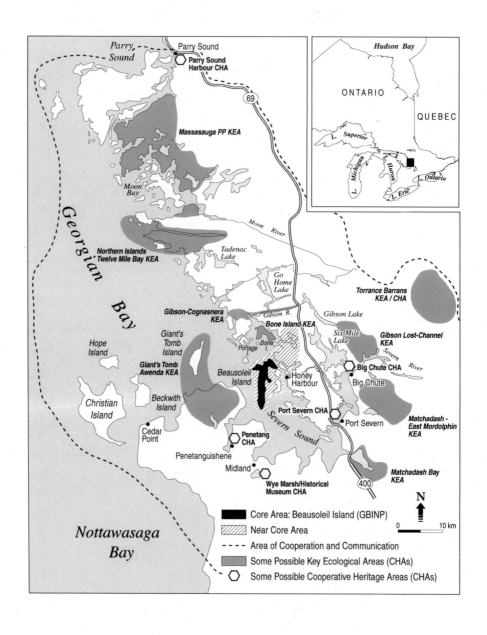

Figure 3.5   Suggested Spatial Framework for the ECP

PLACES

PLANNING, MANAGEMENT, AND DECISION-MAKING

The Georgian Bay Islands National Park study raises the fundamental question of how planning, management, and decision-making are undertaken in regard to land uses in and around national parks and protected areas. Yet protected areas and land-use analysis and planning, management, and decision-making have received relatively little evaluative research to date. Indeed, in this context, it is necessary to provide some information on the meaning of terms such as planning, management, and decision-making. We are using the term *planning* in the general sense of thinking about and preparing for the future (Etzioni, 1967; Friedmann, 1973; Nelson, 1991). Numerous different kinds of planning have been recognized, although generally not in regard to parks and protected areas. Some of the major ones are shown on Table 3.1. These kinds differ quite strongly in character, although all are applicable in one way or another to national parks and protected areas and related land-use changes.

Management, in the general sense, refers to the controlling or direction of activities. The term implies care, responsibility, and accountability. Once again, however, there are different kinds of management (Table 3.2), which can be used in various ways in dealing with land-use changes in and around parks and protected areas.

Decision-making is used in the general sense of how we make choices as individuals, groups, communities, or societies. The term, therefore, includes the various kinds of planning and management noted previously. It also refers to the basic ways of governance, for example, by dictatorial or military methods, by oligarchy, by consensus, or by voting and other democratic means. Decision-making also has been used to refer to broad styles of decision-making – that is, managerial or corporate or shared, participatory and civic (Roseland et al., 1996).

The question is how such theory and thinking applies to planning, managing, and deciding upon land-use changes in and around national parks and protected areas? In the past, stress has been placed on rational or synoptic planning, and on corporate management in national parks and protected areas around the world. Planning and management were concentrated within the boundaries of the protected areas, an approach

Rational or Synoptic Planning	Thinking in terms of goals and objectives, and the use of scientific and related knowledge to attain them.
Incremental Planning	Responding to challenges and opportunities on a step by step basis without any necessary overall goals.
Mixed Scanning	Responding to challenges and opportunities on a step by step basis while guided by longer term goals and objectives.
Advocacy Planning	Planning intended to promote the aims and welfare of particular groups.
Transactive or Civic Planning	Preparing for the future through regular communication with participation of other parties, including other governments, businesses and citizens.

Table 3.1   On Planning Ideas or Methods

Corporate Management	Controlling or directing an agency or group in accordance with a set of goals and objectives set by law, policy, and/or a Board.
Shared, Joint, or Co-management	Sharing of powers and responsibilities to varying degrees and in various ways, for example by legal agreement and memoranda of understanding.
Adaptive Management	Deciding on action through research and experiment, monitoring and assessment and adjusting to the results as deemed necessary.

Table 3.2   Types of Management

that was later referred to by some critics as a fortress mentality. Management, resource conservation, and visitor service plans were to be developed for each park and protected area, with the idea that they would be followed quite precisely in governing the areas in question.

Almost from the outset, however, this command and control system had to be modified because of the need to take account of the reactions, opinions, and ideas of users and citizens. Public hearings and reviews were held on plans and they were often changed. Broad-based advisory committees, or scientific and technical committees, as well as other means of consultation were used for receiving information from the users of the parks and protected areas. Yet challenges developed, particularly in the areas around the parks and protected areas. Here park and protected area policies and practices caused difficulties for surrounding land users and vice versa. For example, elk or bear strayed out of the protected areas onto land set aside for grazing by domestic stock.

Or lumber companies or hunters conducted their external activities up to or even beyond the boundary of parks and protected areas. Given the many other provincial and municipal government agencies and private organizations and owners that Georgian Bay National Park is going to have to deal with in its ecosystem conservation plan, interactive and collaborative planning and shared decision-making will have to mark the way forward.

Another major challenge to rational or synoptic planning and corporate management has been the inevitability of surprises – storms, floods, or political changes not foreseen nor well understood by researchers, planners, and managers. The foregoing challenges have led toward adaptive management with its stress on decision-making as an experiment in which monitoring and assessment is used to discover and adapt to the unforeseen and change course accordingly. In this context a flexible human ecological approach to planning, management, and decision-making through methods such as the ABC resource survey provides the broad accessible information base needed by diverse government, business, NGO, and citizen groups to understand and deal with land-use and other pressures on national parks and protected areas more effectively and equitably in future (Nelson, 1991; Nelson and Serafin, 1992).

In closing, it should be noted that, while the theory and methods described in this chapter were applied mainly to the studies discussed in the remaining chapters of Part I, they are frequently applicable to other chapters and topics presented in Parts II, III, and IV.

NOTES

1   Adapted from J.G. Nelson, R. Serafin, A. Skibicki, and P.L. Lawrence, "Land Use and Decision-Making for National Parks and Protected Areas." In: *National Parks and Protected Areas: Contributions to Heritage Conservation, Tourism, and Sustainable Development*, ed. J.G. Nelson and R. Serafin, 36–56. Proceedings of a NATO International Scientific Exchange Program Advanced Science Workshop, Krakow, Poland, April 26–30, 1996 (Heidelberg: Springer, 1997).

REFERENCES

Bastedo, J.D., J.G. Nelson, and J.B. Theberge. 1984. "An ecological approach to resource use and planning for environmentally significant areas: The ABC method." *Environmental Management* 8(2): 125–134.

Boyd, J.M., and I.L. Boyd. 1990. *The Hebrides: A Natural History.* London: Collins.

Dempster, B., and J.G. Nelson, eds. 2001. "Urban environmental planning, management and decision-making." *Environments* 29(1).

Etzioni, A. 1967. "Mixed scanning: A 'third' approach to decision-making." *Public Administration Review* 27: 385–392.

Forman, R.T.T., and M. Godron. 1986. *Landscape Ecology.* New York: Wiley.

Friedmann, J. 1973. *Retracking America: A Theory of Transactive Planning.* Garden City, NJ: Anchor Press.

Funtowicz, S.O., and J.R. Ravetz. 1993. "Science for the post-normal age." *Futures* 25(7): 739–755.

IUCN. 1980. *World Conservation Strategy: Living Resource Conservation for Sustainable Development.* Gland, Switzerland: IUCN.

McKibben, B. 1990. *The End of Nature.* New York: Anchor Books.

Meyer, W.B., and B.L. Turner, eds. 1994. *Changes in Land Use and Land Cover: A Global Perspective.* New York: Cambridge University Press.

Nash, R. 1967. *Wilderness and the American Mind.* New Haven, CT: Yale University Press.

Nelson, J.G. 1991. "Research in human ecology and planning: An interactive, adaptive approach." *Canadian Geographer* 35(2): 114–127.

Nelson, J.G. 1994. "The spread of ecotourism: Some planning implications." *Environmental Conservation* 21(3): 248–255.

Nelson, J.G., and R. Serafin. 1992. "Assessing biodiversity: A human ecological approach." *Ambio* 21(3): 212–218.

Nelson, J.G., and A. Skibicki. 1997. *An Ecosystem Conservation Plan for Georgian Bay Islands National Park: Planning for Nature Conservation in the Georgian Bay Islands National Park Region.* Waterloo: Heritage Resources Centre, University of Waterloo.

Nelson, J.G., P. Grigoriew, P.G.R. Smith, and J.B. Theberge. 1988. The ABC Resource Survey Method, the ESA Concept and Comprehensive Land Use Planning and Management. In *Landscape Ecology and Management*, ed. M.R. Moss. Proceedings of the First Symposium of the Canadian Society for Landscape Ecology and Management. University of Guelph. Toronto: Polyscience Publications: 143–175.

Nelson, J.G., R. Butler, and G. Wall, eds. 1993. *Tourism and Sustainable Development: Monitoring, Planning, Managing.* Department of Geography Publication Series No. 37. Waterloo: University of Waterloo.

Rackham, O. 1986. *The History of the Countryside.* London: J.M. Dent and Sons.

Roseland, M., D.M. Duffy, and T.I. Gunton, eds. 1996. "Shared decision-making and natural resource planning: Canadian insights." *Environments* 23(2): full issue.

Ross, M., and T.O. Saunders, eds. 1992. *Growing Demands on a Shrinking Heritage: Managing Resource Use Conflicts.* Calgary: Canadian Institute of Resource Law.

Tebeau, C. 1986. *Man in the Everglades: 200 Years of Human History in the Everglades National Park.* Coral Gables, FL: University of Miami Press.

Tubbs, C. 1968. *The New Forest: An Ecological History.* Newton Abbot, Devon, England: Davis and Charles.

Turner, B.L., W.C. Clark, R.W. Kater, J.F. Richards, J.T. Matthews, and W.B. Meyer, eds. 1990. *The Earth as Transformed by Human Action.* Cambridge: Cambridge University Press.

Woodley, S. 1996. "A scheme for ecological monitoring in national parks and protected areas." *Environments* 23(3): 50–73.

World Commission on Environment and Development. 1987. *Our Common Future.* Oxford: Oxford University Press.

4

1987

PLANNING FOR PRESQU'ILE
PROVINCIAL PARK ONTARIO[1]

J.G. Nelson and J. Greig

INTRODUCTION

Presqu'ile Peninsula, first designated as a provincial park in 1922, is one of the oldest parks in Ontario (Figure 4.1) (OMNR, 1980). In spite of its long history, by the late 1980s, Presqu'ile Provincial Park had no official management plan. Ideas about the future of the park had been formulated by each successive park administration, but no long-term planning document was written. One of the key elements of a park management plan is a zoning scheme. Zoning allows special areas within a park to be recognized and appropriate management policies to be applied. The research described here attempted to identify such *special* areas within Presqu'ile Provincial Park – in terms of their environmental significance or constraints – with a final goal of proposing an ecologically sound zoning scheme for the park.

To accomplish this goal, an assessment of the park was carried out using the ABC resource survey approach (Bastedo et al., 1984; Grigoriew et al., 1985; Smith et al., 1986). This involved the mapping of Abiotic, Biotic, and Cultural features and processes, the identification of areas of significance and constraints within the three categories, and the integration of that information to delineate areas of overall environmental significance and constraint. Zoning, or other land management types, could then be applied in a way that recognizes and guides important uses, while still preserving the ecological and historical integrity of the region.

55

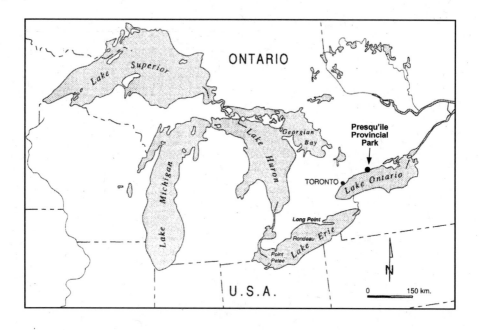

Figure 4.1   Location of Presqu'ile Provincial Park, Ontario, Canada

METHODOLOGY

The ABC method is comprised of four levels of mapping and analysis. The first level involves the collection and mapping of raw or baseline data on the Abiotic, Biotic, and Cultural components of the park. Obviously, not all Abiotic, Biotic, and Cultural variables can be mapped, so those that are particularly important in the ecology and use of the area are chosen, with guidance from previous research, local knowledge, and local people. Both structural and functional variables are mapped. *Structural* refers to actual features such as soil types, vegetation zones, roads or other facilities. *Functional* refers to ongoing processes such as succession or recreational land use. Each variable is mapped separately so that the information remains clear and available for future reference. The final product of the first level of analysis is a set of structural and functional maps for each of the selected Abiotic, Biotic, and Cultural components of the park.

Level II involves the analysis and interpretation of Level I maps to identify areas of significance and constraint within the park. This identification is based on carefully defined criteria, which are decided upon in advance, and reflect ecological and human values. The final product of Level II is two sets of maps, one showing areas of significance and one showing areas of constraint for each of the Abiotic, Biotic, and Cultural components.

In Level III, the Abiotic, Biotic, and Cultural maps are synthesized to produce two maps, one showing areas of overall environmental significance and one showing areas of overall environmental constraints. This synthesis of the Abiotic, Biotic, and Cultural elements reveals areas requiring special management considerations as well as their spatial relationship with other areas. This overall picture aids in the development of a Level IV map, which proposes land-use divisions and policies that protect areas with special management needs as well as reducing potential conflict between different areas. In this study, the final Level IV map is a proposed zoning scheme for the park.

Some general limitations apply to this method of resource assessment, as well as its specific application to Presqu'ile Park. Although the ABC method attempts to be disinterested or unbiased, the choice of variables to map and the selection of criteria for evaluation of significance and constraints reflect the objectives and values of the assessors to some degree. As well, the criteria have to be selected with the size and past history of the area being assessed in mind. At Presqu'ile, the area is a public park, and because its land mass is so small, almost no part of the park lacks several differing and often contending land uses. Finally, the maps in this chapter are in sketch format as prepared by the student at the time of the study.

ABIOTIC ASSESSMENT (LEVEL I)

Five structural variables and one functional variable were included in the Level I Abiotic mapping:

- underlying bedrock
- surficial geology
- topography
- soil types
- moisture regime
- erosion and deposition (functional)

Structural

The underlying geology reflects the creation of the peninsula through deposition of a sedimentary bridge or *tombolo* between the mainland and a former island. This ancient bedrock outlier is underlain by a flat-lying brown shaley limestone of Lindsay formation (OMNRa, 1982). The surficial geology of the park is quite varied, especially on the tombolo (Figure 4.2). The finger-spits on the eastern side are remnants of successively deposited sand and gravel bars which joined the island to the mainland, while allowing a large marsh to develop on the protected eastern side. On the western fringe of the spits is a set of high, mature dunes, formed by wind deposition probably during historically higher glacial Great Lakes levels. Younger dune ridges border the western edge of the tombolo, inland of the beach. Between these two sets of dunes lies a wide, flat, ill-drained lowland or *panne*.

Most of the limestone plain is covered by gently undulating till, with several sets of inland relict dunes. These are aligned parallel rather than perpendicular to prevailing wind direction and may reflect differing wind and water currents, as well as higher water levels in the past. Gull Island and High Bluff Island are both similar in geology to the southern plain or former island, having a thin cover of till and cobble along the shorelines.

Soils of the limestone plain, High Bluff Island and the spits tend to be sandy acidic *podsols* of varying thickness. In both the main marsh

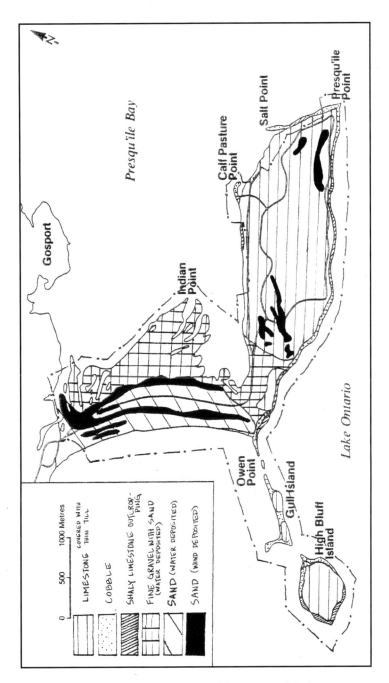

Figure 4.2   Surficial Geology, Presqu'ile Provincial Park

and two smaller marshy areas on Owen Point and near the camp-grounds, decaying plant matter has produced an organic muck. Sand covers much of the tombolo dunes and beaches. In the panne, a thin, ill-drained sandy *gleysol* has formed. The overall moisture regime is shown in Figure 4.3 and is closely related to soil type and topography.

Functional

Erosion and deposition were mapped as one functional variable (Figure 4.4). The dramatic erosional and depositional forces that formed the tombolo originally are not so obvious now, but several areas are still very active. Erosion occurs all along the exposed western and southern shores. Erosion is particularly intense at Owen Point and Presqu'ile Point. Old air photos show that the distance between the lighthouse and the water was considerably greater in earlier years. Deposition and spit formation also occur along the shorelines, particularly at Owen Point, Sebastopol Point on Gull Island, and Calf Pasture Point. Wind erosion and deposition along the dunes are continually modifying their form. The eastern dunes are more stable, but the loss of vegetation along some parts of the ridge has led to large blowouts.

ABIOTIC SIGNIFICANCE AND CONSTRAINTS (LEVEL II)

Following the Level I research, areas of Abiotic significance and constraint were identified and mapped. For Abiotic significance, the following criteria were used:

- uniqueness; or rarity of a feature or process on a regional or provincial scale
- representativeness; or value as a good example of some regionally or provincially typical landform, or as a good example of an Abiotic process.

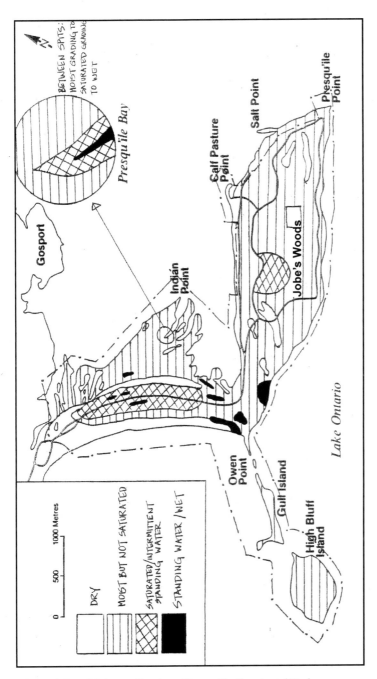

Figure 4.3   Moisture Regime, Presqu'ile Provincial Park

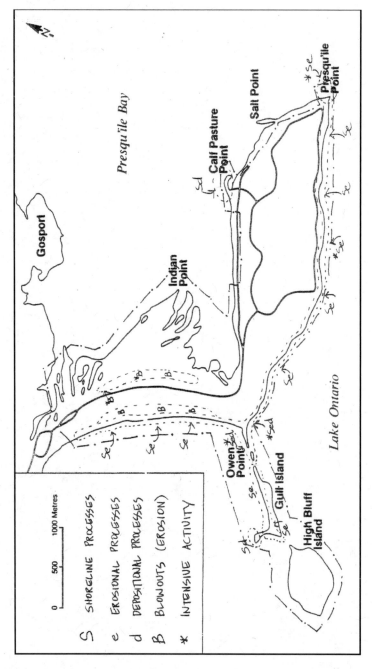

Figure 4.4   Erosion and Deposition, Presqu'ile Provincial Park

Significance

Figure 4.5 identifies several areas of Abiotic significance. The tombolo as a whole has significance on the basis of its uniqueness. Tombolos are uncommon landforms within the region and the province, and the Presqu'ile tombolo is "one of the most complex, best developed, active tombolo systems in the Great Lakes," (OMNR, 1982a). Within the tombolo, the marsh is considered regionally unique, being one of the few large, relatively undisturbed marshes left along the Lake Ontario north shore (OMNR, 1982a). The finger-spits are significant landforms representing the process of tombolo-building in general and particularly the processes of formation specific to Presqu'ile. An area of exposed limestone along the southern shore provides a good example of the erosion process. The relict dunes also are significant as representations of the past nature of the peninsula.

Constraints

Abiotic constraints (Figure 4.6) were evaluated according to the following criteria:

- terrain sensitivity; or susceptibility of an area to ecological damage from use or development, and
- hazardous process; or risks presented either to users or to development.

Areas of terrain sensitivity include the large marsh, the dunes and panne, Jobe's Woods, and the small inland marshes. In Jobe's Woods and the panne, the saturated soil and poor drainage make the soil easily compactable. This could affect vegetation and further disrupt the hydrogeology of these areas. In the marshy areas, development could disturb the build-up and distribution of organic muck, which would affect vegetation patterns and might disrupt the hydrological regime. The dunes are sensitive to wind erosion if vegetation cover is disrupted. Hazardous processes occur along the southern shoreline and in the panne. Seasonal flooding in the panne and the intense wave action at Owen and Presqu'ile Points and along the southern shore could pose

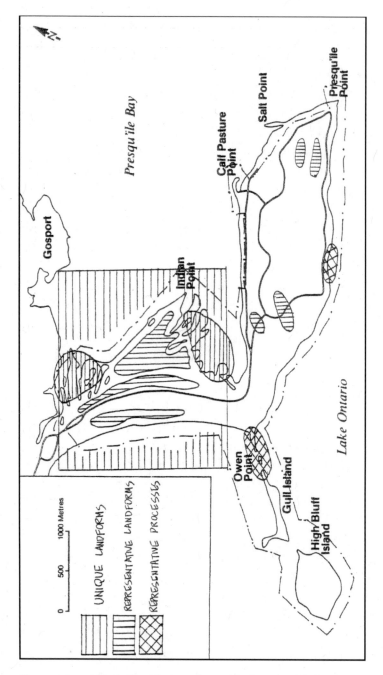

Figure 4.5   Abiotic Significance, Presqu'ile Provincial Park

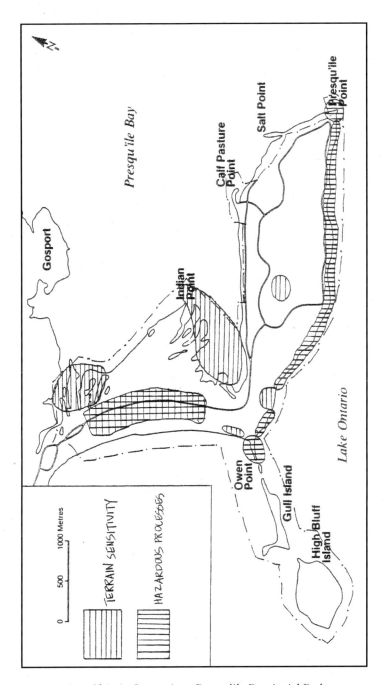

Figure 4.6   Abiotic Constraints, Presqu'ile Provincial Park

risks to development. The shoreline here could also be dangerous to swimmers and recreationalists, through currents and undertows.

BIOTIC ASSESSMENT (LEVEL I)

Two structural and two functional Biotic elements were mapped:

- vegetation zones (structural)
- habitat use by wildlife (structural)
- areas of succession (functional)
- critical habitat for wildlife (functional)

Structural

Presqu'ile vegetation is quite patchy due to variability of terrain and past use by humans (Figure 4.7). On the tombolo, the different vegetation zones are mainly a reflection of the variation in landform from west to east. These zones are quite linear. They begin with an unvegetated beach, succeeded by dune vegetation, panne vegetation, more mature dune vegetation, and coniferous forest, grading on the spits into aquatic vegetation in the marsh. Most of the beach has no vegetation to the first well-developed dune, mainly because of raking during the summer months. At the northern end, beach disturbance is less, with some primary dune succession and the establishment of beach grasses. The southern beach is likewise less disturbed, and several rare species of rush and sedge are found growing there (OMNR, 1982a). Vegetation of the western dunes is composed mainly of young cottonwoods and a variety of groundcover including grasses, goldenrod, wild grape, and poison ivy. Eastern dunes are older and more mature in vegetation, with larger cottonwoods, white cedar, juniper, wild grape, and poison ivy (OMNR, 1982a).

Between the dunes lies the panne, an uncommon habitat in Ontario, especially of this size. Vegetation varies within the panne because of differences in the degree of saturation and past human activity. Vegetation on the western side of the panne, where parking lots were

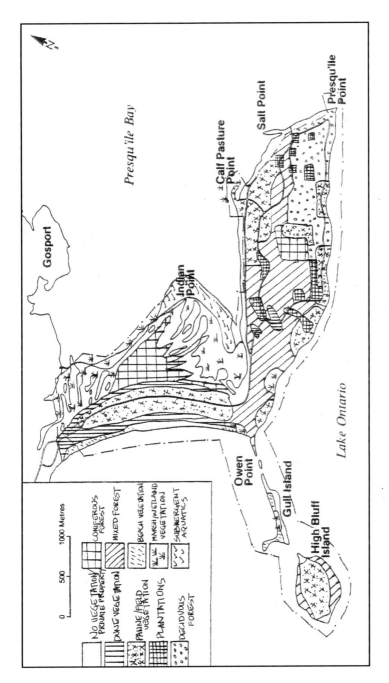

Figure 4.7   Vegetation Zones, Presqu'ile Provincial Park

formerly located, is very different from the surrounding area. One of the old lots is now completely covered by a thick growth of dogwood. In undisturbed areas where water is not continuously standing, vegetation includes scattered white cedar, weed dogwood, purple loosestrife, equisetum, and bulrushes. Cattails and pondweed are found in several isolated areas of standing water. Some rare species grow on the panne, including sedge and grass species, showy dragon's head and lobelia, and because it is an uncommon habitat, some of the plant associations are quite uncommon in Ontario (OMNR, 1982).

On the spits, the coniferous forest consists mainly of white cedar, white spruce, tamarack, and hemlock. Undergrowth is limited, but some notable herbaceous species are found, including several species of orchids, adder's mouth, a shinleaf, and, along the margins, a rare rush (OMNR, 1982a). At the edges of the spits, near open water is a complex gradient of vegetation: conifers give way to shrubs (dogwood and willows), which give way to sedges, to cattails, and finally to open water and submerged aquatics. Within the marsh are several distinct vegetation communities. Near land, cattails are the dominant species. In deeper water with less organic accumulation, bulrushes and some wild rice are found. Submergent aquatics, including pondweed, milfoil, tapegrass, bullhead, and white water lily, occur further out. A rare rush and a rare burreed are also found in the marsh (OMNR, 1982a).

On the limestone plain, vegetation reflects past human activity. A uniform mixed forest probably dominated until human settlement and agriculture began. Now the plain is a patchwork of mature forest, young forest, and old fields. The undulation of the plain causes alternating wet and dry pockets. The drier areas have a canopy of sugar maple, beech, and occasionally white pine or cedar. The understory may be composed of ash, basswood and elm, and striped maple at the southern limit of its range in Ontario (OMNR, 1982a).

Young forests are growing in once-cleared areas. The main tree species are white ash, elm, poplar, and aspen, with a groundcover of Queen Anne's lace, goldenrod, and grasses. Each of these areas differs slightly depending on the length of time it has been regrowing and its specific location. Several old field areas support some shrubs among grasses, goldenrod, thistle, and other herbaceous plants. Plantations, mostly of red pine, and mown lawn make up a portion of the plain as well. On the southern shore, where picnic areas and park buildings are located, the vegetation is mostly manicured grass and trees. Lawns are also maintained around the present location of the park store near Owen Point, and in the campgrounds. High Bluff Island, which was once farmed, has a central portion of old field surrounded by mature forest. Black oak, with a restricted range in Ontario, is found on the island, as is an uncommon cinquefoil in the island's field (OMNR, 1982a).

Varied vegetation communities provide numerous habitats for fauna. Wetlands offer habitat for amphibians and reptiles such as toads and frogs, salamanders, and turtles. Muskrat and beaver also live in the marshes, and several species of fish use the big marsh for spawning and as a nursery area. These include smallmouth bass, pike, sunfish, yellow perch, and carp (OMNR, 1982a). In the forested areas and on the dunes, many species of mammals are found, including red fox, coyote, raccoon, skunk, rabbit, weasel, mink, red squirrel, and smaller mammals such as mice and shrews. The peninsula also supports a sizeable deer herd, although information about exact numbers is lacking.

Presqu'ile is perhaps best known for its varied bird life. Because of its extension into Lake Ontario, many migrating species use the peninsula as a stopover and staging point; 299 species have been recorded in the park. Many species also use the park year-round; over eighty-two species have been recorded on annual Christmas bird counts. Presqu'ile is considered to be of provincial significance for birds (OMNR, 1982a).

Functional

As a result of vegetation patchiness on the peninsula, much successional activity is taking place. Successional areas are important to the ecology of a region because they are generally places where diversity and productivity are high. On the western side of the tombolo, dune succession is the predominant process, although it is somewhat disrupted by beach management activities. In the marsh, several stages of succession are evident. Between the fingers, areas of open water are being filled in by sedges and grasses. Farther from shore, emergent aquatics are becoming established as more organic muck accumulates. On the plain, old field succession is evident in many stages.

The large marshes and the long shoreline stretches favour diverse waterfowl and shorebirds. Shorebirds tend to congregate especially around Owen Point, where accumulated algae supplies abundant food. Several unusual species regularly visit the point, including the piping plover, willet, and marbled godwit, very occasionally the extremely rare shorebird, sulfur-bellied sandpiper. Owen Point may be one of the most important shorebird feeding areas in the eastern part of Lake Ontario. Gull Island has a large colony of ring-billed gulls and herring gulls and attracts other less-common gulls and terns. High Bluff Island has provincial significance for its large double-crested cormorant colony as well as a colony of black-crowned night herons, which do not usually nest in Ontario (OMNR, 1982a). Several species of songbirds also nest in the fields and forest of High Bluff Island; in 1979, fifty-nine species were counted there (OMNR, 1982).

Songbirds also use Presqu'ile Point as an entry and exit point for the rest of the peninsula. Variable vegetation and many edge areas in the plain provide many different habitat types. Presqu'ile is especially well-known for the fall migration of warblers and the many species of sparrow, which are found there. In the marsh, great blue and black-crowned night herons have nested, as well as green herons near the campground marsh. Swallows also gather in large numbers in the marsh to roost.

EVALUATION OF BIOTIC SIGNIFICANCE AND CONSTRAINTS (LEVEL II)

Significance

Biotic significance was determined using the following criteria:

- faunal diversity; referring to the numbers of animal species present,
- community diversity; referring to the number of plant species found and complexity of association,
- community uniqueness; referring to the rarity of occurrence of that community on a regional or provincial scale.

Areas were evaluated for significance by these criteria and were then designated as high, medium, or low in significance, according to how many of the criteria were applicable. For example, if an area was considered to have faunal diversity, community diversity, and community uniqueness, it was rated as high in significance. If it had only community diversity, it was rated low.

Areas with high Biotic significance were Jobe's Woods, located centrally in the southern limestone block of Presqu'ile, High Bluff Island, Owen Point, and the large marsh (Figure 4.8). Jobe's Woods has high faunal diversity as both the typical forest mammals and several species of salamander, frog, and other amphibians occur there. Vegetation composition is quite diverse, especially because of the alternating wet and dry habitats and the corresponding variation of plant life. It also has community uniqueness in that it is a particularly good example of undisturbed mature forest, which is no longer widespread in Ontario.

High Bluff Island has high faunal diversity in its birdlife and both community diversity and community uniqueness due to the mixture of old field/mature forest vegetation and the presence of rare and unusual species. Owen Point has similar characteristics, except that the bird species are mainly shorebirds and the vegetation is more shrubby and marshy. The large marsh has a high diversity of animal life, which includes birds, fish, and mammals, and high vegetative diversity especially

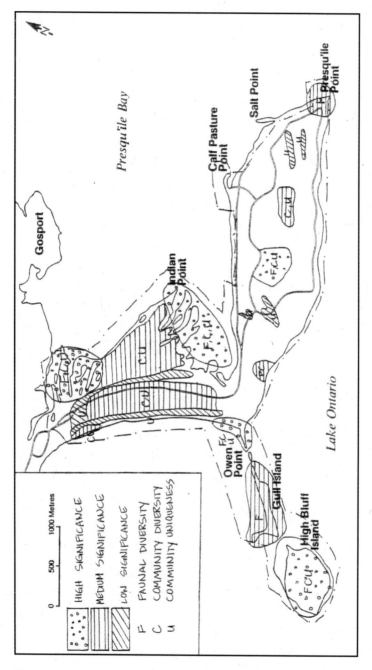

Figure 4.8   Biotic Significance, Presqu'ile Provincial Park

around the ends of the spits. It is unique both due to the presence of several rare species that occur there and in terms of its size and complexity.

Gull Island, the campground marsh, Presqu'ile Point, the panne, the spits, and the northern beach were all rated as medium in significance. Most of those areas are both diverse and unique in their vegetation assemblies. Included here are the northern beach with its cross-section of dune vegetation, the panne with its unusual associations and species, the campground marsh with its variety of aquatic and successional species, and the spits with their mature conifers in the centre and transitional species at the ends. Gull Island and Presqu'ile Point rated medium significance for faunal diversity and as extremely important areas for birds. The main dune ridges and the relict dunes were given low significance because of the uniqueness of the dune vegetation assemblage.

Constraints

Biotic constraints were evaluated using three criteria:

- vegetative recoverability; referring to the ability of the area to regenerate its present vegetation if disturbed,
- fire susceptibility; referring to the degree of fire hazard based on the type of vegetation and the amount of canopy closure,
- faunal habitat dependence; referring to the importance of the area to wildlife for critical life functions such as breeding or feeding.

Areas of constraint (Figure 4.9) were evaluated as being high, medium, or low on the same basis as for significance. Areas of high Biotic constraint include Jobe's Woods and the large marsh. Jobe's Woods, because of its mature trees and closed canopy, would be both susceptible to fire and extremely slow in recovering to its present state. It also provides critical habitat for salamanders and other amphibians, which are uncommon in other areas. The marsh has low recoverability and very high faunal dependence, and thus is rated high for constraints.

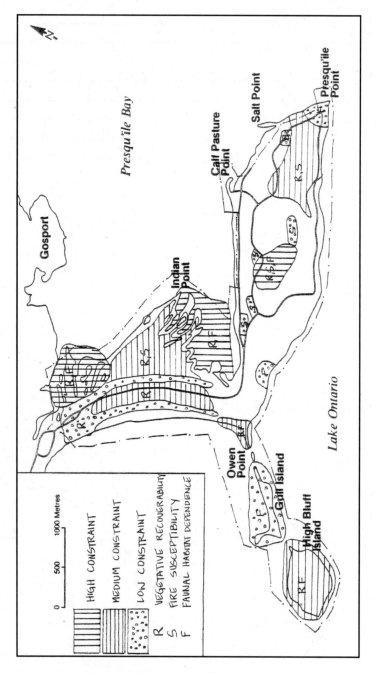

Figure 4.9   Biotic Constraints, Presqu'ile Provincial Park

PLACES

High Bluff Island, Owen Point, the panne, the spits, and the mixed forest at the east end of the plain are all of medium constraint. The forest on the spits and the mixed forests, both mature forests with closed canopies, are susceptible to fire and have low recoverability. The mature forest on High Bluff Island has low recoverability and the island as a whole provides critical habitat for birds. Owen Point also is critical feeding habitat for shorebirds and has low recoverability because of the many rare species occurring there. On the panne the likelihood of the present unusual association of plants becoming reestablished is quite low, and it is consequently rated medium in constraint. Areas of low constraint include Gull Island and Presqu'ile Point for bird habitat dependence, the campground marsh for habitat dependence of wetland animals, the plantations for fire susceptibility, and the dune ridges for recoverability of vegetation.

CULTURAL ASSESSMENT (LEVEL I)

Little is known of early use of the area by native people, although plant collection and seasonal waterfowl-hunting likely occurred for centuries prior to European arrival. The first European settler, Obediah Simpson, came to the peninsula in 1796. In the early 1800s plans were made to build a town, Newcastle, on the peninsula as the centre of the newly formed District of Newcastle. A ship sinking delayed development and the only notable subsequent major nineteenth century events were the 1840 construction of the lighthouse and the transfer of the peninsula to the Government of the Dominion of Canada for lighthouse management purposes.

Around the turn of the century, Presqu'ile became a focus for recreational activities. A hotel and pavilion were opened in 1905, attracting visitors from the immediate area and New York State. The harbour lost its importance for shipping and commerce and the land was transferred to the Ontario Department of Lands and Forests in 1922 for establishment of a government park. Many changes were made to the park, including the building of roads, construction of camping and picnic areas, stocking of the park with deer, and reforestation of previously cleared land. Lots for cottages were also put up for lease. The hotel continued to be a focus for social activities and, between the summer visitors and the cottagers, Presqu'ile was a centre of social and economic activity in the region (OMNR, 1980).

In 1956 Presqu'ile became part of a provincial parks system directed through a Toronto office, and the local parks commission was disbanded. It was Ontario's fifth provincial park, now under the jurisdiction of the Ministry of Natural Resources. Some of the cottage lots were reclaimed by the park, while most of those on the northern shore were sold to private landowners. The emphasis of the park turned to camping, and the park was eventually classed as a Natural Environment park, under the Ontario Provincial Parks classification system (OMNR, 1980). Little of the past history of Presqu'ile remains in any tangible form. However, the past has left a legacy in the present land tenure, in the historical focus at Presqu'ile Point, and in a tradition of recreation that has carried on for almost a hundred years.

Cultural features mapped included:

- structural; park structures, transportation and communication features, and recreational facilities, and
- functional; areas of recreational activity, corridors, and nodes of activity.

Structural

Most of the operational and recreational facilities are concentrated along the western and southern shores of the peninsula (Figure 4.10). West of the main road, which runs through the centre of the panne, are parking lots, washrooms, a concession, the beach, and related facilities. Little has been built east of the road except for the marsh boardwalk trail and associated parking lot, a lightly used trail along one of the finger spits, and duck blinds in the marsh. Facilities are also centred around the base of Owen Point, where trails, picnic areas, washrooms, and the park store are all located. Duck blinds are found on Owen Point, Gull Island, and High Bluff Island. Along the southern shore are located, from west

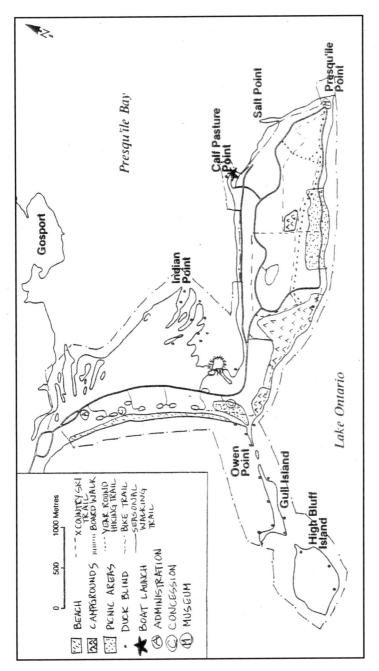

Figure 4.10   Recreational Facilities, Presqu'ile Provincial Park

to east, the campgrounds, picnic areas, park buildings including staff residences, the naturalists' office, and finally the museum, lighthouse, and associated facilities at Presqu'ile Point.

Functional

Activity is concentrated around the beach, the campgrounds, Presqu'ile Point, and, to a lesser extent, the marsh, Jobe's Woods, and the Owen Point-south beach area. The beach is a major attraction for both day users and campers. Swimming and wading were cited as the most popular activities by about 15 per cent of campers, and the beach is one of the most important reasons why day users come to Presqu'ile (OMNR, 1982b). Activity around the marsh and Owen Point appears to be increasing slightly due to increased interest in birdwatching. Use in other areas of the park appears to be stable.

Figure 4.11 summarizes the Cultural information in a corridors and nodes map displaying the major patterns of human development and activities, highlighting the foci for planning. The major corridors within the park are the main road through the panne, the roads to the beach parking lots, and the Lakeshore Drive loop around the plain. Minor corridors include the trails from the campgrounds to the beach and hiking trails and skiing on the panne. Most of the activity occurs in summer, including beach use, camping, picnicking, fishing, and bicycling. Birdwatching is mainly concentrated in the fall and spring during migration. Duck-hunting is restricted to the fall. Hiking and skiing trails are used year-round (OMNR, 1982b).

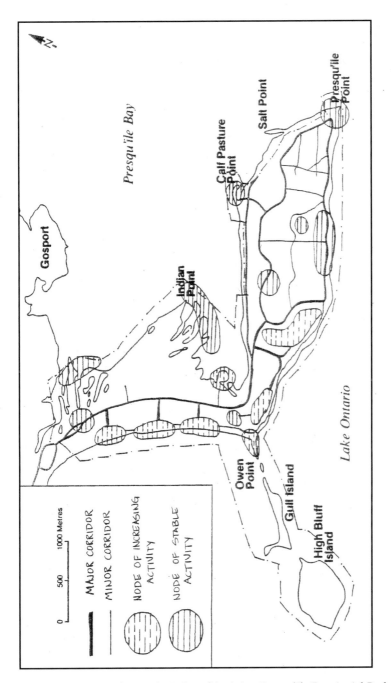

Figure 4.11   Corridors and Nodes of Activity, Presqu'ile Provincial Park

EVALUATION OF CULTURAL SIGNIFICANCE AND CONSTRAINTS

Significance

Cultural significance (Figure 4.12) was determined using four criteria:

- importance for recreation; referring to the use of an area for recreation and the intensity of that use,
- historical importance; referring to the importance of an area as a historical resource on a regional or provincial scale,
- educational potential; referring to having value as a tool for interpretation, scientific research, and related activities, and
- aesthetics; referring to having value for enjoyment on the basis of a pleasing sensual or spiritual experience.

On the tombolo, the beach, including the northern end, the marsh, and the southern beach–Owen Point area were all considered to be culturally significant. The beach has very high importance for recreation, due to intensity of use by both campers and day users for swimming, wading, sunbathing, and sail-boarding. The northern end of the beach is significant for its educational value as it represents dune formation and dune succession processes. The marsh has recreational importance for several groups of users, including birdwatchers, fishermen, and hunters. It is also visited frequently, especially by local residents, for its appealing aesthetics. The educational potential of the marsh is high as well because it is a good example of a marsh ecosystem and contains many different plant and animal species. The southern beach–Owen Point complex has recreational value to hunters and to birdwatchers, and educational potential because of its bird life and the diverse and unusual plant assemblage. The tombolo as a whole also has high educational value on the basis of its diverse landforms and habitats, and its illustration of the process of tombolo formation.

High Bluff and Gull Islands both are significant as recreation areas for birdwatchers and hunters and have educational potential due to their varied bird life and breeding colonies. The campground marsh

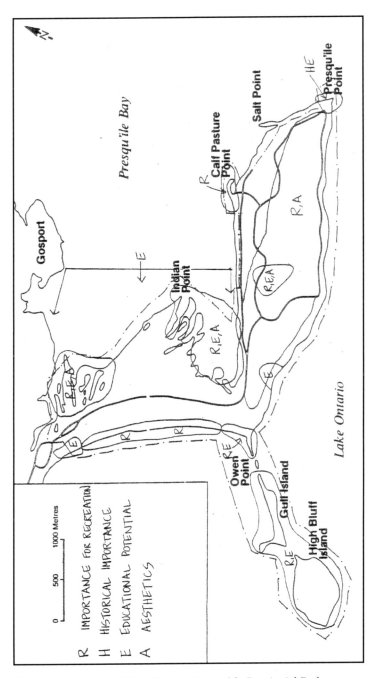

Figure 4.12   Cultural Significance, Presqu'ile Provincial Park

has educational potential in terms of marsh ecology and succession. Jobe's Woods has recreational importance for hikers, bird and wildlife watchers, and skiers. Many people visit the woods for its aesthetic value. Jobe's Woods also has considerable educational potential because of its diversity of vegetation and habitat and also because it is a good example of a relatively undisturbed natural forest, most of which has disappeared in Ontario.

Presqu'ile Point is the only area on the peninsula currently considered to have historical value, since most traces of past history of the area have vanished except for the lighthouse. However, the lighthouse is quite important provincially as one of the few buildings of its vintage left standing on the northern shore of Lake Ontario (OMNR, 1982a). The lighthouse and its associated history have educational value and serve as generally an important entry and exit point for migrating birds.

Constraints

Two criteria were used to evaluate Cultural constraints:

- conflicting land uses; referring to the use of an area by two or more user groups with contrasting intensity, technology, and philosophy, and
- environmental impact; referring to land uses that result in deleterious effects to the ecology of the area.

A Cultural constraints map was prepared on the basis of these criteria (Figure 4.13). Conflict zones include the marsh, the Owen Point-Gull Island-High Bluff Island complex, and the boundary between the private land and the northern side of the park. Conflict in both the marsh and the Owen Point area stems from concurrent usage by both naturalists and hunters. An annual fall duck hunt has been held in Presqu'ile since 1971; the park supplies thirty blinds on a first-come-first-serve basis. The Ontario Federation of Anglers and Hunters (OFAH) is interested in seeing the hunt continue and have been lobbying the OMNR to that end. However, with increasing interest in bird-watching and naturalist activities, considerable interest has been expressed in discontinuing the hunt. Naturalists' groups like the Federation of Ontario Naturalists (FON) feel that the hunt is disruptive to the bird populations and that it preempts other activities. Research is needed on the impact of hunting on bird populations and habitat.

The beach is also a conflict zone, specifically at the southern end which is heavily used by feeding shorebirds. Beach management practices include raking up algae and removing it to an inland disposal site. Since the food sought by the shorebirds appears to be mainly small invertebrates collecting in the strands of algae, removal of the algae may reduce the availability of food and discourage shorebirds from stopping at Presqu'ile. The effects of beach raking on the shorebird population, however, are presently unknown and need study.

Private cottages along the park's north boundary bring conflict. Cottagers are said to at least occasionally dump garbage in the park and allow domestic animals to roam into the park, resulting in the killing of birds and harassment of other animals. The cottagers may also have complaints about the park, but these are unknown.

Tension zones in the park include the majority of the tombolo, excepting the beach, Jobe's Woods, and the algae dump. The tombolo and Jobe's Woods are highly susceptible to disturbance from inappropriate or excessive use. Minor problems such as soil compaction, damage to vegetation, and increased erosion have already occurred. The potential for conflict is there if certain types of use are not discouraged.

At the algae dump, suspicion of mercury contamination alerted park managers to the potential for leaching from the algae in the dump. Although no evidence of mercury contamination was found in a later investigation, more research would be useful. Until the possibility of any type of contamination has been ruled out, the potential for conflict will continue to exist.

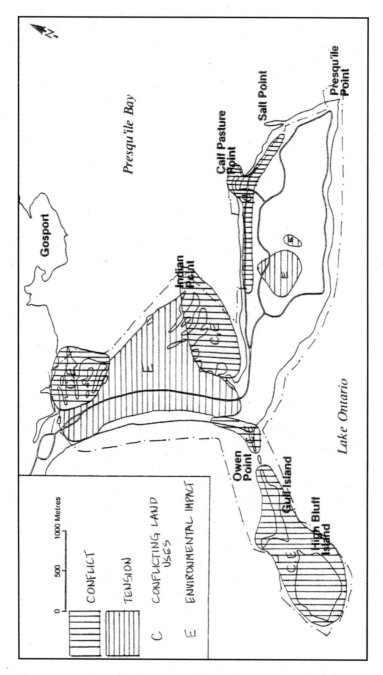

Figure 4.13   Cultural Constraints, Presqu'ile Provincial Park

PLACES

ENVIRONMENTAL SIGNIFICANCE AND CONSTRAINTS (LEVEL III)

By synthesizing the information provided on the significance and constraint maps for the Abiotic, Biotic, and Cultural components, two maps showing areas of significance and constraints for the park were produced. All of the tombolo was considered to be significant to some degree; the marshes at Owen Point, High Bluff, and Gulf Islands are considered highly significant for all three components, Abiotic, Biotic, and Cultural (Figure 4.14). The dunes, Jobe's Woods and Presqu'ile Point were of medium significance and the panne and beach, excepting the northern beach, were judged to be of low significance.

Most of the tombolo is constraining to some extent, with the exception of the main beach area (Figure 4.15). The marsh, the northern beach, and Owen Point are particularly constraining, especially Jobe's Woods, Presqu'ile Point, the campground marsh, and the northern and southern boundaries of the park. High Bluff and Gull Islands are also constraining.

INSTITUTIONAL ARRANGEMENTS: ZONING (LEVEL IV)

Before a zoning scheme can be developed for an area, the different institutional organizations and agencies which have an interest in its management must be determined. It is highly unlikely that the peninsula will be changed from its status as a provincial park, under the Parks and Recreational Areas Branch of the Ontario Ministry of Natural Resources (OMNR). However, the land tenure around the park is quite varied, and several different agencies might have to be involved in negotiations to protect and sustainably use the park.

Figure 4.16 shows the land tenure for the park and its perimeter. Most of the peninsula is controlled by the OMNR. But, the lighthouse is under federal control and the north shore cottages are privately owned. These cottages are under the jurisdiction of Brighton Township, which manages and maintains the main road coming through the panne to the cottages. The park land outside the park gate also abuts the Town

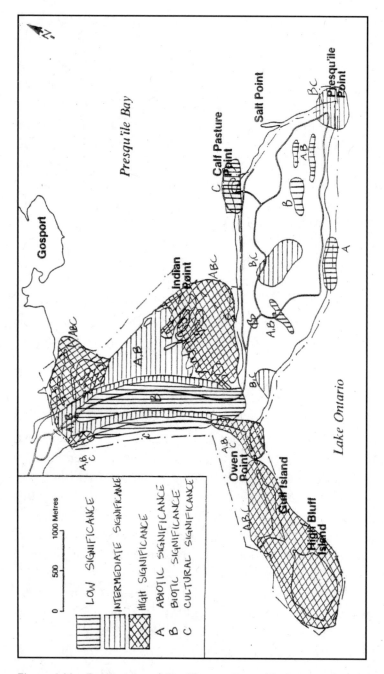

Figure 4.14   Environmental Significance, Presqu'ile Provincial Park

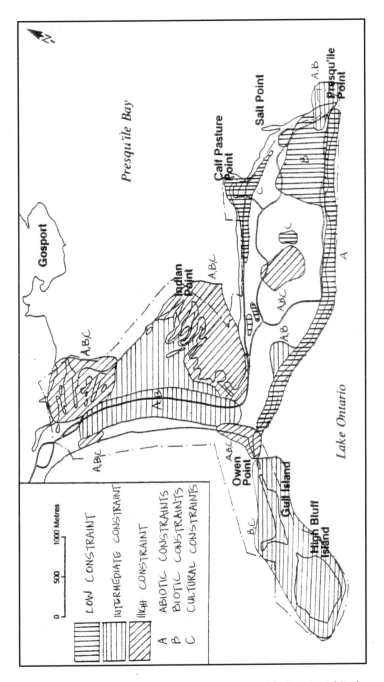

Figure 4.15   Environmental Constraints, Presqu'ile Provincial Park

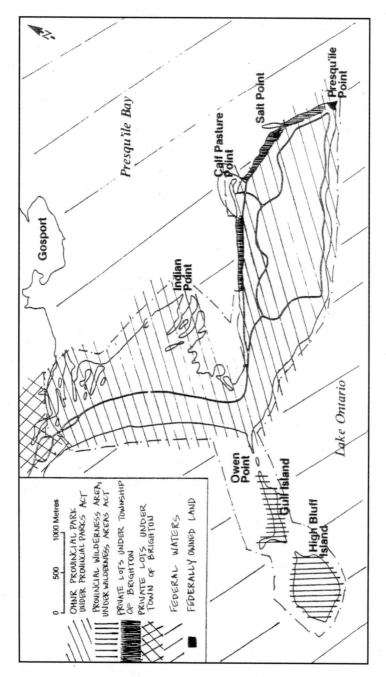

Figure 4.16   Land Tenure, Presqu'ile Provincial Park

PLACES

of Brighton. Within the park itself, High Bluff Island and Gull Island are designated Wilderness Areas under the provincial Wilderness Areas Act. The location of the off-shore boundary around the park is unclear, and research is needed on how far out from the land the boundary should lie in order to have some measure of control over shore-zone ecology and management. The waters around the park are federally controlled, but the province generally enforces regulations there.

Beyond the foregoing, some other organizations and agencies have interests in the park. Several Great Lakes binational and federal-provincial water quality agreements could affect management of the park. The International Migratory Birds Convention could also affect decisions at Presqu'ile. The Napanee District of the OMNR also has specific guidelines for land use and these might influence how Presqu'ile is managed. Other organizations interested in the management of Presqu'ile include the Ontario of Federation of Fishing and Hunting (OFAH) and other local hunting organizations, the Federation of Ontario Naturalists (FON, now Ontario Nature) and other conservation organizations, the Quinte Historical Society, Ducks Unlimited, and others. Some or all of these groups might have to be consulted before a final decision was made about zoning in Presqu'ile Park.

PROPOSED ZONING SCHEME

Presqu'ile Park has been classified as a Natural Environment Park, in accordance with the planning and management guidelines of the Ontario Provincial Parks system (OMNR, 1978). The goal in a Natural Environment park is to provide high-quality recreational experiences in a natural setting. This classification recognizes the dual nature of Presqu'ile; it has long been important for recreation in the region and is an area of diverse and sensitive natural features. Any zoning scheme would have to take these two aspects into consideration and provide for continuation of recreation while protecting areas that are susceptible to ecological disturbance.

Based on information gathered by the ABC method, a zoning scheme is proposed for Presqu'ile (Figure 4.17). The zoning scheme

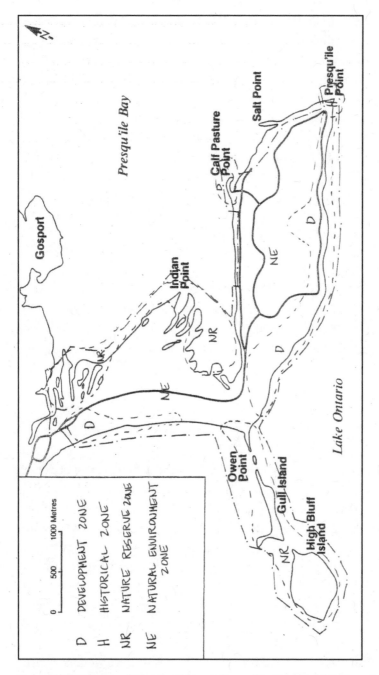

Figure 4.17   Proposed Zoning Scheme, Presqu'ile Provincial Park

and management recommendations are based on the guidelines set out in the Ontario Provincial Parks Planning and Management Policies (OMNR, 1978). It includes one Historical zone, two Nature Reserve zones, three Development zones and a large Natural Environment zone.

Historical

Presqu'ile Point, including the lighthouse, present museum, and immediate area, is proposed as a Historical zone. In a Natural Environment park, development in Historical zones is limited to "trails, necessary signs, interpretive, educational, research and management facilities, means of conveyance appropriate to the historical resource and historical restorations or reconstructions where appropriate. Restorations or reconstructions will conform to high standards of authenticity and will be complementary to and will not interfere with the integrity of the historical resource" (OMNR, 1978). Given the significance of the lighthouse as an authentic and uncommon historical structure, Presqu'ile Point should be conserved as an historical resource. Possibilities for management include restoration of the lighthouse and implementation of a high profile interpretative and educational program. Local historical groups could be encouraged to use the zone for their recreational, educational, and research programs as well. Negotiations on changes to the present status of the lighthouse would have to include the federal government.

Nature Reserve

Two areas within the park are proposed as Nature Reserve zones. Nature Reserve zones are established to include "significant earth and life science features which require management distinct from that in adjacent zones" (OMNR, 1978). In Nature Reserve zones, "development will be limited to trails, necessary signs, minimal interpretive facilities and temporary facilities for research and management" (OMNR, 1978). The two areas chosen for this status are the Owen Point-Gull Island-High Bluff Island complex and the large marsh. The Owen Point area is highly significant in terms of its biota, with shorebird feeding, waterfowl and other bird nesting and breeding, and several rare or unusual plant species. The shore zone processes are also significant. Given the highly sensitive nature of this area, in terms of disturbance to bird populations, special protective management policies should be put in place. Access to the islands should be limited, at least during breeding seasons, and perhaps year-round. Hunting activity should be phased out in accordance with the guidelines for Nature Reserve zones. A trail could be established to the end of Owen Point to allow visitors to view the bird colonies and spit formation from a distance. Trail access to the Point should be preceded by an Environmental Impact Assessment (EIA) and an intensive information program about the sensitivity of the floral and faunal communities.

The marsh is particularly significant as one of a small number of relatively undisturbed, large marshes left on Lake Ontario. It also has a high diversity of plant species and unusual vegetation patterns. Many species of birds, mammals and fish depend on this habitat. Interpretive and educational programs and facilities should be encouraged because of the high educational potential of the marsh, but care should be taken to minimize any impact that these may have on the ecology of the area. The issue of hunting in the marsh is a difficult one, given the intensity of the debate. However, if the marsh is to maintain its importance as a natural area, hunting may have to be phased out with reductions in the intensity of hunting activity over some years.

Development

Development zones "provide the main access to the park and facilities for a wide range of day-use and camping activities" (OMNR, 1978). Facilities in Development zones may include "roads, visitor control structures, day-use facilities, car campgrounds, basic commercial service facilities for visitors including outfitting facilities for back-country users, and orientation, interpretive, educational, research, and management facilities" (OMNR, 1978). Development of the park is currently widespread, extending all along the western and southern shores of the peninsula. To minimize impact on the more sensitive parts of the park, we propose concentrating development activities, especially on the tombolo.

Three Development zones are proposed; one at Calf Pasture Point, one along the southern shore of the plain, and the third at the northern end of the tombolo and the northern half of the beach. Calf Pasture Point is already developed, with a boat launch and picnic and washroom facilities. Further development would cause relatively little ecological damage. Although no immediate need for development at the point is foreseen, this might be an appropriate area for expansion of boating facilities, should that receive more emphasis in the future. If the marsh was to be zoned as a Nature Reserve, the small boat launch could be closed and activity redirected to Calf Pasture Point. The main constraint to development in this location is its proximity to private land, and the cottagers should be included in negotiations before any development takes place.

As with Calf Pasture Point, the southern shore of the plain has numerous facilities and is already quite developed. No immediate development is foreseen, but this could be a good location for additional day-use or camping facilities. Development would pose relatively little ecological damage, since the area is relatively resistant and already somewhat disturbed. It is easily accessible and would be popular with visitors because of its position along the lakeshore.

The most drastic change is proposed in the third Development zone. Instead of access to and facilities for the beach being located all along the western edge of the tombolo, we propose that development be concentrated at the northern end, near the park gate. Parking lots, toilets, and concession facilities would be moved towards the north. Disruption of the panne and the front dunes would be lessened if parking was concentrated at the northern end. Raking of the southern half of the beach should be discontinued. Disturbance of shorebird feeding could be reduced in this way. Moving the park store and picnic areas to the northern end of the tombolo would reduce activity in this area, allowing it to act as a buffer for the Owen Point-Island complex. One way of controlling the movement of users through this sensitive area is to set up a shuttle service from the campgrounds to the beach, reducing both foot traffic across Owen Point and vehicular traffic and parking facilities at the beach.

Concentrating development in the north would provide a major focus for day-use activities. Currently facilities are diffuse, and day-users have little immediate access to information about the park or interpretive services. A small visitor centre could be set up at the northern end of the tombolo, so that visitors who came to use the beach would have immediate access to interpretive and educational material. If these visitors were made more aware of the diverse and sensitive nature of the dunes, the panne, the tombolo, and the park as a whole, their impacts in the park might be considerably reduced.

Natural Environment

The remaining areas of the park should be zoned as Natural Environment zones. Natural Environment zones "include aesthetic landscapes in which there is minimum development required to support low-intensity recreational activities," and development may include "back-country campsites, trail, necessary signs for route identification, minimal interpretative facilities, and similar simple facilities which will support low-intensity recreational activities" (OMNR, 1978). Since Presqu'ile is classified as a Natural Environment park, most of the area of the park should be zoned as Natural Environment. Most of the areas proposed as Natural Environment zones are already being used in this manner. The trails on the plain and the marsh boardwalk on the tombolo are appropriate facilities for this type of zone. Considerable room is available for expansion of interpretive activity on the tombolo, which has much diversity in landform and habitat. However, this development should be carried out in a way that avoids disruption of the natural processes at work there. Another function of Natural Environment zones is to act as buffer zones for more sensitive areas. Especially around the base of Owen Point, and on the eastern side of the tombolo, Natural Environment zoning should minimize the impact of human activity in the Owen Point-Island complex and in the marsh.

RESEARCH NEEDS

The ABC Resource Survey Method is a useful tool for gathering information about Presqu'ile Provincial Park and also reveals how much information is needed for park planning. Numerous research needs have been identified in the application of the method to Presqu'ile. Some of this requires the expertise of trained personnel carrying out in-depth study. Such projects could include research on:

- hydrological patterns on the panne to understand the role of flooding and determine if impeded water flow is adversely affecting vegetation or fauna;
- effects of beach use and beach management practices on natural dune formation and on the ecology of the tombolo as a whole;
- effects of foot and vehicular traffic on the eastern dunes and the extent to which wind erosion is exacerbated by such activity;
- ecology of the deer population to determine the size of the herd, its population dynamics, and critical habitat for survival;
- shorebird populations to determine their feeding ecology and whether beach raking is affecting their survival or visitation to the park;
- nearshore ecology to determine what outside influences are acting on the park and where a water boundary should be located to control impacts on the littoral areas of the park;
- possibility of leaching and contamination of surrounding water from the algae dump; and
- effects of hunting on local and migratory bird populations and habitat.

Some useful monitoring projects could include:

- possible damage/vandalism and other effects by cottagers to determine the need for fencing or other control between the park and private property;
- usage of the eastern dunes to determine extent of human-caused

erosion and to help decide on use policy in the area;

- use of duck blinds and user patterns during hunting season to assist in a possible phase out of the program;
- use of the park by naturalists to determine impacts of bird watchers; and
- use and impacts on other users and the environment as a basis for planning the future of the water.

The park does not have the resources to gather information on all research and monitoring needs. However, it is an ideal place for research by people interested in ecology, geology, park management, and many other areas. The park could facilitate projects by preparing a booklet of research needs, outlining what needs to be studied, and the priority of research. This booklet could be distributed to universities and other research sources. It is important that such research be conducted because a comprehensive body of knowledge is essential in making wise decisions about the future of Presqu'ile Provincial Park.

NOTES

1   Adapted from J. Greig, "A Proposed Zoning Scheme for Presqu'ile Provincial Park using the ABC Resource Survey Method." In *Application of the ABC Resource Survey Method to Presqu'ile Provincial Park*, ed. V. Swinson, J. Greig, J.G. Nelson, P. Grigoriew, and T. Whillans, 35–81. Heritage Resources Center, University of Waterloo, Ontario, Canada, 1987.

REFERENCES

Bastedo, J.D., J.G. Nelson, and J.B. Theberge. 1984. "An ecological approach to resource survey and planning for environmentally significant areas: The ABC method." *Environmental Management* 8(2): 125–134.

Grigoriew, P., J.B. Theberge, and J.G. Nelson. 1985. *Park Boundary Delineation Manual: The ABC Resource Survey Approach.* Occasional Paper 4. Waterloo: Heritage Resources Centre, University of Waterloo.

Ontario Ministry of Natural Resources (OMNR). 1978. *Ontario Provincial Parks: Planning and Management Policies.* Toronto: Ontario Ministry of Natural Resources.

Ontario Ministry of Natural Resources (OMNR). 1980. *Presqu'ile de Quinte, A History of Presqu'ile Provincial Park*. Toronto: Ontario Ministry of Natural Resources.

Ontario Ministry of Natural Resources (OMNR). 1982a. *Presqu'ile Provincial Park Draft Preliminary Master Plan, Background Data, July 1982*. Toronto: Ontario Ministry of Natural Resources.

Ontario Ministry of Natural Resources (OMNR). 1982b. *Provincial Park Camper Survey for Presqu'ile Provincial Park, June to September 1981, Summary of Results*. Toronto: Ontario Ministry of Natural Resources.

Smith, Paul G.R., J.G. Nelson, and J.B. Theberge. 1986. *Environmentally Significant Areas, Conservation and Land Use Management in the Northwest Territories*. Technical Paper 1. Waterloo: Heritage Resources Centre, University of Waterloo.

5

1989

APPLYING THE ABC RESOURCE SURVEY TO THE BRUCE PENINSULA NATIONAL PARK AND ENVIRONS[1]

J.G. Nelson, G. Whitelaw, J. Theberge, and G. Forbes

INTRODUCTION

The primary aim of this study was to test the effectiveness of the ABC method as a planning tool in establishing a new national park. The anticipated benefits included information for park boundary delineation, zoning of the park, land use in the surrounding area, interpretation, education, and research (Bastedo et al., 1984). Establishment of the Bruce Peninsula National Park near Tobermory, Ontario (Figure 5.1), presented an uncommon opportunity to apply the ABC method to an intriguing area of medium size, that is, about 250 square kilometres at a 1:50,000 scale.

STUDY AREA

This includes the lands and waters north and west of Miller Lake on the Bruce Peninsula. The islands and waters north of Tobermory were not included in the survey, which covers an area larger than the proposed park boundaries. This larger area allowed for examination of a "buffer area" adjacent to the proposed park boundaries as well as areas of natural significance located some distance away such as Cape Hurd and Johnston's Harbour. Numerous maps were prepared as part of this study with many place names. For reader referral purposes, their locations are marked as clearly as possible on early maps and then less well on later maps often reduced in size to save space.

HISTORY OF UPPER BRUCE PENINSULA NATIONAL PARK

The idea of a national park appears to have been conceived in the 1950s, although the peninsula was recognized for its outstanding natural and scenic qualities decades earlier (Fox, 1952). Particularly valued were the floristic richness and diversity of the peninsula, its caves and karstic terrain, and the steep scenic limestone cliffs facing Georgian Bay. A study for the proposed park was not announced until 1981 after the federal government of Canada purchased the Tobermory Islands for incorporation into Georgian Bay Islands National Park located to the east along the shores of the bay. Emotions ran high in late 1982 with people against the park contesting seats on municipal councils in St. Edmunds and Lindsay Townships, which were located in the park study area. Subsequently, Lindsay Township withdrew support for a national park while St. Edmunds, the northernmost of the two Townships, remained in support. The Lindsay Township lands, including natural areas such as Cabot Head, were then removed from the park proposal by the federal government. About four thousand hectares of deer yards located on the south side of the park proposal also were left for management by the Ministry of Natural Resources. After extensive consultations with local people, the new Bruce Peninsula Park Reserve was established by the federal Minister of the Environment and the Ontario Ministry of Natural Resources on July 20, 1987.

APPLYING THE ABC METHOD

The ABC resource survey is a four-part process that can be used to delineate protected area boundaries and to derive planning arrangements for protected areas and adjacent lands. For our purposes, the four levels of the overall survey were considered to be: 1) collection of

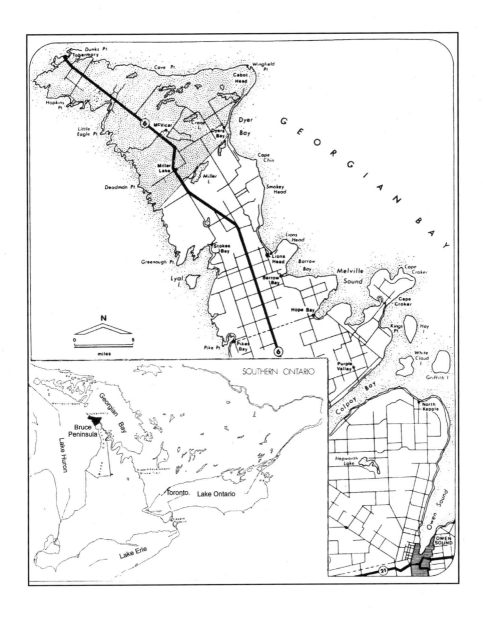

Figure 5.1   Bruce Peninsula National Park Study Area, Ontario, Canada

information on Abiotic, Biotic, and Cultural structures (features) and functions (processes); 2) evaluation and assessment of significance and constraints of Abiotic, Biotic, and Cultural structures and functions; 3) overall integration of information on the Abiotic, Biotic, and Cultural significance and constraints; and 4) planning arrangements for a national park in the Bruce Peninsula (Bastedo et al., 1984; Grigoriew et al., 1985; earlier chapters of this book).

At Level I, certain structures and functions were selected for mapping because they were considered as indicative of the basic character of the Abiotic, Biotic, and Cultural dimensions of the Bruce. Judgments about the selection of these indicators or theme maps were made by assessing the historical importance of the structures and functions as revealed in the literature on the Bruce and in the views of knowledgeable persons. At Level II, similar evidence was used to select criteria for making judgments about the areas of significance and constraint mapped and described for each of the Abiotic, Biotic, and Cultural dimensions of the Bruce. At Level III, overall integration of the Level II information was achieved by use of an overlay and ranking approach. These procedures for Level I, Level II, and Level III are described more completely at appropriate points in this chapter.

ABIOTIC INFORMATION: LEVEL I DATA ON ABIOTIC STRUCTURES AND FEATURES

The Abiotic structures and features of the Bruce were mapped and discussed in terms of the bedrock and major landforms of the area.

Bedrock and Major Landforms

The Bruce Peninsula consists of Middle and Lower Silurian limestones and dolomites and Upper Ordovician shales. The sediments forming these rocks were deposited in ancient tropical seas some 500 million years ago. Over ensuing millennia, the sediments were compressed into limestone, dolomite, and shale. The large inland sea and its deposits had sufficient weight to down-warp the underlying sediments and rocks to create a very large saucer-shaped depression. Today the central part of this syncline, the Michigan Basin, is largely occupied by Lakes Huron and Michigan. The Niagara Escarpment, or questa, at the eroding northern and eastern edges of the syncline dips beneath the lakes and toward central Michigan at about five metres per kilometre (Liberty and Bolton, 1971). The area was glaciated four times during the Pleistocene Epoch. The last and most important glaciation was the Wisconsinian 100,000 to 15,000 years before present (YBP). This three-kilometre-thick ice advanced northeast to southwest and is known as the Georgian Bay/Lake Huron Ice Lobe (Chapman and Putnam, 1984). This great glacier significantly reshaped the landscape.

About 11,000 years ago, ice began to melt differentially, creating post-glacial lake stages in future Lake Huron and Georgian Bay basins. The stages most important to the development of the Bruce Peninsula were Lake Algonquin (12,000 to 10,900 YBP) and Lake Nipissing (6,000 to 3,500 YBP) (Chapman and Putnam, 1984). Their higher shorelines are demarcated by elevated caves, natural arches, wave-cut stacks, and cobble beaches (Figure 5.2).

Glacial meltwater was responsible for accelerated development of karst topography on the northern peninsula. This karst developed for two reasons. First, the ice covering the Bruce removed most soil and overburden, leaving highly soluble limestone and, to a lesser extent, dolomite exposed to water. Second, given the voluminous meltwater, solution weathering and karstification of the rock was high. The only glacial deposits remaining today in the upper Bruce Peninsula are the South Tobermory fluvioglacial deposits and the Dorcas Bay/Cameron Lakes dunes complex (Cuddy and Lindsay, 1976). Glacial erosion features in the study area include bedrock scour marks such as the flutings and striations at Cyprus Lake, plus the "sheep backs" or roches moutonnees at Cabot Head. In addition a few glacial re-entrants, where the ice broke through or indented the Niagara Escarpment, are located along the Georgian Bay shore, including Big and Little Tub Harbours at Tobermory, and possibly Dyer's Bay (Figure 5.2).

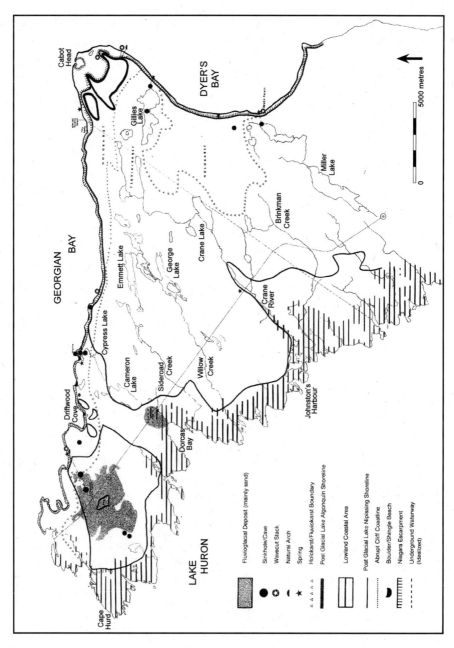

Figure 5.2   Abiotic Structures and Features, Bruce Peninsula National Park

ABIOTIC INFORMATION: LEVEL I DATA ON ABIOTIC FUNCTIONS AND PROCESSES

The Abiotic functions and processes can be discussed in terms of fluvial and drainage processes, mass wasting processes, shoreline erosion, deposition and flooding, karstification, peat formation, and isostatic rebound.

Fluvial and Drainage Processes

Desolving of the limestone bedrock over the millennia produced many caves and natural tunnels. Much of the drainage is subterranean. Surface drainage channels tend to follow bedrock joints with a few meandering streams. Shallow lakes, ponds, and swamps in low-lying areas seldom exceed three to six metres in depth (Cuddy and Lindsay, 1976) (Figure 5.3). Most Bruce lakes are in the upper peninsula west of Cabot Head. These lakes and ponds are drained by short, low-volume streams running along the bedrock slope to Lake Huron or by underground connections to either Lake Huron or Georgian Bay. Gillies Lake, near Cabot Head, does not fit this description, being about forty-six metres deep, oligotrophic, and connected by an underground outlet to Dyer's Bay. This lake is the deepest in southern Ontario, excluding the Great Lakes, and is likely a collapsed cave (Cowell and Woerns, 1976).

Mass Wasting Processes

Mass wasting involves removal of rocks and other debris from slopes and cliffs by collapse, slide, and creep. In the case of the Niagara Escarpment, the face and steeper parts of the brow are largely free of protective vegetation. This leaves the Escarpment rocks vulnerable to breakdown by rain, snow, frost, and temperature changes. The Escarpment is mechanically eroded by running water, ice, or tree roots wedging the rocks apart. Waves undercut the base of the cliff and the passage of people or large animals can trigger rock slides. Escarpment rocks can also be chemically dissolved by acids in lichen and tree roots or by carbonic acid in rain water and groundwater.

Shoreline Erosion, Deposition, and Flooding

Bruce Peninsula shorelines are constantly in flux. Wave energy, especially during the severe October-November storm season, may be so great as to move boulders the size of automobiles. Lake ice aids rock movement, which can erode and undercut the cliffs and nearshore areas. Promontories more commonly undergo this type of erosion. Further evidence of high wave energy along the Georgian Bay shoreline are wave-cut platforms, wave-cut stacks, caves (grottoes), notches, and potholes. The Lake Huron shoreline, with its more gradual slope, is significantly less prone to erosion than the Georgian Bay shore. Erosion is concentrated at headland and unprotected areas. Deposition is concentrated in sheltered bays. Higher sand deposits along the Huron shore testify to the lower energy level there. Water level for Lake Huron/Georgian Bay fluctuates between 580 and 590 feet above sea level (Cuddy and Lindsay, 1976).

Karstification

Glacial erosion left little or no protective overburden on the upper surface of the Bruce Peninsula, exposing soluble carbonate rocks to glacial meltwater, rain, and activating karstification through solution processes. The northern Bruce karst area is characterized by: 1) holokarst, i.e., vertical drainage of water into the bedrock; 2) fluviokarst, or underground river capture by sinkholes, disappearing streams and connecting springs; 3) caves; and 4) rock pavement (Figure 5.3). Rock pavement is produced by rainfall and overland water flow and by lichen growth, which etch pits, rills, and grooves into the rock surface. These features are collectively referred to as *grike*. Groundwater also promotes karstification by weakening subterranean rocks through solution.

Peat Formation and Isostatic Rebound

The one peat bog is in a depression near the centre of the South Tobermory fluvioglacial deposit (Figure 5.3). As the water is typically acidic, plant material decomposition is slow and much peat is produced. The

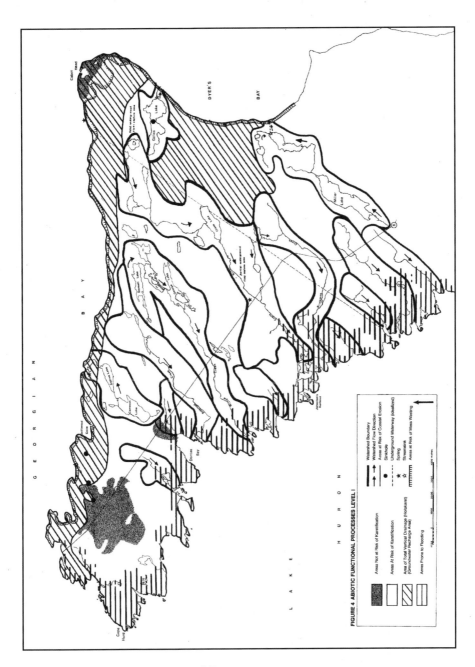

Figure 5.3   Abiotic Functions and Processes

peat inhibits drainage of the bog area. Slow isostatic recovery or land rebound has followed retreat of the great weight of glacial ice. One estimate is a rise of 75 metres over 12,000 years, based on the observation that the wave-cut stack at Cabot Head was formed at 184 metres above sea level during the Lake Algonquin phase. It is now 360 metres above sea-level.

ABIOTIC INFORMATION: LEVEL II – SIGNIFICANT AREAS

Our judgments about Abiotic significance were based upon the criteria of uniqueness and representativeness. The dictionary definition of *unique* implies presence of only one of a particular feature or process. This was found to be too restrictive for practical use here. The definition was therefore extended to include the "rare" and the "unusual," implying that at least some comparable features and processes are found in the Bruce or the general region in which it is located. According to Smith et al. (1986), "unusual" Abiotic features have a localized distribution or are only fully developed at a limited number of sites in a region, in this case, southern and central Ontario. For example, wave-cut stacks are not found elsewhere in southern Ontario, except the Bruce Peninsula and Flowerpot and Bear's Rump Islands in Georgian Bay. However, these features are found along Lake Superior and ocean coastlines of Canada. As these features are restricted to the Bruce Peninsula in southern Ontario, they are deemed to be unique for purposes of this study. Other information on criteria used to define uniqueness and representativeness is presented on Table 5.1.

In fact, the entire Bruce area is unique with respect to southern Ontario, particularly for its karst and cliff features. However, to designate the entire study area as unique would not serve the purposes of our study. Identifying a series of specific sites as unique would be more beneficial to boundary delineation and comparison of areas within and outside the proposed park.

Significance		Constraints
Unique	**Representative**	• Disturbances
• Numerically rare:	• Typical feature of the	• Terrain sensitivity
• found nowhere else in	Bruce Peninsula and	• Hazard Potential
Southern Ontario or Canada.	Southern Ontario.	• Active hazard:
• Best example of feature or	• A typical portion of larger	• Coastal erosion and
process in its unaltered (by	features.	depositional processes
humans) state.	• Best example in	• Mass wasting processes
• Best example of the feature's	southern Ontario found	• Flooding (600 ft.
or process's morphological	in the study area.	contours – OMNR)
development.	• Many examples of	• Karstification
• Fragility (vulnerability) to	typical features in the	• Peat bogs
disruption by humans.	study area.	**Susceptibility to erosion**
• Peripheral distribution in	• The feature or process is	**ranking system**
Southern Ont.	also typical of the Bruce	• 3 overlapping processes:
• Disjunctive from main	Peninsula sub-region of	Severe Constraint
distribution.	Southern Ontario.	• 2 overlapping processes:
• Small, localized of limited		Moderate Constraint
geographic distribution.		• 1 process:
• Abnormally large in size or		Low Constraint
areal extent than others of its		• 0 processes:
kind.		No Constraint
Examples	**Examples**	**Severe Constraint Areas**
• Cabot Head	• Niagara Escarpment	• Cabot Head
• Cabot Head to Overhanging	(except those sections	• Georgian Bay shoreline
Point	designated as being	• Lake Huron shore
• St. Edmund's cave system	unique)	• Tobermory Bog
• Little Cover shore	• Lake Nipissing Stranded	
• Tobermory Bog	Shoreline	
• Gillies Lake	• Lake Huron Shoreline	
• Devil's Pulpit (Monument)		

Table 5.1   Level II: Abiotic Significance and Constraints

No practical method of ranking features and processes for high, medium, or low significance could be found. This was largely due to lack of specific data on comparable features and processes in southern Ontario. The only available data simply delineated areas where similar features are located. Details on the criteria for Abiotic significance are presented in Table 5.1.

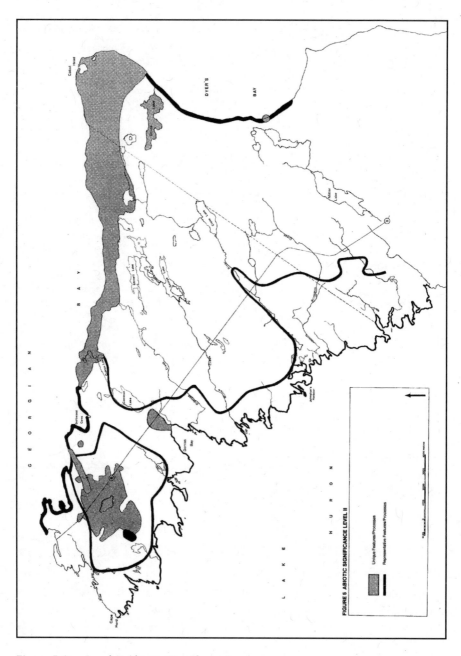

Figure 5.4   Level II Abiotic Significant Areas

Delineation of Abiotic Significance Areas

Areas of Abiotic significance are presented in Figure 5.4. Mostly, these areas are located along the Georgian Bay shore from Cabot Head to Little Cove. This area is a very unusual part of the Niagara Escarpment and is probably the most unique example of cliff shoreline in southern Ontario. The shoreline includes wave-cut stacks carved during three different lake phases (Algonquin, Nipissing, and Huron/Georgian Bay) as well as caves cut during the Nipissing and Huron/Georgian Bay phases. In addition, the shoreline exhibits unusual natural arches, blow-holes, wave-cut platforms, and cobble and shingle beaches.

The cliff shoreline between Cabot Head and Little Cove near Tobermory exhibits the best expanse of bedrock pavement in Ontario and perhaps in the entire world (Cowell, 1976; Cowell and Woerns, 1976). Holokarst reaches its best development in this area and has been considered as the most unique feature of the Bruce (Cowell, 1976). The holokarst area serves as headwaters for many surficial creeks in the north Bruce and is therefore of high hydrological importance (Cowell, 1976). Other unusual features are the South Tobermory fluvioglacial deposit and the Cameron Lake/Dorcas Bay dune complex.

Representative features in the study area are the sections of the Niagara Escarpment not already designated as unique and the raised ancient Lake Nipissing shoreline encircling the fluvioglacial deposits and winding south across the Bruce along the Lake Huron shore. These features are representative of similar features found elsewhere on the Bruce Peninsula and/or southern Ontario.

ABIOTIC INFORMATION: LEVEL II ABIOTIC AREAS OF CONSTRAINT

Areas of constraint are considered to be hazard areas that are easily disturbed by the actions of people or have terrain susceptible to flooding, erosion, or comparable risks. These areas must be carefully managed to prevent or reduce such risks. The various types of constraints and the procedures for their ranking are presented in Table 5.1 along with location of severe constraint areas.

No data were available on sensitivity or susceptibility of the study area to specific erosion processes. Nor were any data available on which erosion processes were more prevalent or severe at any given location. For example, no data existed as to where on the Escarpment the most serious mass-wasting is occurring or might occur. Consequently, mass-wasting was mapped along the entire length of the Escarpment, rendering it a constraint area. However, in the case of shoreline erosion, basic geomorphological principles indicate greater severity in headland and unprotected areas. Shoreline erosion was mapped on this basis. As a result of lack of specific data, Abiotic constraints were ranked as being severe, moderate, or low, according to their spatial overlap (see Table 5.1). The greater the number of overlapping hazards (shoreline erosion, mass-wasting, karstification, flooding, or peat bog) the greater the constraint index value, and the more severe the potential hazards. The cave, collapse, and subsidence areas could constitute hazard areas but available data were not adequate for mapping.

Delineation of Abiotic Areas of Constraint

The entire study area presents numerous Abiotic constraints of varying degrees of severity (Figure 5.5). The Lake Huron and Georgian Bay shorelines and adjoining lands exhibit the greatest active or potential hazards. In these areas, shoreline erosion, flooding, karstification and, on the Escarpment side, mass-wasting, all overlap and create the greatest risk potential. The Tobermory Bog is included as a low-level constraint and possibly a limitation to urban development. The South Tobermory fluvioglacial deposit, outside the bog and the more stable parts of the Cameron Lake/Dorcas Bay dunes complex, are considered the only Abiotically relatively constraint-free parts of the study area.

The large inland tract of land designated as "low constraint" is conditional upon its remaining under forest cover. The trees lessen the risk of accelerated karstification by reducing the impact of falling rainwater on the rock surface. If this forest cover is removed, karstification would likely accelerate, causing potentially severe erosion problems

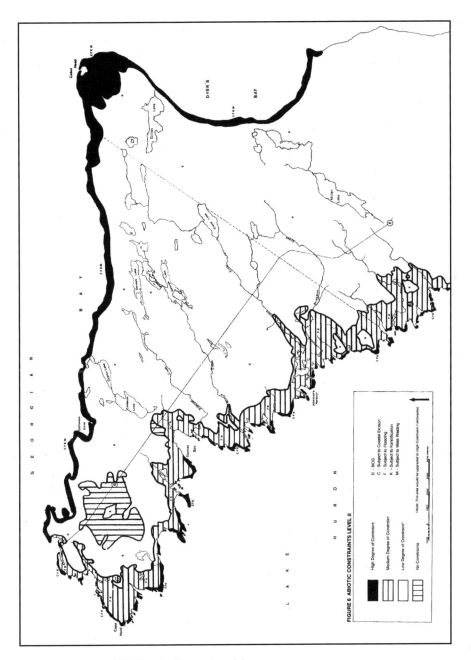

Figure 5.5   Level II Abiotic Constraints Map

(e.g., cave-ins) and water-level subsidence. This area would have to be reclassified to a severe constraint category.<Figure 5.5>

BIOTIC INFORMATION: LEVEL I DATA ON BIOTIC STRUCTURES OR FEATURES

In this study the Biotic features of the Bruce were mapped in terms of vegetation composition and distribution.

Vegetation Composition and Distribution

The large unbroken tracts of coniferous, deciduous, and mixed forest in the Bruce were found to be uncommon in southern Ontario. The vegetation communities within this forest are shown in Table 5.2. This table was prepared from government data, air photos, consultation with knowledgeable persons, and road reconnaissance. Within the wetlands are rock pavements or alvars and fens, which support grass and sedge species as well as a diversity of orchids. Fifteen species of orchids have been found in association with the fen and dune system near Dorcas Bay on Lake Huron. The unimproved pastures near Tobermory and eastward toward Lindsay Township include numerous alien grass and weed species. Many pastures are succeeding to woodlands of trembling aspen, cedar, and ground juniper. More details are given in Table 5.3, Comparison of Area and Frequency of Vegetation Communities.

BIOTIC INFORMATION: LEVEL I DATA ON BIOTIC FUNCTIONS OR PROCESSES

Maps were prepared of both terrestrial and aquatic habitat as a basis for identifying habitats offering vital winter protection, migration or reproduction functions for deer, fisher, trout, pike or other species valued by local residents, visitors, and researchers on the Bruce.

1. Coniferous Forest (>70% tree cover is coniferous)
   a. mixed conifer (no one species occurs over 50%)
   b. cedar dominant (>50% of forest is cedar)
   c. jack pine dominant
2. Deciduous Forest (>70% tree cover is deciduous)
   a. mixed deciduous
   b. poplar/birch association (combination of both exceeds 50%)
   c. hard maple dominant
3. Mixed Forest (conifers and deciduous each contribute 25-75% of canopy cover)
   a. mixed forest
   b. cedar dominant
   c. poplar/birch association
4. Woodland (10-25% of tree cover)
   a. cedar dominant
   b. white birch woodland
   c. poplar woodland
5. Alder Shrubland
6. Wetland (land having water table near, at, or above land surface)
   a. swamp
   b. alvar/fen
   c. marsh
   d. bog
7. Agricultural land
   a. improved pasture
   b. unimproved pasture
8. Meadow (>25% grass or forb cover)

Table 5.2   Vegetation Community Classification (Based on Ontario Ministry of Natural Resources Forest Resources Inventory Maps)

Community*	Frequency %	Rank 1-20	Area %	Rank 1-20	Uniqueness
1a	4.6	10	9.7	16	Low
1b	8.8	18	17.3	20	Low
1c	0.8	4	1.0	7	High
2a	3.4	8	3.4	10	Medium
2b	7.5	15	10.6	18	Low
2c	10.0	19	8.3	15	Low
3a	7.1	14	9.8	17	Low
3b	5.0	13	6.7	14	Medium
3c	8.4	17	15.3	19	Low
4a	8.0	16	4.8	13	Low
4b	2.1	6	2.7	9	High
4c	0.8	3	0.2	2	High
5	4.6	11	0.6	6	High
6a	13.4	20	3.5	11	Low
6b	2.1	5	0.3	4	High
6c	2.9	7	0.6	5	High
6d	0.4	1	0.2	1	High
7a	5.0	12	3.8	12	Medium
7b	4.2	9	2.4	8	Medium
8	0.8	2	0.2	3	High

Rank Values:	Values	Uniqueness
High = 1-6	High/High, High/Medium	= High
Medium = 7-13	High/Low, Medium/Meduim	= Medium
Low = 14-20	Medium/Low, Low/Low	= Low

*Community name is provided in Table 5.2.

Table 5.3   Comparison of Area and Frequency of Vegetation Communities

Habitat	Vegetation communities
Lowland Forest	# 1a, 1b, 3b, 5
Upland Forest	# 2b, 2c, 3a, 3c
Open Shrub Woodland	# 4a, 4b, 4c, 7b
Open Field	# 7a, 8
Cliff Face	Escarpment line from 1:50,000 National Topographic Series map

Table 5.4   Vegetation Communities into Wildlife Habitat

Terrestrial Habitat

The detailed vegetation communities identified in Table 5.2, which are primarily from Forest Inventory maps prepared for logging evaluation purposes, were reclassified into broader ecological communities: upland and lowland forest, open shrub land, open field, and cliff face according to the procedures on Table 5.2, 5.3, and 5.4. The results are displayed in Figure 5.6, the Terrestrial Wildlife Habitat map. Some of the detailed vegetation communities in Table 5.2 are not included in the tabulation and reclassification for Figure 5.6, the Terrestrial Wildlife Habitat map. This is because of their apparently low value for the terrestrial species of interest (Jackpine dominant) and because they were included later on the Aquatic Wildlife Habitat map (Figure 5.7), where they are more relevant than terrestrial habitat.

Winter deer yards were mapped by Ministry of Natural Resources in 1968, 1977, 1979, and 1984, respectively. Size and boundaries of the yards fluctuated somewhat over these years in accordance with snow depth, forage, and other conditions. The winter yards are shown in Figure 5.6, the Terrestrial Wildlife Habitat map, which also includes the lowland forest, upland forest, and other broad ecological communities derived from the detailed Vegetation Communities map. It is apparent that the predominantly lowland forests found in a broad band around Johnston's Harbour on Lake Huron are the preferred winter protection and reproduction grounds for the deer of the study area.

Less data were available on the preferred habitat of the elusive forest predator, the fisher. General information from government sources and local people was used to approximate the boundaries of prime fisher habitat. Figure 5.6 indicates that this habitat was in the relatively isolated upland and lowland forests near Emmett and George Lakes in the north central Bruce. Black bear were also a species of special interest to locals, visitors, and government officials but no reliable information was available on their numbers, distribution, or preferred habitat in the Bruce at the time of our study.

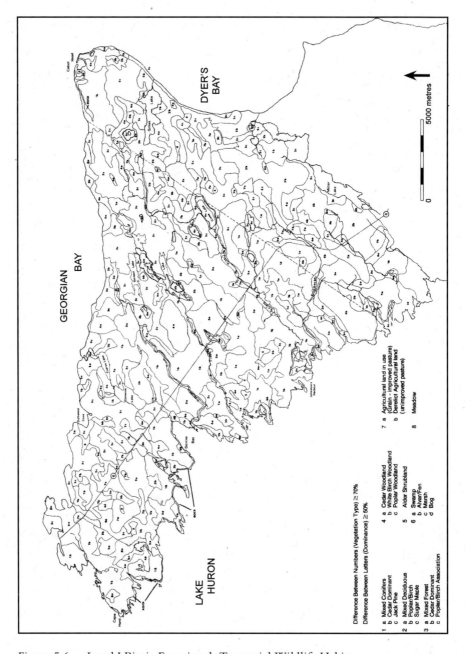

Figure 5.6   Level I Biotic Functional: Terrestrial Wildlife Habitat

PLACES

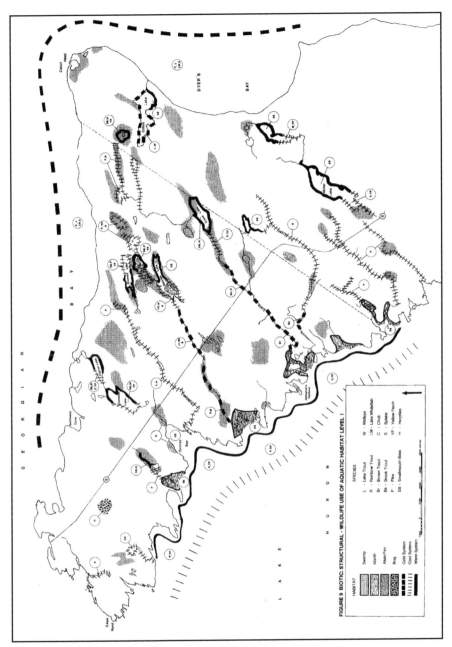

Figure 5.7   Level I Biotic Functional: Aquatic Wildlife Habitat

Aquatic Wildlife Habitat

To prepare this map (Figure 5.7) Ontario Ministry of Natural Resources data were used to classify water bodies (streams, lakes, wetlands and shore zones) as either cold, cool, or warm systems because such temperature differences influence the migration, reproduction, and seasonal habitat of trout, pike, and other fish species. The Crane Lake system produces brown and brook trout in the cold river water, pike and yellow perch in the cool lakes, and bays and smallmouth bass in the warm shallow lakes. The gradually sloping Lake Huron shoreline produces both a near-shore warm water zone and a deeper cool zone. The deep Georgian Bay water north of the Niagara Escarpment forms a cold system with suitable habitat for whitefish, splake, and chubb. Snakes and other herptiles as well as ducks and other waterfowl are concentrated in near-shore marshes, interior swamps, and shallow lakes.

BIOTIC INFORMATION: LEVEL II AREAS OF BIOTIC SIGNIFICANCE

Vegetation community diversity, faunal diversity, terrestrial and aquatic habitat, and community uniqueness were initially selected as significance criteria in our study but lack of relevant data proved to be a barrier to their effective use.

Community Diversity

This was initially calculated according to the number of vegetation communities (Table 5.2) located in three-kilometre sites distributed over the study area. Areas were then ranked as high, medium, or low according to an ordinal scale. This procedure was subsequently considered to have limited value in actually mapping community diversity because of the arbitrary and non-ecological nature of the three-kilometre boundaries. The principle of assigning a high community diversity value to an area with a relatively high number of vegetation communities did, however, prove useful in estimating areas of high Biotic significance.

Faunal diversity also turned out to be of limited specific value in this study because available data were insufficient to determine faunal diversity for each mapped vegetation community. General information from knowledgeable residents and professionals indicated no large difference in animal species numbers among the vegetation communities, although faunal diversity was thought to be highest where the greatest numbers of vegetation communities were located. On this basis, estimates of high vegetation community diversity were considered indicative of an area's high faunal diversity.

Terrestrial and Aquatic Wildlife Habitat

The Terrestrial and Aquatic Wildlife Habitat maps were used as indicators of areas offering important functions or services for valued animals such as deer, fisher, fish, and waterfowl.

Community Uniqueness

The relative uniqueness of a vegetation community was considered to be a function of its size and frequency in the study area. Communities were valued as high, medium, or low according to the frequency and size scales shown on Table 5.3. Mapping of these uniqueness values was considered but the interspersing of many communities over the study area inhibited the clear display of broad patterns of uniqueness. In actual practice, patterns of community uniqueness can be envisioned in terms of the uniqueness categories in Table 5.3.

Delineating Biotic Significance Areas

On the basis of the foregoing selection and analysis of significance criteria, a schematic map of Biotic significance areas was prepared (Figure 5.8). Areas were ranked as high, medium, or low on the basis of how they rated in terms of estimates of occurrence of the principal criteria of vegetation community diversity, terrestrial and aquatic habitat, and community uniqueness, with faunal diversity incorporated into vegetation community diversity. Areas where two or more of these overlapped were given a high rank and areas where the evidence indicated only

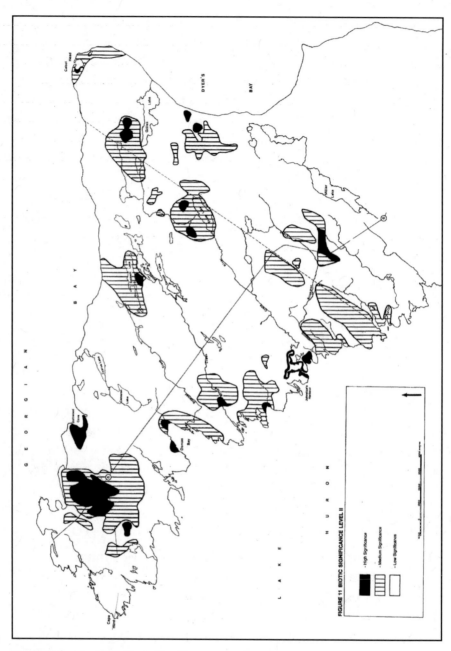

Figure 5.8   Level II Biotic Significance

one occurrence were assigned a medium ranking. The uncertain nature of the data meant that only preliminary mapping of Biotic significance was possible in this study.

The results are shown in Figure 5.8 and can be understood by relating Table 5.3, the Comparison of Area and Frequencies of Communities, Figure 5.6, the Terrestrial Wildlife Habitat map, and Figure 5.7, the Aquatic Wildlife Habitat map. So a succession of areas along the Lake Huron coast were mapped as of high and medium significance because of the occurrence of winter deer yards and pike and other aquatic habitat. Areas near Gillies, Crane, George, and Emmett Lakes were ranked medium to high because of vegetation community uniqueness and aquatic habitat for lake trout, small mouth bass, pike, and other fish species. This is also the area where fisher habitat was approximated, and part of this habitat is included (Figure 5.8). Areas near Tobermory were ranked high and medium because of vegetation community diversity and uniqueness with the highly unique bog and its herptile habitat.

BIOTIC INFORMATION: LEVEL II AREAS OF BIOTIC CONSTRAINT

Criteria for identifying areas of biotic constraints were floral and faunal habitat dependence and species rarity. Areas where floral and faunal species are specialists and specifically dependent on particular habitats present constraints to development, as do those with rare species. Recoverability of vegetation communities was also kept in mind as a third criterion, but not systematically evaluated because all the major vegetation groups are considered to possess low vegetation recoverability after fires, logging, or other disturbances.

Faunal and Floral Habitat Dependence

Generally the Bruce supports relatively few strong faunal habitat specialists as many species use a variety of habitats throughout the area. Some species, such as the rare orchids and sedges, are highly dependent on certain habitats. However, inadequacies in the wildlife distribution

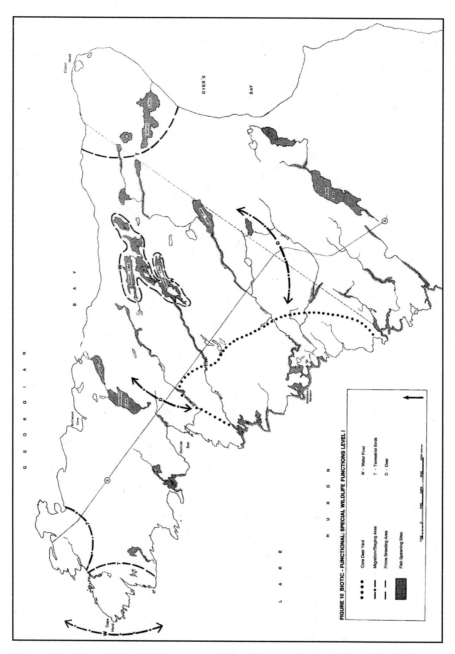

Figure 5.9   Level II Biotic Constraints: Special Wildlife Functions

data severely limit delimitation of areas of habitat dependence for most species.

Figure 5.9 is a Special Wildlife Habitat map, which estimates areas of key habitat for survival of some especially valued species. This map was based on the most reliable data available to us and shows core deer yards and migration routes and fish spawning and breeding areas for waterfowl and terrestrial birds. Important areas of habitat dependence for breeding waterfowl and birds and fish spawning include lakes, streams, and wetlands around Emmet Lake and Cabot Head and for deer the lowland coniferous forest around Johnston's Harbour on Lake Huron. The very specialized breeding habitat of the Henslow's sparrow, a threatened species, is limited to large, uncut fields, which cannot be precisely identified on the Ontario Forest Resource Inventory maps. Potential breeding areas are located in the fields near Tobermory.

Species Rarity

Detailed information on rare species distribution allowed for preparation of the rare species distribution map (Figure 5.10). This map is relevant for identifying Biotic constraint areas but also can be considered in relation to the Biotic significance areas map (see Figure 5.8). In other words, rare species may be considered as representing constraint or significance. For example, the relative abundance of rare species in an area could be used in assessing its significance. The variety of these species in an area also means they require special care in management so they can be seen as constraints. The need for special care to ensure the survival of these valued species was seen as the most important consideration in our study so the rare species were flagged as constraints. All species having the status of provincially or nationally rare were delineated. Information sources included various Ontario Ministry of Natural Resources reports on Areas of Natural and Scientific Interest (ANSIs) and Biologically Significant Areas (Johnson, 1981).

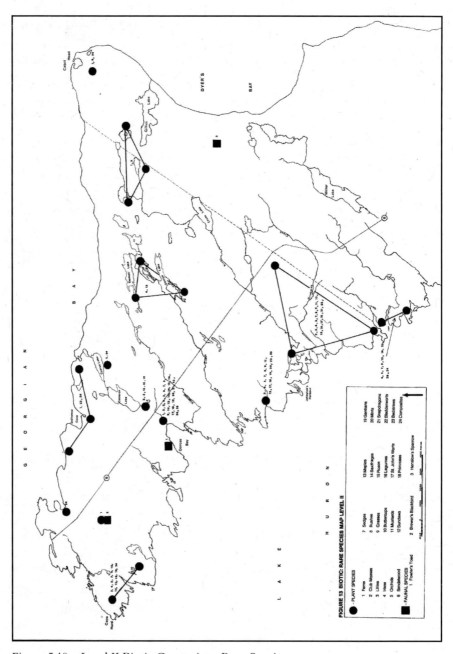

Figure 5.10   Level II Biotic Constraints: Rare Species

Vegetation Recoverability

A typical indicator of vegetation recoverability is the age of the community. Old climax forests take longer to develop than younger ones. Much of the forest on the Bruce is evenly aged (about 60–80 years old) largely because of an extensive fire that occurred in 1908. Much soil subsequently eroded away, and phosphorus was lost from the system. The present forest is stunted and slow-growing as a result and has limited recoverability. Alvar, fen, and bog recovery from disturbance is poor, and recovery efforts need to be focused on these habitats. The rate of organic accumulation in these habitats is slow, nutrient enrichment retarded, regrowth hindered, and many plant species have little resilience to trampling.

Delineating Biotic Areas of Constraint

Data on the criteria for evaluating and delineating Biotically constrained areas were even less amenable to quantification and ranking than those for Biotic significance. All constraint criteria were considered to be of equal importance. An area in which two criteria overlapped scored high as a constraint area. An area with only one criterion ranked low (Figure 5.11). The largest high-constraint area was around Johnston's Harbour. Here a number of rare species are located along with excellent deer habitat. Much Bruce lowland forest was rated medium for Biotic constraint because it is winter habitat for deer. Lakes, streams, wetlands, fens, and alvars were considered sensitive habitat because of fish spawning, orchids, and other rare plants and were mapped as medium constraint. The Tobermory bog was recognized for its uniqueness on the Biotic significance map but should also be recognized here as a constraint because of its association with numerous rare plant and animal species.

CULTURAL INFORMATION: HISTORIC BACKGROUND

Early hunting and gathering peoples were known from archaeological evidence to have lived in the Bruce from 5,000 to 1,000 B.C. Their

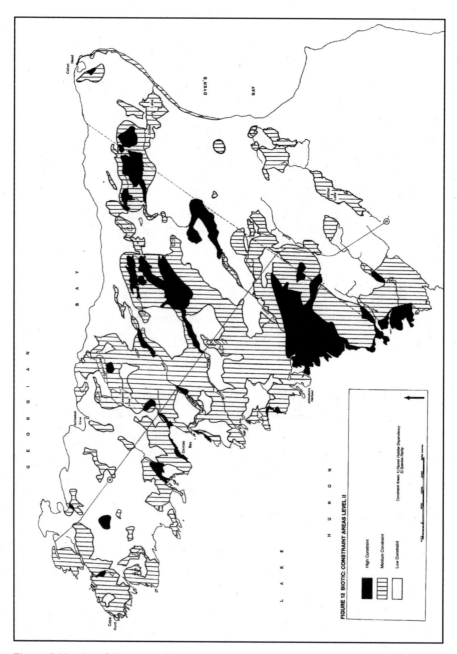

Figure 5.11   Level II Areas of Biotic Constraint

primary locations were near good fishing areas at river mouths on Lake Huron. Archeological finds included seasonal campsites, hunting, fishing, and domestic artifacts. Implements were made from local stone, wood, and hide resources (Carruthers, 1976). Links between early Bruce people and later native groups known to Europeans were not well understood. The Ottawa occupied the Bruce or, as they referred to it, the Saugeen Peninsula, in the seventeenth century (Robertson, 1971). They were later driven out by the Iroquois who were, in turn, routed by the Hurons of the southeast and the Ojibwa who held the peninsula until 1854 (Robertson, 1971; Brown, 1979).

The Ojibwa surrendered the peninsula to the Crown in October 1854 (Robertson, 1971; Brown, 1979). They then settled at Colpoy's Bay on the Cape Croker Indian Reserve, near Georgian Bay. The Ojibwa also obtained a 1,600 ha hunting area in St. Edmunds Township, between the Crane River and Willow Creek, known as the Saugeen and Cape Croker Reserves.

A European survey took place in 1850 and Crown land was divided into farm lots (Robertson, 1971). Initial settlement arose from southern demand for the red and white pine of the region. Robertson noted that "the lumbering resources of St. Edmunds have been exploited to an extent not equalled in any other township" of Bruce County (Robertson, 1971: 259). And this observation could be extended to include much of central and southern Ontario. After logging and realization that farming was impractical in the northern Bruce, largely due to thin soils and exposed bedrock, commercial fishing became the dominant industry. Overfishing and introduction of the parasitic lamprey eel to Lake Huron took its toll. The lake trout fishery was finished by 1956.

After WWI, the automobile opened up the area to cottagers from southern Ontario, New York, Michigan, and Ohio. In the affluent 1960s, people from outside the Bruce began purchasing property throughout the peninsula. The 1970s and 1980s saw a big increase in tourism. St. Edmunds Township has been actively promoting tourism, including promotion of diving and park use and construction of a health clinic for local people as well as seasonal and transient visitors.

Institutional Arrangements and Land-Use Planning and Management

The legislative framework for the Ontario municipal government system is described in the Ontario Municipal Act overseen by the Ontario Ministry of Municipal Affairs (Corpus Almanac and Canadian Source Book, 1985). Under this Act local government consisted of Bruce County with sixteen townships. Two of these were St. Edmunds and Lindsay Townships, which covered our study area. The county's Official Plan established policy for land use and related activities. Actual development decisions for private and municipal lands were the legal responsibility of the townships.

Other influential agencies and levels of government included the Niagara Escarpment Planning and Development Act (NEPDA), which provided for the Niagara Escarpment Commission. This commission was to maintain the rugged uplands, cliffs, and forests of the escarpment and surrounding lands in a natural state through development control measures. The Niagara Escarpment extends from Niagara Falls to the north shore of the Bruce and Georgian Bay. That part of the escarpment falling within the Bruce Peninsula National Park would be protected by National Park legislation and staff.

The Ontario Ministry of Natural Resources had major responsibilities for conservation and appropriate development of fish, wildlife, fuel, and industrial minerals. The Ministry controlled large parts of the Bruce, including land intended for the proposed national park. Native or First Nation traditional lands fell within the proposed national park and other First Nation reserves were located nearby. Numerous other federal and provincial agencies also bore various responsibilities in the Bruce and had to be considered in planning for the proposed park (Government of Ontario, 1987).

CULTURAL INFORMATION: LEVEL I CULTURAL STRUCTURES OR FEATURES

Land tenure, land use, recreational areas, and cultural, historic, and archaeological information were selected for Level I mapping and description of the Cultural structures or features of the study area.

Land Tenure

The tenure pattern reflected the historical development of the northern Bruce (Figure 5.12). Tobermory and Tobermory South were two major areas of permanent human settlement. Cottage and residential development took place at the tip of the peninsula, along the southern shoreline, and on Gillies Lake, George Lake, and Cameron Lake. The north shore was relatively untouched by cottage development, with the exception of Dunk's Bay, because high scarp faces and cobble beaches limited access.

The 1,600 ha Cape Croker and Saugeen Indian Reserves – native hunting lands – were situated between Side Road Creek and the Crane River north of Highway 6, and other lands were subject to First Nation claims. The Ontario Ministry of Natural Resources land holdings involved: Crown land, wildlife management areas, and provincial parks. These lands comprised approximately 6,480 ha of the entire park study area, which was approximately 15,237 ha in size. Private vacant lands accounted for approximately 50 per cent of the land within the national park study area. Bruce County owned an approximately 1,380 ha forest to the northwest of the First Nations reserves. St. Edmunds Township owns some property throughout the study area, including the municipal airport and small parks. The federal government owned one small parcel of land on Highway 6 used for telecommunications.

Land Use

The land-use categories were chosen in accordance with criteria suggested by Grigoriew et al. (1985). These included historic persistence, current extent, intensity of use, economic and cultural significance to

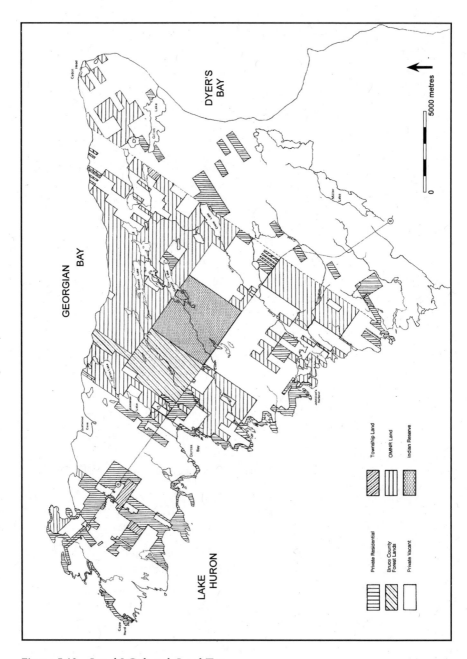

Figure 5.12   Level I Cultural: Land Tenure

PLACES

local people, environmental impact, and potential to generate land-use conflict. The land-use categories are presented on Figure 5.13 and included small areas of hamlet, agricultural, and extractive (aggregates) land along with extensive private residential or cottage areas especially along the Lake Huron shore. In general, recreational opportunities were widespread and included local traditional hunting areas, provincial parks, public and private natural lands, and caving, diving, hiking, and snowmobile areas, notably along the Georgian Bay coast.

CULTURAL INFORMATION: LEVEL I CULTURAL FUNCTIONS OR PROCESSES

Cultural functions such as transport routes, residences, and other patterns were grouped and mapped in terms of corridors, nodes, and hinterland areas (Figure 5.14). This map can guide decision-makers and concerned citizens to areas representing planning challenges notably in the nodes and corridors where numerous, sometimes conflicting, uses come together.

Major Corridors

The major transportation corridor was Highway 6 to Tobermory. Other transportation corridors followed access roads to permanent and seasonal homes on Gillies Lake, George Lake, Crane Lake, and Cameron Lake, seasonal residences on the southern shoreline, the Emmett Lake Junior Ranger Camp, and the former Cyprus Lake Provincial Park. The two mapped recreational corridors along the Georgian Bay coast and winding through the proposed national park were the Bruce Trail and the Bruce Snowmobiling Association Trail. Public recreation sites were scattered through the area.

Core Area Concept

On the basis of the foregoing analysis, a large block in the north central part of the park study area, where roads and recreational and other activities were less intense, stood out as especially suitable for a national

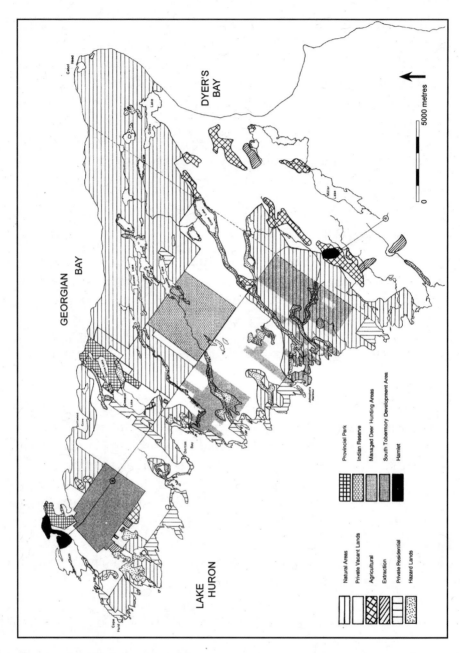

Figure 5.13   Level I Cultural: Land Use

PLACES

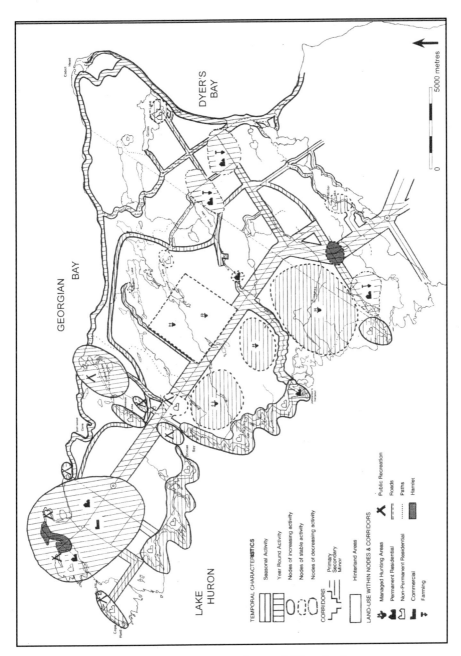

Figure 5.14   Level I Cultural: Nodes, Corridors, and Hinterlands

park (Figure 5.15). This core area was approximately 8,364 ha in size. Seventy-nine percent was owned by the Ontario Ministry of Natural Resources or Bruce County, making land acquisition for a national park quite feasible. In comparison, 86 per cent of the rest of the park study area was privately owned, making acquisition considerably more difficult.

CULTURAL INFORMATION: LEVEL II AREAS OF CULTURAL SIGNIFICANCE

Several criteria were used to map and discuss culturally significant areas. These included low density of development, which favoured nature conservation, the major goal of the proposed national park. Also included were park, recreational, historic, and symbolic significance as well as importance to indigenous people.

Cultural Significance Map

The majority of the study area was considered significant in terms of the foregoing criteria (Figure 5.16). Some significant features included park and former park areas, the Bruce Trail, the Bruce County Snowmobile Trail, various historical areas and sites, deer management areas, areas of interest to indigenous people, and archaeological areas and sites. The Bruce Trail was open in winter for skiing and snowshoeing with camping at Cypress Lake. Seasonal and permanent residential areas and agricultural and aggregate extraction areas were not mapped as significant, being viewed as activities generally incompatible with recreational, historic, and other values.

CULTURAL INFORMATION: LEVEL II AREAS OF CULTURAL CONSTRAINT

In the ABC method, Cultural constraints are determined by degrees of incompatibility among land uses as well as the environmental effects of these uses. Places in the study area were accordingly judged as compatible,

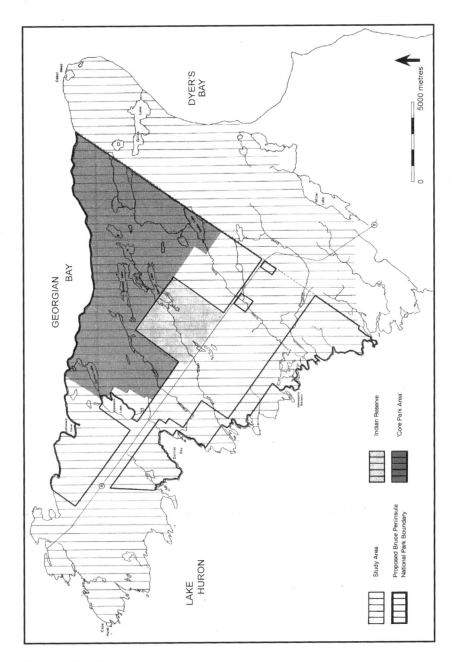

Figure 5.15   Core Park Area Concept

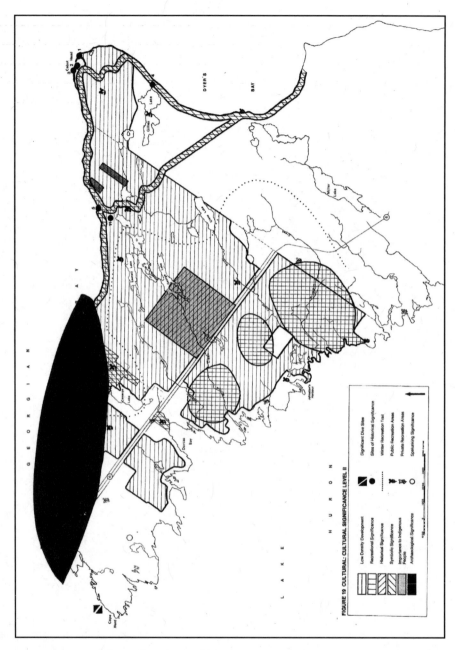

Figure 5.16   Level II Cultural Significance

tension, or conflict areas in terms of the interactions and effects of land use, recreation, nodes, corridors, hinterland patterns, and the core park area, as shown on Figures 5.13 to 5.15. Figure 5.16 can also be usefully compared to these maps in establishing compatibility, tension, and conflict zones.

Cultural Constraint Map

Figure 5.17, the Cultural constraints map, was the result of a comparison of all the foregoing maps. The compatibility area in the north central part of the proposed park was dominated by extensive natural areas, generally less intense recreational activities, relatively few nodes and corridors, and extensive hinterlands. This area of compatibility also overlapped strongly with the core park area identified on Figure 5.15.

The Indian lands north of Highway 6 adjoining the core park area were judged as tension zones because, while on the one hand they were of historic, educational, and cultural significance, on the other hand their use for hunting or other purposes could present management challenges in a national park where no hunting is allowed. The Bruce County Snowmobile Trail had recreational value, but also was seen as a conflict zone because the noise and disturbance of snowmobiles was not in line with park purposes. The Bruce Trail was mapped on the one hand as compatible in terms of its recreational role and on the other hand as a conflict zone in terms of the effects that heavy trail use could have on the natural environment. The areas around Tobermory have been mapped as conflict zones because of the presence of the village, agricultural and extraction activities, and the designation of a South Tobermory Development Area. The reader is left to undertake other comparisons among the various maps in explaining the Cultural constraint patterns shown on Figure 5.17.

LEVEL III: AREAS OF OVERALL SIGNIFICANCE

To identify areas of overall significance and constraint, each of the Level II Abiotic, Biotic, and Cultural significance and constraint maps

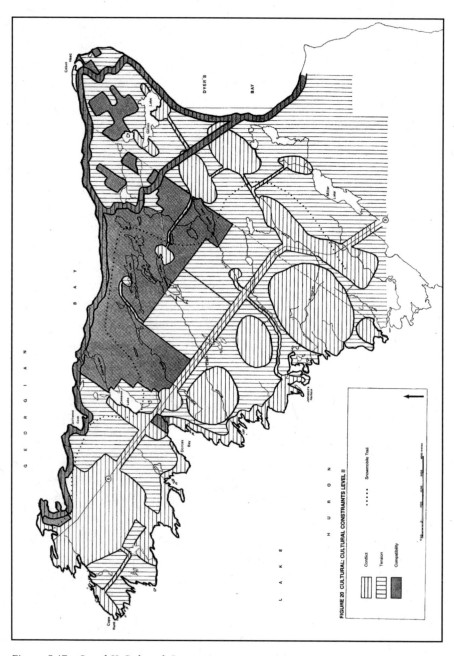

Figure 5.17   Level II Cultural Constraints

PLACES

were overlaid. Areas of overall significance were ranked in terms of the degree of overlap among high, medium, and low values on the significance maps. In integrating the Level II Abiotic, Biotic, and Cultural significance maps, areas of high value on any of these maps were considered as areas of overall high significance. This was done on the principle that an area of high significance should retain its high value whether or not it overlapped with an area on another map which was ranked high, medium, or low in value. This procedure ensured that all the areas of high significance on each of Abiotic, Biotic, and Cultural significance maps retained their values at the overall level of significance. So the overall ranking system was:

HIGH   Any high value

MEDIUM, LOW   At any point of overlap, the higher rank
                   was applied.

Many of the areas of high significance formed a band from Dyer's Bay to Tobermory along the Georgian Bay shoreline (Figure 5.18). This band was given high significance mainly because the area is the most geologically unique part of the entire Niagara Escarpment in Bruce County and surrounding region. In turn, this uniqueness promotes recreational use of the trails and cliff-water interface. The corridor's northern end near Tobermory was highly significant both abiotically and biotically because of the large fluvioglacial deposits as well as the unique bog habitat. Area along the central Lake Huron coast near and south of Dorcas Bay were ranked high and medium significance due to wetland habitat, the deer yard, fish spawning, and other Biotic values as well as high recreational use and potential. Gillies Lake was considered highly significant for both Biotic and Cultural reasons. It is the deepest lake in the study area and the only lake in southern Ontario producing land-locked lake trout. As a result, recreational fishing is intense.

The Overall Areas of Medium Significance included the Indian Reserves, the First Nations hunting area, and biologically productive forest and wetland areas for deer, water fowl, and herptiles. The Overall Areas of Low Significance were basically drier inland areas having

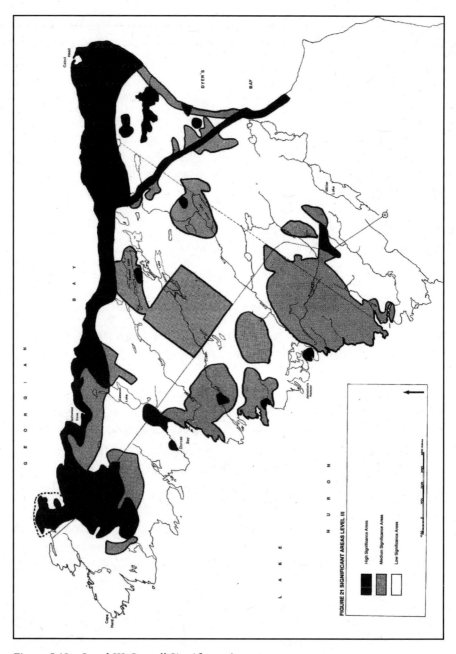

Figure 5.18   Level III Overall Significant Areas

PLACES

no distinguishing Abiotic, Biotic, or Cultural features. Generally they were areas upon which wildlife had low habitat dependence. Karst was present but largely inactive.

LEVEL III: OVERALL AREAS OF CONSTRAINT

The same procedure was used to deal with overall areas of constraint as was used with overall areas of significance. Maps of Abiotic, Biotic, and Cultural constraints were overlaid and ranked in accordance with the system just described for overall significance.

The majority of the study area was classed as either high or medium in constraint (Figure 5.19) largely because of numerous Cultural constraints. The most notable were extensive cottage development and flooding potential along the shorelines: the high density development or potential development areas around Tobermory, Tobermory South, and Highway 6; and the damage susceptibility of important wetlands to hiking and recreational use. Some areas with high Biotic constraints, for example just south of Johnston's Harbour and near Gillies and Emmett Lakes, could have been extended into adjoining areas because of wetland and other Biotic values but were eventually ranked as medium or low constraint in line with the judgments for most of the surrounding area.

Overall Areas of Medium Constraint include the Indian Reserves and much of the private vacant land where uses are currently relatively compatible with national park objectives. Certain activities such as logging or increased hunting are not in line with these objectives and could lead to conflict. Low constraint areas included the public, county, and Crown lands, where use was either of low intensity or high compatibility. The former Cypress Lake Provincial Park, for example, was considered a low constraint area because it had been set aside for recreational use in a natural setting. Recreational use of the former park had been generally in line with use in a national park, having been managed with considerable respect for associated forest, wetland, and natural values. The balance between the intensity of recreational use and the conservation of nature is critical in such an area.

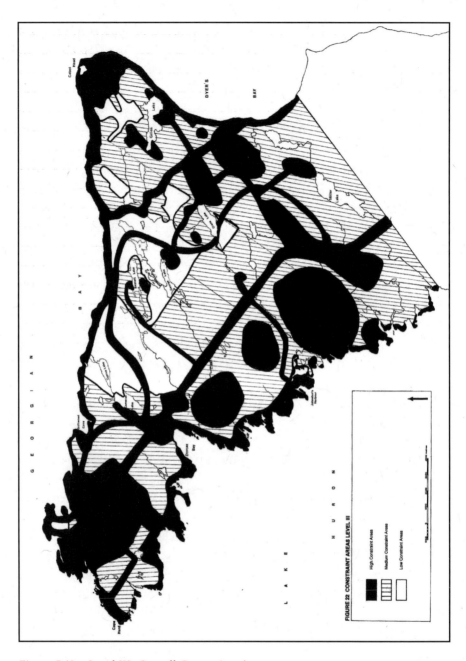

Figure 5.19   Level III: Overall Constraints Areas

LEVEL IV: MANAGEMENT PROPOSAL

The primary aim of this study was to test the effectiveness of the ABC method as a planning tool for a new national park. Interest was focused on collecting, analyzing, and assessing information for boundary delineation, land use within and around the park, interpretation, education, and identifying research needs. Lack of information was often a challenge. For example, spatial data for animal species was limited to "game species."

Another barrier to the achievement of objectives was time and resource limitations, which prevented, for example, collection, analysis, and interpretation of information on the powers, responsibilities, and possible roles of various government agencies and private organizations in working for or against the creation of a national park in the Bruce. Detailed analysis of the mandates and capabilities of such agencies and organizations could not be done in the manner of the Presqu'ile, Aishihik, or East Beaufort studies (Chapters 4, 6, and 7, this volume).

Another challenge was the ongoing work on establishment of the national park. As our study proceeded, the national park was formally announced by the responsible ministers of Canada and Ontario and their agreement included commitments on boundaries and other matters with local residents, for example, the decision to set aside a swath of land extending through the park lands and bordering Highway 6 to Tobermory. Numerous decisions on the inclusion or exclusion of private and public lands were also made, for example, on the deer yard in the southeast part of our study area. These decisions have considerably fragmented the park and left out some areas that our study showed to be significant for park purposes.

RESULTS

In spite of these challenges, the results of this ABC study are valuable to park planning in a number of ways. For example, the results could be used in future refinements of park boundaries, especially for the irregular set of park lands south of Highway 6. Our findings showed the significance of areas such as Cabot Head, which lies just outside the park boundary in Lindsay Township where sentiment has not been in favour of the park. This area is, however, managed as a wildlife reserve by the Ontario Ministry of Natural Resources. This agency and the National Park people should co-operate closely on this area in the mutual interest. Our study also could be applied to zoning the national park. For example, the core area identified in the northern part of the park should be considered for wilderness zoning in the Bruce Peninsula National Park Management Plan. Our information could also be useful in establishing priorities for acquisition of private lands on a willing seller–willing buyer basis. The private lands in the north central part of the park – the core area – would presumably rank high in acquisition programs. And our information would definitely be valuable for park interpretation and education programs, for example, in giving visitors and residents an overview of park resources and values. An example would be an interpretation program on the Bruce Trail, particularly along the Georgian Bay shore, where many significant Abiotic features could be observed, their origin understood and their sensitivity to disturbance and need for protection explained.

RESEARCH NEEDS

Our study also revealed many research and information needs for careful planning and management of the park and surrounding area. These included the following Abiotic, Biotic, and Cultural topics:

Abiotic

- Extent, rate, and susceptibility of mass wasting processes.
- Distribution and linkages of subterranean waterways in karst areas.
- Detailed mapping of geological/geomorphological processes on the Escarpment brow in the holokarst area.
- Severity of shoreline erosion.
- Magnitude, frequency, and natural and cultural effects of shoreline flooding.

Biotic

- Distributional and ecological data on most species.
- Identification of critical faunal habitat.
- Detailed delineation of areas with rare flora.
- Seasonal movement of deer and other species, and identification of critical habitat areas.
- More habitat-specific information on birds that migrate through and breed in the study area. Better data are needed here as well as time and resources for study.

Cultural

- Visitor experience.
- Costs and benefits of recreation.
- Winter recreational use.
- Activities on private vacant lands.
- Effect of future access roads adjacent to park.
- Conflict-resolution studies.
- Effect of coastal access on shoreline sites.
- Institutional and planning arrangements, including analysis of active agencies and organizations, their mandates, capacities, gaps, and needs.

CONCLUSIONS

In general we found the method to be useful and to have the great advantage of flexibility in its application to local circumstances. The method can be modified to accommodate to areas with different land-use and environmental histories, current land-use patterns and scales. This is apparent in comparing this application of the ABC method to those for Presqu'ile, Aishihik, and the East Beaufort Sea (See Chapters 4, 6, and 7).

Numerous challenges apply, however, to our study and the others. One is general difficulty in securing relevant data, especially biological data. Another is difficulty in quantifying and comparing data for ranking purposes. Subjective qualitative scales (high, medium, low) often have to be used. And relating the significance or constraints of Abiotic, Biotic, and Cultural features through, for example, their degree of overlap also makes assumptions about equivalence of values among Abiotic, Biotic, and Cultural features. Lack of overlap of one of these types of features with one of the other two types could result in a low overall ranking for a feature even though it is of high value in its category. Some sort of subjective adjustment often is considered in such circumstances, as in our case when we decided because of their intrinsic value that high values for the Abiotic, Biotic, and Cultural dimensions should remain as such in compiling overall ranking.

This leads to a final important point. Some subjective judgments will generally have to be made in all applications of the ABC method because of inevitable data inadequacies and because of the problems inherent in comparing different kinds of things – "apples to oranges." In this respect careful consultation among research team members and affected parties is essential in arriving at an imperfect but generally useful working conclusion. Considerable consultation was possible among our team members. But much consultation with affected parties was impossible because of time and resource limitations. Our study and many of the maps are therefore only indicative and preliminary but still have considerable value for planning, particularly strategic planning, which involves determining what is known, not known, and needs to be known in understanding more detailed work towards shared goals and objectives.

NOTES

1   Adapted from G. Forbes, M. Bowes, L. Ordubegian, T. Rasmussen, and G. Whitelaw, *Application of the ABC Resource Survey Methodology to the Bruce Peninsula National Park and Environs*. Technical Paper 3, Heritage Resources Centre, University of Waterloo, Waterloo, Ontario, 1989.

REFERENCES

Bastedo, J.D., J.G. Nelson, and J.B. Theberge. 1984. "An ecological approach to resource survey and planning for environmentally significant areas: The ABC method." *Environmental Management* 8(2): 125–134.

Brown, L. 1979. *The Bruce: A Guide.* The Mariner Chart Shop, Tobermory, Ontario.

Carruthers, P.J. 1976. *An Archaeological Transect through Ontario – Heritage Planning – Recommendations for the Niagara Escarpment Development Areas.* Toronto: Ontario Ministry of Culture and Recreation, Historical Planning Research.

Chapman, L.J., and D.F. Putnam. 1984. *The Physiography of Southern Ontario.* 3d ed. Toronto: Ontario Ministry of Natural Resources.

Corpus Almanac and Canadian Source Book, Vol. 2. 1985. Toronto: Southam Communications.

Cowell, D.W. 1976. *Karst Geomorphology of Northern Bruce Peninsula.* Master's thesis. McMaster University, Hamilton, Ontario.

Cowell, D.W., and N. Woerns. 1976. *Earth Science Candidate Nature Reserves in the Niagara Planning Area.* Toronto: Ontario Ministry of Natural Resources, Park Planning Branch.

Cuddy, P.G., and K.M. Lindsay. 1976. *Significant Natural Areas along the Niagara Escarpment: A Report on Nature Reserve Candidates and Other Natural Areas in the Niagara Escarpment Planning Area.* Toronto: Ontario Ministry of Natural Resources, Park Planning Branch.

Fox, W.S. 1952. *The Bruce Beckons: The Story of Lake Huron's Great Peninsula.* Toronto: University of Toronto Press.

Government of Ontario. 1987. *KWIC Index to Services.* Toronto: Queen's Park.

Grigoriew, P., J.B. Theberge, and J.G. Nelson. 1985. *Park Boundary Delineation Manual: The ABC Resource Survey Approach.* Occasional Paper 4. Waterloo: Heritage Resources Centre, University of Waterloo.

Johnson, J. 1981. *Biologically Significant Areas: Lake Huron Shoreline-Bruce Peninsula.* Owen Sound: Ontario Ministry of Natural Resources.

Liberty, B.A., and T.E. Bolton. 1971. *Paleozoic Geology of the Bruce Peninsula.* Memoir 360. Ottawa: Geological Survey of Canada.

Ontario Ministry of Natural Resources. 1986. *Owen Sound District Fisheries Management Plan 1986–2000.* Owen Sound: Owen Sound District Office.

Robertson, N. 1971. *The History of the County of Bruce and the Minor Municipalities Therin.* Owen Sound: Richardson Bond and Wright.

Smith, P.G.R., J.G. Nelson, and J.B. Theberge. 1986. *Environmentally Significant Areas, Conservation and Land Use Management in the Northwest Territories.* Technical Paper 1. Waterloo: Heritage Resources Centre, University of Waterloo.

6

1987

INSTITUTIONAL ARRANGEMENTS FOR INDIVIDUAL ENVIRONMENTALLY SIGNIFICANT AREAS: THE CASE OF AISHIHIK, YUKON[1]

J.G. Nelson, P. Grigoriew, J. Theberge, and B. Bastedo

INTRODUCTION

Here we describe a method of designing appropriate institutional arrangements for safeguarding individual environmentally significant areas (ESAs). It is assumed that an ESA has been identified on the basis of rarity, diversity, representativeness, or other valued aspects of natural and cultural systems, by a wildlife, recreation, or other concerned agency or group. Some type of park, wildlife reserve, or other institutional arrangement may also have been suggested for management of the area concerned. In such circumstances, questions may arise about whether the ESA has been mapped well enough, in terms of its natural and cultural characteristics, to plan for its appropriate management in the long term. More important from the standpoint of this chapter, it may also be asked whether the proposed institutional arrangements are suitable or whether others should be applied to the ESA.

A companion study of the analysis of institutional arrangements for a set of candidate ESAs in a particular region is the next chapter in this book (Chapter 7). The key question in that case is: what institutional arrangements ought to be applied to all the candidate ESAs in the region? Recommendations for each ESA can subsequently be analyzed, on a larger scale and in more detail, by using the method described in the present chapter.

The impetus for these papers arises from research conducted beginning in 1978 in the Yukon and Northwest Territories (NWT) (Theberge et al., 1980; Fenge, 1982; Bastedo et al., 1984; Bastedo, J.D., 1986). In general, the work is in the spirit of the human ecological approach taken by Lusigi (1981) in Africa, the present authors being always very aware of, and sensitive to, the land uses and ways of life of indigenous people. In this context, it is important to realize that many native people in the Canadian North have not made what are referred to as "land-claim settlements" with the federal government. The development of national parks and other management arrangements for lands and waters to which native people lay claim, and which they have traditionally used and occupied, is of great concern to them and their offspring.

BALANCING USE AND CONSERVATION FOR SUSTAINABLE DEVELOPMENT

Our work is intended to contribute to the balancing of development and conservation in the spirit of the World Conservation Strategy (IUCN, 1980). Under various types of institutional arrangements, ESAs may provide for recreation, tourism, education, science, and environmental monitoring – as well as for hunting, fishing, and some other extractive uses – while protecting valued aspects of the environment. ESAs form a basic component in comprehensive use of land and other resources, and of environmental management. Table 6.1 is an attempt to indicate schematically some basic relationships among land-uses, general management classes, and institutional arrangements. ESAs play a strong role in all management classes, but especially in the preservation and protection categories noted in Table 6.1.

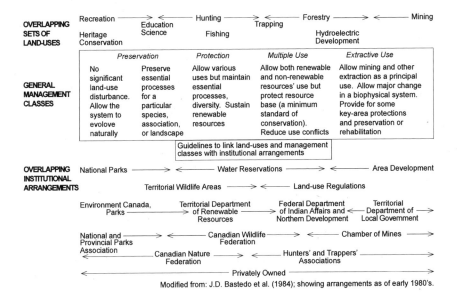

Modified from: J.D. Bastedo et al. (1984); showing arrangements as of early 1980's.

Table 6.1   Balanced Land-use in Northern Canada

INSTITUTIONAL ARRANGEMENTS FOR ESAS

Institutional arrangements refer, among other things, to laws, policies, guidelines, land-management types, regulations, zoning and boundary delineation, as well as to the agencies or groups ('actors') engaged in planning and managing ESAs. Examples in Yukon and NWT are the National Parks Act, territorial park ordinances, federal land-use regulations, and territorial wildlife areas – as well as Environment Canada, Parks (formerly Parks Canada), the Canadian Wildlife Service (CWS), the territorial parks, tourism, and other agencies and groups. Table 6.2 indicates some salient aspects of agencies, legislation, and other institutional arrangements, applicable to NWT ESAs. The last column – IUCN Management Category – refers to the fit between the northern Canadian existing ESA designations and the global protected area classes or guidelines established by the International Union for the Conservation of Nature (IUCN).

In early Yukon work, methods were developed for describing, analyzing, and assessing the strengths and weaknesses of an array of legislation and agencies related to the planning and management of ESAs. Among, the criteria applied to each agency were: (1) mandate as revealed in legislation or other ways; (2) goals; (3) ideology, or conceptual or philosophic orientation; (4) institutional character as indicated through budgets, type of personnel, and assistance programs; (5) land-use types and permitted activities; (6) institutional comprehensiveness or linkages with relevant groups; (7) land access and control methods, for example through leasing; and (8) experience and image. The research resulted in linking thirty-five candidate Yukon ESAs and their varying Abiotic, Biotic, and Cultural, characteristics with what were considered to be appropriate land-management types (Theberge et al., 1980).

Similar procedures were employed in subsequent research in the NWT (Nelson and Jessen, 1984; Smith et al., 1986). In that case attempts were also made to link available management-types to those suggested as global models by international agencies or groups, such as the International Union for Conservation of Nature and Natural Resources (IUCN, 1978) (Table 6.2). It is important to note that, when studied in totality, the IUCN land-management types permit a very wide array of land-uses as well as levels and kinds of conservation.

Environmentally Significant Areas

The term ESA refers to areas judged to be important for natural and/ or cultural reasons. The areas may include unique or rare *structures* or *features* such as landforms, plants, and archaeological sites. The areas may also include particular landforms and biological communities representative of natural regions identified by relevant agencies. ESAs also perform *functions* of natural or cultural importance, for example as aquifers, flood-plains, nesting sites, migrant bird staging areas, calving areas, migratory routes, religious or ceremonial sites, key hunting-grounds, or summer or winter settlements (Grigoriew et al., 1985; Nelson et al., 1985; Smith et al., 1986).

Existing ESA Designations	Proposed ESA Designations	Agency	Legislation or Policy	IUCN Management Category
National Park		Parks Canada[1]	National Parks Act	National Park (II)[2]
National Historic Park		"	"	
	Canadian Landmark	"	Parks Canada Policy	Natural Landmark (III)
	National Marie Park	"	Marine Parks Policy	National Park (II)
Historic Places		DIAND[3]	Historic sites and Monuments Act	
National Wildlife Area		Canadian Wildlife Service	Canada Wildlife Act	Wildlife Sanctuary (IV)
Migratory Bird Sanctuary		"	Migratory Birds Convention Act	"
	Fish and Marine Mammal Sanctuary	Dept. of Fisheries and Oceans	Towards a fish habitat policy	"
	Ecological Reserve	DIAND[3]	Comprehensive Conservation Policy and Strategy	?
Land Withdrawal		DIAND[3]	Territorial Lands Act	Resources Reserve (VI)
Reservation		DIAND[3] and NWT Water Board	Northern Inland Waters Act	Managed Resource Area (VIII)
Natural Environment Recreation Park		Parks and Tourism Division	Territorial Parks Ordinance	National Park (II)
Outdoor Recreation Park		"	"	Managed Resource Area (VIII)
Historic Park		"	"	
Wildlife Preserve		NWT Wildlife Service	Wildlife Ordinance	Wildlife Sanctuary (IV)
Wildlife Sanctuary		"	"	"
Critical Wildlife Area		"	"	"
Development Area		Dept of Local Government	Area Development Ordinance	Managed Resource Are (VIII)

[1] Parks Canada is now called 'Environment Canada, Parks'
[2] Roman numerals refer to IUCN Management Categories
[3] DIAND = Department of Indian Affairs and Northern Development

Source: Smith et al (1987: 379)

Table 6.2   Existing and Proposed ESA Designations in the NWT

In our view, ESAs are the 'nodes' and 'threads' that are key to conserving ecosystems or wider biomes. Thus, nesting grounds or calving areas perform vital functions for birds and other wildlife that are used by humans for hunting, recreation, tourism, or other purposes – often over large surrounding areas and sometimes even involving very distant lands and waters. The identification, delineation, planning, and management of ESAs are, therefore, seen as a fundamental part of comprehensive resource and land–use planning for a region.

THE ABC RESOURCE SURVEY METHOD

In our Yukon and NWT work, the Abiotic, Biotic, and Cultural (ABC) resource survey system, originally proposed by Dorney and Hoffman (1979), has been modified and used to describe the natural and cultural features and processes occurring in the vicinity of an ESA. The results provide a basis for analyzing and assessing an ESA's natural and cultural significance, delimiting boundaries, and deciding upon appropriate institutional or management arrangements.

The ABC method provides for description and analysis of landscape or ecosystem characteristics in terms of Abiotic (geology, geomorphology, hydrology), Biotic (flora and fauna), and Cultural (historic and current land-use, technology, ideology, and policy) aspects. Our modifications of the method mainly involve: (1) more precise development of the Abiotic and Biotic aspects for purposes of mapping, (2) more detailed development of land-use and Cultural mapping, and (3) the introduction of an institutional component (Grigoriew et al., 1985; B.H. Bastedo, 1986; J.D. Bastedo, 1986).

The ABC method culminates in the consideration of laws, polices, agencies, and other institutional arrangements for managing an ESA in relation to its Abiotic, Biotic, and Cultural characteristics, significance, and constraints. In other words, the ESA is first described, analyzed and interpreted in terms of its natural and cultural character. As attempt is then made to find appropriate arrangements for its management from among the range of institutions available in the region or jurisdiction in question. In analyzing available institutions in a region or jurisdiction, gaps or weaknesses may be identified and recommendations made for improvement. Such was the case in early Yukon work, which led to a recommendation that either the territorial or the federal government should introduce an ecological or Biosphere Reserve category (Theberge et al., 1980).

Institutional aspects of the ABC resource survey and of the ESA method are the focus of interest in this chapter, mainly because our systematic treatment of such arrangements is an innovation for which no counterpart has been found in the resource survey, landscape planning, or environmental management literature. Other research has laid stress on methods of describing and integrating Abiotic and Biotic informa-tion, for example, in the Ecological Land Classification systems (East et al., 1979), although land-use and Cultural aspects have generally received little attention in such methods. The systematic description, analysis, and assessment of appropriate institutional arrangements has been neglected as well. This situation has limited the range of institu-tional choice considered appropriate for a candidate ESA and has inhib-ited professional and citizen agreement on the actual establishment and management of candidate ESAs.

ABIOTIC, BIOTIC, AND CULTURAL CHARACTERISTICS OF ESAS

Experience in Yukon and the NWT reveals some basic patterns in Abiotic, Biotic, and Cultural characteristics of ESAs. These patterns bear on deci-sions about institutional arrangements and management. At one end of a spectrum will be those ESAs that are important for one or a few Abiotic, Biotic or Cultural reasons. Examples of this relatively simple pattern would be sites that are rich in certain rare plant species or serve as the yearly calv-ing grounds of certain animal species. Further along the spectrum are more complex areas that are important for many, often interrelated, Abiotic, Bi-otic, and/or Cultural reasons. For such areas, a complex of institutional arrangements may have to be considered. Examples of both the relatively simple and the more complex arrangements for the Yukon and NWT are presented in Theberge et al. (1980) and Nelson and Jessen (1984).

ABIOTIC, BIOTIC, AND CULTURAL PATTERNS AND MANAGEMENT TYPES

In the context of the foregoing discussion of ABC characteristics and patterns, the relatively simple case presents relatively few problems. In the case of a species' calving-grounds, for example, the selection of a wildlife designation of some kind seems quite straightforward and appropriate. In the case of more complex ABC characteristics and patterns, however, two general types of institutional or management arrangements seem appropriate. The first general type is one in which the Abiotic, Biotic, and Cultural patterns are, for the most part, appropriate to the goals and characteristic of a single land-management regime: for example, a national park. The second general type of institutional arrangement involves using a combination of parks, wildlife, or other land management types to administer large areas with diverse Abiotic, Biotic, and Cultural patterns. We refer to the first general type of arrangement as a 'dominant-agency approach,' and to the second as an 'institutional mosaic.'

THE DOMINANT-AGENCY MANAGEMENT TYPE: ZONING AND THE BUFFER

In the case of an ESA that is largely suitable for a single land-management type, and so for management mainly by a dominant agency, variations in resource significance within and without the boundary of the dominant-management unit must still be accommodated. In the case of lands within the management unit, zoning or similar types of land classification can be applied. An example is the five-part system used in national parks by Environment Canada, Parks. The zones are: special preservation, wilderness, natural environment, outdoor recreation, and park services (Parks Canada, 1983). These zones are established to provide for a variety of uses that are deemed appropriate to the different Abiotic, Biotic, and Cultural characteristics and conservation requirements within the management unit. Such zones can be delineated by using the Abiotic, Biotic, and Cultural information and the institutional analysis that is characteristic of the ABC resource survey method. The ABC method has been applied in this manner in Presqu'ile Provincial Park in Ontario (Nelson et al., 1987). (See Chapter 4, this volume.)

In the cases of Abiotically, Biotically, or Culturally significant areas that are left outside of the dominant-management unit, other institutional arrangements should be applied to provide for their appropriate use and conservation. Indeed, some outside areas are the object of very careful consideration when the boundary is being drawn for any dominant-management unit. Such outside areas may be considered as part of the dominant unit in Abiotic, Biotic, or Cultural terms. However, it may not be possible to include them within the dominant unit because of the presence of conflicting and incompatible land-uses and their effects on resources and the environment.

In dealing with outside areas and boundary issues such as the foregoing, we are illustrating the close relationship between boundary delineation and the establishment of an overall set of institutional arrangements for an ESA. We are also dealing with what is often called the 'buffer zone' problem, which arises for various reasons: for example, because animals often migrate outside a national park or other individual management unit, or because watersheds cannot be contained within a dominant-management unit. Native people and other uses also frequently migrate across boundaries in the course of various economic and social activities. In other words, natural and cultural systems may be continuous but usually have to be broken institutionally because of land-use, economic, or other pressures. In this sense, boundaries should not be treated as lines but rather as institutional interfaces superimposed on continuous natural and cultural systems.

Sets of institutional arrangements should be considered and applied in the buffer zone, which will permit uses that are different from those allowed in the dominant land management unit and yet protect significant Abiotic, Biotic, and Cultural resources within the relevant ESA but outside the unit. Institutional arrangements for the buffer zone can be drawn from the range of types that are available in the jurisdiction in question. (See Table 6.2.)

THE INSTITUTIONAL MOSAIC

The foregoing discussion leads to the second general type of arrangement that can be applied to a complex ESA, namely the institutional mosaic. The mosaic generally applies when a range of ABC factors – calving areas, migratory routes, vegetation types, or geological, archaeological, or ethnic features – are divided by a growing network of mining sites, roads, settlement, or other development features and processes. In such circumstances, a set of different institutional arrangements is desirable – to provide for both development and conservation. Means of co-ordinating the work of the different agencies and management types involved is also essential if the institutional mosaic is to be effective overall.

THE EXAMPLE OF AISHIHIK LAKE ESA, YUKON

At this point, the example of Aishihik Lake ESA will be presented in order to illustrate the foregoing discussion. Aishihik Lake ESA covers about 1,944 km^2 (750 mi^2) in the rolling uplands of south-central Yukon, west of Whitehorse (Figure 6.1). The area is occupied chiefly by alpine tundra and subalpine vegetation, with boreal forest and some associated vegetation-types including relict grassland. It has excellent moose (*Alces alces*) and grizzly bear (*Ursus arctos horribilis*) habitats, waterfowl staging-areas, salmonid (*Oncorhynchus*), 'trout' (*Salvelinus namaycush*), and whitefish (*Coregonus*) habitats, wolf (*Canis lupus*) and black bear (*Ursus americanus*) habitats, and populations of muskrat (*Ondatra zibethicus*), otter (*Lontra candensis*), beaver (*Castor canadensis*), mink (*Mustela vison*), sharp-tailed grouse (*Pedioecetes phasianellus*), and upland plover (*Bartramia longicauda*). It is one of the best areas in the Yukon for ducks, geese, and shorebirds.

The area also contains rare plants, highly diverse plant communities, and archaeological sites and is currently used by native people for hunting, fishing, and other purposes. An old village at the head of Aishihik Lake is still used in summer and autumn by native people. Aishihik Lake is also the site of a hydroelectric development, which was completed in the 1970s. The major facilities are located at the south end of the lake and of the ESA, where a small territorial campground is also located. A few cottages and an old road are situated on the eastern lakeshore, leading to an abandoned World War II air-base. The lake is used by Whitehorse and other residents for fishing and boating. Big game outfitting and gold mining are also carried on in parts of the ESA.

A large part of the Aishihik Lake ESA was recommended as an International Biological Programme (IBP) site. Environment Canada, Parks, was also interested in the area as a site for a national park that

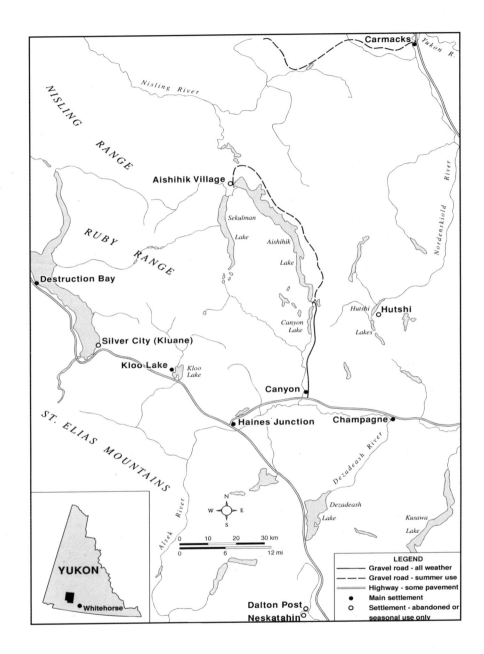

Figure 6.1   Physical and Cultural Setting of Aishihik Lake ESA

would be representative of Natural Region 7 in the agency's national system planning framework. In the process of settling their land-claim, native people have also indicated an interest in part of the area. In recognition of its many important Abiotic, Biotic, and Cultural attributes, it was named as one of thirty-five ESAs in the Yukon in our survey of candidate areas through the territory (Theberge et al., 1980).

With support from Environment Canada, Parks, and other sources, the Aishihik area was subsequently subjected to a detailed ABC survey, and the resulting Abiotic, Biotic, and Cultural data were described, analyzed, and interpreted according to the ABC method. It is not possible to present all the resulting maps here, but Figures 6.2 to 6.7 are included to portray the natural and cultural character of the area and provide a basis for understanding how institutional arrangements were recommended for the ESA (Figure 6.8). Additional figures illustrating the method's application in Aishihik ESA are available in Grigoriew et al. (1985).

Figure 6.2, a functional wildlife map, illustrates the range of animals in the area and their migration range and other requirements. This functional wildlife map can be related to the Biotic significance and constraints maps (Figures 6.3 and 6.4). The western portion of the ESA is roadless, relatively inaccessible, and wild. Figures 6.5 and 6.6 have been included to give an idea of the uses of this remote area. Considerable mineral exploration has occurred, as well as hydroelectric development at the southern end of Aishihik Lake (Figure 6.5). Archaeological, historical, and other features reflect past use by First Nations people and early European migrants (Figure 6.6). The land-use patterns map (Figure 6.7) indicates a range of hunting, trapping, and other uses in the area.

INSTITUTIONAL ARRANGEMENTS FOR AISHIHIK ESA

The set of institutional arrangements recommended for Aishihik Lake ESA will now be reviewed generally. More details on the ESA's boundary delineation and on the recommended institutional arrangements

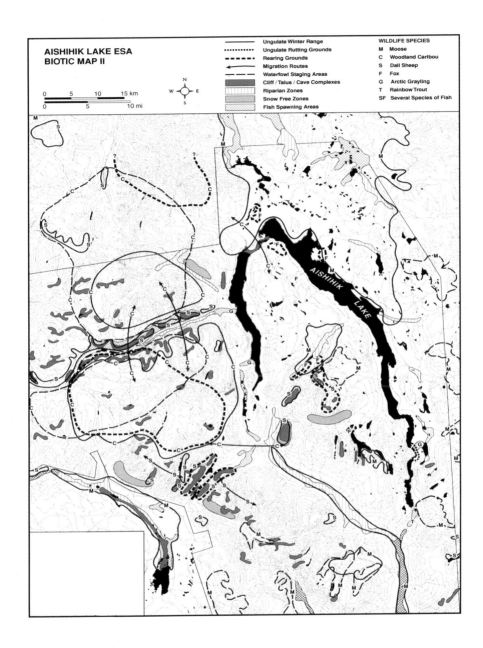

AISHIHIK LAKE ESA
BIOTIC MAP II

Figure 6.2   Wildlife Functional Map

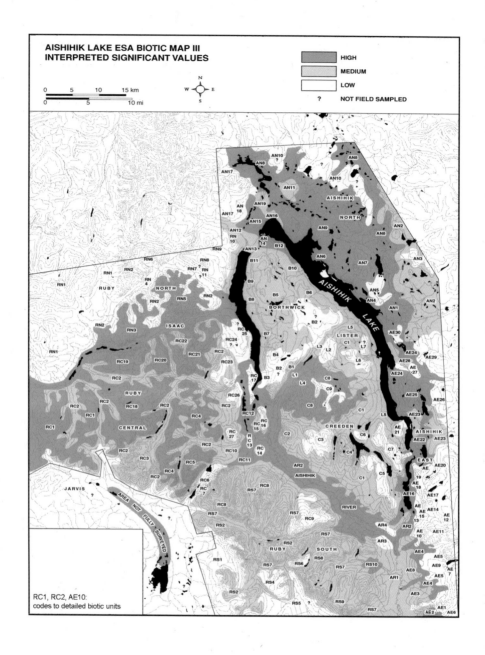

Figure 6.3   Biotic Significance Map

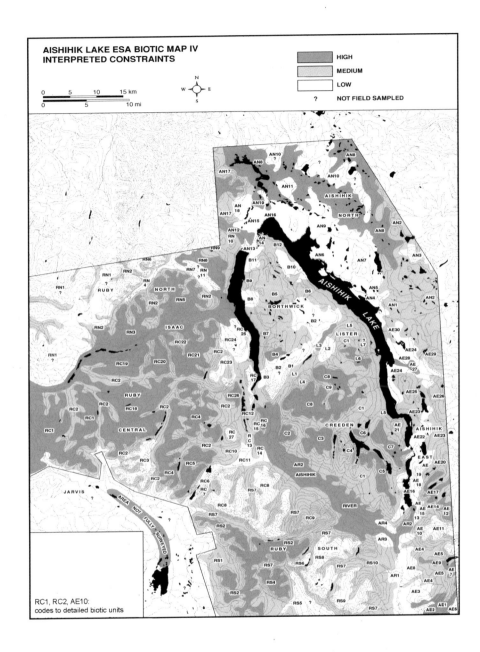

Figure 6.4   Biotic Constraints Map

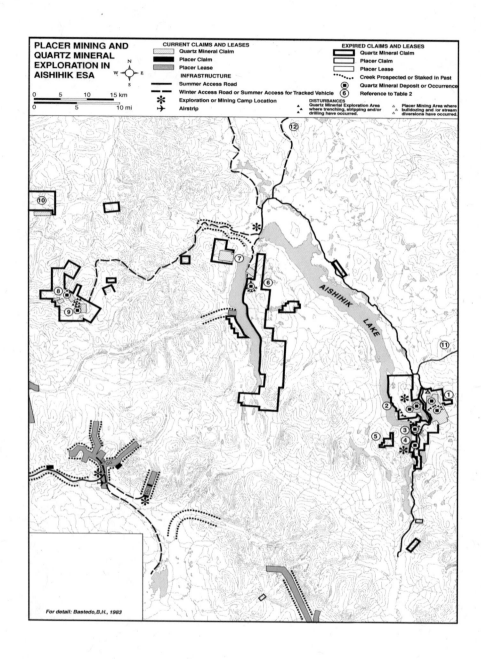

Figure 6.5   Mining and Mineral Exploration Map

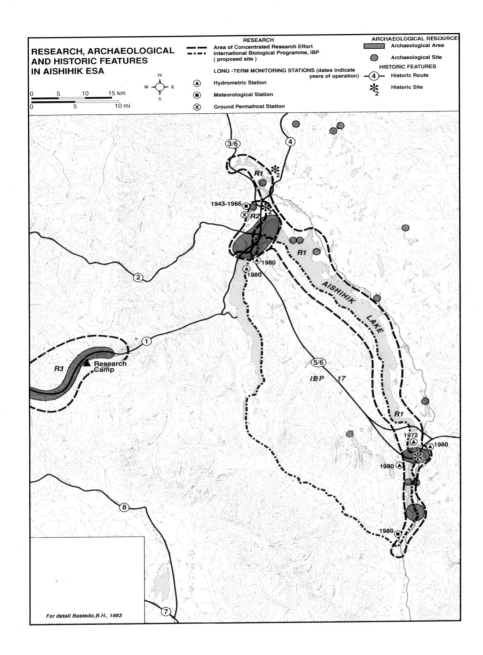

Figure 6.6   Research, Archaeological, and Historic Features

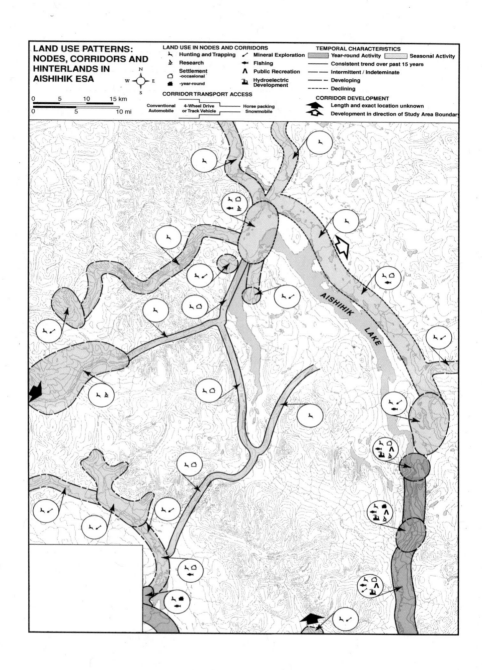

LAND USE PATTERNS: NODES, CORRIDORS AND HINTERLANDS IN AISHIHIK ESA

Figure 6.7   Land Use Patterns Map

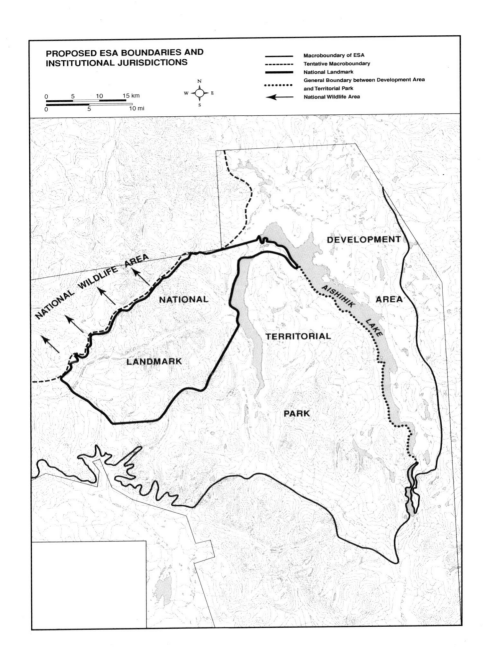

PROPOSED ESA BOUNDARIES AND INSTITUTIONAL JURISDICTIONS

0   5   10   15 km
0   5   10 mi

N
W ⊕ E
S

———— Macroboundary of ESA
------- Tentative Macroboundary
———— National Landmark
••••••• General Boundary between Development Area and Territorial Park
◄——— National Wildlife Area

DEVELOPMENT

NATIONAL WILDLIFE AREA

NATIONAL

AISHIHIK LAKE

AREA

TERRITORIAL

LANDMARK

PARK

Figure 6.8   Proposed ESA Boundaries

can be found in Grigoriew et al. (1985), Bastedo and Theberge (1986), and Bastedo, B.H. (1986)..

In the Aishihik case, it became apparent that many factors militated against the designation of all or part of the area as a national park or other dominant management type. Among these factors were the area's proximity to Kluane National Park, its lack of distinction in terms of ecosystem representativeness, numerous cultural or land-use pressures (notably unsettled native land-claims), the presence and possible expansion of the Aishihik Lake hydroelectric facility, and the encroachment of 'placer' and other mining.

As a result, recommendations were made to conserve and sustainably use the Aishihik area through the application of a set of co-ordinated institutional arrangements or an institutional mosaic, including a national landmark, a national wildlife area, a territorial park, and the Yukon Area Development Ordinance (Figure 6.8). The national landmark designation, termed a Canadian Landmark by Environment Canada, Parks, provides for recreational, scientific, and conservational use of an area north and west of Sekulman Lake (Figure 6.1), which possesses unique geological, geomorphological, and archaeological features.

The national wildlife area designation provides for the use and conservation of the numerous caribou (*Rangifer tarandus caribou*) in western and northern Aishihik. The territorial park provides for protection of the significant Abiotic and Biotic values identified in the mapping, and for scientific, interpretive, recreational, and related uses of the more accessible central and southeastern portions of the Aishihik area. A territorial park can also be more compatible with hunting, mining, and hydroelectric development than a national landmark designation. The Area Development Ordinance is applied around Aishihik Lake itself and allows for large-scale zoning for recreation, transport, and other development purposes, including zones to protect significant Abiotic, Biotic, and Cultural processes and features. Such site-level zoning could be applied east of Aishihik Lake where roads, hydroelectric development, reservoir drawdowns, mining, and other changes militate against park or comparable status, but careful management of some sites is nevertheless very important.

SOME KEY CONSIDERATIONS IN SELECTING INSTITUTIONAL ARRANGEMENTS FOR THE AISHIHIK ESA

One possible constraint to a Canadian Landmark designation by Environment Canada, Parks, is an interest in ownership of all or part of the proposed area by the territorial government. The proposed landmark area is also hunted by the local native people for mountain sheep (*Ovis nidicola*) and other animals. However, under 1980s Environment Canada, Parks, policy such hunting could continue, given appropriate conservation measures. A similar problem is posed by outfitters currently operating in the ESA. But the policy of Environment Canada, Parks, again provides for co-operation and agreement with previous private users of candidate areas. Potentially, therefore, a national landmark could be established through co-operation among Environment Canada, Parks, the territorial government, and traditional users.

In the context of management arrangements for other parts of the ESA, the native people seem most interested in ownership of land near Aishihik Village and the upper part of Aishihik Lake in the northeastern section of the ESA. Those portions of this land that we propose for management under the territorial area development ordinance (Figure 6.8) could qualify for this designation, even through privately owned by the native people. Any First Nations lands that fall within the proposed national wildlife area in the northern and western section of the ESA also could be owned by the native people, as the relevant legislation – the Canada Wildlife Act – empowers the Canadian Wildlife Service (CWS), as the administering agency, to make co-operative management arrangements with other governments or with private owners. An agreement between the CWS and native people for the creation of a national wildlife area could thus provide for technical and other assistance to the people and for co-operation in protecting and using the resources in which both parties are vitally interested. Under territorial parks policy, similar provisions could be made for native co-operation in the management of the territorial park that is proposed for the central section of the ESA (Figure 6.8).

AN INSTITUTIONAL MOSAIC AND THE NEED FOR CO-ORDINATED MANAGEMENT

In reviewing the foregoing recommendations, it is apparent that a complex set of different management types – a veritable mosaic – has been recommended for the Aishihik ESA (Figure 6.8 and Table 6.2). Management will, therefore, require the co-operation of the local people, territorial government agencies, the Canadian Wildlife Service, Environment Canada, Parks, and the federal Northern Affairs Program because of its responsibility for land-use regulations for public land generally in Canada's two territories.

In thinking about co-ordinating these institutional arrangements, it should be recognized that the Aishihik area was originally brought to the attention of ourselves and others because an International Biological Program (IBP) site was mapped near Aishihik Lake. IBP's successor, the Man and the Biosphere (MAB) Program, offers a means of co-ordinating the agencies and groups interested in the entire ESA under a Biosphere Reserve designation (Batisse, 1982; 1985). Such a designation could be applied to the ESA and surrounding lands, and a co-ordinating committee could be set up to manage them co-operatively. Management could build upon the knowledge of Abiotic, Biotic, and Cultural processes revealed through the ABC resource inventory. The Biosphere Reserve designation would also indicate a commitment to the continued learning, research, and adaptive management definitive of the MAB program itself. A co-ordinated Aishihik ESA management system could draw upon research, maintenance, and development funds that might become available through federal-provincial agreements.

It is of additional interest that the Aishihik ESA involves some areas that have been relatively little modified, and some areas that have been rather heavily modified, by humans. Biosphere Reserves are intended to include both wild and human-modified landscapes in order to monitor, improve understanding of, and manage the effects of development programs and projects. The Aishihik Lake ESA offers prime opportunities for such programs.

INSTITUTIONAL ARRANGEMENTS AND THE ABC SYSTEM

This chapter provides an example of the application of appropriate institutional arrangements to an individual ESA as part of the ABC method. An attempt has been made to give enough information to make the method generally understandable and to stress its major characteristics and advantages. These include:

1) Its systematic nature. Judgments have to be made at a number of points; the criteria and basis for these are intended to be clear and replicable by others. While it has not been possible to stress this enough in the text, it is invaluable to receive information and viewpoints from all major affected groups or agencies. This can be achieved by various types of consultation and involvement.

2) Its comprehensive, interactive and dynamic character and compatibility with conservation and sustainable development. Abiotic, Biotic, and Cultural characteristics are linked to analysis of the strengths and weaknesses of available land management agencies and institutional arrangements. This is done in order to secure the best fit for an ESA while providing some flexibility for modification based on further research, changes in land-use, rehabilitation, and other factors. Mapping of the Abiotic, Biotic, and Cultural characteristics, and of significance and constraints patterns, is linked to a system for deciding on the range of institutional arrangements that are needed for conservation and sustainable development in the ESA and surrounding areas.

3) Its capacity to reveal any inadequacies in the intuitional arrangements that will be needed for sustainable use of an ESA and surrounding areas.

4) Its capacity for linking with more comprehensive land-use management and regional planning and development that is being introduced in Canada's North. This linking

occurs primarily through consideration of the kinds of institutional arrangements that will be applied at the margins of the ESA, where it grades into less-significant and more generally usable lands and waters.

5) Its utility in illustrating the need and basis for co-ordinated or shared management of an ESA. Such co-operative management is required even in those types of ESAs where a single land management agency is dominant, and certainly for those where a mosaic is needed to provide for conservation and sustainable development.

The last advantage also underscores a major problem in implementing the ESA method, namely the difficulties in getting agencies to co-operate continuously and effectively. In the Yukon and the NWT, federal and territorial departments and agencies work together only slowly – for a variety of reasons, including tradition, agency loyalty, reward systems, funding, and staffing problems.

Another perceived difficulty with the ESA approach and the method of selecting appropriate institutional arrangements is their apparent complexity. Several reviewers of the method have seen it as too complex for many citizens, as well as for some agency personnel, to utilize. Yet the method reflects the reality of the situation and seems to be what is needed to do justice to the collective Abiotic, Biotic, and Cultural character of those special landscapes or ecosystems that are of central concern to the conservation and sustainable use of the land generally. Further to this perception of its difficulty, we have tested the ABC approach in a practical exercise involving eight university students who learned the system quickly and reported relatively little difficulty in working with it (Nelson et al., 1987) (see Chapter 4, this volume).

NOTES

1   Adapted from J.G. Nelson, and P. Grigoriew, "Institutional Arrangements for Individual Environmentally Significant Areas: The Case of Aishihik, Yukon," *Environmental Conservation* 14(4)
(1987): 347–356.

REFERENCES

Bastedo, B.H. 1986. *Aishihik Lake Resource Survey: Cultural Aspect.* President's Committee on Northern Studies. Waterloo: University of Waterloo.

Bastedo, J.D. 1986. *An ABC Resource Survey Method for Environmentally Significant
Areas, with Special Reference to Biotic Surveys in Canada's North.* Depart-
ment of Geography Publication Series No. 24. Waterloo: University of
Waterloo.

Bastedo, J.D., and J.B. Theberge. 1986. *Aishihik Lake Resource Survey: Biotic Aspects.* President's Committee on Northern Studies. Waterloo: University
of Waterloo.

Bastedo, J.D., J.G. Nelson, and T.B. Theberge. 1984. "An ecological approach to
resource survey and planning for environmentally significant areas: The
ABC method." *Environmental Management* 8(2): 125–134.

Batisse, M. 1982. "The biosphere reserve: A tool for environmental conservation
and management." *Environmental Conservation* 9(2): 101–111.

Batisse, M. 1985. "Action plan for biosphere reserves." *Environmental Conservation*
12(1): 17–27.

Dorney, R.S., and D.W. Hoffman. 1979. "Development of landscape planning
concepts and management strategies for an urbanizing agricultural region." *Landscape Planning* 6: 151–177.

East, K.W., D.L. Day, D. Lesauteur, W.M. Stephenson, and L. Charron. 1979.
"Parks Canada application of biophysical land classification for resources
management." In *Applications of Ecological (biophysical) Land Classification in
Canada,* ed. C.D.A. Rubec. Ecological Land Classification Series, No. 7.
Ottawa: Environment Canada.

Fenge, T. 1982. "Towards comprehensive conservation of environmentally significant areas in the Northwest Territories." *Environmental Conservation*
9(4): 305–313.

Grigoriew, P., J.B. Theberge, and J.G. Nelson. 1985. *Park Boundary Delineation
Manual: The ABC Resource Survey Approach.* Occasional Paper 4. Waterloo: Heritage Resources Centre, University of Waterloo.

International Union for Conservation of Nature and Nature Resources (IUCN). 1978. *Categories, Objectives, and Criteria for Protected Areas.* Gland, Switzerland: International Union for Conservation of Nature and Natural Resources.

International Union for Conservation of Nature and Nature Resources (IUCN). 1980. *World Conservation Strategy.* Gland, Switzerland: IUCN-UNEP-WWF.

Lusigi, W.J. 1981. "New approaches to wildlife conservation in Kenya." *Ambio* 10(2–3): 87–92.

Nelson, J.G., and S. Jessen. 1984. *Planning and Management of Environmentally Significant Areas in the Northwest Territories: Issues and Alternatives.* Ottawa: Canadian Arctic Resources Committee.

Nelson, J.G., and P.G.R. Smith. 1987. "Institutional arrangements for a system of environmentally significant areas: The case of the East Beaufort Sea area, Canada." *Environmental Conservation* 14(3): 201–218.

Nelson, J. G., P.G.R. Smith, and J.B. Theberge. 1985. "Environmentally Significant Areas (ESAs) in the Northwest Territories, Canada: Their role, identification, designation and implementation." *Environments* 17(3): 93–109.

Nelson, J.G., P. Grigoriew, and T. Whillans, eds. 1987. *Application of the ABC Resource Survey Method to Presqu'ile Provincial Park, Ontario.* Waterloo: Heritage Resources Centre, University of Waterloo.

Parks Canada. 1983. *Parks Canada Policy.* Ottawa: Minister of Supply and Services.

Sauchyn, D.J. 1986. *Aishihik Lake Resource Survey: Abiotic Aspects.* Waterloo: President's Committee on Northern Studies, University of Waterloo.

Smith, Paul G.R., J.G. Nelson, and J.B. Theberge. 1986. *Environmentally Significant Areas, Conservation and Land Use Management in the Northwest Territories.* Technical Paper 1. Waterloo: Heritage Resources Centre, University of Waterloo.

Task Force on Park Establishment (Canada). 1987. *Our Parks – Vision for the 21ˢᵗ Century.* Ottawa: Environment Canada, Parks, and Waterloo: Heritage Resources Centre, University of Waterloo.

Theberge, J.B., J.G. Nelson, and T. Fenge, eds. 1980. *Environmentally Significant Areas of the Yukon Territory.* Ottawa: Canadian Arctic Resources Committee.

PART II

PART II:
FOCUSED SUMMARIES OF DETAILED STUDIES

INTRODUCTION

Chapter 6, on Aishihik, sets the stage for the chapters in Part II, which involve Focused Summaries of Detailed Studies using of the ABC method. The focus is on linking summaries of detailed Abiotic, Biotic, and Cultural research with planning management and decision-making challenges and opportunities in a study area. In some cases available information, time or other resources limit linking the summary to planning implications of a detailed study. In other cases, more explicit and complete conclusions can be made about planning and decision-making.

Chapter 7 arises from a detailed ABC application undertaken in the Canadian North during the 1980s struggle over conservation and development. The area of concern is the East Beaufort Sea region on the Arctic Coast east of the Mackenzie Delta. Chapter 7 is intense in its use of selected Abiotic, Biotic, and Cultural information to focus on finding a way of breaking a logjam over different protected area proposals by conservation, First Nations, and industrial interests. With a few key maps as a platform, the chapter lays out procedures for analyzing and assessing the varying capacities and roles of different land-use and conservation agencies and institutional arrangements in creating a technically and socially acceptable system of protected areas for the East Beaufort. In its focus on finding a suitable set of planning and institutional arrangements for a system of protected areas in this large region, Chapter 7 differs from but complements Chapter 6, where the goal was to provide an appropriate plan for a particular environmentally significant area.

Chapter 8 on Canadian Heritage Rivers, with particular reference to the Grand River watershed in Ontario, focuses on the use of significance and constraint maps (Level II) in highlighting planning for an area. These maps were produced as part of a comprehensive and lengthy ABC study of the watershed. The purpose of this two-year research effort by a team of multidisciplinary students was to assess the case for designating the Grand as a Canadian Heritage River, including identifying the major planning challenges that needed to be addressed if this status was to be given to the Grand.

Chapter 9, on coastal planning in Indonesia, is a summary of research, training, and collaborative work undertaken on a part-time basis over approximately a six-year period in the late 1980s and 1990s with the support of the Canadian International Development Agency (CIDA). The work focused on mapping losses of formerly extensive mangrove forests in the Segara Anakan area, south central Java. Research involved mapping changes based on analysis of satellite images taken at different dates. The use of satellite imagery did not involve preparation of theme maps as in our initial approach to the ABC, but rather mapping of land cover or landscape types. These constituted a synthesis or integration of the A, B, and C in one map in the sense anticipated at a later stage (Level III) in our original formulation of the ABC method. The results were analyzed, assessed, and interpreted in terms of significance and constraints for conservation, sustainable use, and planning. The highlights of this complex study are presented in this summary chapter, which encapsulates many of the coastal planning challenges in Indonesia as well as other parts of Asia.

Chapter 10 is a companion piece to the preceding one. It addresses coastal zone planning and management in the Great Lakes. The chapter summarizes a number of separate but interrelated coastal studies. Maps are selected from these studies and presented to highlight flood, erosion, and other processes and their significance as well as biotic issues arising from urban, recreational, and other land-use changes in the coastal zone. This chapter also illustrates how information selected from more detailed studies can be used to improve professional and civic understanding and responses. The chapter can be compared with the previous one on Java to show similarities in coastal challenges in different parts of the world.

7

INSTITUTIONAL ARRANGEMENTS FOR A SYSTEM OF ENVIRONMENTALLY SIGNIFICANT AREAS: THE CASE OF THE EAST BEAUFORT SEA COAST, CANADA[1]

P.G.R. Smith, J.G. Nelson, and J. Theberge

INTRODUCTION

There is a growing awareness of the importance of integrating protected areas into a broader land-use strategy as well as adapting protected area management more closely than is currently practised to local conditions (Gardner and Nelson, 1980; Fenge, 1982; Miller, 1982; Swen and Cahn, 1983; Wright, 1985; IUCN, 1986; MacKinnon et al., 1986). It is in this context that we present a method for matching the natural and cultural values and resource uses of a number of proposed environmentally significant areas (ESAs), with the "best" management arrangement. We illustrate the method with examples from the eastern Beaufort Sea region, an area of approximately 150,000 km^2 lying east of the Mackenzie River delta in the Northwest Territories (NWT) of Canada.

The term 'environmentally significant area' or 'ESA' has been used extensively in Canada and elsewhere to refer to those portions of the landscape that have special natural or cultural value – for instance, ungulate calving areas, raptor nesting habitat, and archaeological sites (Theberge et al., 1980; Fenge, 1982). ESAs can be identified by government or private organizations concerned with parks, wildlife, or natural resources. Criteria and techniques to identify ESAs vary and have evolved rapidly over recent decades (Margules and Usher, 1981; Roome, 1984; Smith and Theberge, 1986; Usher, 1986).

The focus is on formulating the "best" management alternative for each of a set of ESAs in a region. This involves consideration of any initial suggestions, as well as alternative institutional arrangements. In using the terms institutional or management arrangements, we refer to: (1) protected area categories, such as parks and wildlife preserves; (2) legislation, policies, and agencies involved in protected areas and related land management; (3) non-statuatory mechanisms for managing ESAs, for example agreements, leasing, or contracts; and (4) co-ordination or other implementation arrangements, for example joint planning or management committees involving several agencies or groups. This broad, comprehensive approach views all possible means of managing ESAs as a system, each means having its special characteristics which may, for example, suit a particular ESA better than it does the others in the region.

The idea of matching the type of management with the natural and cultural characteristics of each ESA is illustrated quite simply in Figure 7.1. In the matching process, two types of information are brought together, the first of which is the result of an analysis of each ESA's salient natural and cultural attributes. Of particular importance is information on past, present, and potential land and water use in and around the ESA, as well as information on current management and tenure of ESA and adjoining lands and waters. The second type of information is the result of an analysis of the characteristics, strengths, and weaknesses of laws, policies, agencies, protected-area categories, and other mechanisms for management (Nelson and Jessen, 1984; Smith et al., 1986; Nelson and Grigoriew, 1987).

The notion of systematic matching of ESAs with management arrangements can be seen as a logical outgrowth of the IUCN "Objectives, Criteria and Categories for National Parks and Protected Areas" (IUCN, 1978), which defines, in general terms, the natural and cultural features considered appropriate to various categories of protected area, as well as the appropriate type of management and allowable uses. Many studies have also stressed the importance of developing a diversity of

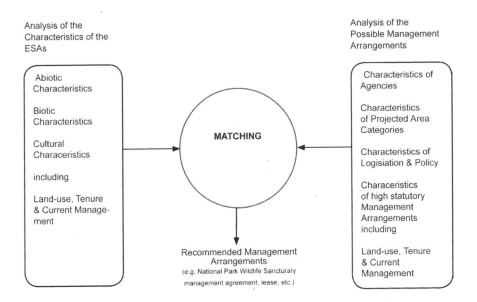

Analysis of the
Characteristics of the
ESAs

Abiotic
Characteristics

Biotic
Characteristics

Cultural
Characeristics

including

Land-use, Tenure
& Current Manage-
ment

MATCHING

Analysis of the
Possible Management
Arrangements

Characteristics of
Agencies

Characteristics
of Projected Area
Categories

Characteristics of
Logisiation & Policy

Characeristics
of high statutory
Management
Arrangements
including

Land-use, Tenure
& Current
Management

Recommended Management
Arrangements
(e.g. National Park Wildlife Sancturary
management agreement, lease, etc.)

Figure 7.1   A Schematic Representation of the Matching Process

management types to suit different conservational objectives and local conditions (MacKinnon, 1981; Fenge, 1982; Miller, 1982; Dingwall, 1984; Mosley, 1984; MacKinnon et al., 1986). However, evaluation of a "candidate" protected-area is often done by a single agency, which is responsible for only one or at most a few of the pertinent management categories. Consequently, anything like the full range of possible management arrangements is, often, not considered at all.

Furthermore, little has been published on how the type of management can be matched to particular areas with due consideration of their specific patterns of use and tenure. Salm and Clark (1984) presented a matrix in which the IUCN protected-area categories are classified as to those categories' primary and secondary objectives. Salm and Clark's method of matching was to define the objectives of a "candidate" protected-area and compare these with the objectives of the protected-area categories in order to find out which was the most appropriate category. Oltremari (1985) presented a method that was based on both the suitability of an area for different conservation objectives and the limitations that were imposed by the exiting ownership and use. Employing a system of subjective scores and weights, the best protected-area category for a particular site was chosen by summing the scores for suitability and then subtracting those for limitations. The category with the highest overall score is inferred to be the best form of management for the site.

The method presented here differs from the foregoing examples in a number of ways. We have analyzed, in some detail, the agencies, laws, policies, and non-statutory measures for managing ESAs in order to identify the strengths and weaknesses of each for different situations. The results are then related to a detailed analysis of the natural and cultural values as well as to the existing and potential uses, management, and tenure of each ESA based on the use of the ABC method. The emerging product is one or more alternatives for the management of each ESA. These alternatives or suggestions can form the basis for informed discussion amongst agencies, local people, and other interested parties before a final decision is taken as to management.

A HIERARCHY OF ESA PLANNING SCALES

Many of the agencies that are concerned with protected area and conservation planning divide their efforts into a series of stages or scales of planning (Parks Canada, 1978, 1979). Figure 7.2 illustrates the relationship between different scales of ESA planning and the types of issues that are dealt with at each scale. Initially, a plan for managing a set of ESAs should be formulated, allowing an evaluation of whether the system as a whole adequately protects the natural and cultural heritage of the jurisdiction or region under study. Matching of ESAs with one or more alternative management arrangements can be done at this stage, as can the delineation of general boundaries. ESAs that are not appropriate in comparison with other candidates can also be identified and perhaps eliminated from the set. Furthermore, ESAs that do not fit any management arrangement in the jurisdictional area in question can also

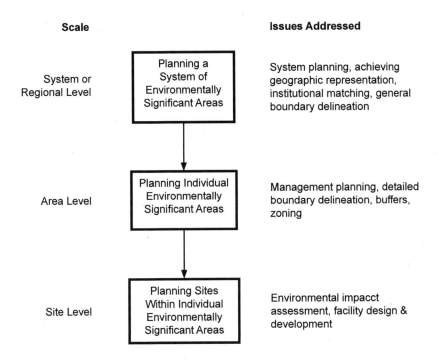

Scale		Issues Addressed
System or Regional Level	Planning a System of Environmentally Significant Areas	System planning, achieving geographic representation, institutional matching, general boundary delineation
Area Level	Planning Individual Environmentally Significant Areas	Management planning, detailed boundary delineation, buffers, zoning
Site Level	Planning Sites Within Individual Environmentally Significant Areas	Environmental impacct assessment, facility design & development

Figure 7.2   A Hierarchy of ESA Planning Scales

be readily identified, whereupon consideration can be given to other institutional arrangements for them.

Following completion of such a systems study as the foregoing, at a scale of, say, 1:2,000,000, the planning of individual ESAs can proceed to address more specific issues – such as a final decision on institutional arrangements, defining the buffer zone, detailed boundary delineation, and zoning of an ESA for different types and levels of use. This level of planning is the subject of a companion study on Aishihik ESA, Yukon, at a scale of 1:125,000 in Chapter 6 (this volume).

Eventually, there will also be a need for detailed or site planning within ESAs. For instance, parks and recreation areas often require camp-sites and other visitor services. Our method has recently been applied to these more detailed site concerns in a study of Presqu'ile Provincial Park, Ontario, at a scale of about 1:30,000 (Nelson et al., 1987) (see Chapter 4, this volume).

THE CONTEXT: CONSERVATION AND SUSTAINABLE DEVELOPMENT

At the heart of our work is the desire to link conservation and development, or to facilitate sustainable development – in this case primarily for the peoples of the NWT. As in other extensive hinterlands that lack a large industrial base, the inhabitants of northern Canada are particularly dependent on the use of renewable resources and consequently on the protection of key habitats and ecosystems. Furthermore, the human treatment of such vital areas must always be in the context that northern peoples are still an integral part of the ecosystems that they use. They have occupied and used the resources of these ESAs for millennia. Thus management of ESAs must integrate use and protection differently from the practices in southern Canada or other, more developed parts of the world.

Special Problems Regarding ESAs in the NWT

Many places in the Canadian north have long been recognized as having special wildlife, vegetation, landform, archaeological, or other qualities. Some of these places are thought to be particularly representative of the character of a region or large part of the North, while others are thought to be unusual or unique naturally or culturally. Such ESAs have not gone unnoticed. International Biological Programme (IBP) sites, "critical, sensitive and unique areas," "key migratory birds," "terrestrial habitat sites," "natural areas and sites of Canadian significance," and yet other types of significant areas, have been identified by non-governmental groups, as well as by federal and territorial agencies.

At the time of this study, in the 1980s, disagreement was widespread about the significance of, and appropriate management status for, such ESAs. Many were used by native people and tied up in the struggle for settlement of land-claims. Oil, mining, and other companies wished to use some ESAs for development purposes, sometimes with the support of government and other agencies. Competition existed between federal and territorial agencies over who should manage particular ESAs. As a result of all these declared interests and of the competition and uncertainty inherent therein, insufficient progress was considered to have been made in placing many ESAs under national park, territorial park, or other appropriate protected-area management status.

The research presented here grew out of an interest in developing a method to break this "logjam." Research began with compilation and evaluation of information on ESAs throughout the Yukon Territory, as well as generally linking this information with the most-favoured management arrangements (Theberge et al., 1980). Subsequent work focused on issues relating to the planning of individual ESAs, and in particular Aishihik ESA in southern Yukon (Bastedo et al., 1984; Nelson and Grigoriew, 1987) (Chapter 6, this volume). In 1982 we began further work on a number of proposed ESAs in the Northwest Territories (Nelson and Jessen, 1984; Nelson et al., 1985; Smith et al., 1986).

In this context, the present application of our method to the eastern Beaufort Sea area must be regarded as more of an illustration than a definitive analysis of ESA management options for the region. Close consultations with local people, and field checks of data obtained in Yellowknife and Ottawa, were not possible, though each would be important steps for 'real life' evaluation of alternative management options.

Types of ESA Management in the NWT

Under a variety of legislation, policies, and programs, a large number of federal and territorial agencies administered different types of protected areas within the NWT and were responsible for proposals for the eastern Beaufort Sea area. Several agencies were also involved in broad-scale land- and water-use planning and management. These included native organizations that owned or, increasingly in the future, might own and manage large tracts of land in the NWT. The characteristics of major existing types of protected areas in the 1980s are summarized in Table 7.1, and the proposals for the eastern Beaufort in Figure 7.3. Further details are available in Fenge (1982, 1985), Nelson and Jessen (1984), and Smith et al. (1986).

Native Organizations and ESAs

The aboriginal peoples of the East Beaufort Sea area and other parts of the NWT had recently settled, or were negotiating, comprehensive claims with the Canadian federal government. The claims were those of the Dene and Métis, First Nations peoples of the southwestern NWT, the Inuit of the Canadian Central and Eastern Arctic as represented by the Tungavik Federation of Nunavut, and the recently settled claim of the Inuvialuit, an Inuit people of the northwestern NWT. Some native organizations integrated well-developed positions on the role of various types of ESA management into their land-claim proposals (e.g., Tungavik Federation of Nunavut, 1985).

Under the 1984 Inuvialuit settlement, over 90,000 km^2 of land in the East Beaufort Sea area and nearby areas were controlled by the Inuvialuit and managed by the Inuvialuit Land Administration. It was too early to determine whether different types of management would be applied to ESAs occurring on Inuvialuit land from those occurring elsewhere. However, the agreement stated that "A basic goal of the ... Settlement is to protect and preserve the Arctic wildlife, environment and biological productivity through the application of conservation principles and practices." Furthermore, "it may be desirable to apply special protective measures ... to lands ... important from the stand-point of wildlife" (DIAND, 1984a).

THE EAST BEAUFORT SEA AREA

Under the land-claims agreement with the Canadian federal government, the several hundred Inuvialuit of the East Beaufort Sea area, who depended largely on wildlife harvesting, acquired large tracts of land with either fee simple (complete ownership) or surface rights. Exploration by the hydrocarbon industry was the other major use of both land

Protected Area Category	Land-Use	Tenure	Designation and Planning	Implementation & Enforcement	Policy Coordination
National Parks etc.					
National Park	No settlement, resource extraction, or hunting, except by native people	Generally must be owned fee simple by federal government	Designation requires amendment of the Act	Park wardens have police powers	Provision for cooperation with other governments
National Marine Park	No commercial non-renewable resource extraction; fishing allowed by traditional users	as above	as above	as above	as above
National Landmark	No resource extraction within site	Federal ownership not required	Through cooperation with other agencies and private groups		
National Wildlife Area	At discretion of minister, but commercial and industrial activities generally disallowed	Flexible; purchase, lease, etc.	Designated by Federal Environment Minister	Wildlife officer has police powers	Provision for agreements and cooperation with other agencies and private groups
Migratory Bird Sanctuary	Hunting or disturbing migratory birds prohibited	No land acquisition or tenure	Designated by Federal Environment Minister	Permits to control use; Game officers have police powers; fines and imprisonment	No provision for joint management
Territorial Parks etc.					
Natural Environmental Recreation Park	Hunting by NWT residents allowed; no industrial or commercial activities except outfitting and guiding	Administration and control by NWT	Federal parliament must designate land for park and transfer control	Park use by permit	Agreements with other governments and private groups
Outdoor Recreation Park	'More active types of recreation' with 'appropriate facilities' i.e. roads, buildings	as above	as above	as above	as above
Historic Park	As for Natural Environmental Recreation Park	as above	NWT Executive member may designate	as above	as above
Wildlife Preserve	Hunting by NWT residents only; no trapping or Polar Bear hunting; resource exploration and development generally allowed; land-use controls through federal legislation	No transfer of lands, only wildlife affected	Designated by territorial council	Wildlife officers have powers of police; fines and imprisonment	General provision for agreements with federal government
Critical Wildlife Area	Non mentioned; land-use controls through federal legislation	as above	as above	as above	as above

Table 7.1   Major Types of Protected Areas in the NWT

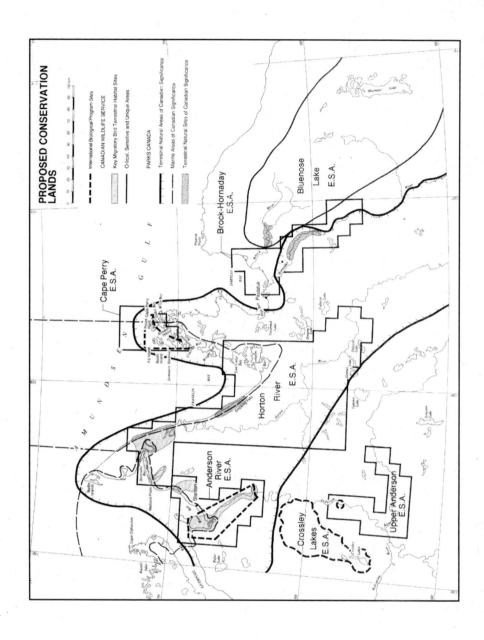

Figure 7.3   Proposed Conservation Areas

and marine areas. Thousands of miles of seismic lines were shot in the 1970s, and a number of exploratory oil-wells were drilled, though all were dry. Nevertheless, several areas were under permit for future exploration. The degree to which exploration and development would go ahead in the near future was uncertain given the prices of petroleum.

The foregoing land tenure arrangements of the Inuvialuit and the oil industry required reconciliation with the proposals for various kinds of ESAs and conservation lands made by relevant government agencies and environmental NGOs. The proposals by different agencies and groups not infrequently overlapped, and the boundaries of the various areas deemed worthy of protected area status tended to differ among the agencies and groups. We differentiated seven more or less separate ESA proposals for which we decided to determine the most appropriate protected area type or management arrangement based on the application of the ABC method (Figure 7.3).

The Abiotic, Biotic, and Cultural significance of the proposed East Beaufort ESAs is summarized in Table 7.2. ESAs are listed along with the criteria used to evaluate significance, namely (1) importance for wildlife; (2) rare plants or rare animals; (3) unusual abiotic features; (4) abiotic representativeness; (5) ecoregion representativeness; (6) biotic diversity; (7) symbolic importance; (8) historic and archaeological importance; and (9) importance to native people. The reasons for using these criteria, and further details on the evaluation method employed, are discussed in Smith et al. (1986). Figures 7.4, 7.5, 7.6, 7.7, and 7.8 are a set of maps selected from the array prepared in the application of the ABC method, to summarize and highlight the salient cultural and natural characteristics of the East Beaufort region. When these maps are overlaid, they show the potential for tension and conflict between nature conservation and development.

Criterion	Upper Anderson	Crossley Lakes	Anderson River	Horton River	Cape Parry	Brock-Hornaday	Bluenose Lake
Biotic and Abiotic Criteria							
Importance for Wildlife	Territorial Significance (Peregrine)		National Significance (Snow Goose, Brant, White-fronted Goose)	National Significance (Caribou, Snow Goose, Peregrine)	National Significance (Thick-billed Murre, Common and King Eiders)	National Significance (Peregrine)	National Significance (Caribou)
Rare Animal Species	National Significance		National Significance	National Significance	National Significance	National Significance	
Rare Plant Species				High			
Unusual Abiotic Features			National Significance			National Significance	
Abiotic Representativeness			High				
Ecoregion Representativeness		High					
Biotic Diversity			High				
Cultural Criteria							
Symbolic Importance				High		High	
Historic and Archaeological Importance	Potential		Potential	Potential	Potential		
Importance to Native People				High	High	High	

Table 7.2   Abiotic, Biotic, and Cultural Significance of the Seven Eastern Beaufort ESAs (Figure 7.3)

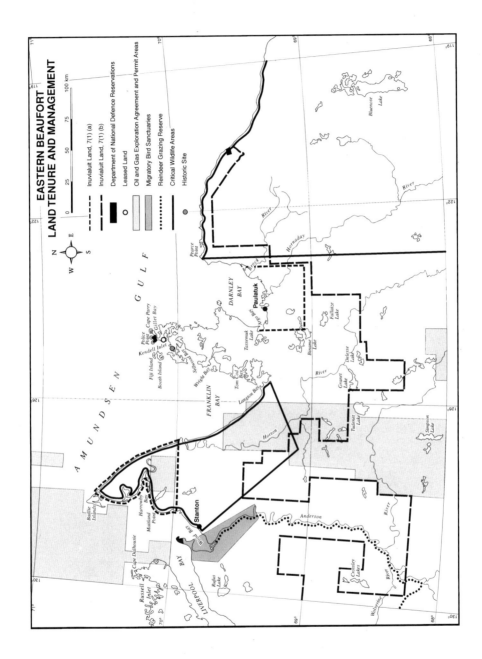

Figure 7.4   Eastern Beaufort Land Tenure and Management

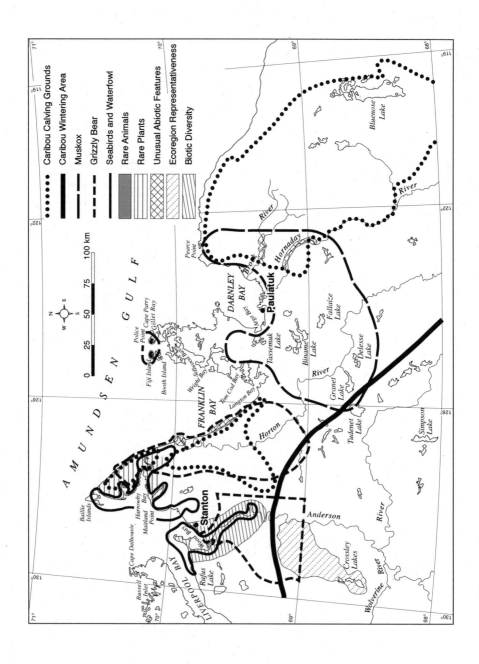

Figure 7.5 Eastern Beaufort Abiotic and Biotic Significance

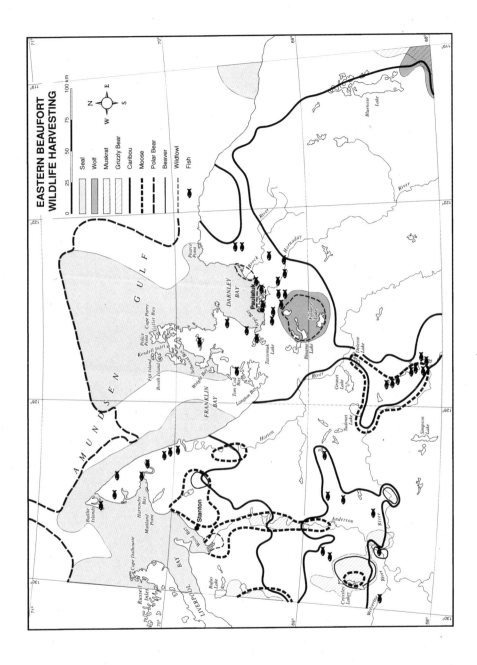

Figure 7.6   Eastern Beaufort Wildlife Harvesting

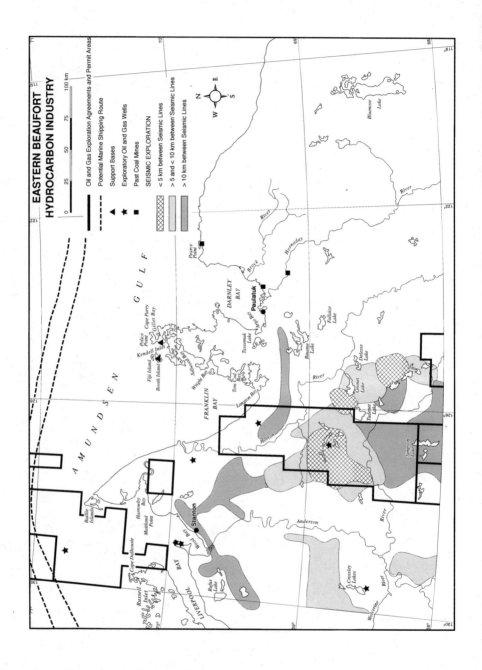

Figure 7.7   Eastern Beaufort Hydrocarbon Industry

PLACES

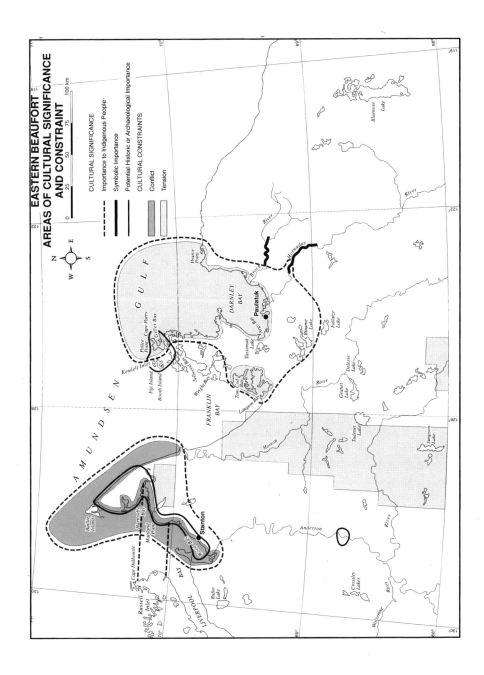

Figure 7.8   Eastern Beaufort Areas of Cultural Significance and Constraint

MANAGEMENT ALTERNATIVES

To formulate the "best" protected area or management alternative for the proposed ESAs (Figure 7.3), we compared the ESA's Abiotic, Biotic, and Cultural significance (Figure 7.5 and Table 7.2), existing and potential uses and values (Figures 7.6, 7.7, and 7.8), and current management and tenure (Figure 7.4), with the attributes of each type of protected area described in Table 7.1. Type of management was matched to existing uses; for example, oil and gas exploration was permitted in migratory bird sanctuaries and critical wildlife areas, but not in national parks. Similarly, existing tenure could be matched to that possible under different legislation or policies. For example, public or private land could be included in national wildlife areas but, under current policy, national parks needed to be publicly owned in fee simple (that is, unlimited as to class of heir). The results of our study are shown in Figure 7.9, which illustrates a considerably simplified set of protected area and management proposals.

PRIORITIES FOR PLANNING AND MANAGEMENT

After suggesting an appropriate means of managing each ESA, it seemed desirable, given the number of candidate areas, as well as funding and staffing constraints, to indicate the priority that could be accorded to implementing each proposed protected area. In this regard, we classified the ESAs into four categories: (1) short-term priority, requiring immediate action; (2) medium- to long-term priority; (3) further information needed: (a) immediately or in the short term and (b) in the medium to long term; (4) no action needed in the foreseeable future. Five criteria were used to assign each of the ESAs to one of the above categories: significance and responsibility; land-use; place in the system; ease of establishment; and social and economic benefits. The results (Table 7.3) should be evaluated by concerned organizations and individuals.

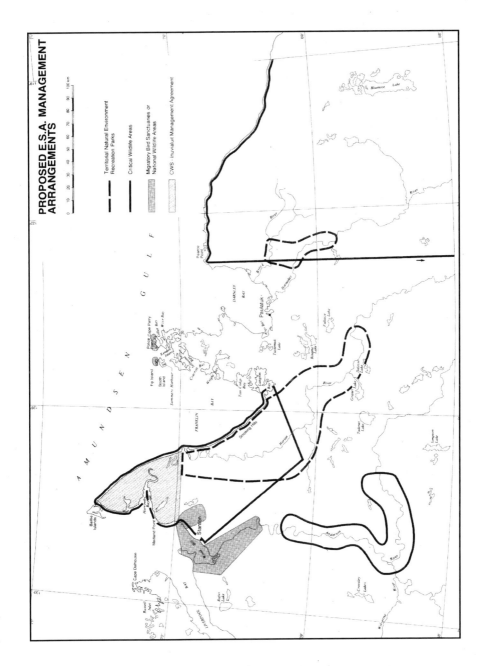

Figure 7.9   Proposed ESA Management Arrangements

	Upper Anderson	Crossley Lakes	Anderson River	Horton River	Cape Parry	Brock-Hornaday	Bluenose Lake
Recommended Management Arrangement	Critical Wildlife Area or National Wildlife Area	No Good fit, private	National Wildlife Area or Migratory Bird Sanctuary	Inuvialuit CWS Management Agreement and Territorial Park (NERP)	Expanded Migratory Bird Sanctuary, National Wildlife Area or Area Development Ordinance	Territorial Park (NERP) or National Landmark	Critical Wildlife Area or National Wildlife Area
IUCN Management Class	Wildlife Sanctuary (IV)		Wildlife Sanctuary (IV)	Natural Monument (III)	Wildlife Sanctuary (IV)	Natural Monument (III)	Wildlife Sanctuary (IV)
General Type of ESA	Species-type: Birds	Representative Landscape	Species-type: Birds	Multiple values	Species-type: Birds	Geologic and Scenic	Species-type: Mammal
Significance and Responsibility	NWT Wildlife Service clearly responsible	No agency clearly responsible	CWS clearly responsible	Several agencies involved	CWS clearly responsible	Several agencies involved	NWT Wildlife Service clearly responsible
Land-Use	Generally compatible	A number of conflicts	Some conflicts	Possible conflicts	Generally compatible	Generally compatible	Compatible
Ease of Establishment	Relatively easy	Difficult	Some impediments to expansion at present	Difficult to assess	Little land involved; simple expansion	Relatively easy	Already exists; a change in management approach
Place in System	Should be part of system of raptor areas	No agency link	Important expansion	Important addition	Important expansion	Important addition	Already part of system
Social and Economic Benefits				High potential for tourism and recreation		High potential for tourism and recreation	Secures a critical renewable resource
Planning and Management Priority	Immediate, Short-term priority	No action needed at present	Medium- to Long-term priority	Immediate, Short-term priority	Immediate, Short-term priority	Immediate, Short-term priority, Medium to Long-term information need for Brock Lagoon	Immediate, Short-term priority

Abbreviations used in the Table: CWS, Canadian Wildlife Service; IUCN, International Union for Conservation of Nature and Natural Resources; NERP, Natural Environment Recreation Park classification of Territorial Parks Ordinance

Table 7.3   Priority Assigned to Each of the Seven Eastern Beaufort ESAs

IMPLEMENTATION OF A COMPREHENSIVE ESA POLICY

Success in implementing an ESA policy depends not only on a method of evaluating ESAs and matching the outcomes with appropriate intuitional arrangements, but also on the means and will to implement it. Yet the available levels of staffing and funding of relevant federal and territorial agencies present a major constraint on NWT ESA planning. Two major institutional problems also impede ESA designation: inadequacies in the policy and legislative framework, and lack of a co-ordinating mechanism. These impediments are discussed briefly below, partly in the spirit of illustrating how our method reveals management issues and partly as a basis for their mitigation in the NWT.

INSTITUTIONAL ARRANGEMENTS, FUNDING AND CO-ORDINATION

The development of "a system of legislative and regulatory tools that can be applied in a comprehensive and coordinated manner to conserve the diverse natural environment of the NWT" was recommended by Fenge (1982). Related to that goal, he also saw the need "to evaluate the ability of existing environmental legislation and regulations to conserve northern ESAs." Our research and the work of the Task Force on Northern Conservation (DIAND, 1984b) involved such an evaluation, which is summarized as follows:

1) One of the most glaring gaps in the 1980s protected-area policy and legislation in Canada was the lack of concern for coastal and marine areas. No legislation or policy enabled the federal Department of Fisheries and Oceans to create or manage coastal and marine ESAs, although efforts were in progress towards remedying this defect (Mills, 1984; Department of Fisheries and Ocean, 1983, 1985a, 1985b). Environment Canada, through Parks Canada, recently had a policy statement on national marine parks approved – a welcome addition, indeed, to the available institutional arrangements. Yet implementation

remained uncertain. Similarly, few means were available to designate freshwater habitats for conservation purposes. Lands and waters could be, but never were, reserved for water conservation purposes under the Northern Inland Waters Act (Fenge, 1982).

2) Policy and legislation regarding wildlife habitat conservation was in a particularly difficult state. The federal Wildlife Service mandate had been increasingly confined to bird species that are protected under the Migratory Bird Convention, even though policy and legislation provide for a broader role. The NWT Wildlife Service assumed responsibility for managing terrestrial mammals and raptors, yet the three types of protected areas available to that Service constituted weak tools for future habitat management. There were no management regulations for Critical Wildlife Areas, and land-use control was affected only through the federal Territorial Land-Use Regulations. The NWT Wildlife Service was reviewing the available designations with the aim of deriving effective means of habitat protection.

3) The absence of a legal basis for Canadian Landmarks left no means within federal legislation to manage geological and other abiotic sites. In addition, Canadian Landmarks were also the only protected category explicitly intended to conserve areas significant for rare plants. Territorial Parks could be used to manage geological sites, but the federal government was still considering transferring many lands to the NWT government for designation as parks. In fact, the Territorial Park Ordinance, with its five parks' types, provided a comprehensive series of management types suited to many kinds of ESAs. On the other hand, the NWT Government reportedly concluded the creation of territorial parks "is not the mechanism of choice to protect ESAs" (Hamre, 1985).

4) The many ecological sites identified by the International Biological Programme (IBP) failed to fit the mandate of any particular agency. Hence, a Territorial Ecological

Sites Act or Ordinance was seen as useful as a basis for managing many IBP sites.

5) Policies and legislation failed to provide for effective management of historic and archaeological heritage resources, though a comprehensive policy and strategy for their management was apparently under development at the time.

6) The Area Development Ordinance was suggested as a powerful basis for wildlife habitat management (Hunt et al., 1979; Fenge, 1982), but the 150 km^2 restriction on the size of a "development area," severely constrained its use in ESA management. Rescinding the size restriction would provide a needed tool for regional as well as ESA planning on a scale more appropriate to Canada.

7) A number of challenges arose from the recent Inuvialuit land-claim settlement. Under Canadian laws, national parks could not be established on private land and were thus rendered inoperative for Inuvialuit lands as well as other native land in the future, although such would not have been the case in northern Australia, for example (Gardner and Nelson, 1981). Furthermore, private land was not subject to the Territorial Land-Use Regulations and the interim protection which they provided for ESAs.

8) Another issue raised by our work was that the full range of institutional arrangements was not used in the NWT. Only IUCN Categories II and IV, namely national parks and wildlife sanctuaries, were emphasized, whereas use of other categories is essential to meeting many conservation objectives. Similarly, non-statutory management arrangements such as leases, management agreements, donation, and purchase were little used. Nelson and Jessen (1984) list twenty techniques, only two of which were employed to any significant degree in the NWT. Federal ownership of over 95 per cent of NWT lands largely accounted for this situation. As land was transferred to

the native peoples and the territorial government, more techniques would probably be used, including some of the less formal means of protection likely more attractive to indigenous people.

9) A fundamental problem was posed by the 1985 and 1986 major federal government budget cuts for land and environmental management agencies such as Environment Canada, Parks, and the Canadian Wildlife Service. The smallness of staff and financial allocations to protected areas planning by NWT agencies also constrained progress in ESA management.

10) All of the above considerations indicated that, while there were, on paper, numerous means of managing ESAs, many of these were not used, could not be used, or would likely not be used – due to legal, policy, funding, and staffing constraints. The agencies were weak overall and limited in their capacity to implement an effective system of ESA management. Ways of working with First Nations were also limited.

11) A comprehensive, integrated, multi-agency mechanism was needed to bring together efforts of the many agencies that are, or should be, responsible for ESAs (Nelson and Jessen, 1984; DIAND, 1984b; Fenge, 1985). Some ESAs could probably only be managed effectively through the co-operation of a number of agencies and local communities. Indeed, the matching of ESAs with the most appropriate type of management was only possible with the assumption of more co-ordination. In any event, only time will tell if these issues are effectively addressed. It would be an interesting exercise to study the situation in the NWT today and determine what changes had taken place.

12) The foregoing challenges are so wide-ranging and significant that regular monitoring and assessment is vital to effective management and planning.

NOTES

1   Adapted from J.G. Nelson and P.G.R. Smith, "Institutional Arrangements for a System of Environmentally Significant Areas: The Case of the East Beaufort Sea Area, Canada," *Environmental Conservation* 14(3) (1987): 207–218.

REFERENCES

Bastedo, J.D., J.G. Nelson, and J.B. Theberge. 1984. "An ecological approach to resource survey and planning for environmentally significant areas: The ABC method." *Environmental Management* 8(2): 125–134.

Department of Fisheries and Oceans. 1983. *Towards a Fish Habitat Management Policy.* Ottawa.

Department of Fisheries and Oceans. 1985a. *Proposed Policy and Procedures for Fish Habitat Management.* Ottawa.

Department of Fisheries and Oceans. 1985b. *Consultations to Develop an Arctic Marine Conservation Strategy.* Ottawa.

Department of Indian Affairs and Northern Development (DIAND). 1984a. *The Western Arctic Claim, the Inuvialuit Final Settlement.* Ottawa: Department of Supply and Services.

Department of Indian Affairs and Northern Development (DIAND). 1984b. *The Report of the Task Force on Northern Conservation.* Ottawa: Department of Indian Affairs and Northern Development.

Dingwall, P.R. 1984. "Moving toward a representative system of protected areas in New Zealand." In *National Parks, Conservation and Development: The Role of Protected Areas in Sustaining Society,* ed. J.A. McNeely and K.R. Miller, 386–393. Washington, D.C.: Smithsonian Institution Press.

Fenge, T. 1982. "Towards comprehensive conservation of environmentally significant areas in the Northwest Territories." *Environmental Conservation* 9(4): 305–313.

Fenge, T. 1985. Conservation of Polar Bear Pass, Bathurst Island, and the emerging comprehensive conservation policy for northern Canada. *Environmental Conservation* 123: 231–240.

Gardner, J.E., and J.G. Nelson. 1980. "Comparing national park and related reserve policy in hinterland areas: Alaska, northern Canada, and northern Australia." *Environmental Conservation* 7(1): 43–50.

Gardner, J.E., and J.G. Nelson. 1981. "National Parks and native people in northern Canada, Alaska and northern Australia." *Environmental Conservation* 8(3): 207–215.

Hamre, G. 1985. Conservation in the Canadian Arctic with special emphasis on territorial parks. In *Arctic Heritage, Symposium Proceedings*, ed. J. G. Nelson, R. Needham, and L. Norton, 557–566. Ottawa: Association of Canadian Universities for Northern Studies.

Hunt, D., R. Miller, and D. Tingley. 1979. *Wilderness Area*. Ottawa: Canadian Arctic Resources Committee.

International Union for Conservation of Nature and Nature Resources (IUCN). 1978. *Categories, Objectives, and Criteria for Protected Areas*. Gland, Switzerland: International Union for Conservation of Nature and Natural Resources.

International Union for Conservation of Nature and Nature Resources (IUCN). 1986. *Review of the Protected Areas System in Oceania: Based on the Works of Arthur Dahl*. Gland, Switzerland: International Union for Conservation of Nature and Natural Resources.

MacKinnon, J. 1981. *National Conservation Plan for Indonesia*, Vol. 1: *Introduction, Evaluation Methods and Overview of National Nature Richness* (Field Report 34). Bogor, Indonesia: Food and Agriculture Organization of the United Nations.

MacKinnon, J., K. MacKinnon, G. Child, and J. Thorsell. 1986. *Managing Protected Areas in the Tropics*. Gland, Switzerland: International Union for Conservation of Nature and Natural Resources.

Margules, C., and M.B. Usher. 1981. "Criteria used in assessing wildlife conservation potential: A review." *Biological Conservation* 21(2): 79–109.

Miller, K. R. 1982. "Parks and protected areas: Considerations for the future." *Ambio* 11(5): 315–317.

Mills, H. 1984. *Arctic Marine Conservation – A Discussion Paper on Responsibilities and Opportunities for the Department of Fisheries and Oceans*. CanadianTechnical Report, Fisheries and Aquatic Science 1242.

Mosley, J.G. 1984. "Protected areas and environmental planning in Australia: The continuing evolution of a diverse range of protected areas." In *National Parks, Conservation and Development: The Role of Protected Areas in Sustaining Society*, ed. J.A. McNeely and K.R. Miller. Washington, D.C.: Smithsonian Institution Press: 267–273.

Nelson, J.G., and P. Grigoriew. 1987. "Institutional arrangement for individual environmentally significant areas: The case of Aishihik, Yukon." *Environmental Conservation* 14(4): 347–356.

Nelson, J.G., and S. Jessen. 1984. *Planning and Management of Environmentally Significant Areas in the Northwest Territories: Issues and Alternatives*. Ottawa: Canadian Arctic Resources Committee.

Nelson, J.G., P.G.R. Smith, and J.B. Theberge. 1985. "Environmentally Significant Areas (ESAs) in the Northwest Territories, Canada: Their role, identification, designation and implementation." *Environments* 17(3): 93–109.

Nelson, J.G., P. Grigoriew, and T. Whillans, eds. 1987. *Application of the ABC Resource Survey Method to Presqu'ile Provincial Park, Ontario.* Waterloo: Heritage Resources Centre, University of Waterloo.

Oltremari J. 1985. "Some criteria for evaluation of resources in a system of protected areas in Chile." *Environmental Conservation* 12(2): 173–175.

Parks Canada. 1978. *Planning Process for National Parks.* Ottawa.

Parks Canada. 1979. Parks Canada Policy, Ottawa: Department of Environment.

Roome, N.J. 1984. "Evaluation in nature conservation decision-making." *Environmental Conservation* 11(3): 247–252.

Salm, R., and J. Clark. 1984. *Managing Coastal and Marine Protected Areas: Principles and Guidelines for Managers of Natural Areas of the Sea.* Gland, Switzerland: IUCN.

Smith, P.G.R., and J.B. Theberge. 1986. "A review of criteria for evaluating natural areas." *Environmental Management* 19(6): 715–734.

Smith, P.G.R., J.G. Nelson, and J.B. Theberge. 1986. *Environmentally Significant Areas, Conservation and Land Use Management in the Northwest Territories.* Technical Paper 1. Waterloo: Heritage Resources Centre, University of Waterloo.

Swen, T., and R. Cahn. 1983. "The politics of parks in Alaska." *Ambio* 12(1): 14–19.

Theberge, J. B., J.G. Nelson, and T. Fenge, eds. 1980. *Environmentally Significant Areas of the Yukon Territory.* Ottawa: Canadian Arctic Resources Committee.

Tungavik Federation of Nunavut. 1985. Land claims, national parks, protected areas and the renewable resource economy. In *Arctic Heritage, Symposium Proceedings,* ed. J.G. Nelson, R. Needham, and L. Norton. Ottawa: Association of Canadian Universities for Northern Studies.

Usher, M. B. 1986. *Wildlife Conservation Evaluation.* London: Chapman and Hall.

Wright, R. G. 1985. "Principles of new park-area planning as applied to the Wrangell-St Elias region of Alaska." *Environmental Conservation* 12(1): 59–66.

8

1991

THE GRAND AS A CANADIAN HERITAGE RIVER[1]

J.G. Nelson

INTRODUCTION

Although the principal concern here is with rivers and heritage, a fundamental underlying theme must be recognized at the outset. This theme is that of the Canadian middle ground that is envisioned as lying geographically, economically, socially, and environmentally somewhere between two general places or images often perceived as personifying Canada. These two general places or images are the wilderness or wildlands and the large cities or urban metropolitan areas, notably Montreal, Toronto, and Vancouver. In southern Ontario and Quebec especially, many middle-sized towns and villages are located amid agricultural, mining, and more natural lands. In this middle ground, under the rapid Canadian economic growth of the last several decades, a struggle has been underway over dominance in land use and landscape. This struggle means more and more care must be taken to plan for appropriate development if we wish to conserve the natural and cultural heritage coming from the past. Such planning should underlie any sustainable development thrust in future. In this context, nothing seems more important than thoughtful planning and management of the rivers, which serve humans and nature in so many ways.

Canada has long been famous for its rivers, which provided the routes along which Indian ways of life were concentrated and European travel, trade, and settlement developed. Rivers were also among the first of Canada's resources to suffer from pollution and the adverse effects and stresses of development. Among the first pollution laws passed in Canada were those intended to control the high oxygen demand and other damaging impacts of sawdust refuse discharged by lumber mills into streams. Canadians have therefore been concerned about stream water quality and quantity for more than a century. In Ontario, conservation authorities were created in the 1940s and 1950s to deal on a watershed basis with matters such as low-flow augmentation and flood control. Concern for pollution in Ontario was highlighted in the 1950s, 1960s, and 1970s with the construction of sewage and waste purification plants in most cities and towns. While the interest in pollution control continues, more recently, concern has arisen over the protection of natural and human heritage resources – old forests, marshes, wildlife, buildings, and structures – threatened by accelerating economic growth.

Concern for river heritage in the broad, natural, and human sense has also been manifest in the United States through the development of the Wild and Scenic Rivers Program beginning in the 1970s. In the ensuing years, a network of these rivers has been developed, which undoubtedly influenced the creation of the Canadian Heritage Rivers Program (CHRP) in 1984. The stated objectives of the CHRP were to give national recognition to the important rivers of Canada and to provide long-term management intended to conserve their natural, historical, and recreation values for the benefit of Canadians now and in the future. In practice, the CHRP has slowly taken on a more broadly human and historic dimension.

At the time of this study in 1990, fifteen rivers or sections of rivers had been nominated or designated in the CHRP since its inception. The CHRP program was co-ordinated by the Canadian Heritage Rivers Board, which consisted of one representative each of Environment Canada (Canadian Parks Service), Indian and Northern Affairs Canada, and the seven provincial and two territorial governments involved in the heritage rivers system. The Board was served by a small secretariat of Environment Canada and had as one of its functions the selection and funding of studies relating to the recognition, nomination, designation, and planning of Canadian Heritage Rivers. The Board reviewed nominations to the system and recommended to the federal Minister of the Environment and the appropriate provincial or territorial minister of the nominating government whether or not a river met selection guidelines for designation as a Canadian Heritage River (CHR). A study was initiated in 1988 to consider whether the Grand River in southern Ontario had the significant natural, cultural, and recreational characteristics to merit its designation as Canadian Heritage River (Nelson and O'Neill, 1989).

GRAND RIVER STUDY

The study of the Grand River valley was undertaken for two basic reasons. The first was to determine whether the river valley had the outstanding qualities required for designation as a Canadian Heritage River along with other famous streams such as the French River in northern Ontario or the Nahanni of the Northwest Territories. The second purpose was to collect and analyze information on Grand River Heritage generally, for use by the Grand River Conservation Authority (GRCA) and other government agencies and private groups involved in the day-to-day planning and managing of the river. In other words, the Canadian Heritage River studies for the Grand River link outstanding heritage resources and provincial and federal agencies with watershed agencies, such as the GRCA, as well as regional and municipal agencies and private interests.

In this respect, it is noteworthy that the Grand River Heritage Study (GRHS) was commissioned by the Canadian Heritage Rivers Board and the Grand River Conservation Authority, with guidance from the Ontario Ministry of Natural Resources. The latter is the lead agency in Ontario, charged with tabling nomination documents and management plans for candidates for Canadian Heritage River status in the province.

A resource and environmental survey is the first step in the process followed by the Canadian Heritage Rivers Board in determining whether a river has the outstanding qualities to become a Canadian Heritage River. As of 1990, the inventory included information on natural and human heritage in the broad sense discussed previously. The inventory also included data on the recreation qualities of the river, because recreation and tourism were seen as generally appropriate ways in which heritage rivers could be used and enjoyed by people. In other words, natural heritage, human heritage, and recreation were the three broad categories or criteria upon which information was collected to determine if a stream had the outstanding characteristics to become a Canadian Heritage River. To attain this status, a river needed to qualify under only one of the three categories.

If the inventory seemed promising, then the second step in the Canadian Heritage River process was to prepare a nomination document. This summarized the inventory information and made the case for heritage river status. The third step in the Canadian Heritage River process was the preparation of a Management Plan for the river. A river could be approved in principle for Canadian Heritage River status but could not be confirmed by the Board until completion of a Management Plan. All the major concerned agencies, groups, and individuals in the river valley should be given an opportunity to be involved in the preparation of this plan.

The foregoing policies and procedures for identifying and designating a Canadian Heritage River have remained generally the same over the years. And the Management Plan continues to be an important document, which specifies how activities will be administered by agencies, groups, and people along the waterway in order to appropriately use and protect the outstanding qualities for which it is designated. In this connection, it is also very important to realize that designation as a Canadian Heritage River does not bring any specific standards or regulations for either use or conservation. In other words, the Canadian Heritage River designation does not impose any water quality, land-use planning, or other requirements of its own. Any regulations, guidelines, policies, or other institutional or management arrangements for the use and protection of the river's heritage are prepared by the agencies, groups, and people in the valley as part of the Management Plan. Many of the arrangements in such a plan may already exist, as is the case in the Grand River valley, as will be shown later in this chapter.

Given the foregoing circumstances, it might well be asked, "What are the values of Canadian Heritage River status?" The first surely is that the designation increases awareness of the natural and human heritage, and the recreational and tourism potential of a river. In the case of the Grand, over the years many communities and groups have forgotten or neglected the heritage of the river. They have turned their backs to it, thinking of and using it primarily for water supply or other development purposes. People expressed concern about this state of affairs at the open house and other meetings held as part of this study. Many people at these meetings expressed appreciation for the information about the Grand and asked for more. Many people also expressed support for stronger efforts to protect the natural and human heritage of the Grand, especially at this time when accelerated development in some areas seemed to be threatening what had come from the past. Other persons were concerned that the recreational, tourism, and associated economic potential of the river was not being adequately developed, for example, in regard to boating and related activities in the lower river, from Brantford to Lake Erie.

Designation as a Canadian Heritage River not only could make local people more aware of the heritage values of the Grand and the need to appropriately use and protect them, but it could increase knowledge of the river in other places. It should help to attract more outside visitors to the Grand River watershed. Designation of the Grand as a heritage river could also promote more co-operation among residents in the different regional municipalities and local governments throughout the watershed. It could prompt local governments to work more closely with citizens' groups, the GRCA, and federal and provincial government agencies, as well as private businesses, in planning for appropriate use and protection of the heritage resources and features along the river valley.

A prime value of Canadian Heritage River status is education. Reports and other information prepared for designation, as well as for planning and management purposes can be used in the schools, colleges, and universities, as well as by interested citizens' groups. The information can become part of the environmental education program of key agencies such as the GRCA. An additional benefit of designating a river, like the Grand, as a Canadian Heritage River is the increase in enjoyment and quality of life that it will bring. Outstanding heritage sites will become better known, more widely used, and the citizens better informed. The recreation and leisure time of citizens will be enriched. The basis for a higher quality of life will be identified, and heritage resources could be more wisely used and protected through management planning.

APPROACH

The study of the Grand began in March 1988, after about one year of negotiation with the Canadian Heritage Rivers Board, provincial government personnel, representatives of the GRCA, and interested citizens notably from the lower reaches of the Grand River. A wide-ranging public consultation process was developed, which focused on three open houses held in the lower, middle, and upper reaches of the river in June 1988. Various visits and presentations were made to groups in different parts of the valley in spring and summer. The major aim of these public consultations and other presentations was to get reaction to ideas and to secure other information and suggestions of value to the study. The summer was a period of intense research, following up on our work and the suggestions of others. A draft background study was subsequently presented to a public workshop and to a members' meeting of the Grand River Conservation Authority in October and November, respectively.

Eight student research assistants worked with the study director to collect and analyze information on Grand River heritage and recreation (Nelson and O'Neill, 1990). This information was organized into the following specific themes:

1) abiotic and geologic (i.e., bedrock, landforms, glaciation, and the like);

2) biotic (i.e., vegetation and animal life);

3) water quality;

4) human heritage, with special reference to native peoples, the watershed's cultural mosaic, and industrial history;

5) Six Nations – past and present;

6) recreation and tourism;

7) parks and protected areas;

8) Grand River valley trail systems;

9) development stresses; and

10) heritage management arrangements.

This information was collected and analyzed in general accordance with the ABC Resource Survey Method (Nelson, 1991). The method was chosen as a comprehensive attempt to understand the Abiotic, Biotic, and Cultural resources of the Grand by describing and mapping them in terms of patterns. These patterns include the roads, buildings, or other artifacts or structures found in the study area. These patterns also refer to processes such as erosion or flooding in the natural sense, or transport or manufacturing in the human sense.

The large amount of information collected by the research team and numerous accompanying maps were published in a comprehensive volume by Nelson and O'Neill (1989). For each of the topics considered by the research assistants and in general accordance with the levels or steps in the ABC method, information was given on context, patterns, significance, constraints, and management issues. Much of this information is very relevant to the question of whether the Grand River merited Canadian Heritage River status. However, only the findings on the more significant resources and constraints can be discussed in this summary.

RESULTS

The purpose here is not to present details on the analysis, assessment, and mapping of the Grand River but rather to focus on the results of the study. The maps and details of the study are available in Nelson and

O'Neill (1989). The study revealed the Grand River as being rich in natural and human heritage, as well as in recreation and tourism opportunities. Much of the heritage, and some recreation and tourism opportunities, were judged to be outstanding on a provincial or national basis. Such judgments were founded on various criteria, for example, certain wildlife or other features are rare in Ontario or Canada. Other features are representative of aspects of natural or human history that have been recognized as provincially or nationally significant by appropriate authorities such as the National Historic Sites and Monuments Board or by the Ontario Ministry of Natural Resources (OMNR) (Nelson and O'Neill, 1989). Among the kaleidoscope of heritage features, and recreational and tourism opportunities, were some considered sufficiently outstanding to make the case for the Grand as a Canadian Heritage River. These outstanding features were natural, human, and recreational in kind. In other words, the Grand River was considered to qualify for Canadian Heritage River status in terms of all three of the basic criteria used by the Canadian Heritage Rivers Board.

Significant Abiotic Resources

The river is one of the oldest in Ontario, underlain by buried river valleys probably carved thousands of years ago, during the last glacial stage. The present river and its valley began with the retreat of Wisconsinan ice some 12,000 years before the present. Along the course of the river valley are found good examples of the major landforms resulting from glaciation. These include: extensive poorly sorted clay, sand, and gravel deposits, or till and undulating ground moraine in the north; hummocky interlobate, recessional, or retreat moraines in the central basin; and old, raised, glacial shorelines and flat lake-bottom deposits in the south (Figure 8.1). In other words, along the Grand River valley is the sequence or suite of landforms and deposits representing much of the evidence for ancient ice advance and retreat. Within the Grand River valley are also found quite rare geologic features such as the giant potholes and old river channels at Rockwood and the canyons of the Elora Gorge. Unusually large aquifers or underground water storage areas

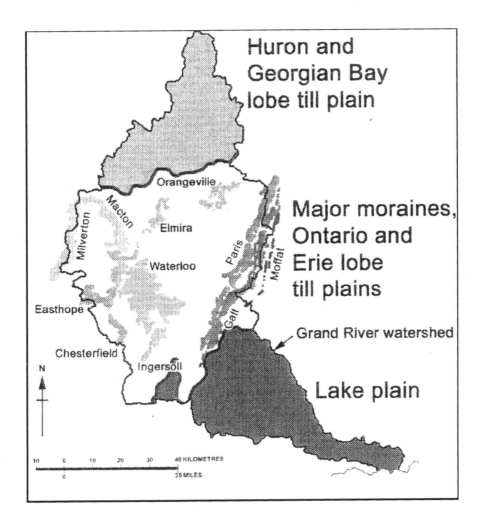

Figure 8.1   Landforms of the Grand River Basin

are also located in the central part of the Grand River valley area. Such aquifers have been the basis for long-time reliance upon groundwater for water supply in many communities in the Grand River basin.

Significant Biotic Resources

Many significant Biotic features are found in various parts of the Grand River valley. An outstanding biological feature is the extensive area of deciduous Carolinian forest (Sudden Bog, Grand River Forest, Spottiswood Lakes) in the central and lower part of the valley below Cambridge (Figure 8.2). The Carolinian forest occurs in Canada only in the most southerly part of Ontario, roughly below a line drawn from Windsor to Toronto. The Carolinian flora are species that occur infrequently or not at all elsewhere in Ontario or Canada, for example, tulip tree, sassafras, flowering dogwood, and various species of hickory. Rare animals such as the opossum and birds such as the prothonotary warbler also are concentrated in the Carolinian zone.

Extensive areas of Carolinian forest are found in and around that part of the valley below Cambridge and also on the Six Nations Indian Reserve. An almost unbroken twenty-kilometre stretch of what is known as the Grand River Forest lies between Cambridge and Paris (Figure 8.3). This stretch of Carolinian forest is not only one of the strongest justifications for Canadian Heritage River status but also the key element in an uneven network of forest, woodlots, and treed strings and patches that link with the Grand River, providing important habitat for the movement and survival of animal life.

The Grand River valley also contains numerous provincially significant marshes and wetland areas. Luther Marsh in the northern part of the valley is also outstanding biologically, for example, with respect to its very high number of breeding bird species and its diversity generally. The Dunnville and Grand River wetlands in the lower valley, near Lake Erie, are also of special interest.

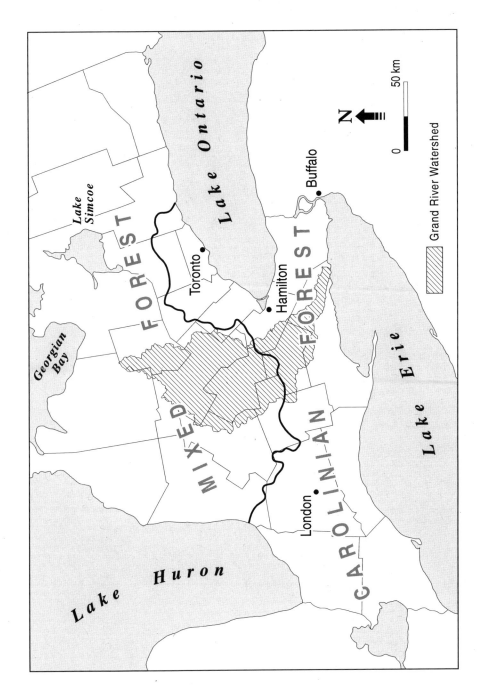

Figure 8.2   Forest Types in the Grand River Basin

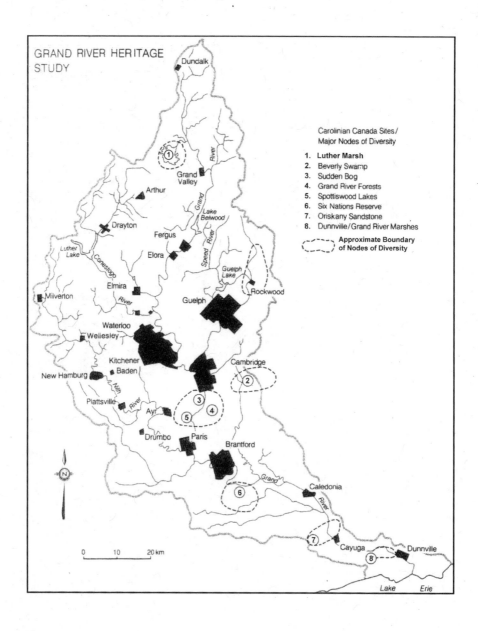

Carolinian Canada Sites/
Major Nodes of Diversity

1. **Luther Marsh**
2. Beverly Swamp
3. Sudden Bog
4. Grand River Forests
5. Spottiswood Lakes
6. Six Nations Reserve
7. Oriskany Sandstone
8. Dunnville/Grand River Marshes

Approximate Boundary
of Nodes of Diversity

Figure 8.3   Biotic Features: Carolinian Canada Sites

Significant Cultural Resources

In human terms, the Grand River valley is an ethnic or cultural mosaic. It contains features and landscapes that reflect the attitudes, values, and effects of a wide variety of people, some of whom are still distinctive in the valley today (Figure 8.4). In the north are descendants of Scots and Irish immigrants. This includes many Scots in towns, such as Guelph, whose presence represents some of the major means of European settlement in Canada, in this case the Canada Land Company and the entrepreneurs who purchased land blocks from it for sale to immigrants. In the central basin are Mennonites as well as descendants of German immigrants of various religious backgrounds. In the lower basin, below Paris, are descendants of United Empire Loyalists, including the native people who came from New York in the 1780s after the American Revolutionary War.

The valley is especially outstanding for the story it tells of the history and current role of native people. Archaeological research in the Grand River area has revealed sites and artifacts that date back thousands of years. Remains of Paleo-Indian people who hunted caribou, bison, and other Pleistocene or Ice Age fauna in southern Ontario some 9,000 to 5,000 years ago are concentrated in the lower valley below Paris. Remains of Archaic and other people who occupied the valley area some 5,000 to 1,000 years before present are also found in the lower and central valley in particular.

Remains of later Woodland peoples, who practised shifting agriculture based on corn, beans, and squash, date from about the time of Christ to about AD 1100. These people lived in transient villages, which have been found primarily in the central valley area. These ancient folk are linked to the native people who live today on the Six Nations and New Credit reserves along the west bank of the Grand, south of Brantford. On the New Credit Reserve are descendants of the Mississauga Indians who succeeded the Neutrals or late Woodland residents of the area.

The Six Nations Reserve is also home to descendants of Iroquois from New York who were awarded land all along the Grand River by the British government for their loyalty in the American War of

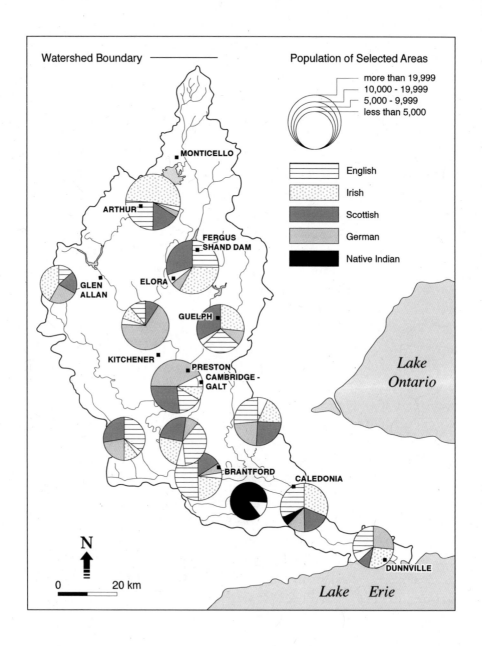

Figure 8.4   Ethnic background of the Grand River Basin, ca. 1871

PLACES

Independence. These people subsequently migrated to Canada where they were led for many years by the well-known Joseph Brant. The history of their interactions with European and American immigrants and the gradual reduction of their reserve is a prominent example of an important theme in Canadian history. As the largest Indian reserve in southern Ontario, the Six Nations–New Credit area represents an unusual manifestation of Indian history and the continuity of the struggle to do well economically, culturally, and environmentally today.

Another outstanding aspect of human heritage in the Grand River valley is its industrial history. Numerous old mills and other historic structures are located along the Grand River, with many of them still being used today as factories, markets, or restaurants. A number of major technological innovations were made at historic sites along the valley as well. Examples are the invention of a rolling mill for grinding grain at St. Jacobs and Alexander Graham Bell's well-known invention of the telephone in Brantford. His house is preserved as an historic site on the Grand River bank in the southern part of the city.

Other examples of industrial history include development of a canal system from Dunnville via Cayuga to Brantford in the period from about 1830 to the 1860s. Paddlewheelers and other craft passed along the Grand and its locks, moving passengers, wheat, and other goods to and from United States ports and other Canadian cities (Figure 8.5). Access to these other cities was facilitated by early nineteenth-century construction of a feeder canal between the lower Grand, Lake Erie, Dunnville area and the Welland Canal, St. Catharines, Hamilton, and other nearby towns.

Remains of the Grand River locks and the Welland feeder canal are quite apparent today. The tourism potential for such industrial history seems good, especially if the interest of lower Grand River people in arranging for construction of a new lock and the development of boating and other tourism activities between Dunnville, Caledonia, and points north comes to fruition. Major efforts are being made to develop tourist and associated facilities relating to industrial and other history in river towns such as Dunnville, Caledonia, and Brantford.

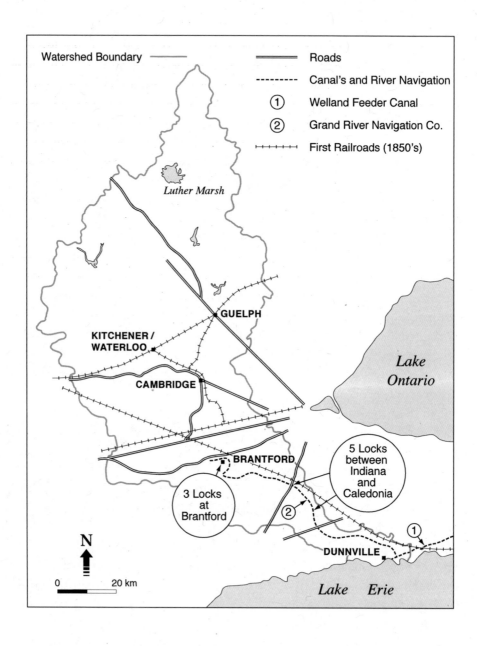

Legend:
- Watershed Boundary
- Roads
- Canal's and River Navigation
- ① Welland Feeder Canal
- ② Grand River Navigation Co.
- First Railroads (1850's)

Luther Marsh

GUELPH

KITCHENER / WATERLOO

CAMBRIDGE

Lake Ontario

BRANTFORD

3 Locks at Brantford

5 Locks between Indiana and Caledonia

②

①

DUNNVILLE

N

0   20 km

Lake Erie

Figure 8.5   Transportation Development in the 19th Century

In terms of recreation and tourism, the Grand River valley offers many resources, facilities, and opportunities. Some of these have been discussed in the foregoing section on industrial history. Many others are described in Nelson and O'Neill (1990). Continuing use and protection of these resources, facilities, and opportunities should contribute to tourism, as well as to recreation and quality of life, not only in the basin, but also through tourist visits from large surrounding areas.

From the perspective of the case for the Grand as a Canadian Heritage River, three areas are considered to possess a combination of recreational opportunities and related natural values that are highly significant for naturalist activities, such as for wildlife viewing, hiking, fishing, and other outdoor activities. These three areas are the Luther Marsh in the upper reaches of the river, the Carolinian forest area in the central part of the basin, probably extending to include the Six Nations Reserve, and the wetlands and marshes near Dunnville and Port Maitland at the mouth of the Grand River. In addition, four areas have been identified as having highly significant clusters or combinations of recreational opportunities, including human heritage appreciation. These are Fergus/Elora/West Montrose, Elmira/St. Jacobs, Kitchener/ Waterloo, and Brantford and area.

Constraints for Planning

Many constraints can limit or prevent the appropriate use and conservation of the natural and human heritage and recreational opportunities along the Grand River. These constraints are described in detail in the various reports that make up the background study, notably that on development stresses (Figure 8.6). The most obvious or direct constraints have to do with recent rapid development in urban areas along the river. Residential, industrial, aggregate mining, and other development can destroy, damage, or otherwise stress heritage resources and recreational opportunities along the Grand. Such development problems are especially acute in Kitchener/Waterloo/Cambridge, Guelph, and Brantford.

In more rural sections of the river, stresses from conflicts among recreational activities and other related uses can threaten the forests,

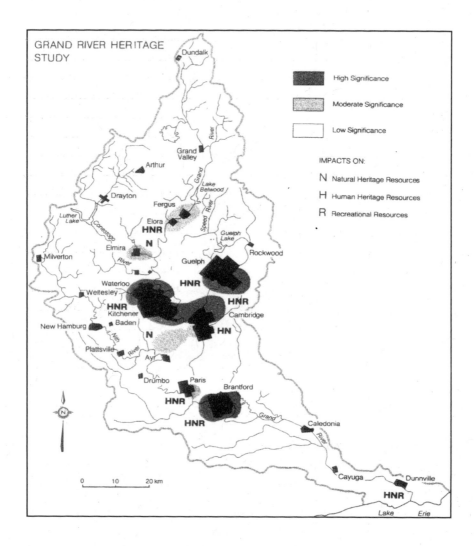

Figure 8.6   Significant Development Stresses

wetlands, landforms, historic structures, land uses, and ethnic patterns, which are the basis for heritage and recreational opportunities in the first place. A major problem in rural areas is the impact of agriculture through clearing of vegetation and habitat for mechanized farming, artificial and tile drainage, and from fertilizer run-off and other non-point sources of river pollution.

Management Arrangements

Fortunately, an array of laws, agencies, policies, guidelines, regulations, and other means are available to eliminate or reduce these constraints upon appropriate use and conservation of heritage resources, and recreational and tourist opportunities in the Grand River valley. Local and regional governments, the GRCA, and a number of provincial and federal government agencies such as the Ontario Ministry of Natural Resources and the Canadian Parks Service can assist with planning and management of heritage, recreation, tourism, and quality of life generally.

Among the means for appropriate use and protection are: floodplain and fill regulations; the land-use and human or historical heritage policies of local governments; conservation areas; Environmentally Significant Areas (ESAs); regional parks; agreement forests; provincial and national parks and historic sites; and, perhaps, international programs such as the UNESCO Man and Biosphere program (MAB).

In addition to these arrangements, interest and activity have been growing in private stewardship, that is, in employing leases, agreements, or other means of encouraging private landowners to use and conserve heritage resources wisely. These arrangements seem particularly desirable in rural areas. A leading example at the moment is the landowner contact and private stewardship program for Carolinian forestlands organized by the University of Guelph and the Ontario Natural Heritage League. Among the management issues frequently put forward about these means or other mechanisms for more appropriate use and conservation is the question of their effectiveness. Research is needed to determine how well these means or arrangements work and how they can be improved.

Another major management issue is how the various laws, agencies, regulations, and other means can be best brought together or coordinated for optimal use and conservation. A major vehicle in this regard could be the Grand River Conservation Authority (GRCA), which consists of municipalities from throughout the watershed functioning under the umbrella of the Ontario Ministry of Natural Resources. The GRCA has played a lead role in areas such as water management. However, more study is required to determine the best means of co-ordination. This applies to co-ordination for conservation as well as uses such as recreation and tourism. Underlying this interest in co-ordination is a concern for integrated planning and management in the Grand River valley.

One of the concerns that has to be addressed in securing Canadian Heritage River status is the means available to maintain the integrity of the features, processes, or resources upon which the CHR designation was based in the first instance. Effective co-ordination in the conservation and use of key features and processes is most important in maintaining this integrity. Compatible policies and procedures are needed throughout the river valley, and ultimately the watershed.

Co-ordination through provincial government bodies, the regional and local governments, and the GRCA has already led to improvements in river water quality in the last two decades or so. The water quality along the river is now considered to be good to very good by the GRCA. Although water quality is not considered to be outstanding enough in its own right to be put forward as a reason for CHR status, it is generally satisfactory as support for the geologic, biologic, and human features and processes upon which the case for designation is made in this study.

The development of hiking trails is another potential way of bringing the various agencies, groups, and people together to provide for the integrity of Grand River valley heritage and recreation. A report on Grand Valley Trails prepared for the background study shows that a very good trail system has been developed in the Grand River valley, notably in the last few years. This system links people and places in the valley and tends to make people more aware of and interested in the heritage qualities and scenic character of valley landscapes.

The foregoing discussion raises another issue that must be addressed in a Management Plan, the delimitation of a boundary or border for the Canadian Heritage River. In other words, we have to identify the zone around the river to which the CHR designation applies. We have not done so in this study because of the complexity of the matter and the desire to get opinions and information on how the border would relate to heritage features and recreational opportunities from the agencies, groups, and people in the basin. They will have to live and work with any boundary, so it seems appropriate that it be decided upon as part of the Management Plan. The delimitation of the boundary may require some innovations in the case of the Grand, for example, it may be desirable to identify different types of management areas along the river, as well as means of co-ordination among concerned agencies.

Another major issue has to do with the level of public awareness and potential support for use and conservation of Grand River heritage and associated recreation and tourism. Over 150 people came to the June 1988 open houses and thousands of people in the course of the work were contacted indirectly. But we are uncertain of the degree of public understanding and commitment to the heritage river idea, although we believe it to be quite strong on the basis of experience so far.

Another important issue is the claim of the Indian people to the bed and banks of the Grand River alongside the Six Nations Reserve. This issue raises questions about river uses, with the native people favouring maintenance and care of spawning areas and fishing opportunities in the context of any recreation or other developments.

A number of the reports prepared for this background study stress the need for more information, so that planning and management can be improved through increased understanding. Examples of this call for further information extended to the biotic, human, and recreation (and tourism) domains. Thus, we need to know more about the Biotic details of key areas such as the Carolinian section of the valley from Cambridge to Paris. We need to know more about the industrial and technical history of the valley, neglected themes in heritage in Canada generally. Many of the recreational and tourism statistics were completed some years ago and should be updated.

CONCLUSIONS

The study showed that the Grand River had the Abiotic and Biotic characteristics as well as the cultural characteristics to merit nomination as a

Canadian Heritage River, although a nomination document and plan were needed to complete the designation process. This study showed that the means for managing heritage resources, recreation, and tourism are present in the valley, although more study is required to find out how these arrangements can work most effectively. The three issues of management effectiveness, management co-ordination, and public awareness and commitment seem to be the major ones to be addressed in the management planning phase for the Grand. The Management Plan should also provide details on how specific heritage resources and recreational and tourist opportunities will be planned for along the length of the Grand River valley. The foregoing comments apply especially to the geologic, biologic, historic, and recreational resources that are truly outstanding and make the case for Canadian Heritage River status for the Grand.

In thinking about awareness of heritage, we should also be thinking about ways of linking heritage use and conservation with recent ideas on development. Use and conservation are increasingly viewed as opposite sides of the same coin. They are essential to one another, as are heritage and development. Currently there is a strong interest in the concept of sustainable development as a philosophy for the future. The idea of sustainability is necessarily based on knowledge of the things that have come to us from the past. Some of these natural and cultural features and processes are essential to acceptable change or development in future. An understanding of geology, vegetation, animal habitats, and other key natural phenomena as well as ethnic, industrial, and other human history is important to the understanding of our present circumstances as well as where we are going in the years ahead. In this fundamental sense, heritage is an essential part of overall planning and management in the Grand River valley and its watershed. Furthermore, the Grand is of special interest in this context, for it is a much more developed river than those designated as Canadian Heritage Rivers previously. The Grand is a kind of test case for the Canadian Heritage Rivers system in that it is not a wild stream in the sense of the northern French or the Clearwater rivers in Canada. It has a much wider heritage in the sense of the natural to human history and

the local, regional, provincial, and national levels of significance atten-
dant upon the many features and processes in the valley. On January 15,
1994, the Canadian Heritage Rivers Board approved the nomination of
the Grand as a Canadian Heritage River.

NOTES

1   Adapted from J.G. Nelson, "Canadian Heritage Rivers with Special Reference to the Grand
     River in Ontario." In *Ontario: Geographical Perspectives on Economy and Environment*, ed. B. Mitch-
     ell, 269–291. Department of Geography, University of Waterloo, Waterloo, Ontario, 1991.

REFERENCES

Nelson, J.G. 1991. "A step toward more comprehensive and equitable information
     systems: The ABC resource survey method." In *Greenways and Green Space
     on the Oak Ridges Moraine: Towards Cooperative Planning.* Occasional Paper
     14, Peterborough, ON: Department of Geography, Trent University.

Nelson, J.G., and P. O'Neill, eds. 1989. *The Grand River as a Heritage River.* Water-
     loo: Heritage Resources Centre, University of Waterloo.

Nelson, J.G., and P. O'Neill, eds. 1990. *Nominating the Grand River as a Canadian
     Heritage River.* Occasional Paper 13. Waterloo: Heritage Resources Cen-
     tre, University of Waterloo.

9

1995

ASSEMBLING, ANALYZING, AND ASSESSING INFORMATION FOR COASTAL PLANNING IN JAVA[1]

J.G. Nelson, E. LeDrew, C. Olive, and Dulbahri

INTRODUCTION

Coasts are increasingly recognized as highly significant areas from a sustainable development perspective. They reflect the interrelationships between development and environment in an exemplary fashion. On the one hand, coasts are sites for major concentrations of human population supported by fishing, farming, mining, industry, waste disposal, tourism, and other activities. On the other hand, coastal estuaries, deltas, mangroves, marshes, fish habitats, waters, and other productive and diverse environments are increasingly stressed by these human activities. The stresses are accompanied by changes, which may be the indirect result of human activities, such as global climatic warming, sea-level rise, and diseases. The sustainability of human populations and activities is therefore a major issue in coastal areas. In light of their great importance for human well-being, it is important that we understand what is happening in coastal areas as fully as possible in order to be able to plan efficiently, effectively, and equitably for environmental and human well-being in these areas in future (World Commission on Environment and Development, 1987).

With this motivation in mind, studies were undertaken in coastal areas of the Segara Anakan area, Java (Figure 9.1), in co-operation with Indonesian colleagues and students. The studies involved a considerable amount

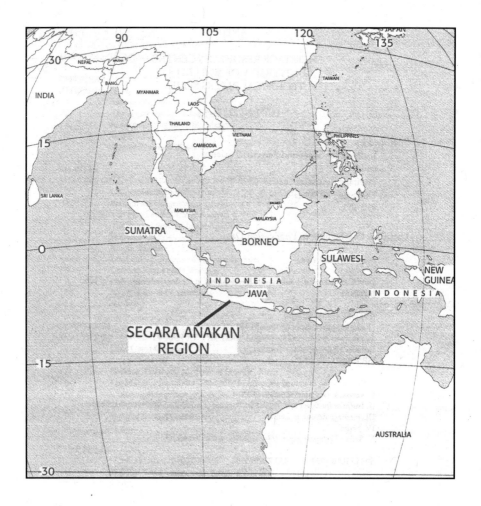

Figure 9.1   Segara Anakan Region

of training and educational activity (Nelson et al., 1992). Their basic
purpose was to provide information of value for sustainable development, where this is defined generally as using and conserving resources
and environments in ways that provide both for present and future
generations. In this context, we used four main objectives or criteria in
thinking about and making judgments on sustainable development:

(1) Preservation of diversity, for example the plants and animals of the mangroves;

(2) Maintenance of essential ecological processes, for example stream flow;

(3) Protection of resource and environmental productivity, for example fisheries;

(4) Provision of equitable access to resources, environments, and socio-economic opportunity for present and future generations, for example water supply.

METHODS

Planning and managing for sustainable development – in terms of the foregoing objectives or criteria – depend upon a wide-ranging knowledge of the environment, resources, and people in an area. Securing such knowledge is a difficult and demanding task as it involves collecting, analyzing, and interpreting geologic, biological, economic, and other information of many different kinds. We concentrated on the collection, analysis, and interpretation of information and not on the specific application of the information to future policy and planning.

A principal interest was in collecting, analyzing, and interpreting as much information as possible in the limited amount of time available through funding from the Canadian International Development Agency (CIDA) and the Social Science and Humanities Research Council (SSHRC). One of our objectives was to assess the usefulness of remote sensing, notably satellite images, in providing information of direct value for sustainable development especially in the Segara Anakan area, Java. A second objective was to assess the utility of the ABC resource survey method as a framework for the collection, analysis, and interpretation of wide-ranging information on the Abiotic (geology and hydrology), Biotic (vegetation and animals), and Cultural (land use, land tenure, and other human matters) characteristics of the area (Bastedo et al., 1984; Nelson et al., 1988).

Since the study was not directly concerned with policy, planning, and institutional arrangements, the focus was on Levels I and II of the ABC method and did not deal with Levels III or IV in any specific way.

In order to provide a focus for fieldwork, satellite images of Segara Anakan were studied in the fall and winter of 1989 and 1990. The only relatively cloud-free images available for comparative study of land cover change were a MSS image for April 25, 1978 (the LANDSAT beginning of the dry season) and a SPOT image for October 11, 1987 (the beginning of the wet season). Much useful information on vegetation, agricultural, and other cover changes was obtained from these images through appropriate digital procedures and field supplement observations (Olive, 1992; Nelson et al., 1992).

In this Indonesian project, the application of the ABC method differed significantly from earlier work (Bastedo et al., 1984; Nelson et al., 1988). Previous projects normally involved preparation of a series of Abiotic, Biotic, and Cultural theme maps at Level I. These were assessed in terms of a set of relevant criteria to ascertain significance and constraints for planning, research, and other purposes. In the Indonesia project, the use of satellite imagery made it possible to map land cover and associated land-use changes directly. The mapping of these changes led to the identification of significance and constraints for research, planning, and other subsequent work.

A basic challenge was to organize the work of Canadian and Indonesian faculty, students, and assistants effectively in a total of about six months field work during the three-year period of active study. We conducted checks of the satellite analysis with field observations, interviews, and supplemental site scale photography. These photos helped considerably with detailed analysis and interpretation. We also collected reports and documents from many government offices, libraries, and other sources so that this information could be used to supplement our field work. In the course of our studies, we held workshops with university and government people at Gadjah Mada University in 1991 and 1992. In this regard, although our work was intended primarily as a co-operative inter-university training and research endeavour aimed at obtaining information in sustainable development, we were sensitive about the need to consult closely with local people as agents of development and sources of information on community characteristics and aspirations. In association with Indonesian students and faculty, the Canadian research team members conducted some consultations with knowledgeable local individuals and in small meetings, for example in schools. However, time and resources did not allow for as much of this as we would have liked. For more specific details on the project and related studies, the reader is referred to Nelson et al. (1992), Harris and Nelson (1992), and Nelson and Harris (1993).

THE STUDY AREA: THE SEGARA ANAKAN

The Segara Anakan area is a low-lying brackish mangrove estuary, which forms part of a larger watershed (Figure 9.2). The Segara Anakan area is located in a highly settled Javanese landscape but exhibits some distinctiveness in having the largest remaining areas of mangrove and rainforest on Java. Historically, the area was settled as a navigational post by the Dutch. Several prisons were also established on the neighbouring island of Nusa Kambangan. Local inhabitants were then moved to villages located in the mangroves and wetlands (Sujastani, 1986). In 1993, three fishing villages, collectively known as Kampung Laut, housed about 10,000 people, of which about 85 per cent live at subsistence level. Cumulative sedimentation is leading to the infilling of the Segara Anakan estuary and has raised questions about the estuary's future state and management (Nelson et al., 1992). Rapid reported rates of sedimentation are highlighted by shoreline accretion from 1900 to 1984 (Figure 9.3). Sedimentation is considered a major driving force of land cover and land-use change in the area.

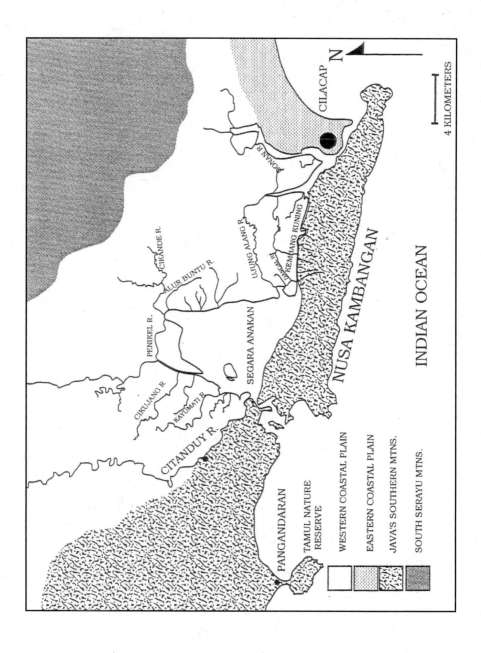

Figure 9.2   Physiographic Regions of the Segara Anakan Region

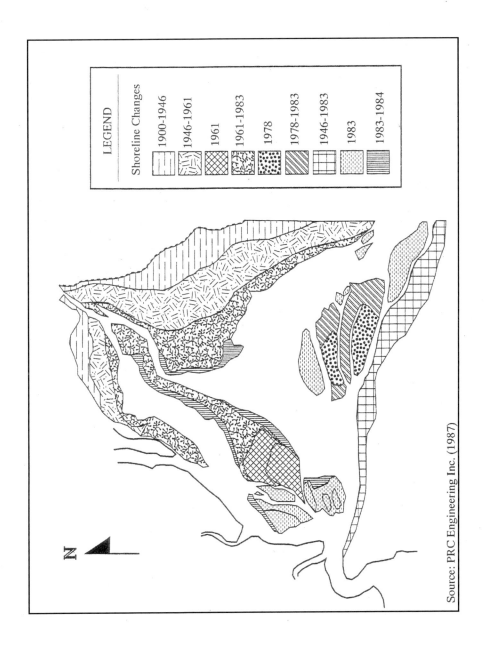

Figure 9.3   Shoreline Accretion in the Segara Anakan: 1900–1984

STUDY SUMMARY

Satellite image analysis led to the identification of a set of land cover patterns that combined Abiotic, Biotic, and Cultural information in a manner quite unlike previous ABC studies, which focused on a set of thematic maps. The satellite image analysis produced the combined landscape mapping normally described in Level III of the ABC method. Information on land-use activities was collected during follow-up field studies conducted to identify the actual bedrock, landform, forest, natural vegetation, crop patterns, settlements, and other Cultural features shown in the patterns on the satellite imagery. This field work and other supplementary research is described in the following summary of the overall results of the study. The focus in the summary is on land-cover and land-use change and its implications for conservation and sustainable development. The cover of the Segara Anakan area consists of beaches, tidal mudflats, estuaries, mangroves, rice fields *(sawah)*, settlements, and newly formed lands. Extensive areas of rainforest are located on bordering Nusa Kambangan, although limited access to the island prohibited field mapping.

Mangrove deforestation and newly formed lands are two major forms of land-cover change. Rates of deforestation and new land formation were estimated from the basis of satellite image analysis and field checks. Between 1978 and 1987, approximately 3,131 ha were deforested of a total of about 14,000 ha of mangrove (1987). *Sawah* cultivation (rice/paddy field) and other agricultural activities were major encroachments into the mangroves, which are highly valued for fish, bird, and other wildlife habitat. From 1987 to 1991 additional mangrove lands had been cut, but the quantity and extent were uncertain. The mangrove forest also is cut by local residents who require wood for fuel and construction material. Figure 9.4 is an estimate of the condition of the mangrove in 1988. Since then, much of the relatively undisturbed mangrove may have been cut to some degree, so that the protection and sustainable use of the mangrove is clearly a high priority planning concern.

From 1978 to 1987, approximately 1,834 ha of the Segara Anakan estuary are estimated to have been converted to new lands. These new

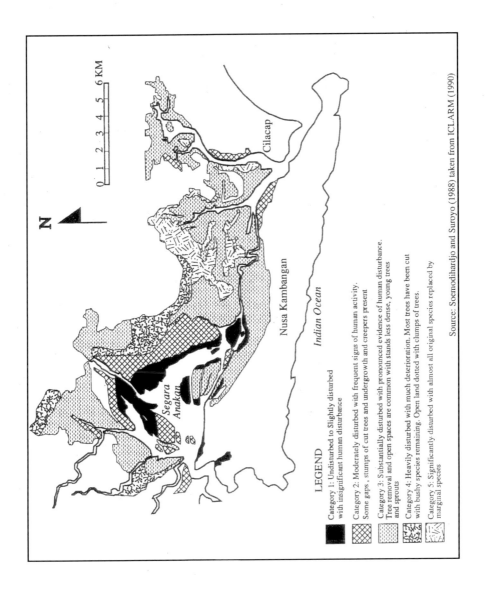

Figure 9.4   Condition of the Segara Anakan Mangrove Forest, 1988

lands are likely forming because of rapid siltation due to agricultural clearing and erosion in upland areas. The history of sedimentation is not completely understood; however, volcanic uplift and easily erodible volcanic soils may be important influences over the long term. The newly formed lands in the estuary are generally fertile and quickly colonized by mangrove trees. Some uncertainty exists as to which lands on the satellite images are actually newly formed lands and which are mudflats uncovered at lower tidal levels. Some newly formed lands are a source of conflict among rice, forestry, and other interests and therefore constitute an important issue in planning for sustainable development.

Significance and Constraints

Figure 9.5 is a combined Abiotic, Biotic, and Cultural significance map of the Segara Anakan area. The map represents work at Level 2 in the ABC method and shows estimates of the significance of different parts of the Segara Anakan area based on the criteria of biodiversity, essential ecological processes such as nesting and spawning, and productivity for fish and other species. The estimates of significance are also based upon judgments about the current and long-term importance of parts of the area for socio–economic purposes, for example fishing by the village people of the estuary. The estuary and its adjoining waters and the mangrove forest of the Segara Anakan area are highly significant in these terms.

Some of the stresses or constraints upon sustainable development of the Segara Anakan indicate areas of tension or conflict over mangrove, newly formed lands, and other resources (Figure 9.6). Due to cloud cover on available satellite imagery and lack of access to air photos and Nusa Kambangan, it has not been possible to map, analyze, and interpret the island rain forests, which is unfortunate because of the rarity of such forests on Java. Of the extensive rainforests remaining on Nusa Kambangan, it is not clear how much is primary forest and how much is secondary and successional to earlier clearing and rubber or other plantation activities by the Dutch. It is also uncertain how much has been cleared by prison work programs, by recent encroachment for rice agriculture, by military manoeuvres and other uses. The potential

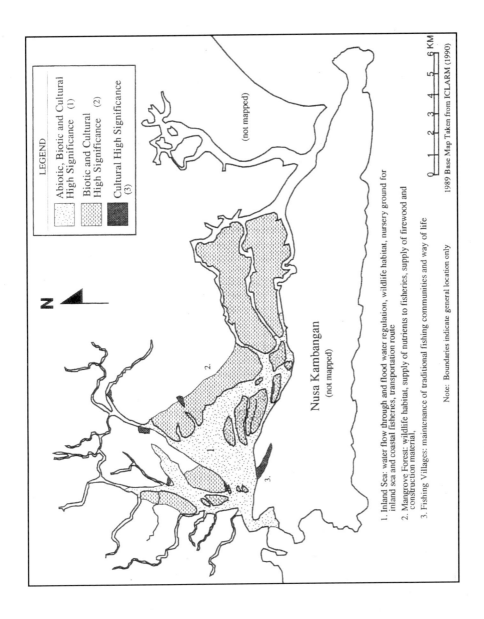

LEGEND

Abiotic, Biotic and Cultural High Significance (1)

Biotic and Cultural High Significance (2)

Cultural High Significance (3)

N

Nusa Kambangan
(not mapped)

(not mapped)

1. Inland Sea: water flow through and flood water regulation, wildlife habitat, nursery ground for inland sea and coastal fisheries, transportation route

2. Mangrove Forest: wildlife habitat, supply of nutrients to fisheries, supply of firewood and construction material,

3. Fishing Villages: maintenance of traditional fishing communities and way of life

Note: Boundaries indicate general location only

0 1 2 3 4 5 6 KM

1989 Base Map Taken from ICLARM (1990)

Figure 9.5   Abiotic, Biotic and Cultural Significance of the Segara Anakan

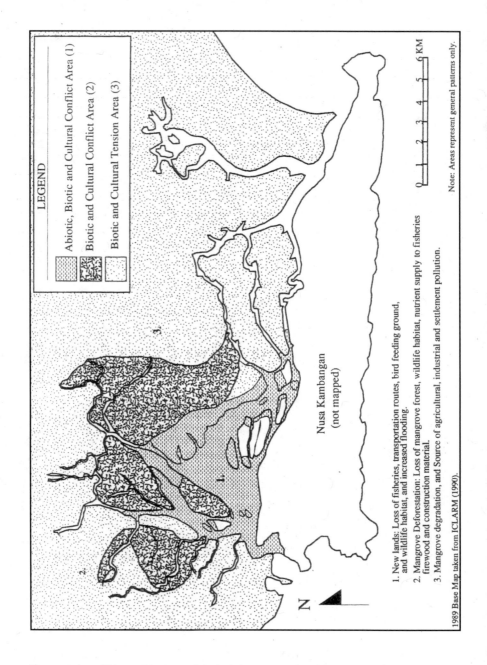

LEGEND

Abiotic, Biotic and Cultural Conflict Area (1)

Biotic and Cultural Conflict Area (2)

Biotic and Cultural Tension Area (3)

Nusa Kambangan
(not mapped)

0 1 2 3 4 5 6 KM

Note: Areas represent general patterns only.

N

1. New lands: Loss of fisheries, transportation routes, bird feeding ground, and wildlife habitat, and increased flooding.

2. Mangrove Deforestation: Loss of mangrove forest, wildlife habitat, nutrient supply to fisheries firewood and construction material.

3. Mangrove degradation, and Source of agricultural, industrial and settlement pollution.

1989 Base Map taken from ICLARM (1990).

Figure 9.6   Abiotic, Biotic, and Cultural Constraints of the Segara Anakan

of the island for conservation of rare rainforest species and communities, and for biodiversity, is high as is the potential for ecotourism and other potentially significant economic activities. It is very important that every effort be made to secure information on the state of the forests before the most valuable parts are cut over and lost. The forests are especially important in the context of the agreement on a Global Convention on Biodiversity at the Earth Summit in Rio de Janeiro in 1992.

A major constraint upon sustainable development in the Segara Anakan area is the fragmented institutional arrangements that apply to the area. Figure 9.7 outlines the various management arrangements and some of the tensions and conflicts associated with them. Nusa Kambangan is publicly owned, with the northern shore being a source of conflict among the Justice Department, which is responsible for the prisons, Perhutani or the State Forestry Corporation with its interest in social forestry, and local people who wish to settle and grow rice. An area on the east side of the Segara Anakan area is subject to some conflict between local residents interested in agriculture and fishing and Perhutani with its interest in social forestry. A large area on the north and northeast sides of the Segara Anakan is subject to some conflict between the district (BAPPEDA), which supports rice agriculture and settlement, and Perhutani with its forestry interests. Some attempts have been made to resolve tensions and conflicts through co-ordinated planning but they do not yet appear to be succeeding in terms of preventing damage to mangroves, maintenance of wildlife habitat, conservation of productivity for fish and other species, and sustainability of the way of life of the fishing villages.

CONCLUSIONS

The use of remotely sensed data, field observations, and the ABC Resource Survey provides an effective method for identifying and measuring land-cover changes and understanding some of the underlying processes affecting environments and sustainable development in the Segara Anakan area, Java. Satellite data are particularly beneficial in

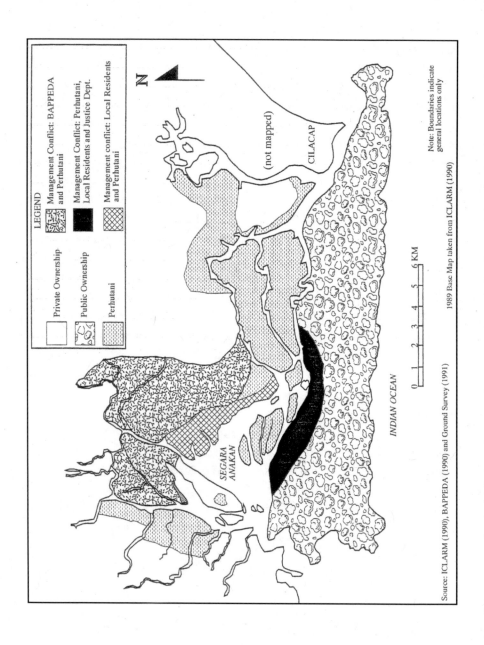

Figure 9.7   Institutional Map of the Segara Anakan

PLACES

several aspects. First, the imagery provides for a rapid reconnaissance of the entire study area. General patterns and distributions of land cover are distinguishable and extent can be estimated for each land-cover type. Second, analysis of multitemporal satellite data identifies areas of possible land-cover changes, which can be checked by field observations.

Land-cover change information is useful in identifying some of the important management issues occurring in the study area, such as mangrove deforestation and sedimentation of the inland sea. Limitations of satellite data for resource surveys include: 1) mapping detail is limited to the spatial resolution of the satellite data; 2) all land-cover types may not be digitally separable for classification and mapping purposes; 3) cloud cover obscures areas for interpretation; and 4) satellite imagery can only provide information on the visible landscape, and thus must be supplemented by information on land use and human activities to provide for comprehensive understanding.

The ABC Resource Survey provides an effective framework for collecting and integrating satellite and other data in order to analyze and evaluate land-cover changes and associated land uses. The ABC approach can accommodate the extensive variety of information types needed to plan and manage for sustainable development. If the information is not available from remote sensing, ground survey, or secondary sources, however, it requires a substantial amount of time to collect by numerous experts. The main limitation of this research occurs from the information gaps, for example cloud cover on satellite imagery and lack of access to aerial photography for the island of Nusa Kambangan. Additional research is essential for the understanding of changes in the rainforest of Nusa Kambangan. Overall, the general constraints to sustainable development in the Segara Anakan area are mangrove deforestation and sedimentation and newly formed lands, which are having a negative effect on the fisheries, wildlife habitat, and other aspects of the natural and human environment. A major constraint in regard to more effective planning for sustainable development is lack of agreement among local people and local and senior government agencies about conservation and future use of the mangroves, rainforests, and other resources significant for sustainable development.

This work demonstrates that satellite image analysis can be valuable in producing information for use in planning and managing for sustainable development. The utility of the satellite images is enhanced by analyzing them in the context of a comprehensive resource and environmental survey system such as the ABC method. This provides for the collection, organization, analysis, synthesis, and interpretation of a wide range of geologic, biological, land-use, and other information needed for thinking about sustainable development. Undertaking more detailed socio-economic resource and environmental surveys and assessments at the local level in parallel with regional survey also yields information of value in planning for sustainable development at the village or site level. Regional survey and more detailed associated local studies can be applied efficiently and effectively along many parts of the Indonesian coast, an area of great economic, social, and environmental significance, which is now increasingly under stress from tourism and other activities.

NOTES

1   Adapted from J.G. Nelson, E. LeDrew, C. Olive, and Dulbahri, "Information for Sustainable Development: Coastal Studies in Java and Bali." In *Bali: Balancing Environment, Economy and Culture*, ed. S. Martopo and B. Mitchell, 297–322. Department of Geography Publication Series, University of Waterloo, Waterloo, Ontario, 1995.

REFERENCES

Bastedo, J., J.G. Nelson, and J.B. Theberge. 1984. "An ecological approach to resource survey and planning for environmentally significant areas: The ABC method," *Environmental Management* 8(2): 125–130.

Harris, J., and J.G. Nelson. 1992. *Monitoring Tourism from a Whole Economy Perspective*. University Consortium on the Environment (UCE) Publication Series, Reprint No. 4. Waterloo: University of Waterloo.

Nelson, J.G., and J. Harris, eds. 1993. *Tourism and Its Effects on the Settlement of Pangandaran, Java, Heritage in an Urban Context*. Occasional Paper 23. Waterloo: Heritage Resources Centre, University of Waterloo.

Nelson, J.G., P. Grigoriew, P.G.K. Smith, and J.B. Theberge. 1988. "The ABC resource survey method: The ESA concept and comprehensive land use planning and management." In *Landscape Ecology and Management*, ed. M. Moss, 142–161. Montreal: Polyscience Publications.

Nelson, J.G., E. LeDrew, Dulbahri, J. Harris, and C. Oliver. 1992. *Land Use Change and Sustainable Development in the Segara Anakan Area of Java, Indonesia: Relevant Information from Remote Sensing, On-ground Survey and the ABC Method*. Technical Paper 7. A joint publication of the Earth-Observations Laboratory of the Institute of Space and Terrestrial Science and Waterloo: Heritage Resources Centre, University of Waterloo.

Nelson, J.G., R.W. Butler, and G. Wall, eds. 1993. *Tourism and Sustainable Development: Monitoring, Planning and Managing*. Department of Geography, Geography Publication Series No. 37. Waterloo: University of Waterloo.

Olive, C. 1992. *The Application of Remote Sensing, Ground Survey and the ABC Resource Survey to Assess Land Cover Change and Its Effects on Sustainable Development in the Segara Anakan Area, Java*. Master's thesis, Department of Geography, Faculty of Environmental Studies, University of Waterloo, Waterloo.

Sujastani, T. 1986. *Environmental Profile of Segara Anakan-Cilacap Coastal Region* (Final Report of Consultant Prepared for the Indonesian ASEAN-US Aid Coastal Resources Management Project, Jakarta).

World Commission on Environment and Development. 1987. *Our Common Future*. New York: Oxford University Press.

IO

1994

A HUMAN ECOLOGICAL APPROACH TO COASTAL MANAGEMENT IN THE GREAT LAKES[1]

J.G. Nelson and P.L. Lawrence

INTRODUCTION

Coastal zone planning and management in Canada and other countries are plagued by difficulties and slow progress on a number of fronts (CCREM, 1978; Dorcey, 1983; Harrison and Parkes, 1983; Hildebrand, 1989). The very idea itself is subject to questions. What do we mean when we speak of the coast and the shore or shoreline, especially in terms of outlining scope and associated government and private responsibilities for planning and management? Many coastal activities continue to be dealt with ineffectively in terms of their economic, social, and environmental impacts (Davidson-Arnott and Kreutzwiser, 1985; Day and Gamble, 1990). Examples include conflicts among competing land uses, loss of wetlands and other environmentally significant areas, pollution and decreasing water quality, and continuing flooding, erosion, and other hazards (Day et al., 1977; Jessen et al., 1983).

Many reasons have been given for slow progress on coastal problems. A notable one is lack of understanding of the dynamic and interested processes at work in coastal areas. Others include fragmentation of planning and management among many federal, provincial (state), and local agencies, lack of awareness of the importance of the coast economically, socially, and environmentally, and failure to learn from historic experiences (Sorenson et al., 1984; Hildebrand, 1989;

RCFTW, 1992). Of particular concern in regard to coastal management is the tendency to repeat maladjustments of the past, particularly in regard to flooding and erosion hazards (Needham and Nelson, 1978; Kreutzwiser, 1987; Clark, 1983). Without careful analysis and assessment, residential or other new developments push human occupancy into wetlands, dunes, and flood and other high risk areas and bring economic, social, and environmental losses in their wake (Nelson et al., 1975; Kreutzwiser, 1988; Dilley and Rasid, 1990).

In this chapter we wish to highlight briefly studies that a group, mainly geographers, at the University of Waterloo has undertaken to deal with shore or coastal zone problems more effectively in the Great Lakes basin (Figure 10.1). The studies are based on what we call a human ecological approach. By this we mean an approach that is comprehensive, dynamic, interactive, and adaptive (Nelson, 1991a). By 'comprehensive' we mean inclusive, at least conceptually, of all activities, features, and processes. Ideally, the approach recognizes geologic and hydrologic (Abiotic), plant and animal (Biotic) economic, technical, social, and cultural processes and groups involved in the complex coastal zone, laying the bases for improved overall understanding and planning. By 'dynamic' we mean keyed to understanding changes in processes and patterns through time. It is important to know the history of change. By 'interactive and adaptive' we mean communicating and learning from as many sources as possible, including science as well as local knowledge.

Our aim is to help prepare people of differing backgrounds to deal with coastal issues by collecting and analyzing information with and for them. It is our belief that planning and management will be made more effective if as many affected parties as possible learn about and deal with the situation together, on the basis of as comprehensive an information base as possible. This statement presents something of an ideal. It is of course not always attainable because of time or money constraints, political circumstances, or other factors. Given these limitations, it is important in our view to be as open and co-operative as possible throughout each study or project in order that as much learning as possible is available to many interested groups and persons. We are

Figure 10.1   Great Lakes Study Sites

actively working on this human ecological and civics approach in the Great Lakes area and can offer highlights of some recent coastal projects to illustrate the nature of the work and its implications to date. All of these projects were conducted using the ABC method (Bastedo et al., 1984; Nelson et al., 1988; Nelson, 1991b). All projects involved wide-ranging application of the ABC method, although only certain aspects of the work are reported on here.

FRENCHMAN'S BAY, LAKE ONTARIO

The first example is a study of a relatively small area, Frenchman's Bay, on the eastern edge of Toronto's urban region. In this case we were asked by the Toronto Waterfront Commission's office for an assessment of the effects of proposed condominium and related developments on the bay. We were asked also to provide views on the long-term capacity of the bay to accommodate such development. The project involved a report to the Commission's office based upon available reports and literature. The project did not provide support or direction for public meetings nor for other citizen involvement during the research, although it was understood that the results of our study would be published and so be widely available for public scrutiny. This project began on April 1, 1991, and was completed rapidly by a team consisting of four graduate students and a university professor by June 10, 1991 (Nelson et al., 1991).

The Frenchman's Bay case illustrates that a comprehensive array of information can be collected and analyzed quickly in terms of significance and constraints bearing on a public issue. The ABC analysis and assessment found that development or urbanization in the area had contributed to stresses on shoreline erosion and geomorphic processes (Figure 10.2). Development during the past forty years had also led to loss or decline of many valued opportunities, such as the natural, recreational, and economic ones associated with the wetlands that have become more and more fragmented over time (Figures 10.3 and 10.4). Historical or cultural values, like those associated with the old port and fishing history of the bay, were considered likely to be impacted by the proposed new residential and marina projects, along with the bay's wetlands and other natural habitats.

With this in mind, the assessment recommended a development moratorium for one year and called for further studies to consolidate and review information on natural and cultural values of the bay in a more comprehensive, interactive co-ordinated manner. Following the completion of the study, it was immediately used in discussion among provincial and municipal governments and other stakeholders, leading to public purchase of key bay wetlands.

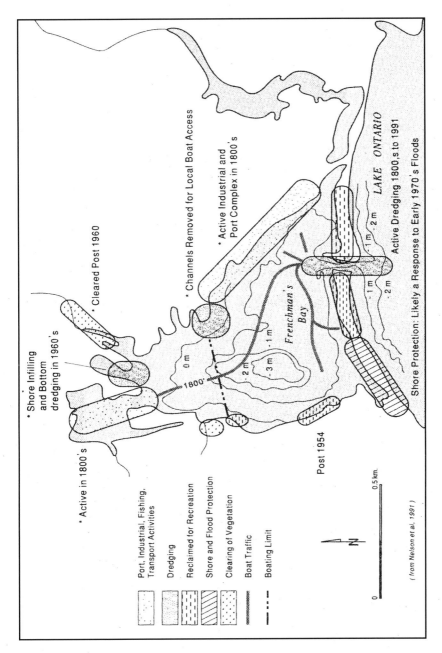

Figure 10.2   Human Features and Impacts on Abiotic Domain, Frenchman's Bay

The following labels appear on the map:

* Shore Infilling and Bottom dredging in 1960's
* Cleared Post 1960
* Channels Removed for Local Boat Access
* Active Industrial and Port Complex in 1800's
* Active in 1800's
LAKE ONTARIO
Active Dredging 1800,s to 1991
Shore Protection: Likely a Response to Early 1970's Floods
Frenchman's Bay
1800'
0 m
- 1 m
- 2 m
- 3 m
- 1 m
- 2 m
1 m - 2 m
Post 1954
0.5 km.
N
(from Nelson et al, 1991)

Legend:
Port, Industrial, Fishing, Transport Activities
Dredging
Reclaimed for Recreation
Shore and Flood Protection
Clearing of Vegetation
Boat Traffic
Boating Limit

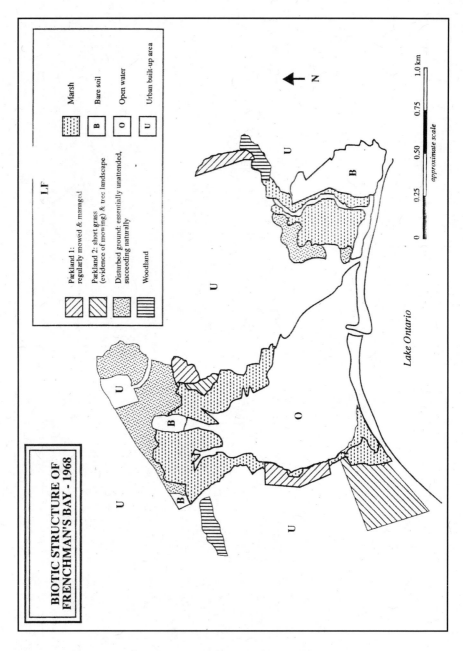

Figure 10.3   Vegetation and Marsh, Frenchman's Bay 1968

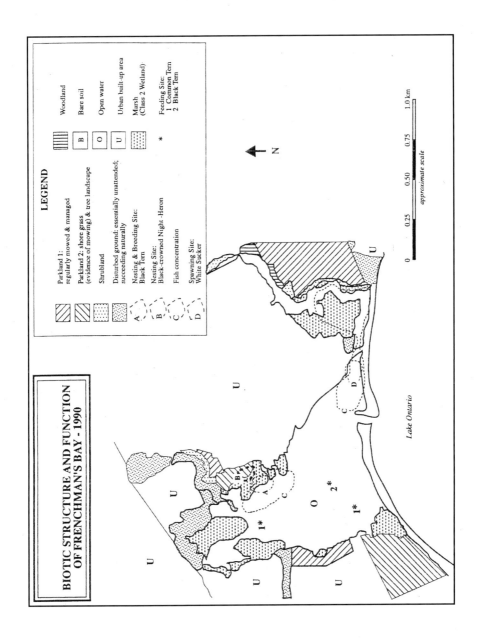

Figure 10.4   Vegetation and Marsh, Frenchman's Bay 1990

LAKE HURON COAST, SAUGEEN WATERSHED

The second project on the Saugeen coast of Lake Huron was conducted in partnership with the Saugeen Valley Conservation Authority (SVGA) from May 1991 to March 1992. In this case, the SVGA had requested assistance in the preparation of a shoreline management plan. From the outset, the study was conducted in an open and interactive manner involving concerned governments, agencies, and citizens. Early discussions with SVGA and various agencies and citizens groups resulted in a decision to develop background documents to assist in preparing for planning rather than a plan itself. Subsequently, a series of public meetings and numerous consultations were held with many government officials and the public. The resulting information was used to complete comprehensive background documents (Lawrence and Nelson, 1992). During the project, the schematic for the ABC method was modified in an attempt to help with citizen understanding (Figure 10.5).

Significant Abiotic features and processes were mapped such as sediment transport patterns, beach/dune complexes, and stream flow (Figure 10.6). Significant Biotic areas were mapped on the basis of criteria such as uniqueness, rarity, diversity, functions, and aesthetics. Landscape and land-use change research revealed that four main land-use changes occurred in the study area from 1954 to 1990: forest fragmentation, rural residential (cottage) extension, rural industrial development, and urban growth (Figure 10.7).

The research team identified several areas of tension where significant conflicts among conservation and development interests were either already evident or likely to develop in the future (Figure 10.8). These areas needed special attention in any future coastal planning exercise. Issues were also identified that initially had not been anticipated as major ones by the research team, the SVGA, or local people. A notable example is the extent to which coastal forests and woodlands are being fragmented by various developments.

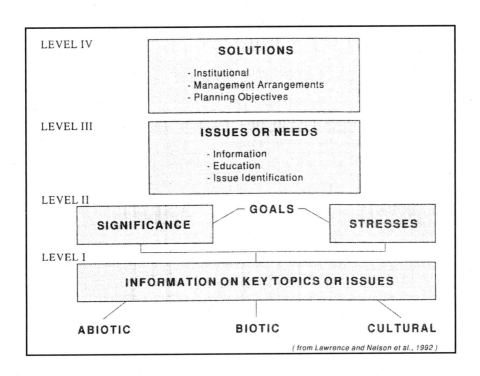

Figure 10.5   Modified ABC Resource Survey Method

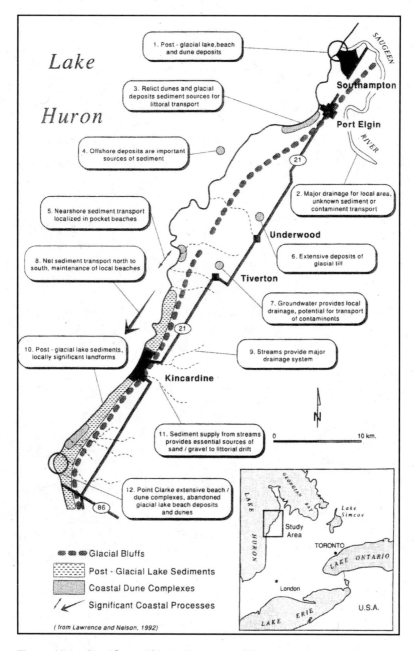

Figure 10.6   Significant Abiotic Features and Processes

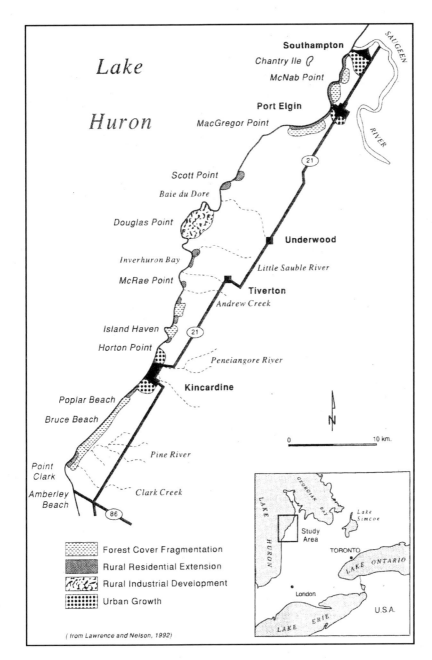

Figure 10.7   Significant Land Use Changes: 1953–1990

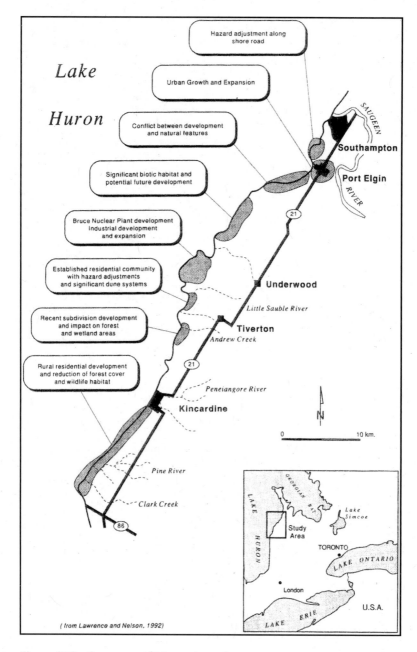

Figure 10.8   Summary of Management Issues

PLACES

LONG POINT, LAKE ERIE

The third project was for the Long Point area, Lake Erie. The Canada/ Man and the Biosphere (MAB) Program approved the nomination of Long Point as a World Biosphere Reserve in June 1985. In 1986, the reserve was officially designated by the UNESCO MAB Program (Francis, 1985). The reserve consists of a core protected area (Long Point National Wildlife Area), buffer area (defined by the 10-metre depth contour offshore and the regulatory 1:100 year flood line onshore), and an undefined "zone of co-operation" (Canada/MAB, 1990).

The shoreline is postglacial and is characterized by 30- to 40-metre-high eroding clay bluffs to the west, a central 40-kilometre-long sandy spit with associated dune and wetland systems, and low-lying beaches, wetlands, and bluffs to the east (Figure 10.9). The dune and wetland systems have a rich mix of habitats consisting of shallow bays, sand bars, dunes, forests, ponds, and marshes (Canada/MAB, 1990).

The Long Point complex is a major staging area for migrating waterfowl and small migratory birds. The complex also has a long history of human use, notably for fishing, waterfowl hunting, cottaging, and other recreational and tourism purposes (Francis, 1985). The Point is also well known for economically damaging flood and erosion hazards. The decline of tobacco farming, historically an economic mainstay, has led to the development of other economic opportunities, including numerous marinas, recreational facilities, and activities (Nelson et al., 1993). Their effects on wetlands and other resources of Long Point and the Inner Bay are not well understood.

The aim of the Long Point project was to produce an environmental folio as a means of synthesizing and graphically displaying natural and human information to assist agencies and local citizens in understanding planning and management (Nelson et al., 1993). The preparation of the folio had approval and support of the local Long Point Biosphere Reserve Committee, which consists of government officials and people living in the area. The Committee wanted to have available information on the area put in a form where it is more widely intelligible and useful than is currently the case with scientific and scholarly articles and bibliographies. Maps and text were prepared on a

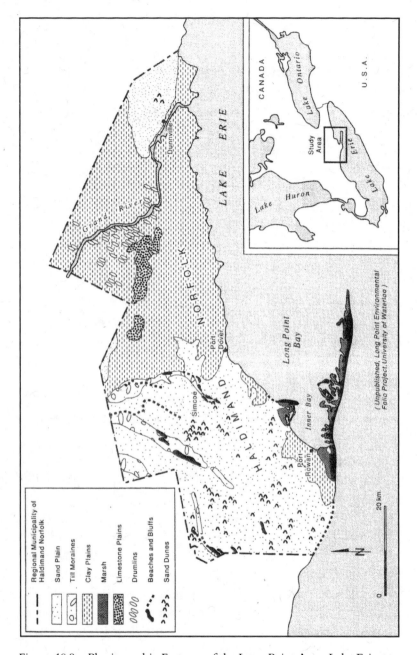

Figure 10.9   Physiographic Features of the Long Point Area, Lake Erie

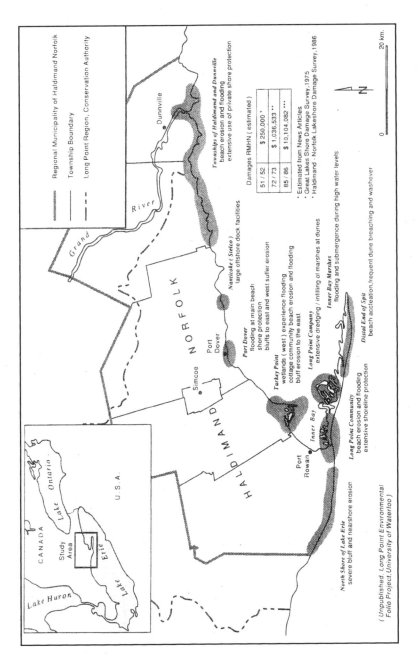

Figure 10.10 Shoreline Flooding and Erosion

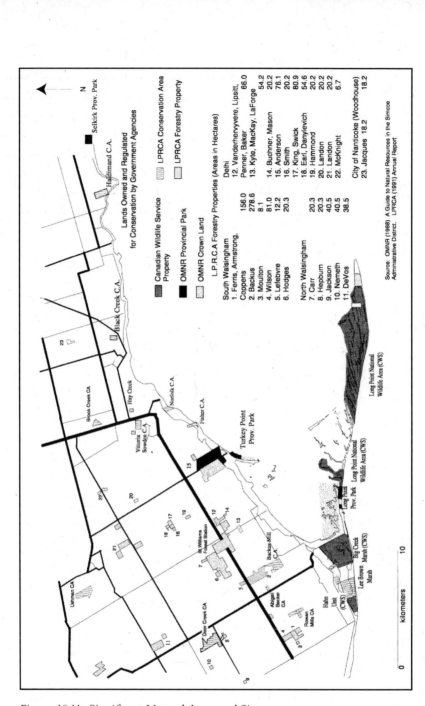

Figure 10.11 Significant Natural Areas and Sites

wide range of Abiotic, Biotic, and Cultural topics, including geology, landform, vegetation and wildlife, archaeology, Caucasian settlement, economic history, and institutions. Illustrative maps are shown here for two topics or issues of high relevance to the Biosphere Committee and many citizens: shoreline flooding and erosion (Figure 10.10) and significant natural areas and sites (Figure 10.11). After its publication, the folio was placed on a website by local people for use in schools and civic affairs.

DISCUSSION

These summaries of three comprehensive case studies demonstrate use of the ABC approach in assessments aimed at better professional and civic understanding of topics and issues of concern along the Great Lakes coast. The studies also set the stage for more broadly informed and participatory decision-making. Issues such as forest fragmentation, habitat loss, disruption of natural processes, flood and erosion hazards, and land-use conflicts are identified and assessed in at least a general way, laying the basis for improved communication and action by governments, non-government organizations, and citizens. Understanding and knowledge are a vital part of long-term, proactive planning of the coast.

NOTES

1   Adapted from J.G. Nelson and P.L. Lawrence, "Preparing for Coastal Management: A Human Ecological Approach" In *Public Issues: A Geographic Perspective*, ed. J. Andrey and J.G. Nelson, 311–335. Department of Geography Publication Series Number 41, University of Waterloo, Waterloo, Ontario, 1994.

REFERENCES

Bastedo, J., J.G. Nelson, and J. Theberge. 1984. "Ecological approach to resource survey and planning for environmentally significant areas: The ABC method." *Environmental Management* 8(2): 125–134.

Beazley, K.F. 1993. *Forested Regions of Long Point: Landscape History and Strategic Planning*. MA thesis, Department of Geography, University of Waterloo, Waterloo.

Canadian Council of Resource and Environmental Ministers (CCREM). 1978. *Proceedings of the Shore Management Symposium*. Victoria: British Columbia Ministry of Environment.

Canadian Man and the Biosphere (MAB) Committee. 1990. *Biosphere Reserves in Canada*. Ottawa: Canadian/MAB Secretariat.

Clark, J.E. 1983. *Coastal Ecosystem Management*. New York: John Wiley & Sons.

Davidson-Arnott, R.G.D., and R.D. Kreutzwiser. 1985. "Coastal processes and shoreline encroachment: Implications for shoreline management in Ontario." *Canadian Geographer* 29(3): 256–262.

Day, J.C., and D.B. Gamble. 1990. "Coastal zone management in British Columbia: An institutional comparison with Washington, Oregon, and California." *Coastal Management* 18: 115–141.

Day, J.C., J.A. Fraser, and R.D. Kreutzwiser. 1977. "Assessment of flood and erosion assistance programs: Rondeau coastal experience, Lake Erie." *Journal of Great Lakes Research* 3(1–2): 38–45.

Dilley, R.S., and H. Rasid. 1990. "Human response to coastal erosion: Thunder Bay, Lake Superior." *Journal of Coastal Research* 6(4): 779–788.

Dorcey, A.H.J. 1983. "Coastal management as a bargaining process." *Coastal Zone Management Journal* 11(1–2): 13–40.

Francis, G.F. 1985. *Long Point Biosphere Reserve Nomination*. Submitted to the Man and the Biosphere Program, Ottawa.

Harrison, P., and J.G.M. Parkes. 1983. "Coastal management in Canada." *Coastal Zone Management Journal* 11(1–2): 1–11.

Hildebrand, L.P. 1989. *Canada's Experience with Coastal Zone Management*. Halifax: Oceans Institute of Canada.

Jessen, S., J.C. Day, and J.G. Nelson. 1983. "Assessing land use regulations in coastal wetlands: The case of Long Point area, Lake Erie, Ontario." *Coastal Zone Management Journal* 11(1–2): 91–115.

Kreutzwiser, R.D. 1987. "Managing the Great Lakes shoreline hazard." *Journal of Soil and Water Conservation* 42(3): 150–154.

Kreutzwiser, R.D. 1988. "Municipal land use regulation and the Great Lakes shoreline hazard in Ontario." *Journal of Great Lakes Research* 14(2): 142–147.

Lawrence, P.L., and J.G. Nelson. 1992. *Preparing for a Shoreline Management Plan for the Saugeen Valley Conservation Authority*. A joint study of Waterloo: Heritage Resources Centre, University of Waterloo, and Hanover, ON: Saugeen Valley Conservation Authority.

Needham, R.D., and J.G. Nelson. 1978. "Adjustment to change in coastal environments: The case of fluctuating Lake Erie water levels." In *Coping with the Coast, Proceedings of the Fourth Annual Conference of the Coastal Society* 196–213. Arlington, VA: The Coastal Society.

Nelson, J.G. 1991a. "Research in human ecology and planning: An inter-active, adaptive approach." *Canadian Geographer* 35(2): 114–127.

Nelson, J.G. 1991b. "A step towards more comprehensive and equitable information systems: The ABC resource survey method." In *Greenways and Green Space on the Oak Ridges Moraine*, Occasional Paper 14, 27–34. Department of Geography, Peterborough, ON: Trent University.

Nelson, J.D., R.A. Battin, and R.D. Kreutzwiser. 1975. "The fall 1972 Lake Erie floods and their significance to resources management." *Canadian Geographer* 20(1): 35–58.

Nelson, J.G., P. Grigoriew, P.G.R. Smith, and J. Theberge. 1988. "The ABC resource survey method: The ESA concept and comprehensive land use planning and management." In *Landscape Ecology and Management, Proceedings of the First Symposium of the Canadian Society for Landscape Ecology and Management*, ed. M.R. Moss, 143–175. Montreal: Polyscience Publications.

Nelson, J.G., A.J. Skibicki, R.E. Stenson, and C.L. Yeung. 1991. *Urbanization, Conservation and Development: The Case of Frenchman's Bay, Toronto, Ontario.* Technical Paper 5. Waterloo: Heritage Resources Centre, University of Waterloo.

Nelson, J.G., P.L. Lawrence, K. Beazley, R. Stenson, A. Skibicki, C.L. Yeung, and K. Pauls. 1993. *Preparing an Environmental Folio for the Long Point Biosphere Reserve and Region.* Long Point Environmental Folio Publication Series Working Note 1. Waterloo: Heritage Resources Centre, University of Waterloo.

Royal Commission on the Future of the Toronto Waterfront (RCFTW). 1992. *Regeneration – Final Report.* Toronto: Government Printer of Ontario.

Sorenson, J.C., S.T. McCreary, and M.J. Hershman. 1984. *Institutional Arrangements for Management of Coastal Resources.* Coastal Publication No. 1. Columbia, SC: Research Planning Institute.

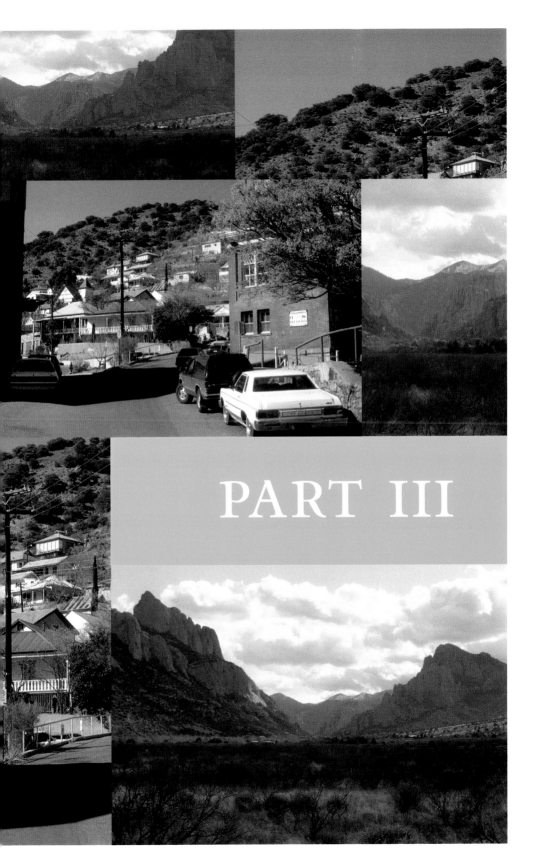

PART III

PART III:
COMPREHENSIVE OVERVIEWS
AND ASSESSMENTS

INTRODUCTION

Part III consists of four chapters that involve less detailed and systematic applications of the ABC method than those in Part I. The ABC method is used as a framework for organizing and assessing a wide range of information in an interrelated way to facilitate integrated understanding and planning of various regions or places. Fewer maps are prepared and these less systematically than in the more detailed applications in Part I. Often the maps are taken from what is available in existing publications and reports and fitted into the method rather than being prepared especially for it.

Chapter 11 on the history of planning for the Bruce National Park area is included to show how the ABC can provide an implicit or embedded framework for collecting, analyzing, assessing, and integrating the changing natural and cultural history and landscape of a place. This chapter was completed in 2006 about twenty years after a 1980s ABC analysis and assessment of the proposed national park (Chapter 5, this volume). Chapter 11 uses the ABC as an underlying framework for describing the history of planning for the park and surrounding area, or greater park ecosystem since that time. The chapter also outlines the current status of planning and the challenges facing the park and its fit with the surrounding area. In reviewing this chapter and comparing it to Chapter 5, it is apparent that key decisions have been made about boundaries for areas such as the First Nations hunting reserve. It is also apparent that many of the challenges foreseen in the 1980s remain, for example tension over the southern boundary from Highway 6 up to Cabot Head. The core area identified in the 1980s as requiring a high level of protection through zoning or other means has not achieved such status.

Chapter 12, on the arid San Pedro river valley in Arizona, describes curiosity-driven research conducted during five visits, each of one to two weeks duration, during the 1990s. Information was collected from published and unpublished documents and from field observations and informal interviews with various government officials and citizens. The ABC method was used to organize and assess this information and paint a general picture of the fascinating natural and human history and multifaceted landscape of the valley. The use of the method also facilitated identification of significance and constraints for conservation and sustainable use as well as for planning needs.

Chapter 13 is a 1990s study of land-use history, landscape change, and planning for the lake country in the interior of south central Ontario. This study of Fairy and Peninsula Lakes region was prepared at the request of the provincial Ministry of Natural Resources as part of a more comprehensive interdisciplinary assessment of environmental and land-use conditions in this area. The Fairy Lake–Peninsula Lakes study and the larger study of which it was part were both envisioned as analytic studies that would integrate diverse natural and cultural information for assessment and planning purposes. More detailed planning, management, and decision-making findings and recommendations were expected to follow from this research. The Fairy and Peninsula Lakes study used the ABC as a framework for analyzing geologic, hydrologic, biotic, land-use, economic, and other changes through time as a basis for understanding and dealing with present and future challenges.

Chapter 14, on ecoregional planning in the Carpathian Mountains in central Europe, arises from a request to complete an evaluation or assessment of an ecoregional planning approach led by the World Wildlife Fund in co-operation with government agencies and private groups in seven countries: Austria, Czech Republic, Slovakia, Poland, Hungary, Ukraine, and Romania. The task was to assess, in approximately six months in 2002–2003, how well the complex Carpathian Ecological Initiative (CEI) had done in the first phase of its work. The use of the ABC method greatly facilitated this study, which focused on existing information mainly from the CEI and interviews with partici-pants. The results were to be used in planning the second stage of the project. This chapter is of special interest because the ABC method was linked with planning theory to analyze the approach used by the CEI and to make comprehensive recommendations on future planning.

II

2005

TWENTY YEARS OF EFFORTS TOWARDS ECOSYSTEM PLANNING IN THE BRUCE PENINSULA NATIONAL PARK, ONTARIO, CANADA: 1987 TO 2006[1]

P.L. Lawrence and J.G. Nelson

INTRODUCTION

After amendments to the National Parks Act in 1988, national parks in Canada were mandated to ensure the maintenance of ecological integrity by reducing the undesirable effects of human activities in the region around national parks as well as within the parks themselves. The Panel on Ecological Integrity of National Parks (2000) proposed that "An ecosystem has integrity when it is deemed characteristic for its natural region, including the composition and abundance of native species and biological communities, rates of change and supporting processes."

National Parks are to complete Ecosystem Conservation Plans (ECPs) to identify problems, issues, and concerns that need to be addressed in order to maintain ecological integrity. Ecosystem Conservation Plans (ECPs) are intended to conserve plants, animals, and other essential elements and processes in the surrounding ecosystem. The system of which a national park is part does not stop at the park boundary. It is, therefore, necessary to prepare a plan that considers not only the national park but the surrounding lands and waters or Greater Park Ecosystem (GPE). In this context, according to Parks Canada,

ECPs are to provide a "reasoned course of action" for a national park's ecosystem management program (Zorn et al., 1997). The national park and its neighbours must deal together with a number of transboundary concerns such as wildlife movements, waterflow and drainage, hiking and recreational uses, and the effects of land and resource uses inside and outside of the park boundaries.

Parks Canada defines an Ecosystem Conservation Plan (ECP) as a dynamic document that provides specific goals for maintenance of a national park's ecological integrity and management of its ecosystem (Parks Canada, 1992). The goals of the ECP are based on the Park Management Plan or Interim Management Guidelines, which historically stressed planning for the park lands and not surrounding lands and waters. The ECP is to present a documented, integrated, and priorized program for the management of a national park's natural resources and the natural evolution of surrounding park ecosystems (Parks Canada, 1992). Several ECPs have been completed for national parks in southern Ontario, including St. Lawrence Islands National Park, Georgian Bay Islands National Park, and Point Pelee National Park. Nelson et al. (2000) provides an overview and assessment of the development of ecosystem conservations plans by Parks Canada.

The aim of this chapter is to review and assess various efforts to develop ecosystem-based planning for the Bruce Peninsula National Park, Ontario, Canada (Figure 11.1). Since the establishment of this national park in 1987, several steps have been made towards a more comprehensive planning approach. The major planning activities to be examined in this chapter include: the park management plan (1988 interim draft and 1996 final approved version); efforts by a study team from the Heritage Resources Center at the University of Waterloo to prepare for an ecosystem conservation plan; the completion of an ECP by Parks Canada in 2001; and recent related implementation activities. A detailed discussion of the HRC study provides a context for describing the evolution of ecosystem planning in the national park during the twenty years from 1987 to 2006.

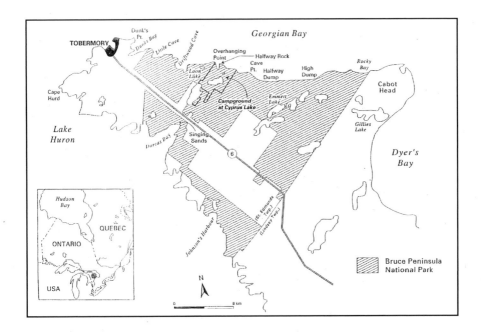

Figure 11.1   Bruce Peninsula National Park

BRUCE PENINSULA NATIONAL PARK

Discussion about the establishment of a national park in the northern Bruce Peninsula had been ongoing since the 1960s. However, it was not until the completion of a federal study in 1981 that serious consideration arose among governments and local citizens. Public consultation by Parks Canada during 1982 revealed concern about a number of issues, including land ownership and rights to conduct traditional land uses such as hunting, fishing, lumbering, and recreation within the proposed national park. A number of individuals and citizen groups voiced strong opposition to the establishment of a national park. Following local municipal elections and a public referendum, one of the two affected local municipalities, Lindsay Township, decided not to support the creation of a national park. As a result of these and other concerns, a federal-provincial agreement was developed leading to the establishment of Bruce Peninsula National Park in St. Edmunds Township in 1987 (Government of Canada/Government of Ontario, 1987).

Bruce Peninsula National Park (BPNP) was initially formed from the transfer of control of provincial land by the Ontario government to the Canadian government. After over two decades of studies and consultation, establishment was based on acknowledgment of the outstanding significance of the natural features and resources in the northern Bruce Peninsula area and the need to conserve and maintain these values for future generations. Proposed boundaries were agreed upon with the intent that the area within them would be acquired by Parks Canada and added to the national park in ensuing years. The national park contained private and provincial lands and economic and other activities at that time and still does to varying degrees today.

The Fathom Five National Marine Park (FFNMP) was also established from provincial land beginning in 1987 along with the Bruce Peninsula National Park (BPNP). Although these are separate parks, they adjoin one another and share many common park management and planning activities, related programs, and Parks Canada staff. For the purposes of this study, the focus will be on the Bruce Peninsula National Park, but the reader should also be aware that ecosystem conservation planning undertaken for BPNP often included FFNMP.

The federal/provincial agreement for BPNP involves provisions stipulated by the Township of St. Edmunds including the definition of strict boundaries for the national park (Government of Canada/Government of Ontario, 1987). The park area of BPNP (140 km) includes the former Cyprus Lake Provincial Park, provincial Crown Land holdings, and private lands within St. Edmunds Township. Several large sections of adjacent land were left out of the park area due to conditions in the federal-provincial agreement. These excluded lands include: a commercial development corridor along Highway # 6; a 4,000 ha area to be maintained as a deer hunting area by the Ontario Ministry of Natural Resources; and a 1,600 ha Native Hunting Reserve of the Chippewas of Nawash and Saugeen First Nations.

Approximately 22 per cent of the lands are still under private ownership (CPAWS Wildlands League, 2005). The remaining lands are either under direct ownership of the federal government or are managed by Parks Canada under agreement with the Province of Ontario, including existing Ontario Ministry of Natural Resources Crown Land holdings. Parks Canada has a land-acquisition program to buy the remaining private land within the park boundaries on a buyer-willing and seller-willing basis. However, the amount of funding available for purchase has been limited by budget reductions. For example, from 1992 to 1996, a total of $1.65 million was spent by Parks Canada to acquire thirty-one properties totalling 1,500 hectares within the area designated for BPNP. Land-acquisition efforts by Parks Canada to secure additional properties within the designated national park boundary are ongoing.

Park Management Plan (1987 to 1996)

Upon the establishment of the Bruce Peninsula National Park (BPNP), an interim park management plan was prepared. The 1996 approved park management plan was finally completed in 1996. The plan provides the general framework for managing the natural resources and human activities associated with the national park. The preparation of the plan included consultations with the local community, members of the park advisory committee, and the local First Nations. The plan is intended as a "strategic framework within which management decisions, more detailed planning, and subsequent implementation will take place" (Parks Canada, 1996: 1).

The purpose of the park management plan is to "provide long term guidance for the protection, operation, and public experience of the park" (Parks Canada, 1988: 1). The plan refers to the need to consider an ecosystem approach to the national park to complement other planning undertaken by various adjacent land management agencies and organizations. These include: the Federation of Ontario Naturalists; Ontario Ministry of Natural Resources; several local municipalities; and the First Nations. The provincial designation of the Niagara Escarpment, which passes through the national park, as a special planning area under the authority of the Niagara Escarpment Planning and Development Act, and as a World Biosphere Reserve by the UNESCO

Man and the Biosphere Program designated in 1990, underline the case for a co-ordinated approach to management within the national park and surrounding region. The national park is also part of the Niagara Escarpment Parks and Open Space System, a series of over a hundred parks and protected areas located along the escarpment from Niagara Falls to Tobermory. The route of the 780-kilometre-long Bruce Trail also runs through the national park.

According to the park management plan, the mission of the national park is "to protect the natural and cultural heritage within the Park and to work with allies outside the Park to conserve the Upper Bruce Peninsula Ecosystem" (Parks Canada, 1996: 8). This concept of the Upper Bruce Peninsula Ecosystem eventually was linked with consideration of the Greater Park Ecosystem in subsequent park conservation planning activities. The management plan provides a vision for the future of the park. This vision includes providing opportunities for research and monitoring, and co-operative management to protect natural and cultural resources and the environment.

One important management aim is to enhance the extent of unfragmented forest cover at a level no less than that of 1994. Thus the northeastern portion of the national park from Halfway Dump to Rocky Bay is to be managed to enhance forest cover and provide the highest quality wilderness experience for visitors in the national park (Parks Canada, 1998). Monitoring programs and visitor management are being developed to address potential impacts of public activities within the national park.

Of particular note in the park management plan is the issue of park zoning. In most national park management plans, spatial zoning in a common signal of Parks Canada's intentions for conservation and public use. However, in the case of the Bruce Peninsula National Park, the management plan does not include the standard park zoning system with its five zones for permitted activities. The decision not to complete a park zoning system was made because land acquisition within the park area was not complete and would not be for many years (Parks Canada, 1996). The park management plan does include the identification, classification, and mapping of "resource values" within the national park.

The resource values rank the significance of key natural features and processes, such as tree cover, rare species, wetlands, old-growth cedar forests, landforms, and escarpment features.

The main interest within the park management plan is protection against the human impacts of visitors on lands owned by Parks Canada and under its active management control. Although the park management plan provides general guidance for greater park ecosystem planning beyond the park boundary, it offers little specific guidance in this respect. These greater park ecosystem concerns are to be addressed in Ecosystem Conservation Plans.

Preparing for Ecosystem Conservation Planning (1996 to 1998)

As a result of 1988 changes to the National Parks Act, which focused on maintenance and enhancement of ecological integrity, the Heritage Resources Centre (HRC) at the University of Waterloo was initially contracted to prepare an Ecosystem Conservation Plan (ECP) for the Bruce Peninsula National Park (BPNP). The HRC study team completed a series of reports, relating to the development of the ECP by Parks Canada. The ABC Resource Survey Method was utilized to assist in the organization and evaluation of information for use in preparing the ECP (Nelson et al., 1988). A comprehensive, dynamic, and interactive approach to land-use mapping and research is ultimately desirable and useful for learning and general understanding, as well as for planning, management, and decision-making. The land-use, resource, and environmental survey and assessment system known as the ABC resource survey method was developed with the desired characteristics of comprehensiveness, dynamism, and interaction in mind (Nelson et al., 1988). The ultimate goal is to map, analyze, and assess human relations with the environment. Working toward this goal requires studies, not only of geologic and biological aspects of the environment, but also the values, ideas, technology, policies, and land-use activities that humans use to adapt to and change the world around them (Nelson et al., 1988).

ECP STUDY APPROACH

The first step was the preparation of a Background Information Study (BIS) (Lawrence et al., 1997). This was intended to provide information for the ECP by producing a summary of information on the study area needed by agencies, groups, and individuals to participate in the development of the ECP. The BIS was also intended to highlight information on problems, issues, and concerns (PICs) related to the ECP. A Synopsis of the BIS was subsequently prepared, which summarized key information, interpretations, and results from the BIS report (Lawrence et al., 1997).

A large amount of geologic, biologic, land-use, historical, economic, and other information has been produced on the Bruce Peninsula in the last century and particularly in the last two decades. To be useful in preparing the ECP for BPNP, this information had to be screened and organized to address the problems, issues, and concerns (PICs) that Parks Canada wanted identified for the ECP planning process in place at the time of our work. Several different methods were used for collecting existing information and organizing it to address PICs. These methods included:

1. examining previous studies conducted by Parks Canada for BPNP;

2. reviewing the Parks Canada Geographic Information System (GIS) database for BPNP;

3. assessing relevant information on the area around the national park as provided by various planning agencies, local groups, and others;

4. reviewing the ECPs prepared for other national parks in Ontario; and

5. interviews and consultations undertaken in preparing a Communication Strategy (CS) for the ECP.

Much of this information focused on the lands and waters within the national park area, thereby limiting the extent to which planning could be undertaken for the Greater Park Ecosystem around the park. During its work the study team frequently consulted with a Project Review Group and the Park Advisory Committee for BPNP. The Project Review Group consisted of the HRC study team, Parks Canada staff, and some members of the Park Advisory Committee. The Park Advisory Committee includes about fifteen individuals representing private organizations and groups concerned about the management of BPNP.

The study team developed a Communication Strategy for the ECP, which involved consultations with stakeholders affected by the plan. Thirty-five interviews and numerous meetings and workshops were conducted with groups and individuals involved in land-use, resource and environmental affairs in the BPNP area (Black and Nelson, 1997). The study team reached out to as many concerned agencies and groups as possible in order to locate information and gain assistance in the identification of problems, issues, and concerns to be addressed in the ECP.

ECP STUDY RESULTS

Initially the information was organized in terms of the categories in the ABC method. This resulted in the identification of numerous PICs that differed in complexity, scale, salience, and other details. It was consequently difficult to come to an understanding of what the fundamental concerns were and how to deal with them in an equitable, efficient, and effective way. The next step therefore was to identify some general or basic PICs with the idea that careful planning for these would encompass and address the more detailed ones. With this in mind, the PICs were organized in terms of the following topics:

Communication: Discussion with stakeholders, including local citizens, developed slowly for the national park. People agreed that communication was a major challenge for Parks Canada as well as other agencies and parties concerned about the national park.

Recreation and Tourism: The distribution and potential effects of current land uses and human activities on valued natural and cultural resources and the natural environment had to be addressed. Recreation and tourism seemed to be especially significant in these respects.

Transport and Infrastructure: Roadways, boating routes, trails, buildings, and other structures are distributed throughout the study area and have significant environmental effects, notably fragmentation of habitats.

Resource Uses: Various resource uses have affected the natural environment of the national park. Examples include forestry, fishing, and agriculture.

Environmental Conditions: Understanding the character of Abiotic (geology, soils, and landforms) and Biotic resources (vegetation, wildlife) is necessary to know how they are changing and how they could be affected by resource and land uses.

Land-Use Planning and Management: To decide how to respond to human activities and their effects, existing land-use planning and management arrangements in the study area had to be examined. This included land tenure and ownership, land-use zoning, identification of environmental sensitive areas, and municipal planning arrangements.

After organization into these general groups, the PICs were sorted according to whether they were considered to be Stresses, Effects, or Responses. The Stresses included recreation and tourism, transport and infrastructure, and land and resource use generally. The Effects included invasive alien species, loss of wetlands, habitat fragmentation and other impacts on the environment. The Responses mainly involved approaches to land-use planning, management, and decision-making, although communication is of underlying and basic importance to all of these.

Land and Resource Use Stresses

Understanding the types and locations of historic and current resource and land uses is important in addressing potential stresses and effects in the study area and especially in identifying Areas of Concern for planning and management responses. Major uses were considered to be forestry, commercial fishing, sand and gravel extraction, tourism and recreation, and residential development.

Early settlement brought extensive commercial logging to the northern Bruce Peninsula. Cutting, processing (mills), and transport (mainly by water routes) were the principal economic activities in the northern Bruce Peninsula from the mid-1800s into the early 1900s. By that time extensive clearing and a series of large forest fires had removed the primary forest cover, and logging underwent a major decline. Selective and small-scale lumber operations still occur on private lands, although data on the level of this activity are not readily available. The Ontario Ministry of Natural Resources in an arrangement with the County of Bruce, practices forest management on three County Agreement Forests in St. Edmunds Township and Lindsay Township (County of Bruce, 1995).

Commercial fisheries were another important early resource use. By the late 1800s and early 1900s, fishing involved over twenty boats operating out of Tobermory. The number of boats operating on Georgian Bay peaked by the early 1930s and fell thereafter as the fish catch declined substantially (County of Bruce, 1995). By the late 1990s only four commercial fishing boats operated out of Tobermory. Data from the 1991 Census indicated that only ten individuals were employed in this industry in St. Edmunds Township. The main market for the current commercial fishing industry was local sales of whitefish to residents and tourists from a few retail outlets.

Due to great distance from major markets for stone and aggregates (sand and gravel), surface quarries were not yet a major resource use. Nine main sand and gravel pit operations with a total licensed area of 105 ha were located outside the national park in St. Edmunds Township. Future expansion of this industry is possible, with increased demand in southern Ontario for construction materials and the gradual decline in alternative supplies within the province. The Niagara Escarpment Planning and Development Act restricts future expansion of this industry in the Niagara Escarpment Plan Area.

The single largest land-use activity in the study area is tourism and recreation. Beginning with improvements in transportation (roads and ferries) in the 1940s, the area around BPNP has been a focus for cottages and seasonal vacations. Recreational features and activities include trails (hiking and snowmobiling), tour boats, dive sites (snorkeling and scuba), campground sites (national parks and private sites), a golf course, parking lots, and picnic areas. The Georgian Bay shoreline from Cabot Head to Little Cove, the community of Tobermory, and waters adjacent to the main islands in Fathom Five National Marine Park, are main areas for tourism and recreation activities. More research is needed on the character, growth, and effects of these activities as well as the adequacy of planning and management responses.

Highway #6 passes through BPNP and will continue to serve as a development corridor because the Federal/Provincial Agreement leaves it out of the national park area. A number of other roads lead from Highway #6 and fragment the national park. More information is needed to understand the evolving patterns and effects of transport and communication systems and the adequacy of related planning and management responses.

Waterfront cottages comprise over 60 per cent of total residential buildings in the Tobermory area. All types of seasonal cottages account for almost 80 per cent of the total. Trends for 1978 to 1993 indicate peak periods for development applications occurred in 1978, 1987, and 1989. New developments requiring planning approval were less than four per year since 1989. Building permits – indicating levels of new construction activities, renovations, or demolition of existing structures – peaked in 1989 (52) and have ranged from 12 to 28 since 1990 (County of Bruce, 1995).

One way of generally estimating and understanding the cumulative pattern of land use and resource stresses is to map concentrations of roads, trails, cottages, marinas, and other facilities in the form of nodes and corridors of human activity. The resulting patterns can be used to estimate potential effects on natural processes and features essential for ecological integrity or health. Figure 11.2 is an initial attempt to outline the various resource and land patterns for the study area. Three general levels of development of nodes and corridors were identified to reflect the different scales of activities. Where three or more uses occur at a node, a major ranking was given. Nodes consisting of one or two uses were given a medium ranking. Nodes with one main resource or land use were given a low rank. The corridors were ranked in a similar manner according to the estimated level of use.

Environmental Effects

Resource and land uses can have various effects on the natural environment. One way of describing or understanding these current or potential effects is to map the natural processes and features deemed essential to the maintenance of ecological integrity in the national park and surrounding lands and waters. The study team identified and mapped the location and distribution of significant Abiotic and Biotic features and processes. Earlier research has identified a number of Abiotic (geological, hydrological, and landforms) features in the study area that are considered to be significant primarily because of their limited occurrence or distribution in Ontario (Geomatics Inc., 1994; Kor, 1994). The surface geology and landforms of the Bruce Peninsula range from extensive surface exposures of Paleozoic bedrock to remnant glacial features, including drumlins and till (Figure 11.3). Prominent among these significant features are beaches, dunes, alvars, caves, and cliff/talus. These features are of interest in their own right. They also provide for interpreting and understanding the range of geologic, hydrologic, and other earth science processes that have shaped and are shaping the lands and waters of the study area.

The region is also one of high biological significance. The national park is located within a large woodland area encompassing 50,000 ha from Whippoorwill Bay to Tobermory on the Bruce Peninsula. In the northern Bruce Peninsula region, 75 per cent of the land cover consists of forests (CPAWS Wildlands League, 2005). Within the national park area, four main plant or biological habitat types were identified on the

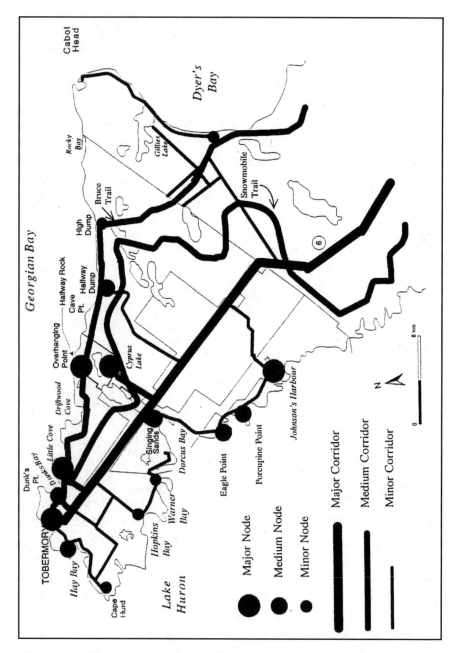

Figure 11.2   Nodes and Corridors

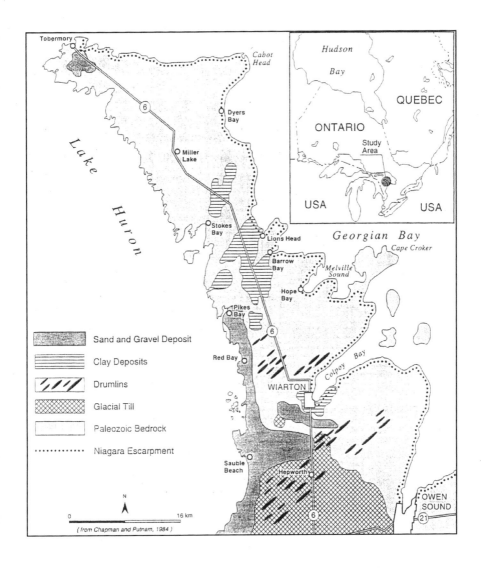

Figure 11.3   Surface Geology and Landforms

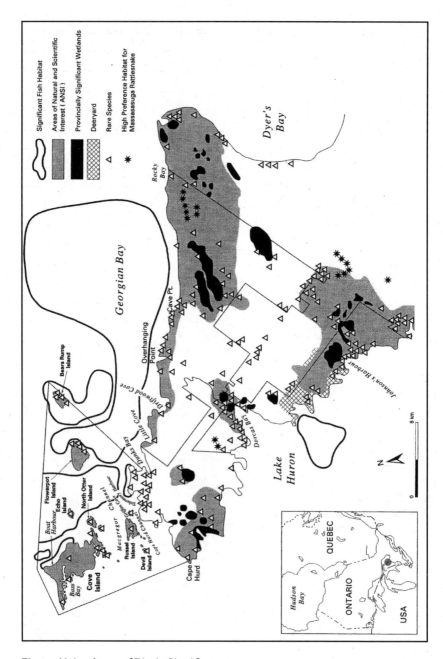

Figure 11.4   Areas of Biotic Significance

PLACES

basis of dominant vegetation, including upland coniferous (coniferous canopy greater than 75%); upland mixed (coniferous or deciduous canopy greater than 25%); uplands deciduous (deciduous canopy greater than 75%); and wetlands (tall shrub thicket swamps, marshes, and fens). In addition to these main habitat types, numerous other smaller or more specialized habitat areas were mapped such as escarpment cliffs and talus slopes, cleared lands, alvars, sand dunes, and cobble and sand beach communities.

The range of habitats supports a rich and diverse community of life. Thus far, 872 taxa of plants, 36 species of mammals, 26 species of herpetofauna, almost 300 species of birds (including migrants) and over 40 species of fish have been recorded within the study area (Lawrence and Nelson, 1998). The distribution of plant and animal species has been found to be closely associated with available habitats. Biotic features and functions that have been identified as significant include: areas with seasonal concentrations of animals; areas with rare or specialized habitats and communities; areas with rare species; significant wetlands or fish habitat; and provincial Areas of Natural and Scientific Interest (ANSIs) (Figure 11.4).

Management and Planning Responses

The history of management, planning, and decision-making is important in understanding how to deal with resource and land uses and environmental effects in the study area. It has only been within the last twenty years that local land-use planning and management have developed in Bruce County and Township of St. Edmunds. During this time the study area has been affected by major provincial land-use policies such as the establishment of the Niagara Escarpment Plan, a series of major changes to the Ontario Planning Act, and the creation of the national park. The fact that the Niagara Escarpment has received international designation as a World Biosphere Reserve also highlights the natural and ecological significance of the region. It is important that the Niagara Escarpment Plan and World Biosphere designation receive careful attention in future planning and management for ecological integrity by Parks Canada.

Within the study area, the Bruce County Official Plan (County of Bruce, 1996) establishes land-use policies to direct the future types and locations of new development. The land currently within the national park is designated as major open space with the majority of the surrounding area designated as rural lands. The Official Plan also identifies natural environment areas outside BPNP. These include: environmental hazard lands (flood and erosion susceptibility, steep slopes); regionally significant wetlands; and areas of ecological significance. Opportunities exist for linking and co-operatively planning for all these areas within the national park and surrounding land and waters.

The Tobermory and Area Community Land Use Plan is intended to manage future growth and development within and adjacent to the community of Tobermory. The plan is associated with the broader goals and objectives of the Strategic Plan for the Township of St. Edmunds. A series of eleven land-use designations and associated management bylaws have been established and mapped for the area, including residential, commercial, extractive, industrial, and community and recreational zones. The ECP must build on judicious linking of these diverse land-use designations with the conservation goals of the adjacent BPNP.

BPNP is also partially located within the Niagara Escarpment Plan Area. Plan policies contain seven land-use designations that indicate acceptable types of development and where they can be located: Escarpment Natural Area; Escarpment Protection Area; Escarpment Rural Area; Minor Urban Centre; Urban Area; Escarpment Recreation Area; and Mineral Extraction Area. These areas have been mapped along the length of the escarpment and are used by the Niagara Escarpment Commission (NEC) in conjunction with local municipalities to review and approve land-use changes within the Escarpment Plan Area.

In addition to the foregoing planning arrangements, several important special environmental policies apply to the study area and the Bruce Peninsula generally. These include municipal Environmentally Significant Areas (ESAs), provincial Areas of Scientific and Natural Significance and Interest (ANSIs), and Provincially Significant Wetlands. Other relevant policies and arrangements include the designation of the Niagara Escarpment Plan Area as a World Biosphere Reserve by the UNESCO and new tax and other stewardship incentives made available to private landowners by the Ontario government. These policies provide new means of conserving and sustainably using lands and waters around the national park. These new arrangements could make substantial contributions to conservation and sustainable development in the study area as well as to the ecological integrity of the lands and waters within BPNP.

Areas of Concern

In order to facilitate planning, areas were identified where the interaction of stresses, effects, and responses seemed to require early attention in order to maintain ecological integrity. Areas where stresses seem to be having undesirable effects on Abiotic and Biotic resources of BPNP were termed 'Areas of Concern.'

The identification of Areas of Concern was intended to present priorities for future management, planning, and decision-making by Parks Canada and other stakeholders in the study area. Areas of Concern could be monitored, assessed, and dropped from this status as effective planning and management responses were developed to deal with them. For planning and management purposes, six Areas of Concern were identified (Figure 11.5). These areas were considered high priority for further studies and assessments by Parks Canada and other concerned agencies, groups, and individuals. These studies and assessments could build on existing management plans or lead to new management or action plans.

PARKS CANADA ECOSYSTEM CONSERVATION PLAN AND IMPLEMENTATION ACTIVITIES (1998 TO 2006)

Since the completion and submission of a report by Nelson (1998) on the preparation of an ecosystem conservation plan (ECP) for the Bruce Peninsula National Park, Parks Canada made a decision to move away from the identification of problems, issues, and concerns (PICs) as a focus in preparing ECPs in favour of a broader strategic approach. For this

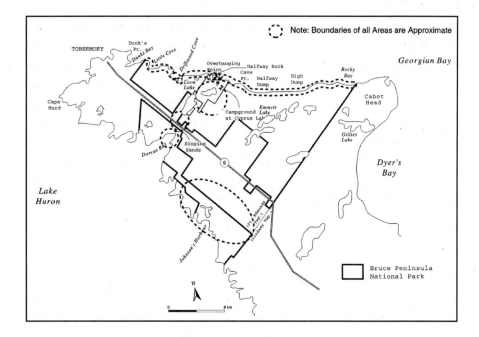

Figure 11.5   Areas of Concern

and other reasons, subsequent to the submission of the Nelson (1998) report, BPNP staff decided that they would complete the final ECP. It would be built around the development and implementation of goals, objectives, indicators, and targets for ecological integrity and the establishment of relevant monitoring indicators and measures (BPNP, 2001) in the Greater Park Ecosystem.

Under the new policy, an ECP is intended to "provide a decision-making support system to assist park and natural resource management in ensuring the long-term viability of [the] ecosystem" (BPNP, 2001). Within the ECP, six ecosystem integrity goals were developed with indicators, objectives, and targets established for each. The six goals were: maintain viable populations; represent all community types; maintain evolutionary and ecological processes; work with others to protect the ecosystem; maintain functional ecological connections; and protect cultural resources. The implementation of the ECP includes specific planning and technical provisions for each ecosystem integrity goal and provides detailed descriptions of priorities, budget information, and scheduling of tasks. The ECP can be seen as a framework or work plan for conducting monitoring within the national park geared to maintaining ecological integrity.

Also, starting in 2000, Parks Canada staff in the National Park began development of a State of the Park report (Parks Canada, 2004). The 2004 Report provides an assessment of the current status of ecological integrity based upon the eight measures for which monitoring is to be conducted (Parks Canada, 2004). Of the eight measures, one (stewardship) is assessed as having a positive contribution to the ecological integrity of the national park. The measure of species diversity has been assigned a moderate assessment due to the presence of numerous alien invasive species. Changes in land cover have resulted in a moderate assessment of the measure on terrestrial ecosystem function. Continued human activities leading to natural area fragmentation resulted in the moderate assessment of the habitat-change indicator. Ongoing impacts associated with back-county campsites and increased park visitor numbers have led to deteriorating ecological integrity in areas where those activities are present in the national park (Parks Canada, 2004). Due to the insufficient information, and lack of monitoring, three of the eight measures were not reported upon.

Budget and policy changes over the last few years within Parks Canada have also provided opportunities to implement some aspects of ecosystem conservation planning. Budget 2005 provided Parks Canada with $60 million nationwide in new ecological integrity funding over five years, followed by $15 million in new annual ongoing funding. Parks Canada will use the funds to broaden its ecological monitoring and reporting work, augment its current ecological expertise, and undertake new initiatives to ensure the long-term ecological health of Canada's national parks. Efforts will be made to restore key ecosystems, involve Aboriginal communities, and educate the public about ecological integrity.

Efforts are underway in the Bruce Peninsula National Park to secure access to these funds to support ongoing ecosystem research and environmental monitoring programs, including studies of black bears, eastern Massasauga rattlesnakes, lake water quality, and forest management. Also in July 2006, after over a decade of planning, a $7 million visitor centre for the Bruce Peninsula National Park was opened in Tobermory, providing an excellent forum for ecosystem interpretation, public awareness, education, and community outreach activities. In a separate but related effort, the Canadian Parks and Wilderness Society – Wildlands League Chapter – has recently completed a community ecosystem atlas for the northern Bruce Peninsula (CPAWS, 2005). The atlas provides a general overview of the ecosystem, land use and development, and related conservation efforts in and around Bruce Peninsula National Park.

CONCLUSIONS

A major challenge in ecosystem planning is the need to provide useful information for planning and decision-making. Much information is often available in a variety of sources, including professional consultation, the public, and the scientific community. A challenge facing decision-making is how to more efficiently and effectively collect, evaluate, and present this information. The ABC method addresses this challenge.

Planning for the maintenance of the ecological integrity of Bruce Peninsula National Park requires understanding of a range of complex and often interrelated management issues. The Nelson (1998) study examined a vast range of research studies, published reports, and databases as well as reporting on extensive public consultation with stakeholders in and around the national park. This work focused on moving beyond an initial list of problems, issues, and concerns (PICs) to the development of a Stress, Effects, Response planning framework and the identification of Areas of Concern. The aim was to assist Parks Canada and other concerned parties in addressing ecosystem conservation issues within the national park and surrounding lands and waters.

The twenty-year history of ecosystem planning efforts in the BPNP reflects a range of policy changes within Parks Canada, including changes to the National Park Act and also administrative and procedural changes within the agency. In addition, new scientific ideas, information, and technologies have emerged as well as growing appreciation of local community contributions within and around the Bruce Peninsula National Park. A broader approach to planning based on ecological integrity and heightened awareness of the greater park ecosystem has emerged with Parks Canada playing a lead role.

NOTES

1   Adapted from P.L. Lawrence and J.G. Nelson, "Twenty Years of Efforts towards Ecosystem Planning in the Bruce Peninsula National Park, Ontario Canada: 1987 to 2006," *The Great Lakes Geographer* 12(2) (2005): 27–44.

REFERENCES

Black, H., and J.G. Nelson. 1997. *Building Bridges through Communication: Communication Strategy Report for Bruce Peninsula National Park and Fathom Five National Marine Park Ecosystem Conservation Plans.* Cornwall, ON: Parks Canada, Ontario Region.

Bruce Peninsula National Park (BPNP). 2001. *Ecosystem Conservation Plan.* Bruce Peninsula National Park. Tobermory, Ontario.

County of Bruce. 1995. *Tobermory and Area Community Land Use Plan and St. Edmunds Township Strategic Plan: Background Report.* Planning and Economic Development Department, County of Bruce, Wiarton, Ontario.

County of Bruce. 1996. *Bruce County Official Plan.* Planning and Economic Development Department, County of Bruce, Walkerton, Ontario.

CPAWS Wildlands League. 2005. *Northern Bruce Peninsula Ecosystem Community Atlas.* Toronto.

Geomatics Inc. 1994. *Surface Geomorphological Inventory: St. Edmunds Township, Cabot Head and Islands Between Tobermory and Manitoulin.* Cornwall, ON: Parks Canada, Ontario Region.

Government of Canada/Government of Ontario. 1987. *Federal/Provincial Agreement for the Establishment for the Establishment of the Proposed National Park in the Township of St. Edmunds.* Ottawa: Parks Canada.

Kor, P.S.G. 1994. *An Earth Science Inventory and Evaluation of Cabot Head Provincial Nature Reserve and Area of Scientific Interest (Lindsay Township Portion).* Ontario Ministry of Natural Resources Open File Geological Report #9401. Aurora, ON: Ontario Ministry of Natural Resources, Southern Region.

Lawrence, P.L., and J.G. Nelson, eds. 1998. *Synopsis of the Background Information Study for Bruce Peninsula National Park and Fathom Five National Marine Park: A Summary and Interpretation for Ecosystem Conservation Planning.* Waterloo: Heritage Resources Centre, University of Waterloo.

Lawrence, P.L. J.G. Nelson, S. Wilcox, H. Black, and H. Olive. 1997. *Ecosystem Conservation Plans for Bruce Peninsula National Park and Fathom Five National Marine Park – Background Information Study.* Waterloo: Heritage Resources Centre, University of Waterloo.

Nelson, J.G. 1998. *Preparing for an Ecosystem Conservation Plan for Bruce Peninsula National Park.* Waterloo: Heritage Resources Centre, University of Waterloo.

Nelson, J.G., P. Grigoriew, P.G.R. Smith, and J.B. Theberge. 1988. The ABC Resource Survey Method, the ESA Concept and Comprehensive Land Use Planning and Management. In *Landscape Ecology and Management,* ed. M.R. Moss, 143–175. Proceedings of the First Symposium of the Canadian Society for Landscape Ecology and Management. Toronto: Polyscience Publications.

Nelson, J.G., P.L. Lawrence, and H. Black. 2000. "Assessing ecosystem conservation plans for Canadian national parks." *Natural Areas Journal* 20(3): 280–287.

Panel on Ecological Integrity of National Parks. 2000. *Unimpaired for Future Generations?: Conserving Ecological Integrity with Canada's National Parks – Final Report of the Panel on Ecological Integrity of National Parks.* Ottawa: Parks Canada.

Parks Canada. 1988. *Bruce Peninsula National Park Interim Draft Management Plan.* Tobermory, Ontario.

Parks Canada. 1992. "Ecosystem Conservation Plan." In *Natural Resource Management Process Manual.* Cornwall, ON: Parks Canada, Ontario Region.

Parks Canada. 1996. *Bruce Peninsula National Park Management Plan.* Tobermory, Ontario.

Parks Canada. 2004. *Bruce Peninsula National Park State of the Park Report for the Bruce Peninsula.* Tobermory, Ontario.

Zorn, P., B. Stephenson, and P. Grigoriew. 1997. *Ecosystem Management Program and Assessment Process.* Cornwall, ON: Parks Canada, Ontario Region.

12

2002

SAN PEDRO RIVER, ARIZONA: LAND-USE HISTORY, LANDSCAPE CHANGE AND PLANNING FOR A UNITED STATES RIPARIAN NATIONAL CONSERVATION AREA[1]

J.G. Nelson

INTRODUCTION

This overview of land-use history, landscape change, and planning for the San Pedro Riparian National Conservation Area (NCA), Arizona, is generally organized in terms of an Abiotic, Biotic, and Cultural (ABC) approach, which integrates the natural and cultural history of the San Pedro valley NCA and surrounding country. The overview reveals the highly significant history and character of the San Pedro landscape geologically, biologically, and culturally. The overview ends with the cultural section, which includes some planning and research recommendations.

River valleys or riparian areas are increasingly recognized as important for the conservation of migratory fauna and flora as well as habitat for many resident wildlife populations. Riparian areas are also increasingly of commercial interest for aggregate mining, irrigation projects, hydroelectric power facilities, livestock grazing, and other enterprises. In few places is the conflict between these two broad sets of values and interests more apparent than in the American Southwest, including the State of Arizona. In the close to five centuries since the

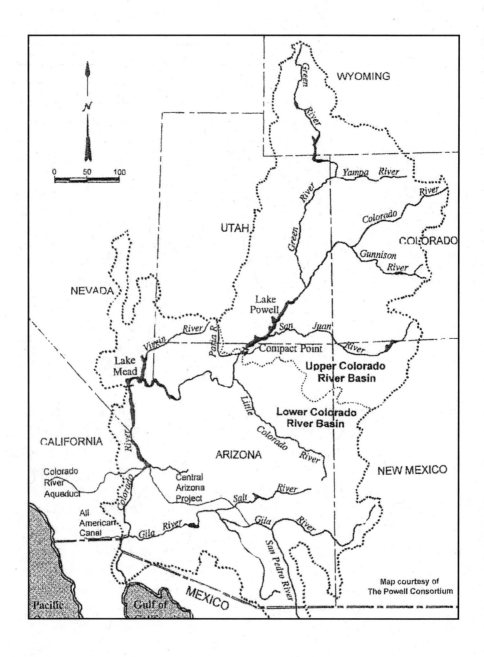

Figure 12.1   The San Pedro and the Colorado River Watershed

PLACES

invasion of the area by Spanish, and later other Caucasians, the river valleys have been subject to growing pressure for development. By the 1980s, few major river valleys in Arizona remained close to what might be called a natural state. One of these was the San Pedro River corridor, which had not been as heavily exploited as other desert stream habitats along the Gila, the Salt, and the Santa Cruz in the Colorado River Basin (Figure 12.1).

SAN PEDRO RIVER

Concern about the future of the San Pedro rose sharply in the 1980s as a result of increasing pressure for grazing, gravel mining, and housing developments for the growing influx of immigrants and visitors. On November 18, 1988, the U.S. Congress responded to this concern by passing an act setting up the San Pedro Riparian National Conservation Area (NCA) to be managed by the U.S. Bureau of Land Reclamation (BLM) (Friends of the San Pedro River, San Pedro Riparian National Conservation Area, n.d.). This NCA was established to conserve, protect, and enhance the riparian ecosystem, a rare remnant of what once was an extensive network of similar riparian systems throughout the arid Southwest. The San Pedro Riparian NCA supports over 350 species of mammals, two indigenous and several introduced species of fish, more than forty species of reptiles and amphibians, as well as thousands of species of plants (Friends of the San Pedro River, n.d.; Bureau of Land Management, 1989; Hanson, 2001).

Although some in-holdings still exist, as of 2002, the San Pedro Riparian NCA consists of approximately 56,000 acres of public land assembled by the BLM along about forty miles of the upper river between the Mexican–U.S. border and St. David, a Mormon settlement dating from about the turn of the nineteenth century (Figure 12.1). The headwaters of the river are in Mexico where the catchment is exploited for cultivation, grazing, mining, and other uses. Efforts have been underway for several years to co-operate with the people of Mexico in introducing more effective conservation measures in their part of the watershed.

The main management measures put in place by BLM since 1988 include controls on grazing, gravel mining, and housing developments, as well as roads and other facilities. Various types of recreation are encouraged including hiking and naturalist activities, notably birding. All Terrain Vehicles (ATVs) and other recreation technology are subject to controls. A hiking trail parallels the full length of the Riparian NCA and seems to be used frequently by locals and visitors alike (Figure 12.2). An excellent guide to the upper San Pedro has been prepared by the naturalist and executive director of the Sky Islands Alliance (Hanson, 2001). No reliable data are known to be available on the number of visitors to the NCA.

Thousands of birders visit the area annually as it is renowned for the high population and diversity of its avifauna. The focal point for birders is the San Pedro House, a historic cabin occupied and renovated by the BLM and the Friends of the San Pedro River, a volunteer non-profit, non-political organization providing support for the Bureau in the stewardship of the NCA. The San Pedro Riparian NCA was designated as the first Globally Important Bird Area in North America in 1995, being joined not long thereafter by the Long Point Biosphere in Ontario and a site in southern Mexico.

A wide range of conservation activities has been introduced by the BLM and it's supporters to enhance the degraded habitat of the NCA since its creation in 1988. The removal of cattle grazing and hay production has led to the restoration of extensive floodplains and grasslands. Areas disturbed by ploughing, surface mining, and other similar activities are returning to grass and other cover. Growth of cottonwood, willow, sycamore, and other trees and shrubs along the stream banks and adjoining floodplain areas has been impressive. Mesquite has begun to encroach onto the floodplain areas, with some limitations on this as a result of accidental and controlled burning. Water quality is also said to have improved. The difficulty, however, is that relatively little systematic monitoring of the ecosystem changes appears to been undertaken, largely because of lack of resources by BLM and others. The lack of this data could pose significant problems when some aspects

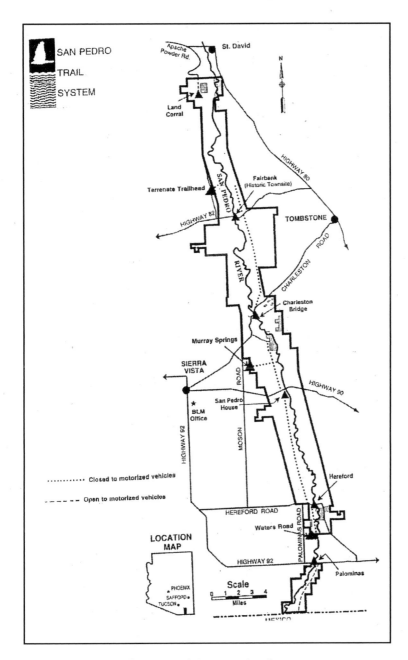

Figure 12.2   San Pedro National Conservation Area

of the agreement for the conservation of the San Pedro Riparian NCA come up for review and possible renewal.

This review of the land-use and landscape history of the San Pedro region provides the basis for an assessment of past and future planning, management, and decision-making for the San Pedro Riparian National Conservation Area. The study is based on six annual field visits to the area in 1990s and early 2000s, as well as interviews and conversations with numerous people from relevant government and non-governmental organizations, including numerous tourists and local residents encountered during visits. Extensive research was also undertaken in libraries, notably the Bisbee Mining Museum and the Douglas Public Library. The natural and cultural history of the San Pedro is quite complex and cannot be considered in detail here. The San Pedro Riparian NCA is affected, not only by activities and processes occurring within its more immediate vicinity, but also by those in more distant parts of the watershed and beyond. It is, however, possible to highlight San Pedro's history by focusing on some key aspects of its evolution from early geologic times to the present day.

THE ABC SURVEY METHOD

The San Pedro valley and surrounding area are of outstanding interest for a number of interrelated natural and cultural reasons. From the natural standpoint, the area is highly significant in terms of both earth science and biological attributes. From a cultural standpoint, the area is highly significant in terms of the great length of human occupancy, the diverse array of changing ethnic and cultural groups, and their frequently profound impacts on vegetation, wildlife, landscapes, and ecosystems generally. These ecosystem changes are a result not only of human activity but also of post-glacial climatic and natural changes and their interaction with human activities.

To describe, analyze, and assess such characteristics and changes, it has been useful to follow the ABC or Abiotic, Biotic, and Cultural method (Bastedo et al., 1984). This method was developed to facilitate comprehensive resource and environmental surveys and assessments for planning purposes. The method provides a broad framework for organizing, describing, mapping, analyzing, assessing, and integrating diverse information from an array of disciplines and sources. The method is useful in dealing with historic as well as current information and ongoing research.

The ABC method can be undertaken in considerable technical detail as well as in a more general way. The latter approach is the one followed here where the method basically provides a framework for collecting, analyzing, and presenting information on the San Pedro Valley on a comprehensive basis. Accordingly, the study considers salient aspects of the geology, hydrology, and climate, or Abiotic, the plants, animals, and habitats or Biotic, and the human or Cultural characteristics of the San Pedro area. The Cultural characteristics include land-use, economics, social, institutional, and other aspects of learned human behaviour and activities. The salient Abiotic and Biotic characteristics are considered first, followed by a stage-by-stage discussion of changing human influences, their interaction with the surrounding environment, and some implications for planning, especially conservation planning.

Abiotic Resources

The San Pedro watershed and surrounding country are located amid the great deserts of the U.S. southwest and northern Mexico (Figure 12.3). The deserts lie in the general vicinity of 30° north latitude, a dry zone subject to strong seasonal shifts in atmospheric circulation and storm trends (Shreve and Wiggins, 1946; Larson, 1977). In the winter, storms and weather originating in the west over the Pacific move eastward and inland. These moisture-laden systems encounter, are pushed upward, and are cooled by the Coast Ranges, the Sierra Nevada, and the Sierra Madre Occidental Mountains. The result is that the western part of the desert receives predominantly winter precipitation.

In the spring the atmospheric circulation and storm trends move north with the sun. The eastward flow from the Pacific becomes weaker and monsoon-type circulation and storm tracks move into the increasingly hot interior from the southeast and the Gulf of Mexico.

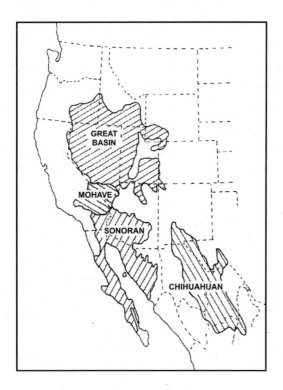

Figure 12.3   North American Deserts

In consequence, much of the precipitation in the eastern part of the southwestern desert falls in the summer in contrast to the winter peak in the west.

In the central parts of the desert, the two seasonal precipitation patterns overlap. These areas receive both summer and winter precipitation. This is true for the country around the San Pedro watershed. Tucson, about 100 miles west and north of the San Pedro NCA, receives about one half its 275 mm (11 inches) annual average in winter and about half in summer (Larson, 1977: 35). The availability of this precipitation is reduced by high evapotranspiration rates, which result from temperatures frequently exceeding 40°C (100°F) in summer. Temperatures tend to fluctuate considerably around the mean. Weather and climate also vary in accordance with variations in geology and topography. Temperatures and precipitation have also varied during past climate changes.

The geological history of the Southwest United States and adjoining parts of Mexico is a very long and convoluted one. Much of the structure of the present landscape arises from the Middle Tertiary and Later Tertiary phases (Figure 12.4). According to Coney (1978: 288), the mid-Tertiary was "the most bizarre and varied period of tectonic activity in the entire history of the region." The bedrock was deformed, domed, extended, and metamorphosed. Of special interest is a Cordilleran-wide sequence of volcanism, which extended from the Pacific Northwest to southern Mexico (Sierra Madre Occidental Mountains), leaving a landscape buried in ash and punctured by great pits or calderas (Coney, 1978: 288).

In Late Tertiary, between about 15 million and 6 million years ago, widespread faulting and extensive vulcanism produced the characteristic southern Arizona and northern Mexican landscape of fault-block mountains. These are separated by basins, such as Sulphur Springs and the San Pedro Valley, filled with thousands of feet of sediment. Figure 12.4 shows the major kinds of faults and structural features making up the region.

The San Pedro area is also of unusual interest because of its Quaternary history of the last several million years. Huge ice sheets advanced across Canada and the United States a number of times, causing changes in climate throughout the continent. In the Southwest, these northern ice advances and retreats resulted in alpine cool-wet, or pluvial climates, alternating with interpluvial or semi-arid climates.

Evidence for these changes is found in remnants of formerly extensive lakes in the region. An example is pluvial Lake Cochise, which was located in what is now called the Wilcox Playa near the town of that name in the Sulphur Springs Valley on the western fringe of the Chiricahua Mountains (Schreiber, 1978) (Figure 12.4). Using old beach lines, core analysis and other field methods, Schreiber and his students determined that former Lake Cochise covered about 190 km^2 around the present smaller and ephemerally flooded playa.

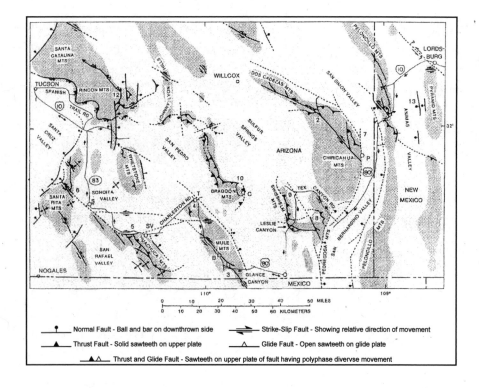

Figure 12.4   Major Structural Features of southeastern Arizona

A 43-m core from the middle of the former lake was examined by P.S. Martin, a pollen expert. C^{14} dates were also obtained on carbon from this core. According to Schreiber (1978: 281), Martin interpreted high pine counts in the core as indicating more extensive growth of forest and woodland and a cool-wet pluvial climate induced by ice advances in northern North America. He interpreted low pine pollen counts, or poor pollen preservation and oxidized sediment, as indicating drier interglacial or interpluvial climates induced by ice retreat in northern North America.

Similar evidence of former lakes has been found elsewhere in the southwest and has been interpreted as indicating widespread fluctuations in climate, flora, and fauna in the Basin and Range region during the Pleistocene (Bezy, 2001). The general picture in the pluvials is one in which upper-level spruce, fir, and pine forest are seen as moving downslope along with mid- and lower-level oak savannah and grasslands. In the drier interpluvials these vegetation zones are interpreted as moving upslope again. Such fluctuations continued until about 12,000 years ago when the ice sheets underwent massive retreat and climate and vegetation patterns generally similar to current ones were established.

Glacial or pluvial Lake Cochise was present in the Sulfur Springs Basin as recently as 10,500 years ago (Bezy, 2001). At that time, the basin had open stands of ponderosa pine and herds of mammoth, horse, and camel. This interpretation is in line with evidence from the San Pedro basin to the west, where excavations have revealed such early fauna in association with human artifacts. In fact, the upper San Pedro Valley is generally considered to have the highest number of early man or Paleo-Indian sites of any comparable area in North America. Of particular note are the Naco and Double Adobe sites on the east fringe of the San Pedro as well as the Escalupe, Lehner, and the Murray Spring sites in the San Pedro Valley NCA, just north the Mexican border. Archaeological excavations at all three sites reveal bones of now-extinct Pleistocene animals in association with stone tools and debris interpreted as having been worked by humans. All these sites have also been dated by C^{14} and other geologic methods as about 11,000–12,000 years BP (Bronitsky and Merritt, 1986: 54–55).

Biotic Resources

According to MacMahon (1985: 65–69), the San Pedro area lies toward the eastern edge of the Arizona Upland, in the Sonoran desert region. Many shrubs occur at various heights in this upland. In very general terms, one vegetation layer is less than eighteen inches high, another is about three feet, and beyond that is an upper layer of sub-trees. This array of plants includes creosote bush, foothill palo verde, iron wood, and many species of cacti whose diversity is high. They include prickly pear, barrel cactus, and various species of cholla such as buckthorn, cane, and jumping cholla.

This vegetation assemblage is associated with an array of animals, of which birds are of special interest for scientific, recreational, and other reasons. At least five hundred bird species have been reported in the Sonoran, approximately half of all the bird species reported for the continental United States or Mexico (Nabhan and Holdsworth, 1998). In the desert shrub and semi-desert grassland habitats, however, the per unit area diversity of breeding birds is not especially noteworthy, approximately 30–150 pairs per forty hectares. Typical Sonoran desert sites generally have less than twenty-five breeding species (Nabhan and Holdsworth, 1998). However, wooded and shrub-lined valleys or riparian corridors may play host to as many as four hundred species for breeding, over-wintering, and migrating. This constitutes approximately 75 per cent of all the bird species that migrate between the United States and Mexico (Nabhan and Holdsworth, 1998: 15).

Species diversity and productivity are also high for species other than birds in the Sonoran. Overall the species richness of mammals known for the San Pedro Riparian Natural Conservation Area is estimated at eighty-six species including twelve at risk. This richness is thought to be unsurpassed for any landscape of similar size in the United States (Nabhan and Holdsworth, 1998: 13). The Sonoran region's reptile diversity is also high, although the same cannot be said for amphibians and fish.

Cultural Resources

PALEO-INDIANS

The Murray Springs and other archaeological sites have been carefully excavated and studied by professional archaeologists and other scientists, and the results highlight the significance of these finds (Anonymous, 1982; BLM, Lehner Mammoth Kill Site, n.d.; BLM, Murray Springs Clovis Site, n.d.; Bronitsky and Merritt, 1986). In 1952 extinct mammoth fragments were found in terrace deposits at what is now known as the Lehner Mammoth Kill Site, located above the current river not far from the Mexican border. This site was excavated in 1955–56 and again in 1974–75. Archaeologists identified thirteen worked stone points similar to the Clovis points found earlier in New Mexico. In addition to these points, which were likely used on long lances to kill mammoth, the archaeologists also found stone butchering tools, chips, and other stone debris as well as fire hearths (BLM; Lehner Mammoth Kill Site, n.d.; Hauny et al., 1959). These hearths contained carbon, which was dated at about 11,000 BP. Animal bones identified at the site included those of twelve immature mammoths, one horse, one tapir, several bison, one camel, one bear, several rabbits, and a small snake. Botanists identified pine, ash, and oak in the charcoal from the hearths. From this and other evidence, they deduced that the site was used by humans in the interval between the end of the Pleistocene and the beginning of recent drier times.

Such evidence from the Lehner, as well as the Murray Springs and nearby similar sites, indicate that ancient people, the so-called Paleo-Indians, were big game hunters who moved regularly in pursuit of mammoth and other sources of food (Kurdeka, 1982; BLM Murray Springs, n.d.; Bronitsky and Merritt, 1986; Amann et al., 1998). They were successful in killing large Pleistocene animals and are considered by some scholars to have been largely responsible for their extinction (Martin and Klein, 1984; Amann et al., 1998). Others are of the view that the change from a cool-wet or pluvial climate to a drier post-glacial one damaged or destroyed habitat, thereby leading to extinction. Still others have concluded that extinction was due to several causes, including both climate change and over-hunting (Amann et al., 1998). The high number of young or immature mammoth at sites such as the Lehner has been interpreted by some scientists as indicating that extinction likely was caused by these early people preying heavily on more vulnerable, younger animals. On the other hand, faunal extinctions at the end of the Pleistocene included some animals and plants not known to have been used by humans, who do not therefore seem likely causes of their extinction (Amann et al., 1998: 8).

PALEO-INDIAN TIMES TO THE ARRIVAL OF THE SPANISH

This long interval extends from the end of the Paleo-Indian times, about 10,000 years ago, to the entrance of the Spanish into what later became Mexico and the American Southwest by about 1540. This very lengthy period has been subject to confusing and uncertain interpretations by archaeologists and other scientists (Bronitsky and Merritt, 1986: 100). Hundreds of relevant sites have been excavated in the southwest and the general region of the San Pedro Valley.

These sites have been interpreted as representing various complexes and stages of what is generally thought of as Archaic or Desert cultures. These people developed a range of stone, bone, and other tools that permitted a hunting and gathering lifestyle in the Southwest, including the San Pedro Basin. For the most part, the Archaic or Desert cultures were migratory, hunting deer, coyote, rabbit, antelope, and other currently existing animals, as well as gathering, grinding, and processing mesquite, beans, and other plants. They may have moved about in bands of about twenty to thirty, although their overall numbers in the southwest and the San Pedro area are unknown.

Fire may also have been used in burning grass and vegetation to drive deer and other game, as was done in more recent times by people living with similar technology and lifestyles (Cornett, 2000: 26; de Golia, 1993: 6; Hanson, 2001: 84). It has also been suggested that these people might have encouraged the growth of wild plants to collect for food, introducing a kind of incipient or early stage of agriculture (Bronitsky and Merritt, 1986: 113). Cumulatively through hunting, plant selection, and other activities over about nine thousand years or four hundred generations (10,000 BP–2,500 BP), these early people probably caused many unappreciated changes in the fauna, flora, and ecosystems of the San Pedro and other areas.

With the development of sedentary agriculture, however, the scene was set for major impacts on the environment. The evidence for agriculture revolves around the three relatively well-known indigenous crops; maize, squash, and beans. Carbon dates have been obtained for the earliest occurrences of maize and squash at the Bat Cave, Tularosa Cave, and Cienega Creek sites in west central New Mexico and eastern Arizona. These plant remnants are said to be associated with Chiricahua stage artifacts and have been dated at between about 4,200 and 3,500 BP by C^{14} analysis. Beans from later San Pedro stage levels at Bat Cave have been dated as early as 3,000 BP. Maize was also recovered from these San Pedro levels. This corn was a crossbreed between early maize and a teosinte form of the plant, likely introduced from antecedents in Mexico (Bronitsky and Merritt, 1986).

Slowly increasing use of the new maize and other crops led to a gradual shift to a more sedentary and elaborate lifestyle. Domestic structures, such as storage pits and cooking hearths, as well as human burials, suggest a trend to sedentism. The existence of settled villages in certain parts of the area, by about 1,500 years BP or AD 500, is seen as a result of these trends (Bronitsky and Merritt, 1986: 114). These villages gradually elaborated into those of people known as the Hohokam with their well-built mud and stone homes, as well as kivas, other ceremonial areas, ball courts, and other architectures. These villages and settlements were associated with the production of corn, beans, and squash through irrigation as well as farming based on natural sources of water. In some cases, irrigation canals, sluices, gates, and other structures were built. In other cases, the crops were grown on floodplains or through diversion of floods and high waters. Evidence of Hohokam agriculture and irrigation apparently has not been found in the upper San Pedro or current NCA. Where sedentary indigenous agriculture and irrigation did develop, this began the process of land clearing, soil disturbance, stream and water diversion, salinization, and other environmental effects that may have been of considerable significance locally but only heralded the larger-scale changes yet to come with the introduction of elaborate irrigated farming in European times.

THE SPANISH

The next phase of San Pedro Valley history is the Spanish period from about the 1530s to the 1850s (Bannon, 1974; Meyer, 1984; Walker and Bafkin, 1979). For our purposes, this three-century span includes the time of Mexican independence from 1821 to 1856, when the U.S. Congress completed its acquisition of the current state of Arizona and other parts of the U.S. Southwest through the Gadsden Purchase. The Spanish found and invaded what is now Mexico in 1521. By the 1530s and 1540s, expeditions in search of gold, silver, and other metals were underway in the present state of Arizona, as well as New Mexico and

Texas. The best known of these expeditions was that of Coronado in the early 1840s.

One wave of Spanish invasion was religious in nature. The Jesuits, and later the Franciscans and other orders of the Roman Catholic Church, moved into the study area to convert the natives to Christianity. Serious attempts to establish missions were made from northern Mexico in the mid- to late 1600s. Some of these efforts were successful, for example in the Santa Cruz Valley west of the San Pedro. These successes included well-known sites such as Tubac and Tucson (BLM, Presidio Santa Cruz De Terrenate, n.d.).

Efforts to establish missions and presidios, or military posts, in the San Pedro Watershed were largely unsuccessful, particularly in the southern or upper parts of the valley. Some success was achieved for a few years at Quibari (Quivari) and the nearby Terrenate Mission. However, these posts were eventually abandoned because of the hostility of nomadic hunting groups such as the Apache and the withdrawal of the Sobraipuri and other collecting and gathering people, whose cultures are thought to resemble those of the archaeological Archaic.

The Spanish introduced many exotic plants and animals into the southwest (Bronitsky and Merritt, 1986; Bahre, 1991; Bennett et al., 1996). Expeditions such as Coronado's in the 1540s included hundreds of horses, cattle, and other stock, many of which were lost. Such animals also were taken to missions like those along the Santa Cruz, for use by the Spanish as well as natives. Wheat and European crops were introduced for similar purposes. Over the decades and the centuries, many of these animals and plants went wild and spread through southwestern ecosystems. Water diversion and irrigation systems were expanded by the Spanish. The invaders also introduced new germs and diseases to the natives, causing epidemics that killed thousands over the years. The development of missions, presidios and silver and other mining camps brought larger populations and settlements and accelerated ecosystem and landscape changes.

THE AMERICANS

The next phase of interest, the American, grew sharply with the 1849 California gold rush. Explorers and traders from the United States had been active in Arizona decades earlier. James Battie, an American Mountain Man, explored and worked the Gila River for beaver and other furs in the 1820s, following the river to the vicinity of the Gulf of California (Bronitsky and Merritt, 1986: 273–276; Walker and Bufkin, 1979). He is known to have been active in the lower San Pedro Valley, close to its entrance to the Gila. Neither he nor other American trappers are known to have reached the upper San Pedro and the vicinity of the current NCA.

Traders, prospectors, and other invaders from the United States came in increasing numbers to Tucson area and other parts of current Arizona, New Mexico, and California in the 1830s and 1840s. War with Mexico let to U.S. acquisition of much of the American Southwest in 1848 and the rest through the Gadsden purchase of 1856. Some predecessors of the California Gold seekers of 1849 passed through the upper San Pedro Valley, but travel increased greatly with the rush of prospectors and others from the east. These travellers used a number of routes through Mexico and the southwest, including one that ran more or less along the border and up the San Pedro Valley to the Gila River, Tucson, and beyond (Bronitsky and Merritt, 1986: 283–284).

After 1856, an array of U.S. economic activities began to boom in the southwest and the San Pedro Valley watershed. Prospectors swept the region looking for gold, silver, lead, copper, and other minerals. Some were found often in short-lived deposits, lasting only a few years. Some rich finds were eventually made, including Tombstone, Bisbee, and a number of sites in the mountains on the fringe of the San Pedro Valley (Schwantes, 1992; Leaming, 1998). These sites lasted well into the twentieth century and spawned mills and settlements such as Fairbanks and Charleston, in the upper San Pedro, in what is now the NCA.

Other settlers moved in to ranch and raise cattle, horses, and other stock for the mining settlements (Bronitsky and Merritt, 1986: 283–284). Some of these outfits were in place in the 1860s, including the

Kitchen Ranch on the lower Santa Cruz, the Slaughter Ranch in the San Bernardino Valley, and the Hooker Ranch in the lower or northern San Pedro Valley, closer to the Gila (Stewart, n.d.: 9–12). Other ranching operations began in the upper San Pedro in the vicinity of the NCA, for example on the Babocomari Creek, a tributary of the San Pedro just north of the present town of Sierra Vista. The Babocomari and other ranches developed on land grants made by the Spanish and Mexican governments prior to the 1840s (Walker and Bufkin, 1979). These ranches were generally ill-defined open range outfits whose cattle ranged over many square miles.

The incursions of travellers, miners, and ranchers led to increasing conflicts with the Apache. One major result was an increasing number of U.S. troops and military posts. These troops numbered in the tens of thousands and had to be fed and housed. This provided big opportunities for cattle and stockmen as well as irrigators and agriculturalists. The extent and intensity of ranching, grazing, and other activities placed rising pressures on the desert environment. In his remarkable book, *A Legacy of Change,* which deals with the historic human impact on vegetation in the Arizona borderlands, Conrad Bahre (1991) describes the effects of grazing, mining, and other activities in detail, with support from historic photographs.

Exploration and development activity took on new vigour in the twentieth century. One major reason was the growth of recreation and tourism. Another was the entrance of rising numbers of retirees from other parts of the United States. In addition, the southwest and the San Pedro watershed became increasingly important for military installations and activities. Recreation and tourism have been growing since the late nineteenth century through hunting and related outdoor activities. Guided hunts for lions, jaguars, and other large animals rose after World War I. Aldo Leopold and his family described hunts for deer, turkey, and other animals along the Gila and the Sierra Madre of northern Mexico in the 1920s and 1930s (Leopold, 1953).

Recreation and tourism began to boom after World War II with the arrival of the entertainment industry. This involved the establishment of gambling casinos, large hotels, and convention centres, as well as filmmaking and family automobile tourism to the deserts and the great mountains of the Southwest. These developments in turn, led to rapid increases in urbanization and rising demand for water and other resources over much of southern Arizona, including the upper San Pedro Valley.

A large and growing military base, Fort Huachuca specializes in electronic systems and houses thousands of troops with more planned for the future. Fort Huachuca borders on the rapidly growing city of Sierra Vista on the western side of the San Pedro Valley. Sierra Vista was almost non-existent in 1958 and exceeds 20,000 today. Other nearby growing areas include the town of Benson, which is close to the north border of the San Pedro NCA. Its damaging impacts on the floodplain, the riparian habitat, and other parts of the valley stand in strong contrast to the protected areas in the NCA to the south.

Today, large numbers of cattle and other stock have led to direct competition for range with antelope, deer, and other animals. Ranching resulted in extremely hard times for the grizzly bear, puma, jaguar, bob-cat, and other predators, for they have been seen as threats to domestic stock. Extensive campaigns to eliminate them were undertaken beginning in the late nineteenth century. These led to government hunting, poisoning, and other efforts in the 1920s and 1930s. As a result, animals such as the wolf, grizzly, and jaguar have been completely or nearly eliminated from the area. As recently as 1996, however, a jaguar was photographed by hunting guides in one major mountain range east of the San Pedro watershed, the Peloncillo Mountains on the New Mexico–Arizona border just north of the Mexican line (Brown and Gonzales, 2001: 1).

Other exploitive activities such as lumbering and clearing of vegetation were wide-ranging by the mid- to late nineteenth century because of the need for wood for mining, railroad, and other construction, as well as for use in making charcoal and other fuel for mining, industrial, and domestic purposes. Extensive areas were cut-over, although, in this case, considerable reforestation has taken place as a result of measures such as the creation of National Forests and other protected areas to conserve trees, control run-off, and protect water supply. The establishment of the San Pedro National Conservation Areas (NCA) itself is a recent expression of attempts to protect the environment, reduce destructive exploitation, and develop more sustainably. Much has been done through the NCA to protect and restore plant and animal habitat within its borders.

PLANNING FOR CONSERVATION AND SUSTAINABLE USE

What is known today as "active conservation management" is practised in the NCA. This includes allowing wild fires to burn to some extent without attempts to extinguish them. It also includes some use of controlled burns to limit the growth of mesquite and other vegetation that has encroached on grassland areas. Certain indigenous animals are also being re-introduced, including the beaver. The fur trapper James Battie reported that, as a result of trapping by himself and others, this animal has been removed from the lower part of the San Pedro near its entrance to the Gila, by the late 1830s (Bronitsky and Merritt, 1986: 273). He probably was referring to the commercial extinction of the animal in the sense that it no longer paid to hunt it in terms of the costs and benefits of Battie's time. As a result of long-continued trapping, drainage of wetlands, dynamiting of dams and habitat, the beaver had virtually disappeared from the lower San Pedro NCA by the 1920s (Hanson, 2001: 123). It has been re-introduced there in recent years.

Such restoration measures are controversial, even within the conservation community. For example, to allow wild fire and take the risk of the escape of a controlled burn could lead to damage or destruction of riparian forests and shrub communities that have developed along the river since the creation of the NCA in 1988. The re-introduction of the beaver also poses a threat to this riparian community and especially to cottonwood and sycamore because the beaver tends to fell such trees in large numbers for its use in building dams and houses and for food.

I observed the extensive felling of trees bordering a pool in an old gravel pit on the San Pedro floodplain in April, 2002. Such pools can be vestiges of former wetlands known as '*cienegas*,' which reportedly were very extensive along the river in earlier Spanish and American times. To restore fire or beaver under such circumstances is risky. Such situations seem to call for an adaptive management approach of the type advocated by Holling and his associates (Gunderson et al., 1995). In such an approach, selected policies and practices are pursued on an experimental basis and are carefully monitored and assessed for their effects before final decisions are made. To follow such an approach in the San Pedro NCA may, however, be difficult because of staff and budget shortages. Collaborative efforts involving the universities, colleges, schools, and volunteers from the Friends of the NCA or other volunteer organizations would seem promising here.

Growing use of groundwater as well as drainage and other activities have reportedly led to reductions in the water table as well as changes in surface run-off (Anonymous, 2000). These changes have contributed to the loss of *cienegas*. Few of these wetlands now remain, one being a Research Area established by the BLM in the NCA near St. David. Interest in conserving and restoring the *cienegas* as "natural sponges," in order to reduce the rates of run-off and other hazards such as floods, encounters challenges. A major challenge is the downcutting that has occurred in many stream valleys of the San Pedro and other parts of the Southwest, mainly since the late nineteenth century. Prior to that time, relatively few *arroyos* apparently could be found in the study area. Vegetation patterns also seem to have been quite different than now, with much less mesquite or scrub desert, fewer trees along the streams including the main stem of the San Pedro, and more grassland and open country. Considerable evidence is available to suggest that such changes have mainly occurred in the region since the 1880s (Bahre, 1991).

Various causes have been put forward for these changes, including overgrazing of the ranges, removal of tree cover for fuel and other purposes, climate changes, drainage, reduction in wild fires, and elimination of beaver. Another possible cause that does not appear to have received much attention is earthquakes and tectonic activity. A major quake is known to have occurred in 1887, exceeding 7.5 on the Richter scale, and apparently causing uplift and earth movement over a large area. Overall, however, it seems unlikely that any one of these changes is alone responsible for downcutting and other changes in stream patterns in the study area. More likely, the changes interact with one another in some poorly understood way.

Two other fundamental points should be made before concluding this chapter. The first involves the basic assumptions and strategy upon which ecosystem or landscape management of the San Pedro Riparian NCA is to be based, particularly with regard to vegetation. Historic analysis shows that the current riparian forest and shrub vegetation that has developed to a considerable degree since the creation of the NCA in 1988 is different that an earlier nineteenth-century landscape dominated by grasslands and related plant communities along the main stream. As noted previously, to introduce active conservation management based on the idea of a return to that earlier landscape would mean reversing the protectionist policy that has led to the growth of the present gallery forest as well as the rich habitat for resident and migratory birds and other fauna so valued by local people and other visitors today. At least one prominent conservationist in the area has raised this problem and has argued for conservation of the present landscape while cautioning about the effects of burning and beaver restoration (Hanson, 2001).

The second fundamental point is that the major challenge to the health of the San Pedro Riparian NCA and surrounding areas today is urban and military development in the Sierra Vista–Fort Huachuca area along the west side of the river, as well as growing settlements in other parts of the valley. These developments will continue to consume large amounts of groundwater since precipitation and run-off in the area are insufficient to meet the demand. Lowering of the water table is recognized as a problem. Continued development poses a risk to the flow of groundwater to the San Pedro River and so to the maintenance of the riparian ecosystem. With leadership from the BLM, a committee of regional interests has been working for a balanced and sustainable approach to this ultimate water challenge. Commitment to growth continues to be very strong, however, for example, the Garrison commander at Fort Huachuca outlined plans for very large-scale expansion of the military over a seven-year period beginning in 2002 (Spinks, 2002: 1).

IMPLICATIONS FOR PLANNING

The San Pedro Riparian National Conservation Area is highly significant for national and cultural heritage and related conservation, education, research, recreation, tourism, and other purposes. Some of the major reasons for this significance are:

1) The highly complex geologic history and diversity of sedimentary, metamorphic, and volcanic rocks and associated land forms, notably the highly faulted and pronounced basin and range topography.

2) A series of recent sediments, terraces, playas, and other landforms, which provide an unusual record of geologic, climatic, vegetation, animal, and other changes resulting from the advance and retreat of northern and alpine glaciers during the last several million years.

3) A complex desert flora and fauna consisting predominantly of Sonoran vegetation exhibiting high diversity on at least a national scale, as well as breeding, migratory, and wintering habitat vital to the survival of some four hundred species of birds, numerous species of reptiles, and other life. In terms of species richness of mammals, the San Pedro Riparian Natural Conservation Area is considered to be unsurpassed for any landscape of similar size in the United States.

4) The San Pedro Valley is possibly the most significant archaeological area in North America, with four Paleo-Indian sites dating from approximately 11,000 BP in or close to the NCA. The archaeological and historic record reveals traces of many indigenous cultures and peoples up to the Spanish, Mexicans, and Americans of more recent centuries. The NCA and nearby areas are very rich in cultural diversity.

5) The San Pedro Riparian National Conservation Area and surrounding country contain an unusual comprehensive record of the Post-Pleistocene evolution of a changing natural landscape and the complex array of

effects that humans appear to have had on that landscape. Early changes include: the extinction of the mammoth and other Pleistocene fauna; vegetation changes through climate change; human use of fire; collecting and gathering; incipient agriculture and the introduction of exotic plants such as maize. Later changes and effects include: accelerated erosion and gullying; changes in sedimentation and landforms through flood farming, irrigation, and water diversion; introduction of numerous European plants and animals; heavy livestock grazing and associated vegetation change; lumbering and deforestation; drainage of wetlands; gravel and other mining and habitat disturbance. Recent increases in recreation, tourism, retirement and military facilities, and urbanization have led to habitat fragmentation and rising pressures on surface and groundwater.

6) Some attempts have been made to counteract these changes and effects, a recent example being the San Pedro Riparian Natural Conservation Area. The NCA was established in 1988 to protect rare riparian habitat by controlling livestock grazing, gravel mining, housing developments, and other exploitive uses of the San Pedro floodplain and adjoining terraces while principally providing for hiking, birding, and other forms of low-tech recreation and tourism. A main goal was nature conservation and some success has been achieved through protection of riparian forests and other vegetation as well as bird and other habitat. The planning implications of these changes and associated conservation efforts are highly significant and include:

a. Undertaking more detailed monitoring, assessment, and reporting of the effects of the NCA and disseminating the results on a widespread regional, national, and international basis. The success of the NCA to date makes it a useful example for conservation programs in other riparian areas and in both dry and humid regions.

b. Reviewing and strengthening the NCA and extending the concept to other rare and threatened riparian systems in Arizona and other parts of the southwestern deserts in the United States and Mexico.

c. Dealing with current questions associated with an active conservation planning and management approach, such as controlled burns and beaver re-introduction, through an adaptive management approach and close interaction and consultation with citizens who can supplement the knowledge, values, and resources of the BLM.

d. Building natural corridors and linkages with significant surrounding habitats such as the Huachuca Mountains and continuing efforts to extend principles and programs associated with the NCA across the border into Mexico.

e. Considering working to have the NCA designated as a World Heritage Site because of its uniqueness and diversity geologically, biologically and culturally.

Some moves have already been made in these directions. As early as 1989 a San Pedro Riparian Management Plan was introduced by BLM. The plan involved some consultation with the public about the selection of one of four major alternatives. These alternatives were very general, ranging from relatively strict conservation management to heavy emphasis on recreation and tourism. The selected alternatives involved balancing resource protection and public use of the San Pedro NCA area. The Environmental Impact Statement (EIS) prepared for the proposed planning alternatives contains numerous comments and criticisms of the plan and the preferred alternatives, mainly from citizens.

The preferred alternative of the NCA office included a number of actions aimed at areas of major concern such as recreation, water, wildlife, soils, and the watershed. These actions were preparatory in nature or are guidelines or statements of principle. For example, the wildlife actions included inventory of terrestrial and aquatic plants and monitoring to determine the condition and status of wildlife and their habitat (BLM, 1989: 2). The planned actions also included: allowing commercial uses only if compatible with the management of the

San Pedro; developing interpretive displays and facilities; restricting campfires to designated locations; and developing a limited number of campgrounds. It has not been possible to assess the implementation and effects of such actions for this study. To do so would be difficult in any event because of their general nature, which leaves considerable discretion with the management agency, BLM.

Since the creation of the NCA and the beginning of planning, water conservation and use have become major, if not the major issues in the NCA and surrounding areas. In this context, it is clear that the growth of military activities, urbanization, and settlement pose significant threats to availability of water for use, not only by humans, but by all life in the region. It has also become obvious that the future of water as a resource and as an essential element in maintaining ecosystems is outside of the control of BLM, any other management agency, or landowners. Much of the water needed to maintain the San Pedro River and the NCA, originates via surficial or groundwater flows from surrounding areas. And agencies and owners of these surrounding areas are also affected by the use of water by their neighbours.

Such interrelationships led to the formation of the Upper San Pedro Partnership in the late 1990s. The partnership was formed to facilitate and implement sound water resource management and conservation strategies in the Sierra Vista Sub-Watershed of the San Pedro River. The partnership is a consortium of agencies that own land or control land or water use in this Sub-Watershed. It also includes agencies that can provide significant resources to help the partnership attain its purposes. Fourteen agencies are part of the partnership and include Cochise County, Sierra Vista and other local organizations, the Arizona Department of Water Resources and other state agencies, the Bureau of Land Management, Fort Huachuca and other federal organizations, and the Nature Conservancy, an NGO. The partnership reflects the interests of a range of organizations operating at local to national scales. The partnership involves combined top-down–bottom-up approach, with a focus on community and citizen involvement.

The partnership has only existed for a few years and it is early to evaluate its progress. The first priority of the partnership is the development of what at times is called a Water Resources Plan and at other times an Upper San Pedro Conservation Plan. The Conservation Plan involves three broad strategies: reducing human and natural water consumption to the minimum necessary to meet the needs of people and nature; reclaiming used water or effluent; and improved rainfall harvesting techniques (Anonymous, 2000).

Further research is needed to ascertain how the partnership and plan have worked to date and what the major challenges are. Two aspects of the work of the partnership deserve special mention at this time, however. One is the growing use of an experimental or adaptive management approach to water policies and actions. Pilot projects on testing and monitoring are included in planning (Anonymous, 2000).

Another potentially very significant aspect of the partnership's approach is linking water conservation and use with wildlife conservation, principally through the work of an Open Space Sub-Committee. An Open Space program is seen as contributing both to conserving water resources and in providing essential natural links or corridors between the nearby mountains and the San Pedro River. Such linkages are seen as facilitating wildlife migration, conserving habitat, and preserving the social values in the area (Anonymous, n.d.: 11). In adopting this approach, the partnership is explicitly linking the traditional field of water resources management with the traditional field of wildlife management in the context of a broad ecosystem approach.

NOTES

1   Adapted from J.G. Nelson, "Landscape Change, Land Use History and Planning for the San Pedro Riparian National Conservation Area, Arizona, USA." In *Parks and Protected Areas Research in Ontario 2002*, ed. C. Lemieux et al., 127–152. Parks Research Forum of Ontario, University of Waterloo, Waterloo, Ontario, 2002.

REFERENCES

Amann, Jr., A.W., J.V. Bezy, R. Ratkevitch, and M.W. Witkind. 1998. *Ice Age Animals of the San Pedro River Valley, Southeastern Arizona.* Tucson: Arizona Geological Survey.

Anonymous. n.d. Upper San Pedro Partnership: Organization Structure. BLM, Sierra Vista, AZ.

Anonymous. 1982. Issue on Archaeology. *Cochise Quarterly* 12(2).

Anonymous. 2000. Upper San Pedro Partnership Semi Annual Report. N.p.

Bahre, C.J. 1991. *A Legacy of Change: Historic Human Impact on Vegetation in the Arizona Borderlands.* Tucson: University of Arizona Press.

Bannon, J.F. 1974. *The Spanish Borderlands Frontier 1513–1821.* History of the American Frontier, ed. R.A. Billington. Albuquerque: University of New Mexico Press.

Bastedo, J., J.G. Nelson, and J.B. Theberge. 1984. "An ecological approach to resource survey and planning for environmentally significant areas: The ABC method." *Environmental Management* 8(2): 125–134.

Bennett, P.S., R.R. Johnson, and M.R. Kunzmann. 1996. *An Annotated List of Vascular Plants of the Chiricahua Mountains, Swisshelm Mountains, Chiricahua National Monument and Fort Bowie National Historic Site.* Special Report No. 12. United States Geological Survey, Biological Resources Division, Co-operative Park Studies Unit. Tucson: School of Renewable Resources, University of Arizona.

Bezy, J.V. 2001. *Rocks in the Chiricahua National Monument and the Fort Bowie National Historic Site.* Arizona Geological Survey. Down-to-Earth 11. Arizona Geological Survey. Tucson, AZ.

Bronitsky, G., and J.D. Merritt. 1986. *The Archaeology of Southeast Arizona: A Class I Cultural Resource Inventory.* Cultural Resources Series No. 2. Phoenix: Bureau of Land Management.

Brown, D., and C.A. Gonzales Lopez. 2001. *Borderland Jaguars.* Salt Lake City: University of Utah Press.

Bureau of Land Management – U.S. Department of the Interior. n.d. Empire Cienega Resource Conservation Area. Bureau of Land Management. Tucson Resource Areas. Tucson, AZ.

Bureau of Land Management – U.S. Department of the Interior. n.d. Fairbank Historic Townsite – U.S. Department of the Interior. San Pedro Riparian National Conservation Area. Sierra Vista, AZ.

Bureau of Land Management – U.S. Department of the Interior. n.d. Hereford Bridge Access Point. Bureau of Land Management. San Pedro Riparian National Conservation Area. Sierra Vista, AZ.

Bureau of Land Management – U.S. Department of the Interior. n.d. Lehner-Mammoth Kill Site. Bureau of Land Management San Pedro Riparian National Conservation Area. Sierra Vista, AZ.

Bureau of Land Management – U.S. Department of the Interior. n.d. Millville and Charleston. Bureau of Land Management. San Pedro Riparian National Conservation Area. Sierra Vista, AZ.

Bureau of Land Management – U.S. Department of the Interior. n.d. Murray Springs Clovis Site. San Pedro Riparian National Conservation Area. Sierra Vista, AZ.

Bureau of Land Management – U.S. Department of the Interior. n.d. Presidio Santa Cruz de Terrenate. Bureau of Land Management San Pedro Riparian Conservation Area. Sierra Vista, AZ.

Bureau of Land Management – U.S. Department of the Interior. n.d. St. David Cienega. Bureau of Land Management. San Pedro Riparian Natural Conservation Area. Sierra Vista, AZ.

Bureau of Land Management – U.S. Department of the Interior. n.d. San Pedro House Trails. Bureau of Land Management. San Pedro Riparian National Conservation Area. Sierra Vista, AZ.

Bureau of Land Management – U.S. Department of the Interior. 1989. San Pedro Riparian Management Plan and Environmental Impact Statement. Safford District, Safford, AZ.

Callender, J.F., J.C. Wilt, and R.E. Clemens, eds. 1978. *Land of Cochise, Southeastern Arizona*. New Mexico Geological Society in co-operation with the Arizona Geological Society. 29th Field Conference. Nov. 9–11, 1978.

Coney, P.J. 1978. "The plate tectonic setting of southeastern Arizona." In *Land of Cochise, Southeastern Arizona*, ed. Callender et al., 285–290. New Mexico Geological Society.

Cornett, J.W. 2000. *Indian and Desert Animals*. Palm Springs, CA: Natural Trails Press.

De Golia, J. 1993. *Fire: A Force of Nature: The Story Behind the Scenery*. Las Vegas, NV: KC Publications.

Friends of the San Pedro River, n.d. San Pedro Riparian Conservation Area. Sierra Vista, AZ.

Friends of the San Pedro. 2002. San Pedro. *River Roundup* 15(2).

Gunderson, L.H., C.S. Holling, and S.S. Light, eds. 1995. *Barriers and Bridges to the Renewal of Ecosystems and Institutions*. New York: Columbia University Press.

Hanson, R.B. 2001. *The San Pedro River: A Discovery Guide*. Tucson: University of Arizona Press.

Haury, E., W.E.B. Gayles, W.W. Wasley, E. Anteus, and J.F. Lance. 1959. "The Lehner Mammoth Site." *American Antiquity* 25(1): 1–41.

Heald, M.F. 1981. *The Chiracahua Mountains Formerly: The Sky Islands.* Tucson: University of Arizona Press.

Kurdeka, J.L. 1982. "Traces of Early Man in Cochise County with Bibliography." *Cochise Quarterly* 12(2): 3–15.

Larson, P. 1977. *The Deserts of the Southwest.* A Sierra Club Naturalist's Guide. San Francisco: Sierra Club Books.

Leaming, G.F. 1998. *The Story of Mining in Bisbee.* Marana, AZ: Free Geos Library.

Leopold, L., ed. 1953. *Round River: From the Journals of Aldo Leopold.* Oxford: Oxford University Press.

Martin, P.S., and R.G. Klein. 1984. *Quaternary Extinctions.* Tucson: University of Arizona Press.

McMahon, J.A. 1992. *Deserts.* New York: Alfred A. Knopf.

Meyer, M.C. 1984. *Water in the Hispanic Southwest: A Social and Legal History, 1550–1850.* Tucson: University of Arizona Press.

Nabhan, G.P., and A.R. Holdsworth. 1998. *State of the Desert Biome: Uniqueness, Biodiversity, Threats and the Adequacy of Protection in the Sonoran Bioregion.* Tucson, AZ: The Wildlands Project.

Schreiber, J.F., Jr. 1978. "Geology of the Willcox Playa, Cochise Country, Arizona." In *Land of Cochise, Southeastern Arizona,* ed. J.F. Callender, J.C. Wilt, and R.E. Clemens. New Mexico Geological Society in co-operation with the Arizona Geological Society. 29th Field Conference. Nov. 9–11, 1978.

Schwantes, Carlos A., ed. 1992. *Bisbee Urban Outpost on the Frontier.* Tucson: University of Arizona Press.

Shreve, F., and I.L. Wiggins. 1946. *Vegetation and Flora of the Sonoran Desert.* 2 vols. Stanford: Stanford University Press.

Smithsonian Migratory Bird Center. n.d. *Western Rivers: Magnets for Migrants.* Washington, D.C.: Smithsonian Migratory Bird Center, National Zoo.

Spinks, Lee M. 2002. "Garrison commander outlines seven-year expansion proposal." *Mountain View News* 9(25). Sierra Vista, AZ. March 27, 2002, p. I.

Stewart, Janet Ann. n.d. *Arizona Ranch Houses, Southern Territorial Styles, 1867–1900.* Historical Monograph No. 2. Tucson: Arizona Historical Society.

Walker, P., and Don Bufkin. 1979. *Historical Atlas of Arizona.* Norman: University of Oklahoma Press.

13

1998

FAIRY AND PENINSULA LAKES, ONTARIO, CANADA: LAND-USE HISTORY, LANDSCAPE CHANGE, AND PLANNING[1]

P.L. Lawrence, J.G. Nelson, A. Skibicki, and K. Wilcox

INTRODUCTION

Fairy and Peninsula Lakes have experienced numerous ongoing and imperfectly understood use changes since European settlement in the 1800s. The direct and indirect effects of these land-use changes are thought to have been considerable but are also incompletely understood.

This study was undertaken as an initial step in analyzing and interpreting land-use changes and their impacts on the physical state of the two lakes and their near-shore environments (Figure 13.1). The aim was to organize information from various historical, scientific, economic, and other sources and to present it in accessible ways for concerned government and non-government organizations, groups, and individuals. The idea was to link or integrate geological, hydrological, biological, economic, land-use, and other information to stimulate the diverse interests of the various stakeholders.

The project was a fundamental part of the 1990s Fair and Peninsula Lake Assessment Plan initiated by the Ontario Ministry of Natural Resources as a basis for improved planning and management of the Fairy Peninsula Lake area. The objectives of the assessment were: 1) to establish baseline data for research design and future monitoring; 2) to

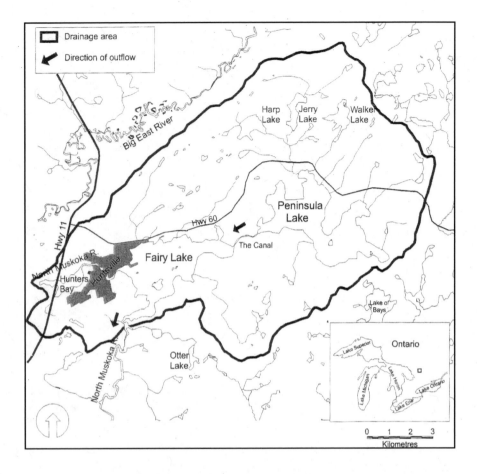

Figure 13.1   Fairy and Peninsula Lakes, Ontario, Canada

study relationships, such as pathways and processes between the riparian zone and Fairy and Peninsula Lakes; and 3) to establish methodologies for assessment of the impacts of sediment on the two lakes (Cornelisse and Evans, 1999).

ABC METHOD

Our study of land-use history, landscape change, and planning of the two lakes was undertaken as an underpinning for and a contribution to the larger Ministry of Natural Resources (MNR) study. As a fundamental exercise in linking human and natural changes, our study lent itself readily to the application of the cross-disciplinary ABC method. Information for the project was collected from an array of published and unpublished documents and reports, interviews, and numerous public meetings with different stakeholders. The following summery generally follows the ABC method. Only selected illustrative maps could be included because of space and other constraints.

Abiotic Resources

The bedrock formations in the vicinity of the lakes are of Precambrian age (3.7 billion to 570 million years ago) (Hewitt, 1967) (Figure 13.2). Few economically exploitable mineral deposits have been identified within the area. Industrial minerals of some interest include diatomite, mica, feldspar, garnet, copper, and gold, but no large deposits of value have ever been discovered (Springer, 1978; Villard et al., 1984). The area does contain valued deposits of flagstone, which is used in the construction industry. Present mining activity is confined to industrial minerals, building stone, road stone, clay products, and sand and gravel.

The area was subjected during the Pleistocene (1.8 million to 11,000 years ago) to major advances and retreats of the Laurentian ice sheets (Barnett, 1992). Thicknesses of glacial deposits vary greatly throughout the region with many upland areas having only thin or no glacial till. Following ice retreat, the area was submerged under the waters of glacial Lake Algonquin, an ancestral body of water of Lake Huron and other Great Lakes. Lake Algonquin drained from the area about 10,400 years ago (Warner, 1978). Following Lake Algonquin, the area was characterized by periodic rising of water levels and submerging of the land surface leading to flooding, inundation, and lacustrine deposition. Glacial delta deposits were laid down near the Big East River, north of Huntsville (Warner, 1978).

The physiography of the area can be characterized as of rough relief with rounded knobs and ridges 15 to 60 m high with occasional ridges up to 150 m in elevation (Chapman and Putnam, 1984). The

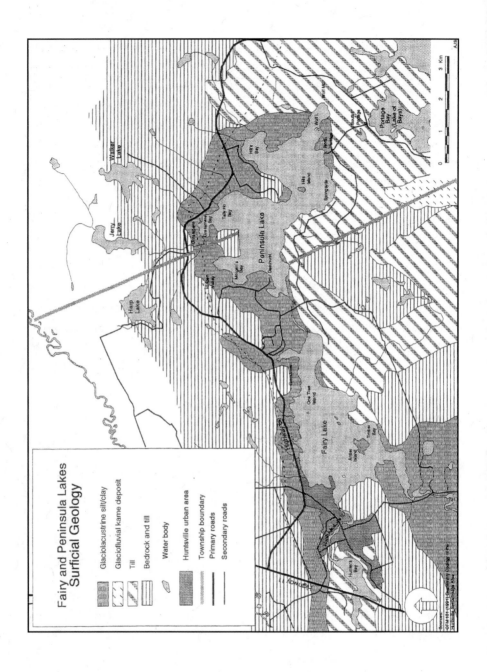

Figure 13.2   Surficial Geology

soils are generally shallow, stony, sandy, and acidic, with frequent bedrock outcrops. A few short discontinuous moraine deposits of sandy till and glaciofluvial sand and gravel occur north of Huntsville. Valley and river beds contain outwash sands and gravels. Soil potential for agriculture in the region is generally low (Classes 4–7 of the Canada Land Inventory).

Biotic Resources

The area is considered to contain some of the most productive mixed forests in central Ontario (District of Muskoka, 1989). Tolerant hardwoods, such as sugar maple and yellow birch, are dominant over much of the area. Poorly drained areas tend to be dominated by black ash, red maple, eastern white cedar, white spruce, black spruce, balsam fir, and tamarack. Conifers, such as spruce and balsam fir, are found mostly in lowland areas between hardwood covered hills. Eastern hemlock has been shown to serve as shelter habitat for white-tailed deer along lakes and major streams and is seen as a limiting factor for deer (District of Muskoka, 1989). During the past forty years many locations around the lakes, mostly old and abandoned farm lands, have been planted and reforested with eastern white pine. As well, many old abandoned fields have succeeded to mature hardwood forest stands, thus adding to the area's forest cover.

Figure 13.3 shows areas of wildlife habitat. Both the Ontario Ministry of Natural Resources and the District of Muskoka have identified white-tailed deer wintering areas (District of Muskoka, 1989). Mapping completed in the early 1970s for the Canada Land Inventory (CLI) identified and ranked areas in terms of habitat suitability for ungulates and for waterfowl. Although the area around the lakes is considered to have generally strong limitations for the production of ungulates, major river valleys offer somewhat better production capabilities and are superior to upland areas. Both Fairy and Peninsula Lakes are considered to have severe limitations for the production of waterfowl due to the depth of the waters and the steepness and drop-off of the nearshore, which offers no shallow areas upon which extensive wetlands may form.

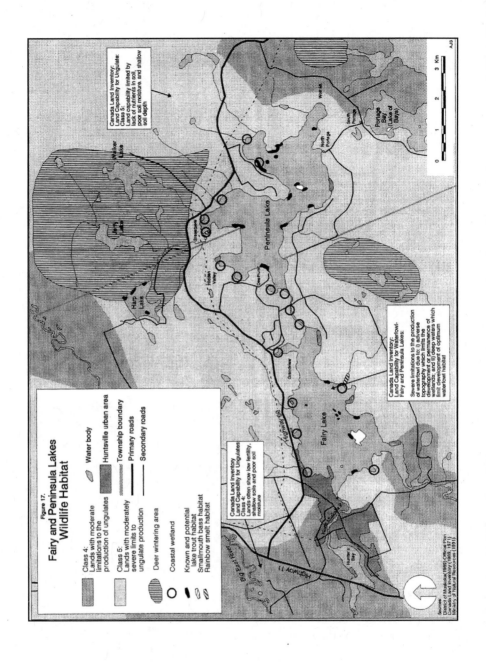

Figure 13.3   Wildlife Habitat

The shorelines of the lakes were extensively cleared for agricultural, recreational, and urban development. This clearing undoubtedly resulted in increased erosion and sedimentation in the lakes, although the extent to which this has occurred is not known. Increases in sediment in the lakes could have resulted in adverse effects on wetlands, fish spawning areas, and water quality. Clearing of tree fall and other debris in nearshore waters could have reduced bass and other fish habitat considerably over the years.

Fish species recorded in Fairy Lake and Peninsula Lake include lake trout, brook trout, lake whitefish, lake herring, white sucker, longnose sucker, smelt, northern pike, smallmouth bass, yellow perch, trout perch, bullhead, blacknose shiner, bluntnose shiner, bluntnose minnow, and golden shiner. Eastern parts of Peninsula Lake are thought to be poor for lake trout production due to shallow depths, lower oxygen profiles, and comparatively warmer waters (Foy, 1991). MNR (1991) observed no lake trout on shoals during a 1990 survey. Stocking of fish in the lakes to supplement recreational angler demands began as early as 1901 with the introduction of smallmouth bass into Fairy Lake. Declining fish stocks were noticed around the turn of the century and may have been caused by heavy recreational fishing pressures (Peninsula Lake Association, 1993) as well as damage to habitat. Lake trout began to be regularly stocked in both lakes beginning in 1917–18. Other stocked species included brook trout and rainbow trout (Allen, 1995).

In assessing the impacts on water quality in Fairy and Peninsula Lakes, critical factors affecting phytoplankton and macrobenthos have to be identified. Of these limiting factors, sedimentation and nutrient enrichment are expected to have the largest effect on water quality, mainly because of their reduction of sunlight penetration and the resulting effect on macrophytes and other organisms. In this respect, the widespread removal of forest and other protective vegetation along much of the lakeshore zones has caused changes in water quality and fish and wildlife habitat, although the amount of this change is unknown.

Cultural Resources

The area was extensively used by Native peoples and fur trappers. Shorelines along Peninsula Lake were sites of seasonal hunting camps by Native peoples (Peninsula Lake Association, 1993). The extent and impact of pre-European occupation by Native peoples in the area is uncertain and not well understood. Fairy and Peninsula Lakes were first officially opened for European settlement in 1868, although several small agricultural homesteads were already in existence to the west of Fairy Lake. French and other fur traders also had been in the area decades before this time. An early map from 1879 showed that most of the land around the lakes was in some form of private ownership and land clearance was likely being undertaken in many of these areas, although the extent is not well known (Research Committee of the Muskoka Pioneer Village, 1986).

Use of the land for agriculture began to decline around the 1880s, barely twenty years after initial settlement. This was due mostly to the harsh, rocky nature of the land and small economic returns. Many cleared areas were left abandoned and allowed to revert to their original forest growth. With the disappearance of many farms, numerous grist mills were closed down. Some farmsteads were converted to inns and hotels to cater to the increasing popularity of Muskoka to tourists and outdoor recreationalists.

Tourism activities around the two lakes increased when the Northern Railway reached Huntsville in 1886 and a canal was dredged between Fairy and Peninsula Lakes in 1888. In addition to the new forestry operations, the diversity of industry in Huntsville was increasing. A leather tannery was opened in 1891 and a hardwood products manufacturing plant in 1900. With the increase in industrial activities and related population growth, water quality problems became more apparent around the turn of the century. To address the problems with the drinking water supply, a water purification plant was built around 1910 (Hutcheson, 1972).

Cottage growth around the lakes grew substantially from the 1890s to the 1920s. Pen Lake Farms golf course opened in 1912 and soon became a social gathering place for cottagers living around Peninsula Lake.

Personal motor boats grew in use and gave cottagers greater mobility on the lakes. Automobiles enabled access to cottage lots from county roads rather than solely by boat. By the late 1930s, tourists were coming more by car than by express train, and municipalities were faced with improving road conditions for motorized traffic. Float planes began to appear in the mid-1920s, enabling visitors to come to area resorts from ever more remote locations (Peninsula Lake Association, 1993).

Muskoka's image as an international resort began to change in the 1940s and 1950s. More and more, it became a "backyard playground" for "working class" families from Southern Ontario (Warankie, 1990). Cottages were purchased or built for seasonal use by people driving up from Toronto and urban areas in Southern Ontario. The completion of Highway 11 in the early 1970s increased the ease with which families could commute from urban centres to the south.

Improved transportation links, hydro-electric power, and expanding municipal services resulted in the increased conversion of seasonal cottages to permanent year-round use during the 1960s and 1970s. Winterizing of cottages meant that septic systems reached their capacities much quicker. Septic systems operating during winter months also showed reduced efficiency due to slower breakdown of waste products. Operation of septic systems year-round also eliminated a period of "down-time" when septic systems could process wastes accumulated during the warmer seasons (Warankie, 1990).

The community of Hidden Valley was built during the 1960s and soon became the focus for resort expansion and recreational developments along the northwestern shoreline of Peninsula Lake. Hidden Valley Resort hotel was opened in 1968, representing an increase in the scale of resort establishments in the area. Inadequacies in the construction and supervision of a sewage lagoon system for the new resort resulted in the first major known water pollution from sewage effluents serving the area's resorts. The problem precipitated legal battles between residents, resort operators and the Ontario Ministry of the Environment (O'Keefe, 1978).

Older, more traditional resorts, such as Deerhurst and Grandview also began expanding, winterizing, and seeking a wider user clientele.

The introduction of winter activities such as skiing and snowmobiling has today placed year-round pressures on water quality and the environment. Lakeside lots on some of the more popular lakes in the District of Muskoka became difficult to purchase for most by the 1980s. Development pressures began on less prominent and less easily accessible lakes as average buyers sought more affordable second homes. The Town of Huntsville ensured a new stage of development with the extension of water and sewage services along Highway 60 to the lakes area in 1982. The servicing solved the sewage effluent problems associated with the Hidden Valley Resort Hotel but set the stage for an unprecedented of growth of resorts in this area.

The growth of the resorts coincided with an overall housing and development boom in the town of Huntsville in the mid- to late 1980s. The main areas of growth were north of town and along the Highway 60 corridor towards Grandview. Large condominium-centred communities were planned for the north shore of Fairy Lake. The high rate of growth and development placed pressures on the existing sewage treatment facility. In the late 1980s, regular overflows of plant effluent into the North Muskoka River were a common occurrence. The problem was compounded in the early 1990s when provincial funding for new municipal sewage facilities became uncertain. One result was numerous delays in the completion of Huntsville's new sewage treatment plant, which was finally finished in February 1995.

In recent years, a steady and considerable increase has occurred in urban, cottage, and resort land uses along the shorelines of Fairy and Peninsula Lakes shorelines, mostly at the expense of old farmlands but also forests and wetland (Figure 13.4). Of particular note has been the rapid development of recreational resorts in the western basin of Peninsula Lake with the expansion of golf and ski facilities. Most development was facilitated by expanding transportation networks and increasing municipal water and sewage services. Natural drainage along the shoreline was disrupted and habitat removed as a result of cottage, housing, and commercial developments. By 1987 to 1995, the majority of the north shore of Fairy and Peninsula Lakes consisted of housing or recreational developments. Extensive sections of the south shore and

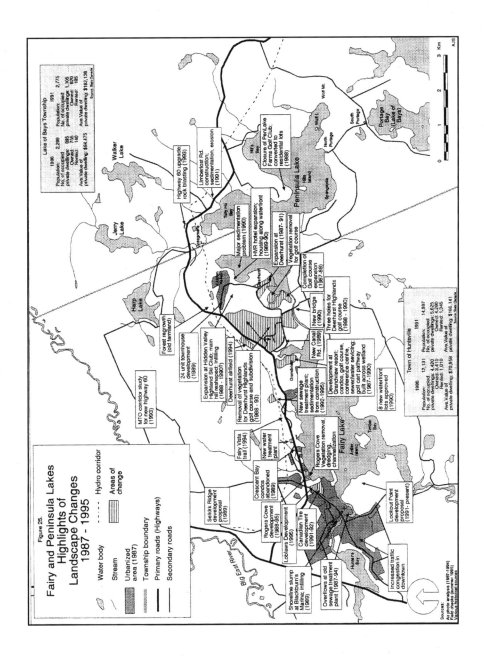

Figure 13.4   Highlights of Landscape Changes 1987–1995

the eastern end of Fairy Lake were occupied by seasonal residential cottages. The southeastern end of Peninsula Lake and some southern sections of Fairy Lake are the main undeveloped natural shorelines left along the lakes.

Significance and Constraints

In order to assist with community planning and decision-making, the results from the landscape history and land-use change analysis were studied in order to identify areas of significance and constraint for planning, management, and decision-making. In mapping significance, a combination of Abiotic, Biotic, and Cultural criteria were used:

- least developed areas from 1947 to 1995;
- rare features or process uncommon to the area (e.g., shore wetlands, geological features, habitat type);
- diverse areas of habitat or terrain type;
- productivity (i.e., areas more productive than surrounding lands for wildlife);
- significant habitat areas for wildlife;
- human heritage value (e.g., recreational value, historic value, possible aesthetic value);
- educational value; and
- social equity (e.g., public access to significant features and processes).

As shown in Figure 13.5, the least-developed areas or areas least affected by land-use changes include many areas inland from the lakes. Land-use changes have been most pronounced along the northern shore of Fairy Lake and the northwestern shore of Peninsula Lake. The least developed area along both shorelines is around Wolf Island and Wolf Mountain. Rare features found along the lakes include pockets of shoreline wetland. Such pockets are most common along the northern shorelines of both lakes and are quite productive in the range of animal and plant species they support. Many of the larger wetlands, such as those found around Grandview and Deerhurst Resorts, show a diverse

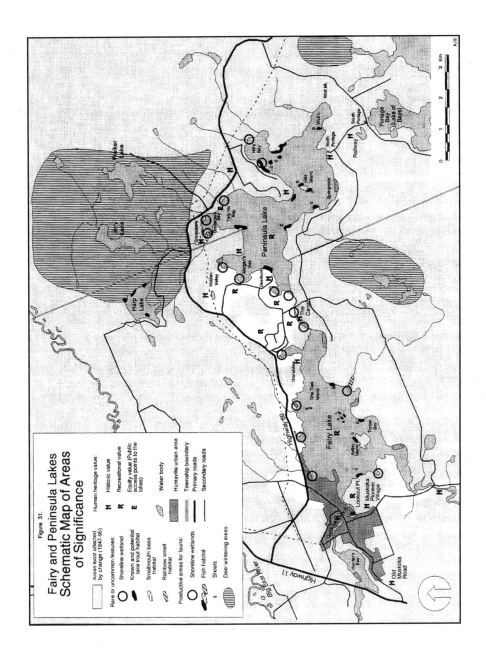

Figure 13.5   Areas of Significance

range of wildlife habitat and are important for birds, mammals, and other aquatic and terrestrial life.

Significant habitats for wildlife include shoals and other areas of known or potential lake trout habitat. Significant habitats for other fish species such as smallmouth bass and rainbow smelt are found along the shorelines or at the mouths of a number of tributary creeks. Within interior forests, three major white-tailed deer wintering areas have been identified by the MNR and the District of Muskoka. White-tailed deer are also known to use river, stream, and creek corridors as travel or movement corridors.

Areas showing significant human heritage value include historic sites such as the Muskoka Pioneer Village, the old Muskoka Road, the Brunel Lock and Dam, downtown Huntsville, the location of the old railroad between North Portage and South Portage, the Canal linking the two lakes, the older resorts in the area, and the communities of Hidden Valley, Grassmere, and Hillsdale. Areas of high recreational value include the lakes themselves, the resorts, and Lookout Point Park. Areas of high equity value include the two public docks on the lakes, which provide public access to these waters.

Constraints for planning serve to identify areas of most pronounced change as well as areas that may present the greatest challenge in planning for the ecological health and sustainability of these two water bodies. The criteria used to identify areas of constraints were:

- most developed areas from 1947 to 1994;
- areas of possible future growth or development;
- impacts on rare or uncommon natural features or processes;
- impacts on natural areas;
- areas of past and possible future sedimentation or erosional impact;
- limitations of land-use policies and programs; and
- lack of information or knowledge of features or processes.

Urban growth associated with the Town of Huntsville has been most pronounced along the northern Fairy Lake shoreline. Areas of possible future growth and expansion include possible urban growth to the

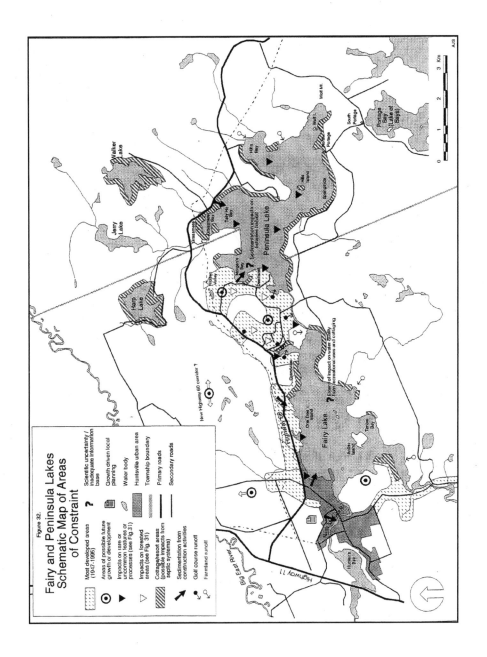

Figure 13.6   Areas of Constraint

north of Huntsville, subdivision developments south of Lookout Point, further growth and expansion of resort facilities in Hidden Valley, and a possible new four-lane highway route through the northern part of the study area (Figure 13.6).

Impacts on rare or uncommon natural features and on natural areas more generally, such as shoreline wetlands, and fish habitats, are of various types. Construction activities associated with land uses and human activities have resulted in sedimentation, erosion, and other adverse effects on water quality and fisheries habitat. The numerous cottages and resort units, which line the shorelines of both lakes and other tributary water bodies such as Harp Lake and Walker Lake, serve as sources of pollution from substandard septic systems. Farmlands close to the shore could also be sources of run-off and soil erosion into the lakes.

Other major constraints include the lack of information on the physical state of the two lakes and uncertainty over the range and nature of human and natural processes, which affect such things as water quality and biological production. This scientific uncertainty is one factor that has tended to hinder the capabilities of area resource and land-use management agencies to address water quality problems on the lakes. As well, a major overall constraint to sustainable development in the area has been the pro-growth-driven planning agenda of local municipal governments.

CONCLUSIONS

Overall, the results of this study indicate that the traditional government-driven approach to planning and management has major challenges. These include the limited capacity of government departments in the face of the rising scale of growth and budget cuts as well as the theoretical, methodological, and funding limitations of science in dealing with the problems associated with such growth. On the other hand, it is clear that resort and commercial operators, local governments, cottagers, and other people have generally supported growth and development of one kind or another without sufficient understanding of or interest in the consequences. This study should help increase this understanding. Similar findings have been made about land-use, resource, and environmental challenges in other areas, and this has led to calls for an implementation of stronger private stewardship programs and more co-operative, civic activities among all stakeholders in the interests of sustainable development.

A clear need exists to adopt ecosystem management and sustainable development approaches to land-use planning in the area by all levels of government. This should entail the development of long-term growth strategies embodying a wide range of socio-economic and environmental concerns and involving a wide range of government agencies, non-government organizations, and citizens in goal definition, strategy formulation, and implementation.

Environmental monitoring and a regular State of the Lakes report are needed for the lakes. Such a report should focus on more than just reporting or water quality. Issues to be addressed include urban and rural growth, cumulative effects of ongoing and proposed developments on water quality, and the overall quality of life. Monitoring and reporting should assess current institutional arrangements used to control or influence growth and development impacts on the lakes. Issues need to be freely brought forth to stakeholders and interested members of the public so that new and innovative approaches may be taken, preferably those that combine traditional agency management mechanisms with private and local stewardship capabilities. Regular environmental monitoring and state of the lakes reports should lead to the development of a conservation strategy for the area.

NOTES

1   Adapted from A. Skibicki, J.G. Nelson, K. Wilcox, and P.L. Lawrence, *Assessing Environment and Development: Fairy and Peninsula Lakes 1995*. Heritage Resources Centre Technical Paper 13, University of Waterloo, Waterloo, Ontario, 1998.

REFERENCES

Allen, Y. 1995. *Timeline: Fairy and Peninsula Lakes*. Ontario Ministry of Natural Resources. Unpublished. Bracebridge, ON.

Barnett, P.J. 1992. "Quaternary Geology of Ontario." In *Geology of Ontario*, ed. P.C. Thurston, H.R. Williams, et al. Special Volume 4: 1011–1091. Toronto: Ontario Geological Survey.

Chapman, L.J., and D.F. Putnam. 1984. *The Physiography of Southern Ontario*. Special Volume 2. Toronto: Ontario Geological Survey.

Cornelisse, K.J., and D.O. Evans. 1999. *The Fairy and Peninsula Lakes Study, 1994–1998: Effects of Land Use on the Aquatic Ecosystem*. Final report for the Fairy and Peninsula Lakes Management Committee. Peterborough, ON: Ontario Ministry of Natural Resources.

Deyne, G. 1993. Background to the Development of a Request for Research Fairy and Peninsula Lake. Bracebridge, ON: Ontario Ministry of Natural Resources.

District Municipality of Muskoka. 1989. *Official Plan of the Muskoka District Area*. Bracebridge, ON.

District Municipality of Muskoka. 1995a. *State of the Lakes: Fairy Lake, Town of Huntsville*. Fact Sheet available at the District Office. Bracebridge, ON: District Municipality of Muskoka.

District Municipality of Muskoka. 1995b. *State of the Lakes: Peninsula Lake, Township of Lake of Bays*. Fact Sheet available at the District Office. Bracebridge, ON: District Municipality of Muskoka.

Foy, M. 1991. *An Evaluation of the Ontario Ministry of Natural Resources Document entitled: "Protection of Lake Trout Habitat Lakeshore Capacity Monitoring Program District Municipality of Muskoka Discussion Report."* Report produced for the District Municipality of Muskoka. King City, ON: LGL Ltd..

Hewitt, D.F. 1967. *Geology and Mineral Deposits of the Parry Sound-Huntsville Area*. Toronto: Ontario Department of Mines.

Hutcheson, G.F. 1972. *Heads and Tales*. Bracebridge, ON: Herald Gazette Press.

Ministry of Natural Resources (MNR). 1969. *Fairy Lake Bathymetry Map*. On file at Bracebridge District MNR.

Ministry of Natural Resources (MNR). 1970. *Peninsula Lake Bathymetry Map*. On file at Bracebridge District MNR.

Ministry of Natural Resources (MNR). 1991. *Protection of Lake Trout Habitat*. Lakeshore Capacity Monitoring Program District of Municipality of Muskoka. Discussion Report. Bracebridge Area Office.

Nelson, J.G., and R. Serafin. 1992. "Assessing biodiversity: A human ecological approach." *Ambio* 21(3): 212–218.

Nelson, J.G., P. Grigoriew, P.G.R. Smith, and J.B. Theberge. 1988. "The ABC resource survey method: The ESA concept and comprehensive land use planning and management." In *Landscape Ecology and Management*, ed. M.R. Moss. Proceedings of the First Symposium of the Canadian Society for Landscape Ecology and Management, 143–175. Montreal: Polyscience Publications.

O'Keefe, C.J. 1978. An evaluation of the Ontario approach to environmental assessment: The Hidden Valley experience, Huntsville, Muskoka. BES thesis in Geography. University of Waterloo, Waterloo.

Peninsula Lake Association. 1993. *Pen Lake.* Erin, ON: Boston Mills Press.

Research Committee of the Muskoka Pioneer Village. 1986. *Pictures from the Past: Huntsville – Lake of Bays.* Erin, ON: Boston Mills Press.

Skibicki, A., J.G. Nelson, P. Lawrence, and K. Wilcox. 1998. *Assessing Environment and Development: Fairy and Peninsula Lakes 1995.* Technical Paper 13. Waterloo: Heritage Resources Centre, University of Waterloo.

Springer, J. S. 1978. *Ontario Mineral Potential, Huntsville sheet, Districts of Parry Sound, Nipissing, Muskoka, and Counties of Haliburton and Hastings.* Scale 1:250,000. Toronto: Ontario Geological Survey.

Villard, D.J., R. Keevil, and A. Hogg. 1984. *The Gold Potential of the Huntsville-Parry Sound Area of Ontario.* Open File Report No. 5521. Toronto: Ontario Geological Survey.

Warankie, E.J. 1990. *Review of Waterfront and Seasonal Residential Development Policies in the Town of Huntsville.* BES thesis in Urban and Regional Planning. University of Waterloo, Waterloo.

Warner, B.G. 1978. *Origin and Depositional History of the East River Glacial Delta, Huntsville, Ontario.* BES thesis, Department of Geography, University of Waterloo, Waterloo.

14

2004

THE CARPATHIAN ECOREGION INITIATIVE:ASSESSING LARGE-SCALE LANDSCAPE PLANNING IN CENTRAL EUROPE[1]

J.G. Nelson

INTRODUCTION

In the 1990s the World Wide Fund for Nature (WWF) added a new ecoregional approach to its long-standing efforts to conserve nature. One of the areas that became an early focus of this approach was the Carpathian Mountain system, a lengthy multinational region of rugged peaks, rolling hills, valleys, and forests in central and Eastern Europe. This summary of a recent assessment of the planning of the ensuing Carpathian Ecoregion Initiative (CEI) begins with a brief description of the Carpathian system, organized in terms of the ABC Resource Survey Method. The ABC system is used as a framework for organizing, describing, and analyzing the varied information made available on the Carpathians through the CEI network as well as related field work and readings. The planning procedures used in developing the CEI were assessed in terms of planning theory, notably interactive and adaptive or civic planning (Hudson, 1979; Dempster and Nelson, 2001).

THE CARPATHIANS

The Alps are undoubtedly the most renowned mountain system in Europe. Yet the lesser-known Carpathians are worthy of equivalent, if not greater, recognition (CEI, 2001). This comparatively young (Tertiary) mountain system rises north of Vienna on the Danube River and extends in a great 1,500 km arc through the Czech Republic, Slovakia, Poland, Hungary, Ukraine, and Romania (Figure 14.1). The peak of the system is the high Tatras of Poland and Slovak, with Mt. Gerlach at 2,653 metres above sea level. The width of the system is about 250 km in the northwest, 100 to 120 km in Ukraine, and 340 km in the southeast, in Romania (Voloscuk, 1999: 9). Overall the Carpathians cover an area of about 210,000 square km, approximately five times greater than the area of Switzerland.

The mountains exhibit complex geology, magnificent scenery, vast tracts of forests and meadows, and a wealth of natural diversity (biodiversity) unparalleled in Europe. The mountains also have a rich human history and cultural heritage reflecting thousands of years of human interaction with the land. One significant manifestation of this is the extensive high grasslands and meadows created by clearing upper-level forests for sheep grazing since about the fifteenth century.

ABIOTIC RESOURCES

Climate

The climate of the Carpathians varies from west to east (Voloscuk, 1999). Maritime influences are stronger in the west, along with higher frequencies of cyclonic weather and storms. Continentality increases to the east, with distance from the moderating influence of the Atlantic, bringing decreases in precipitation and temperature. Mediterranean influences increase toward the south where a north–south seasonal shift in atmospheric pressure systems and weather patterns results in drier hotter summers with more anticyclonic activity and wetter cooler winters with westerly winds and cyclonic storms. Elevation, topography, aspect, slope, and other factors complicate these general climatic patterns. Broadly speaking, the mean July temperature in the western Carpathians is 19°C and in the southern Carpathians, 22°C. Precipitation generally

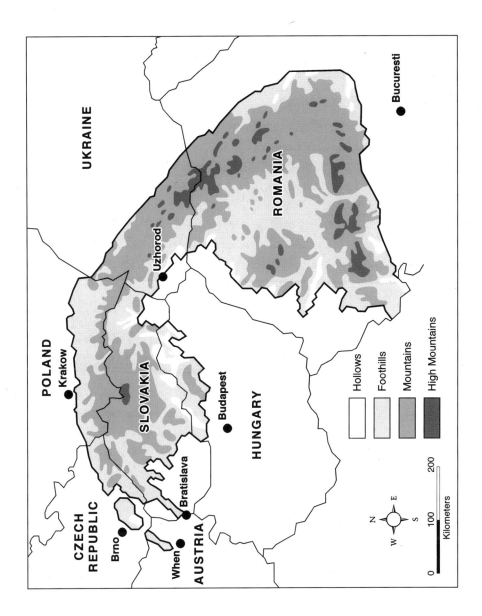

Figure 14.1   Landforms in the Carpathians

falls from an annual average of 2,000 mm in the west to 600 mm in the southeast.

Geology and Landforms

Formed primarily since the early Tertiary, approximately 70 million years ago, the Carpathians are comparatively young mountains (Voloscuk, 1999; CEI, 2001). Generally they rise to less than 2,000 metres, with only about 5 per cent extending above the tree-line. The mountains can be divided into the Western, Eastern, and Southern Carpathians. The Western Carpathians include areas such as the White Carpathians but can be divided structurally and lithologically into Outer, Central, and Inner Ranges (Figure 14.1).

The Outer Mountains are composed mainly of interbedded sandstones and shales known as "flysch." The Central Mountains consist of more crystalline igneous rocks such as the granites of the High Tatras. The mountains have been subject to intense glaciation, with numerous cirques, arretes, cols, and other landforms as well as more than a hundred tarns and glacial lakes. This is an area of rugged relief, magnificent scenery, numerous endemic species, and other features justifying the designation of the core of the High Tatras as two national parks straddling the Slovak and Polish border.

To the south the Inner Range of the Western Carpathians includes more limestone and dolomite and karst topography. Excellent examples are found in the Bukk National Park, Hungary and Slovak Karst Biosphere Reserve in Slovakia. These, and other karst areas, frequently contain large, extensive cave systems, festooned with stalagmites, stalactites, and travertine terraces and provide habitat for bats and other life. The nearby Polana Biosphere Reserve contains volcanic rocks left by Tertiary eruptions. Many areas are less than a thousand metres and grade south into the extensive plains or alfold of southern Slovakia and Hungary.

The Eastern Carpathians stretch from the borderlands of Poland and Slovakia through Ukraine into northern Romania. The Eastern Carpathians include a number of mountain groups, including the Bieszczady Mountains. These are located in a Polish National Park as well as being part of the trinational Eastern Carpathians Biosphere Reserve in Poland, Slovakia, and Ukraine. The Ukrainian part of the Eastern Carpathians is about 280 km long and consists mainly of sandstone and flysch, although volcanics, dolomites, limestones, and granites are also found here. Aside from the significance of their bedrock and landforms, the Eastern Carpathians are valued for a number of endemic species as well as the largest old-growth beech and beech-fir forests in central Europe.

The Southern Carpathians are located in Romania and comprise about one third of the area of the Carpathian system. The mountains swing south and then southwest from the Ukrainian border to the narrows at the Iron Gate on the Danube River. The mountains consist of a mix of sedimentary, metamorphic, and igneous rocks, including granites, which rise to 2,500 metres above sea level in the Priata Craiului National Park. Further south and east, the Retezat National Park and Biosphere Reserve includes part of the Retezat Massif. This consists predominantly of crystalline granodiorites, schists, and biotites, with sedimentary rock such as reef limestones on the southern flank. The Tetezat Massif has numerous peaks over 2,400 metres above sea level. Alpine glaciation has left its mark in these mountains, for example, fifty-eight permanent glacial lakes arc found between 1,700 and 2,300 metres in the National Park (Voloscuk, 1999).

Hydrology

The importance of the Carpathians as a catchment or source area for rivers flowing into more-populated surrounding lands is generally described in the CEI reports and data. Ultimately 90 per cent of the Carpathian waters are said to flow into the Black Sea and 10 per cent into the Baltic. The Carpathians serve as source areas for the Vistula, the Tisza, the Prut, and other major streams of Poland, Hungary, Ukraine, and Romania. Over one third of the flow of the Vistula reportedly originates in the Carpathians, which are also the source of 80 per cent of Romania's freshwater resources if the Danube is excluded (CEI, 2001). The network of mountains, lakes, and streams supports a wide diversity of mammals, fish, invertebrate, plant, microbial, and other species, including birds. Carpathian rivers support the otter, a highly valued symbolic carnivore that lives only in clear, unpolluted aquatic habitat. More than a hundred fish and lamprey species live in Carpathian rivers, including ten endemics. The lakes, streams, and wetlands are important breeding and migratory areas for waterfowl and other birds. In the Duna-Ipoly National Park in Hungary, for example, lakes and marshes, as well as water storage reservoirs, serve as staging areas on a major seasonal migratory route for birds (CEI, 2001).

Mining, lumbering, and grazing are centuries old in the Carpathians (Johnson, 1996; Perzanowski and Augustyn, 1997; Augustyn, 1997). Pollution problems are not new but multiplied with the growth of smelting, manufacturing, and other industry in and near the Carpathians after World War II. Heavy metals such as lead and other toxics have directly entered streams. Forests, soils, environmental quality, and human health have been directly affected by sulphur, ozone, and other airborne emissions, including acid rain. Forests, such as those in the Beskidy Mountains in the western Carpathians, continue to be affected by pollution with indirect effects on run-off and water quality. Closure of iron and steel and other high-cost industries in areas such as Silesia, following loss of markets and support after the collapse of the Communist regime, has reduced these impacts, but they remain as threats today and in the future.

BIOTIC RESOURCES

The Carpathians are home to the largest remaining natural beech and beech-fir forest ecosystems and the largest area of relatively undisturbed forest left in Europe outside Russia (Figure 14.2). Together with semi-natural habitats such as meadow pastures and hay meadows, which are the result of centuries of traditional use of the land, the Carpathians harbour a richness of natural diversity that is unsurpassed in Europe outside Russia (CEI, 2001). No less than one third of European vascular plants can be found in this region: 3,988 plant species, 481 of which are found only in the Carpathians (Figure 14.3). The mountains form a "bridge" between Europe's northern forests and those in the south

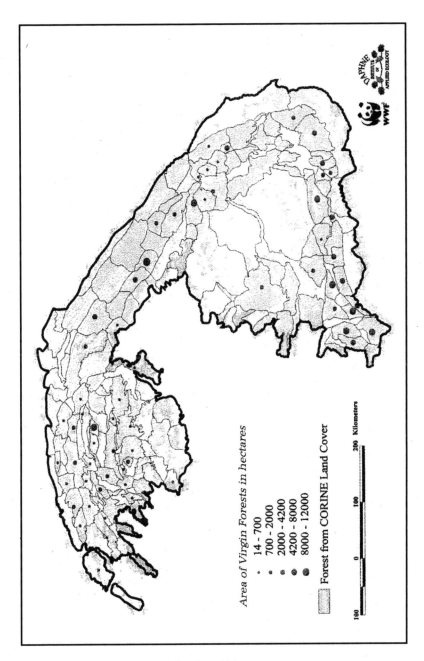

Figure 14.2   Forest Cover in the Carpathians

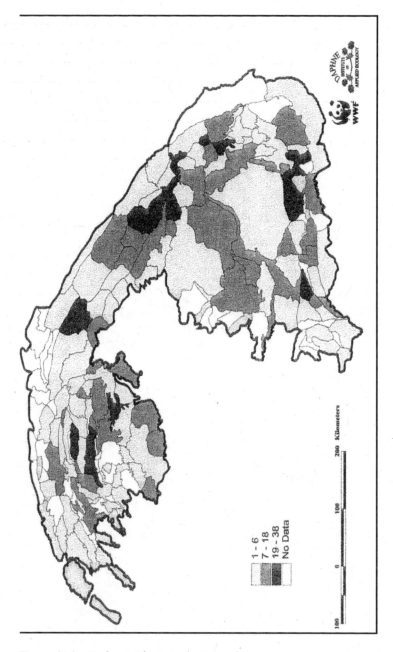

Figure 14.3   Endemic Plants in the Carpathians

PLACES

and west and are a vital corridor for the dispersal of plants and animals throughout Europe. The brown bear, wolf, and lynx are all still to be found in the Carpathian forest. The European bison is gone, although efforts are being made to re-establish this animal, for example, in the Bieszczady foothills and mountains of southeast Poland.

The brown bear was formerly very extensive in Europe and large numbers still remain in the Carpathians. About 5,500 individuals are estimated in the forests of Romania, about 1,000 in Slovakia, and others are scattered in Ukraine, Poland, and nearby countries. In Romania, bear numbers grew from 1,500 in the late 1960s to approximately 8,000 in 1988, protection being high in this period largely because of the strong hunting interest of the president and other state officials. After the political revolution of 1989, the bear population fell because they caused "significant damage to agriculture and people" and because of poaching, illegal use of poison, and a high level of legal hunting, with a strong interest in trophies. Of concern for protection is the uneven distribution of relevant laws and policies among the Carpathian countries as well as poaching, habitat changes particularly through road building, low reproduction rates, and lack of involvement of non-governmental conservation organizations in protecting bears (CEI, 2001).

The grey wolf (*Canis lupus*) is now exterminated in nearly all western and central European countries, the Carpathians being "the largest remaining stronghold" outside Russia. More than 3,000 are estimated for Romania, and scattered remnants are found in Poland (approximately 250), Slovakia (300–450), and Ukraine (350), with a few in the Czech Republic and Hungary. The Romanian population alone is considered to constitute 35 per cent of Europe's wolf population. Consultations during the research for this assessment indicated some difference of opinion about the accuracy of the wolf and other population estimates. They seem to be indicative, but continuing research and monitoring is required.

The Carpathians are home to one of the few populations of lynx left in Europe. Experts estimate that there are more than 1,500 lynx in Romania, 400–500 in Slovakia, approximately 300 in Ukraine and a scattered few (10–20) in both the Czech Republic and Hungary. With the survival of the Eurasian Lynx in Western Europe presently hanging in the balance, their protection in the Carpathians is vital. In recent years, European lynx from the Carpathians have been used in re-introduction programs in places where they were formerly eradicated – in the Vosges and Jura Mountains, the Alps, Slovakia, and Croatia. Only in those areas where extensive forests remained – Switzerland and Slovakia – have the introductions succeeded. In many instances, sheepherders and hunters have opposed the re-introduction of the lynx, and illegal poaching has taken place where the animal has been re-established (CEI, n.d.: 13).

Over 300 bird species use the Carpathians region for nesting, migrating, and wintering. These species include 30 per cent of the entire population of the White-backed Woodpecker, 20–45 per cent of the European population of the globally threatened Imperial Eagle, and 40 per cent of the Lesser Spotted Eagle. Other species include the uncommon Capercaillee and the Corncrake, a bird that is found in the Carpathian agricultural meadows, which have been in decline for two decades. These species prefer a variety of habitats, including old-growth forests, and are threatened by logging, air pollution, intensification of agriculture, and the spread of monocultures (CEI, 2001).

CULTURAL RESOURCES

In addition to their high natural diversity, the Carpathians also are significant because of their high national and ethnic diversity (Johnson, 1996; Langer, 2001). They are home to diverse groups such as Czechs, Slovaks, Poles, Ukrainians, Moravians, Romanians, Walachs, Bohemians, Boykos, and others. Although this national and ethnic diversity has been recognized in general terms in the work of the Carpathians Ecoregion Initiative, relatively little detail is given on the human dimensions of the Carpathians and surrounding areas, which have a long and rich human history.

The Carpathians and surrounding regions are the site of significant Paleolithic discoveries dating back well into the Pleistocene (Lecha and Partyki, 2001). Extensive remains of Neolithic agricultural and mining activities as well as former villages and settlements have also been found in the vicinity of the mountains. Archaeological and literary evidence points to widespread settlement and trade prior to and during Roman and later times. The Carpathians hold traces of the advance of Gothic and other peoples into and following the Roman Empire. The marks of invaders from the east, such as the Huns, the Magyars, the Mongols, and the Turks, have been left on this culturally rich landscape.

Penetration of the mountains appears to have deepened and intensified in the Middle Ages, with Barons and noble families claiming extensive tracts for hunting, forestry, and other purposes. In the Renaissance between approximately the fourteenth and the sixteenth centuries, major efflorescences of technical and cultural development arose in Vienna, Krakow, and other nearby areas. Grazing, mining, lumbering, and other activities accelerated in the mountains in the 1700s, 1800s, and early 1900s. With the rise of industrialization in the nineteenth century, railroads were constructed to mining and other centres in the Carpathians (Figure 14.4).

The Carpathians also became a contended zone between emerging Empires and Nations, especially in the nineteenth and twentieth centuries (Johnson, 1996; Kaplan, 1994). The borders of Prussia, later, Germany, the Austrio-Hungarian Empire and its descendants, Poland, Russia, Ukraine, the USSR, and Romania advanced and retreated across the region. Under Soviet dominance after World War II, the eastern Carpathians were, for some years, a battleground among Poland, Ukraine, and USSR. Large areas were depopulated. In many areas grasslands and rural landscapes gave way to forests and wildland. Private lands were nationalized and operated as co-operative enterprises or as protected areas and hunting grounds for the elite of the Communist Party. Bears and other game were frequently fed with hunting in mind. In some areas, isolated high alpine settlements remained comparatively undisturbed. Under the Soviet regime, the various Carpathian countries lost much of their autonomy and were linked to Moscow. Trade and contact among the Carpathian countries was strictly controlled.

After the fall of the Berlin Wall and the Communist system in 1988–89, numerous hitherto repressed forces were unleashed, including

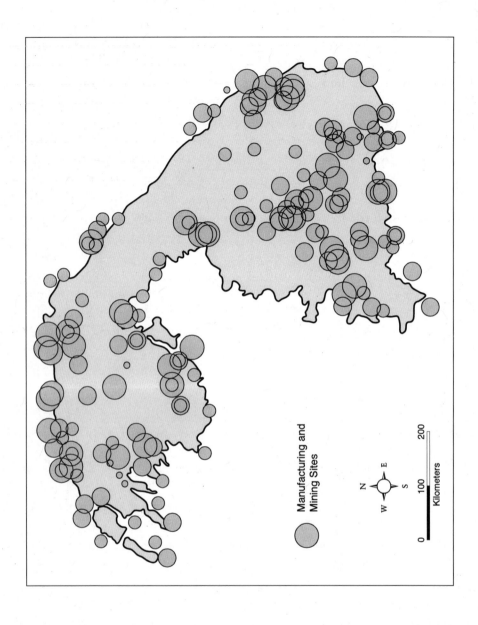

Figure 14.4   Mining and Manufacturing Sites in the Carpathians

interest in recovering private property lost to the public or communal ownership of the Soviets. People began to re-enter, reclaim, and re-inhabit the mountains. Forests, wildlife, and animals began to change again. All this human history is significant from the standpoint of those who value cultural heritage and the understanding it gives us of the past, where we have come from, and where we might be going. However, this human history is also highly significant to those interested in the current state of the forests and landscapes of the Carpathians. Obviously these have changed in numerous ways many times over the centuries, often as a result of the long continued, yet fluctuating ideas and activities of humans.

ASSESSING THE CARPATHIAN ECOREGION INITIATIVE (CEI)

The Carpathians are one of the Global 200 ecoregions classified as endangered by the World Wildlife Fund (WWF). The ecoregion designation indicates that an area is considered highly significant from a biodiversity standpoint and that it is subject, or potentially subject, to high pressure from human development. In the late 1990s, staff of the WWF Danube-Carpathian Project in Vienna made the decision to launch an ecoregion program for the Carpathians. The development of the initial concept occurred between December 1988 and June 1999 and the program was implemented from 1999 to 2001. The CEI staff decided to do an assessment of the Carpathians Ecoregion Initiative (CEI) in late 2001. The author, the CEI co-ordinator, and the director of the associated Danube River Conservation program subsequently agreed to an assessment of the CEI, although this was not to include any earlier work on the Danube River nor connections between CEI and other programs and offices of the WWF.

In the late stages of the assessment, this limitation was associated with major difficulties in completing the work. Conflict between the CEI and its umbrella office, the Austrian WWF, led to a cessation of operations in April 2002. This made it necessary to complete this assessment as a personal enterprise, which has been done largely because the CEI was emerging as a highly successful program up to the time of cessation, one from which valuable lessons can be drawn by others concerned with ecoregional plan elsewhere in the world.

The assessment methods used in this study included:

1. Reviewing existing documents from CEI, additional background from the WWF and other conservation organizations and the CEI website;
2. Attending several meetings of the CEI;
3. Preparation of a questionnaire for wide distribution among the CEI network in advance of fieldwork;
4. Field visits to the Czech and Slovak Republics, Poland, and Romania; and
5. Personal interviews with selected-people.

THE THEORETICAL OR CONCEPTUAL FRAMEWORK FOR THE ASSESSMENT

General theories that seem potentially applicable to assessing the planning of the CEI are rational or synoptic planning, mixed scanning, transactive planning, and interactive and adaptive planning (Hudson, 1979). Rational planning tends to be exclusive rather than inclusive of other interests. Decisions on goals, objectives, resources, timelines, and other essential details are made internally within the lead agency and these are carried forward with appropriate marketing, education, and other programs to elicit support from the affected or general public. Analyzing and assessing a program based upon rational or synoptic planning normally can be done in terms of the original goals and objectives and the degree to which they were met. The CEI was not planned this way but evolved more opportunistically in relation to the general goal of biodiversity conservation.

The CEI can best be understood in terms of mixed scanning or interactive and adaptive planning. The situation in which the CEI began was not really conducive to a rational planning approach. Much of the scientific and general knowledge was diffuse and uncertain. Nor did the originating group yet understand its goals, objectives, and interests well. It did not have the staff and resources to try to proceed in a relatively exclusive and direct manner to design and implement a program. Rather, the CEI involved building on the new and imperfectly defined notions of biodiversity conservation and the ecoregional approach. It involved beginning in a situation marked by considerable social, economic, and political uncertainty. There were questions about how the CEI might be initially defined, who would support and work with such an evolving concept, and whether the necessary knowledge and resources were available.

In accordance with the foregoing circumstances, this assessment of the CEI is based upon a set of principles or processes that underlie participatory, interactive, adaptive, and civic planning. These seven processes are: understanding, communication, assessment, planning, management, monitoring, and adaptation. All these processes are considered to be essential to an efficient, effective, and equitable planning approach. The processes are not thought of as proceeding in any logical or step by step sequence but rather as working together in response to planning challenges. When a challenge presents itself, a planner generally tries, more or less simultaneously, to understand, communicate, assess, plan, manage, monitor, and adapt to the situation in deciding how to deal with it. These essential processes were used as general criteria for analyzing and assessing the CEI.

Evolution of the CEI

The first stages of the CEI planning process involved lead staff in the Danube office collecting background information on relevant government and non-government activities in the Carpathians area and preparing a proposal for WWF International. This led to an initial workshop (9–10 May 1999) in Hungary, involving participants from governments and non-government organizations (NGOs) of six Carpathian countries plus some WWF staff and consultants. Here a number of challenges were recognized but a range of participants from the Carpathians area generally agreed to go ahead with a basic methodology, principles, and a proposal for funding, which was prepared and submitted to WWF-Netherlands in June. At that time, WWF

US had embraced the ecoregional approach, which was initially called Ecoregion Based Conservation (ERBC). WWF was developing ERBC in several exercises in different parts of the world. This approach was accepted by the participants in the initial workshop of the CEI. The idealized WWF methodology consisted of a series of basic steps: reconnaissance, biodiversity assessments, socio-economic assessments, a vision and/or conservation strategy, and action plans for application on the ground. Between July 1999 and approximately December 2001, the CEI undertook the first three of these steps, generally guided by a timetable agreed upon by participants.

The CEI made numerous adaptations during the unfolding of the foregoing planning procedure. The biodiversity and socio-economic assessments were not done in sequence but rather by separate but interrelated groups working at the same time. This seems to have provided for more effective interaction and exchange among the two groups. This interaction and the linking of the information was also enhanced by setting up a Geographical Information System (GIS) group to map the data so far as possible electronically. This, in turn, made it possible for the GIS group to analyze the biodiversity and socio-economic data in collaboration with the other groups and identify thirty Priority Areas for Biodiversity Conservation. These areas had high natural diversity values and were under pressure from transport, forestry, and other land-use changes. The development of the Geographical Information System data and the maps was very challenging and laborious because of differences in data among the countries, varying levels of response to data requests, and other factors. The computer and analytical expertise and efforts of the Slovakia NGO Daphne were crucial in the completion of this work.

As the planning process proceeded, the CEI added two other working groups on Communications and Sustainable Development respectively. The CEI also established a framework for the necessary data collection and analysis on a cross-Carpathian or ecoregional basis. Country co-ordinators were selected for their general knowledge of each of the countries involved, as well as expertise in a field such as biodiversity, socio-economics, or GIS. Country co-ordinators with a broad background and visionary outlook served as members of the CEI Co-ordination or Steering Group (Samec, personal communication). The country co-ordinators were also to recommend knowledgeable people in their countries who would be members of multinational working groups on biodiversity, socio-economics, and communications.

Summary of Major Findings

The major accomplishments of the CEI can be summarized as follows.

1. Creating an integrated vision of the Carpathians as an ecoregion among the divided countries and peoples of the region;

2. Completing a series of interrelated wildlife, vegetation, and other studies, which made it possible to delineated Priority Areas for Biodiversity Conservation in the Carpathians;

3. Completing socio-economic studies that provided primary identification of pressures on the Priority Areas for biodiversity conservation as well as contributing to ecotourism and other activities with high potential for a role in sustainable development;

4. Planning and implementing a wide-ranging information strategy including a website, as well as information and training sessions, workshops, a CD-ROM, and other means of creating interest in and capacity for biodiversity conservation and sustainable development in the Carpathians;

5. Creating a small grants program to build capacity for biodiversity conservation and sustainable development at the local level;

6. Facilitating a growing network of government and non-government conservation organizations involved in biodiversity protection and restoration, and to varying degrees in cultural conservation and sustainable development; and

7. Participating in the high-level summit at Bucharest, Romania, in April 2002, where the Carpathians countries reached a general agreement on an Environmental and Sustainable Development Accord for the Carpathians. This agreement led to a May 2003 Framework Convention on the Protection and Sustainable Development of the Carpathians.

Recommendations

These are major accomplishments, but significant adaptations are needed if the CEI is to proceed as well in the future as in the past. CEI has a prime role in promoting the image of the Carpathians as an ecoregion among scientists, scholars, professionals, and citizens. The CEI office can promote more specialized and comprehensive understanding of the Carpathians ecoregion through conferences, workshops, and other educational and media activities, which would frequently be led by other allied organizations. In this context, the CEI office should also take a key role in organizing exchanges of scientists, scholars, professionals, youth, and citizens among communities in different parts of the Carpathians.

The CEI project should also take a lead role in promoting, organizing, and monitoring research in biodiversity conservation and related fields in the Carpathians. This research would largely be cross-disciplinary and go beyond the specialized research already underway in various organizations and research bodies in the region. The universities in and around the Carpathians could play a much stronger role than they have in the past, perhaps through an Association of Universities for Research on the Carpathians. The CEI could undertake to promote such an Association as well as applications and funding for related research and planning projects. The CEI could also serve as a depository for project proposals and research results in the Carpathians. Comparable organizations have been created in countries such as Canada, for example, the Association of Canadian Universities for Northern Studies and the Park Research Forum of Ontario

The CEI needs to remain flexible, responding directly to or organizing collaborative responses to challenges and opportunities for biodiversity conservation throughout the Carpathians. In this respect, CEI should be prepared to respond at different scales ranging from the national to the local as well as to the different needs and circumstances in various parts of the Carpathians. In the more eastern areas such as Romania, for example, CEI and WWF are said by residents to be needed as a political voice at both the national and local levels because relatively few NGOs are active in that country as yet. This contrasts with the situation in the western part of the Carpathians where numerous NGOs are present and there is more need and opportunity for CEI and WWF to consult, co-ordinate, and delegate. Also, throughout the Carpathians, there is a role for CEI in conflict resolution and in facilitating work with governments and especially businesses, which have had less attention to date.

Greater recognition will have to be given by WWF and other external organizations to the differences in environmental and human histories in the Carpathians – and other parts of Europe in comparison to those in North America and other regions. These differing histories have led to differences in the way concepts such as biodiversity and sustainable development are understood and applied by scientific, government, and private conservation organizations in the Carpathian region, as opposed to WWF and others influenced by U.S. experience and views. Important differences have appeared in the understanding of concepts such as "biodiversity," which tends to be defined in terms of wilderness and the indigenous in much of North America. In contrast, biodiversity often includes the historic effects of humans in the Carpathians in Europe, as for example in the case of centuries of grazing of upland meadows.

Ultimately, the people and natural systems of the Carpathians are too complex, dynamic, and challenging to encompass in an overall management plan in the form of a multi-year blueprint implemented centrally through a number of specific action plans. This complexity, dynamism, and challenge is underlain by a set of historic, economic, social, and political relationships in the Carpathians that must be recognized as likely to have uncertain and long-lasting effects on the Carpathian countries as they all work independently and interactively toward a better future. Here CEI can play a key role in diffusing information and identifying common interests and concerns among the diverse countries, organizations, and natural and human communities of the region. This role, and the associated work of WWF and other national and international organizations, will, however, have to involve greater recognition of the evolving indigenous efforts of Carpathian governments and peoples in stewarding and sustaining environment and quality of life in the region, as for example through the new Framework Convention on Conservation and Sustainable Development.

NOTES

1   Adapted from J.G. Nelson, *The Carpathians: Assessing an Ecoregional Planning Initiative*. Environments, University of Waterloo, Waterloo, Ontario, 2004.

REFERENCES

Augustyn, M. 1997. "Exploitation of forests and its influence on local environment along valleys of Upper San and Solinka in XIXth and the first half of XXth century." In *Selected Ecological Problems of Polish-Ukrainian Mountains. Proceedings of the Scientific Session within the 2nd Annual Meeting of The International Centre of Ecology, Polish Academy of Sciences. August 18–21, 1997.* Bieszczady, Poland: 7–14.

Carpathians Ecoregion Initiative (CEI). n.d. *Ecoregion Conservation in the Carpathians*. Vienna: World Wildlife Fund International (WWF).

Carpathians Ecoregion Initiative (CEI). 2001. *The Status of the Carpathians*. Vienna: World Wildlife Fund International (WWF).

Dempster, B., and J.G. Nelson, eds. 2001. "Urban environmental planning, management, and decision-making." *Environments*. Special Issue 29(1).

Hudson, B.M. 1979. "Comparison of current planning theories: Counterparts and contradictions." *American Planning Association Journal* 35: 387–398.

Johnson, L. 1996. *Central Europe Enemies, Neighbours, Friends*. New York: Oxford University Press.

Kaplan, R.D. 1994. *Balkan Ghosts: A Journey Through History*. New York: Vintage Books, Random House.

Langer, J., ed. 2001. "Ethnologia europae centralis." *Journal of Ethnology of Central Europe*. Brno, Czech Republic.

Lecha, J., and J. Partyki, eds. 2001. "Z. Archeologii Ukrainy: Jury Ojcowskiej." In *The Archaeology of Ukraine and the Ojcow Jura*. Ojcowski Park Narodowy, Ojcow, Poland.

Magris, C. 1997. *Daube: A Sentimental Journey from the Source to the Black Sea*. London: Harvill Press.

Nelson, J.G., and R. Serafin. 1994. "Environmental and resource planning and decision-making in canada: A human ecological and a civics approach." In *Canada in Transition: Results of Environmental and Human Geographical Research*, ed. R. Vogelsang, 1–25. Bochum: Universitäts Verlag.

Nelson, J.G., and R. Serafin. 1997. "National parks and protected areas." In *Proceedings of the NATO Advanced Research Workshop on Contributions of National Parks and Protected Areas to Heritage Conservation, Tourism and Sustainable Development. Krakow, Poland. August 20–30, 1996*. NATO Series Vol. 40. Berlin: Springer.

Perzanowski, K., and M. Augustyn, eds. 1997. *Selected Ecological Problems of Polish-Ukrainian Carpathians. Proceedings of the scientific session within the 2nd annual meeting of the International Centre of Ecology, Polish Academy of Sciences*. Bieszczady, Poland.

Voloscuk, I., ed. 1999. *The National Parks and Biosphere Reserves in Carpathians. The Last Nature Paradises*. Tatranska Lomnica, Slovak Republic: Association of the Carpathian National Parks and Biosphere Reserves.

PART IV

PART IV:
RAPID RECONNAISSANCE STUDIES

INTRODUCTION

Part IV consists of four chapters intended to illustrate the use of the ABC method in rapid reconnaissance studies that highlight the natural and cultural characteristics of valued places as well as conservation and development challenges associated with them. These studies were done quickly, usually in days or weeks, albeit with as much reading and preparation in advance as possible. Contact with and assistance from locally knowledgeable people is invaluable in these circumstances in guiding the researcher through what can be a major cross-disciplinary, cross-sectoral, cross-cultural, and language challenge. The studies in Part IV tend to highlight significance and constraints for conservation and development planning. The application of the ABC is not as complete, systematic, and detailed as the studies discussed in Parts I and II nor as comprehensive as those in Part III. These four studies demonstrate the value of a basic understanding of the ABC method in thinking about the natural, land-use, and cultural qualities of a person's home area or others through which he or she travels.

The first study, Chapter 15, is on the Great Arc, an international initiative involving concerned people in Canada and the United States. The Great Arc project is intended to promote greater cross-border recognition and planning for the cliffs and rugged terrain of what is generally known as the Niagara Escarpment in Ontario and the ridge or ledge in its swing through New York, Michigan, Wisconsin, and Illinois. The chapter is a quick summary of part-time research conducted for several months mainly by graduate students. The intent was to identify the degree to which the Great Arc had been recognized as a landscape feature in geologic, wildlife, land-use, recreational, and other terms. The results were incomplete but identified information gaps and led to ensuing international co-operation on the Great Arc project through information sharing and co-operation.

Chapters 16 and 17 are rapid one- to three-week studies that use the ABC method to collect and organize the Abiotic, Biotic, and Cultural information needed to understand the natural and human interactions underlying the unique Mai Po and New Forest landscapes in greater Hong Kong and England respectively. The maps and information are from available sources and the results are incomplete. But they do give insights into understanding the significance and constraints for conservation and sustainable use of these unusual landscapes as well as leading to some general planning recommendations such as Biosphere Reserves.

Chapter 18, on the Great Sand Dunes of Colorado, is the result of rapid research for about a week during several visits in the 1990s. Considerable information was available from two principal sources, the U.S. National Park Service and Nature Conservancy offices and personnel. The study relied on existing maps and detailed studies with no systematic research undertaken in the field other than reconnaissance and open-ended interviews, notably with National Park and Nature Conservancy staff. The focus was on understanding a complex and interactive exercise in multi-agency and civic planning aimed at protecting water, landform, plant, and animal resources through the creation of a national park. The interagency and intergroup efforts were interesting in their own right and in terms of assessing the tools, experience, and approaches available in the United States as compared to Canada.

15

2002

PLANNING FOR THE GREAT ARC IN THE GREAT LAKES REGION[1]

J.G. Nelson and P.L. Lawrence

INTRODUCTION

The Niagara Escarpment is a well-known landform in Ontario and to a lesser extent in other parts of Canada and the United States. What is not so generally recognized, however, is that this landform is part of a landscape that begins in north central New York State and extends in a Great Arc through southern Ontario, Manitoulin Island, and the states of Michigan and Wisconsin into Illinois and Iowa (Figure 15.1). The Great Arc is therefore a transnational or continental scale feature that has considerable significance for scenic, recreational, natural, and cultural reasons.

The geologic, forest and other natural attributes of the Great Arc have been recognized in Ontario and have been given special protection against quarrying and other disturbing land uses through the Niagara Escarpment Protection Act and the Niagara Escarpment Commission since the 1970s. On the other hand, the extent to which the Great Arc has outstanding natural or cultural features that have been recognized and protected in other areas such as Manitoulin Island or the United States is not so well known. With this question in mind, we have been doing research on the recognition and mapping of the natural and cultural features of the Great Arc since 1998. This work has been a part-time activity focusing initially on the Great Arc in Ontario (Nelson et al., 1999).

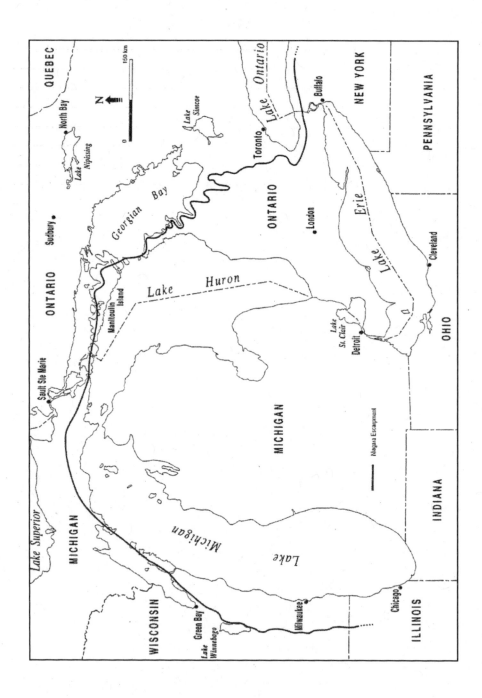

Figure 15.1   The Great Arc in the Great Lakes Region

The interest in the Great Arc has been inspired by bioregional, corridor, or landscape approaches undertaken elsewhere in North America as well as other parts of the world during the last two decades. This planning effort has been driven by changes in ecological science, notably landscape ecology, biological conservation, and the study of biodiversity. Examples include the Yellowstone to Yukon (Y2Y) (Locke, 1997) and the Sky Islands in Arizona and nearby regions in the western United States and Mexico (Sportza, 1999). An example in eastern North America is the Algonquin to Adirondack corridor between Ontario and northern New York State. The World Wildlife Fund and other organizations are promoting similar work outside North America, for example in the Carpathian Mountain region of Eastern Europe.

ABC METHOD

Initial work on the Great Arc primarily focused on determining the extent to which the scholarly, scientific, conservation, and planning literature has identified and characterized the Great Arc, particularly in Ontario (Nelson et al., 1999). A central question was how geologists, biologists, geographers, planners, and others have recognized and dealt with the Great Arc in terms of their own specialized perspectives. In other words, how aware are members of these fields of knowledge of the feature we call the Great Arc and how is it expressed in their work? In considering this question, the ABC Resource Survey Method has been used as a scoping device in organizing and preparing a set of theme maps at a scale appropriate to the entire length of the Great Arc as a transnational feature within the Great Lakes basin. In all cases, this work has been undertaken on a part-time basis by graduate and undergraduate students at the University of Waterloo.

Abiotic Resources

Summarizing the results briefly, the Great Arc has only been recognized and mapped as a distinctive transnational feature on the basis of geology

(Tovell, 1992; Telford and Johnston, 1996). The Great Arc is recognized as forming the margins of a large Paleozoic sedimentary feature called the Michigan basin (Figure 15.2). The bedrock consists generally of relatively resistant dolomites and limestones. These frequently form resistant caprocks over softer underlying more erosive shales, leading to numerous scarps and cliffs along the Arc, although the topographic character or shape of the Great Arc can vary considerably from place to place. In some areas the Great Arc appears as cliffs, for example, the Niagara region in Ontario or the Door Peninsula near Green Bay, Wisconsin.

The Great Arc – or Niagara Escarpment as it is called between Tobermory at the tip of the Bruce Peninsula and Niagara Falls in Ontario – has been divided into four landscapes: the Marine Scarp of the Bruce Peninsula, the Ridges and Valleys in the Owen Sound–Blue Mountain area, the Earthen Scarp in the Blue Mountain to Milton area, and the Southern Scarp from Milton to Niagara Falls (Kosydar, 1996). Reconnaissance field work in New York shows that the Escarpment does not continue far beyond Lockport, gradually becoming lower and more obscure toward Rochester and central New York. The Great Arc is similarly uneven in relief in Michigan, Wisconsin, and Illinois.

Considerable information is available on glaciation and its effects on the Great Arc, but this does not reflect an image of the Great Arc as a distinct glacial feature throughout its length. A distinctive assemblage of geologic and landform features does seem to occur in greater frequency and prominence along the Great Arc than in other areas within the Great Lakes Basin (Cowell et al., 1996; Riley et al., 1997). These features include caves, alvars, and cliff faces or promontories as shown in Figure 15.3. Recent research has revealed numerous submerged cliffs, stream beds, waterfalls, and ancient forest remnants of a lower water level stage in the glacial history of Lake Huron and Georgian Bay (Blasco et al., 1998). Similar features likely occur under the waters between western Manitoulin Island, Michigan, and Wisconsin. These features are an invaluable record of Great Lakes glacial history, perhaps eventually revealing artifacts and other evidence of the human presence thousands of years ago. The features represent an internationally significant scientific, educational, recreational, tourism, and cultural resource.

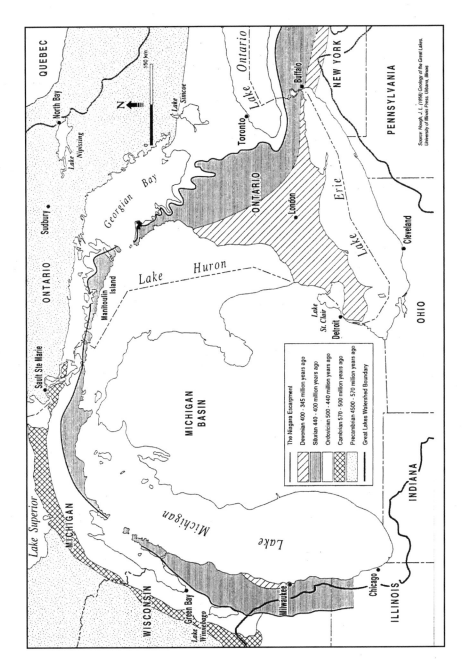

Figure 15.2 Geology of the Great Arc

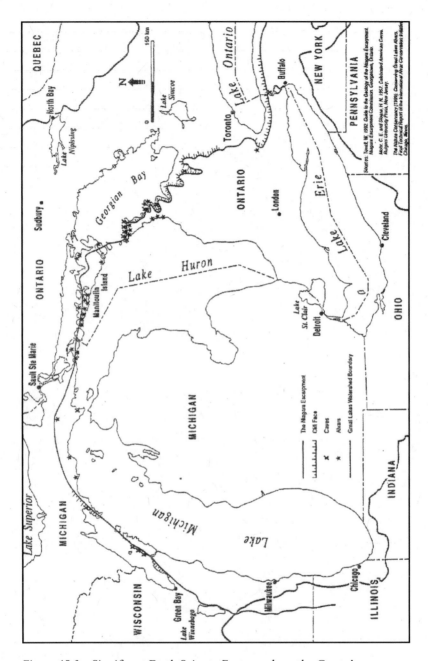

Figure 15.3   Significant Earth Science Features along the Great Arc

Our work on hydrology of the Niagara Escarpment in Ontario has not been very rewarding to date. Little information seems to be available on stream and water patterns of the Niagara Escarpment, although the Escarpment is popularly recognized as an important source of water for surrounding lands. The data that are available, for example though the Ontario Conservation Authorities, are being examined but seem to be inconsistent, incomplete, and not readily comparable along the Great Arc as a whole.

Biotic Resources

The Niagara Escarpment and Great Arc are not generally recognized in vegetation mapping at the regional or Great Lakes scale. Available maps identify vegetation patterns in terms of broad associations or bioregions that cover large areas and tend to cut across the Arc without any specific recognition of it as a region.

Much of the available mapping does not represent present vegetation conditions but rather those thought to have occurred before disturbance from European settlement. To date we have not found any maps that show current vegetation or wildlife habitat patterns along the entire length of the Escarpment in Ontario or the Great Arc in the Great Lakes Region. Various areas have been represented in satellite images, but they do not seem to have been classified and interpreted in terms of vegetation or wildlife habitat maps.

In parts of the Great Arc, research has been done on several distinct and significant vegetation types, which seem to concentrate along and distinguish the Niagara Escarpment in Ontario. These include cliff-edge cedar forests as well as alvar, cave, karst, and associated plant and animal species (Larson and Kelly, 1991; Cox and Larson, 1993; Catling and Brownell, 1995; Matheson, 1995; Schaefer, 1995). Available data, for example, on the biodiversity of ecoregions along the Great Arc do suggest high biodiversity (Figure 15.4). A limited amount of data has been found that indicates animal habitats believed to be definitely associated with the Great Arc. Parts of the Great Arc are known as a hawk migratory bird corridor in Ontario and Wisconsin. Ongoing

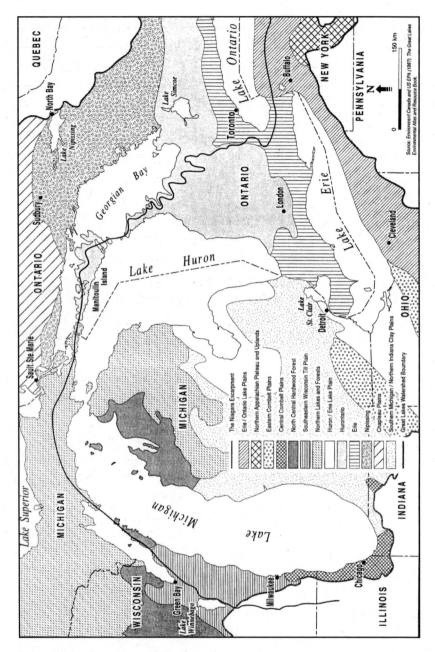

Figure 15.4   Ecoregions of the Great Arc

Parks Canada research suggests that the caves and cliffs of the Bruce Peninsula area may provide key wintering habitat for black bears.

Cultural Resources

We have searched for information and mapping of the human history, land uses, and institutional characteristics of the Great Arc, notably in Ontario. In this context, we have examined and are examining information related to archaeology, land and resource uses, population, settlement patterns, recreation, parks and protected areas, and planning (e.g., Reid, 1977; Mac Vivo, 1994; Fox, 1995; Lusted et al., 1997). We wish to trace the types, locations, characteristics, and effects of human use of the Great Arc by First Nations and subsequently by European settlers.

Paleo-Indian, Archaic, and Woodland sites along the Escarpment span the centuries from about 8000 BC to the sixteenth century AD (Nelson and Porter, 2002). Some areas show greater frequency of sites than others, for example those of the horticultural Woodland people near the shores of Lake Ontario. Similar sites reportedly occur in Wisconsin and Michigan and archaeology seems to be a common interest throughout the length of the Arc (personal communication, Eric Fowle).

A basic question is whether the Great Arc can be characterized in whole or in part on the basis of human uses and cultural landscapes as reflected in factors such as archaeological and historic sites and land and water uses. Recent work on the history of European settlement along the Escarpment in Ontario has revealed considerable data and numerous maps (Preston, 2002). These studies demonstrate the feasibility of doing settlement studies aimed at characterizing the Niagara Escarpment, and the Great Arc, in terms of similar or dissimilar historic land-use and other patterns through time. This settlement information will also provide the basis for more detailed studies of communities along the various parts of the Escarpment and of the perceptions, attitudes, values, and interests that people have had in the region over time.

In terms of institutional arrangements, the Niagara Escarpment in Ontario has been subject to planning and development controls since the 1970s (Government of Ontario, 1973). Any new development along the Escarpment and adjacent areas must meet the regulations of the Niagara Escarpment Plan Area (Niagara Escarpment Commission, 1984). In 1990, UNESCO designated the Escarpment in Southern Ontario as a World Biosphere Reserve, and this has led to some increase in environmental monitoring, research, and educational activities in line with the objectives of a World Biosphere Reserve (Borodczak, 1995). At the time of this work, we know of no other regional land-use or conservation plans, policies, or regulations for other parts of the Great Arc, although some work towards this end has been done in Wisconsin (personal communication, Eric Fowle). A number of geographic information systems (GIS) have been developed for areas of the Niagara Escarpment in Ontario by various regional governments, conservation authorities, and provincial and federal bodies such as the Ontario Ministry of Natural Resources and Parks Canada. However, these data also seem to be inconsistent, incomplete, and not readily comparable so that it may be difficult to construct land cover or other patterns for large parts or all of the Escarpment and the Great Arc from these or comparable systems in the United States. Another challenge is difficulty in gaining access to data in these systems because of costs, proprietary concerns, and other factors.

In terms of overall significance of the Great Arc, over one hundred parks and protected areas have been created along the Great Arc to recognize and provide for its conservation, recreation, and tourism values (Figure 15.5). Four major United States and Canadian federal parks and protected areas are located along the Great Arc: the Hiawatha National Forest (Michigan), Horican Marsh Natural Wildlife Refuge (Wisconsin), Bruce Peninsula National Park (Ontario), and Fathom Five National Marine Park (Ontario). On a state or provincial basis, our information is best for Ontario where numerous provincial parks, conservation areas, and local protected areas are located along the Niagara Escarpment. Much of the area of the Great Arc in northern Michigan is within state or national forests and a system of national, state, and local parks exists at least in Wisconsin. In New York and Pennsylvania, the Great Arc could also be linked to National Forest and other protected areas in the Alleghany Mountains.

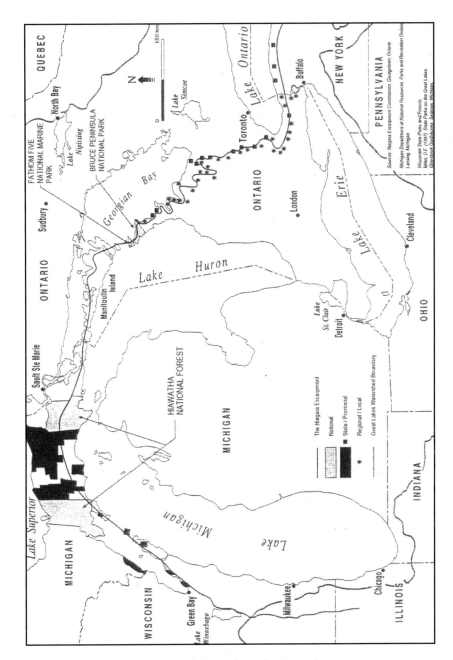

Figure 15.5   Parks and Protected Areas along the Great Arc

CONCLUSIONS

The Great Arc is highly significant in terms of the richly diverse geology and landforms found along its entire length and the biodiversity of plants and animals, including birds and old-growth cedar forests found there. The Great Arc has been widely recognized as significant for recreation and tourism including hiking, camping, skiing, cottaging, and other uses. More detail is needed on these activities and the opportunities, constraints, and challenges they provide mainly for conservation and sustainable use. A hiking trail, the Bruce, runs along the 700-kilometre length of the Escarpment in Ontario. Similar trail systems exist in New York, for example along the Erie Canal and the Hudson River as well as in Michigan and Wisconsin. There is no question therefore of the significance of the Abiotic, Biotic, and Cultural resources of the Great Arc, but more work is needed on the natural and cultural details and impacts of human activities, including land use, and other constraints for conservation and sustainable development.

Use of the ABC Resource Survey method to date has revealed that the Great Arc has primarily been recognized and characterized in geologic terms. In other words, the image that generally exists in many scientific, planning, and civic minds is a predominately narrow geologic one, although the forests and scenery are valued in a general way as well. On the other hand, the Great Arc appears to have characteristics of the kind that have promoted planning for large natural corridors or bioregions such as the Yukon to Yellowstone Initiative (Y2Y) or the Sky Islands between Canada and the United States, and the United States and Mexico respectively.

Furthermore, when the Great Arc is positioned and mapped, it reflects great significance at the continental scale. The Great Arc links many parts of the Great Lakes Basin and in so doing provides potential connections with a number of other large-scale bioregional projects in the eastern New York, New England, the central Appalachians, and northwestern Great Lakes. We are therefore highly motivated to continue work on the Great Arc. Our efforts to date show, however, that the incomplete and inconsistent nature and availability of the data in government and other standard sources is unlikely to yield good mapping, analytical, and planning results without a very high cost in terms of scientific, scholarly, and professional effort. We therefore plan to continue our team work but place more emphasis on the planning and holding of workshops and meetings in various parts of the Great Arc in order to increase and encourage greater general interest in and contributions to what will likely long remain as an unfolding enterprise.

POSTSCRIPT

Work has continued on the Great Arc since this paper in co-operation with Canadian agencies such as the Niagara Escarpment Commission and agencies and groups in the United States, notably the East Central Wisconsin Regional Planning Commission and the U.S. National Forest Service. Two collaborative workshops have been held in Ontario and on in Wisconsin with proceedings available. Other workshops are planned as part of this informal co-operative initiative by the Great Arc group (Nelson and Porter, 2002; Nelson and Peter, 2005).

NOTES

1   Adapted from J.G. Nelson, "Planning for the Great Arc in the Great Lakes Region." In *Managing Protected Areas in a Changing World*, ed. S. Bondrop-Nielson and Munro, 609–621 (Halifax: Science and Management of Protected Areas Association, 2002).

REFERENCES

Blasco, S.M., S.E. Janusas, S. McClellan, and A. Amos. 1998. "Prehistoric drainage across the submerged Niagara Escarpment." In *Proceedings of Leading Edge '97 The Edge and the Point: Niagara Escarpment and Long point World Biosphere Reserves*, ed. S. Carty et al., 218–228 Georgetown, ON: Niagara Escarpment Commission.

Borodczak, N.1995. "Ontario's Niagara Escarpment (Ontario, Canada): Implementing the biosphere reserve concept in a highly developed region." Paper presented at the *International Conference on Biosphere Reserves*. Sevilla, Spain, March 20–25,1995.

Catling, P.M., and V.R. Brownell. 1995. "A review of the alvars of the Great Lakes Region: Distribution, floristic composition, biography and protection." *Canadian Field Naturalist* 109(2): 172–181.

Cowell, D.W., M.J. Sharp, and M.E. Taylor. 1996. "A natural heritage system for the Niagara Escarpment Plan area." In *Proceedings of the Leading Edge '95 Conference: A Conference Exploring the Connections and Interrelationships between Environment, Use and Culture in the Niagara Escarpment Biosphere Reserve*, ed. S. Carty et al., 74–78 Toronto: Ontario Ministry of Environment and Energy.

Cox, J.E., and D.W. Larson. 1993. "Spatial heterogeneity of vegetation and environmental factors on talus slopes of the Niagara Escarpment." *Canadian Journal of Botany* 71(2): 323–332.

Fox, M.A. 1995. "The Northern Niagara Escarpment cultural landscape." In *Proceedings of the Leading Edge '94 Conference: A Conference Linking Research, Planning and Community in the Niagara Escarpment*, ed. S. Carty et al., 81–94 Toronto: Ontario Ministry of Environment and Energy.

Government of Ontario. 1973. *Niagara Escarpment Planning and Development Act.* Toronto: Queen's Printer for Ontario.

Kosydar, R. 1996. *Natural Landscapes of the Niagara Escarpment.* Tiereeron Press. Dundas, Ontario.

Larson, D.W., and P.E. Kelly. 1991. "The extent of old-growth Thuja occidentalism on cliffs of the Niagara Escarpment." *Canadian Journal of Botany* 69: 1628–1636.

Locke, H. 1997. "The role of Banff National Park as a protected area in the Yellowstone to Yukon mountain corridor of western North America." In *National Parks and Protected Areas: Keystones to Conservation and Sustainable Development*, ed. J. G Nelson and R. Serafin, 117–124. NATO ASI Series G: Ecological Sciences, Vol. 40. Berlin: Springer.

Lusted, J., I. Quick, and J. Shapeott. 1997. *Evaluating Land Cover and Land Use Change in the Northern Niagara Escarpment Plan Area between 1975 and 1996.* Report prepared for Ontario Ministry of Environment and Energy, Toronto.

Mac Vivo Consultants Inc. 1994. *Monitoring Cumulative Environmental Effects in the Niagara Escarpment Plan Area: Phase I Report.* Report to Ontario Ministry of Environment and Energy, Environmental Planning Branch, Toronto.

Matheson, U.J. 1995. "The structure and ecological role of avian and mammalian fauna on cliff-faces of the Niagara Escarpment." In *Proceedings of the Leading Edge '94 Conference: A Conference Linking Research, Planning and Community in the Niagara Escarpment*, ed. S. Carty et al., 116–124. Toronto: Ontario Ministry of Environment and Energy.

Nelson, J.G., and J. Peter, eds. 2005. *Heritage-based Recreation along the Great Arc.* An Environments Publication. Waterloo: Faculty of Environmental Studies, University of Waterloo.

Nelson, J.G., and J. Porter, eds. 2002. *Building the Great Arc: An International Heritage Corridor in the Great Lakes Region.* Occasional Paper 29. Waterloo: Heritage Resources Centre, University of Waterloo.

Nelson, J.G., P.L. Lawrence, and C. Beck. 1999. "Building the Great Arc in the Great Lakes Region." In *Proceedings of the Leading Edge '99 Conference: Making Connections,* ed. S. Carry et al., 116–124. Toronto: Ontario Ministry of Environment and Energy.

Niagara Escarpment Commission. 1984. *The Niagara Escarpment Plan.* Georgetown, ON: Niagara Escarpment Commission.

Preston, S.M. 2002. "Ontario's Niagara Escarpment as a cultural landscape." In *Building the Great Arc: An International Heritage Corridor in the Great Lakes Region.* Occasional Paper 29. Waterloo: Heritage Resources Centre, University of Waterloo.

Reid, I. 1977. *Land in Demand: The Niagara Escarpment.* Agincourt, ON: Book Society of Canada.

Riley, J.L., J.V. Jalava, J.L. Varga, and P.S.G. Kor. 1997. *Ecological Survey of the Niagara Escarpment Biosphere Reserve.* Peterborough, ON: Ontario Ministry of Natural Resources, South Central Region.

Schaefer, C. 1995. "Plant communities and environmental factors of alvars of the Bruce Peninsula and a comparison of alvars with Niagara Escarpment cliff faces." In *Proceedings of the Leading Edge '94 Conference: A Conference Linking Research, Planning and Community in the Niagara Escarpment,* ed. S. Carty et al., 386–421. Toronto: Ontario Ministry of Environment and Energy.

Sportza, L. 1999. "Regional approaches to planning for protected areas and conservation." *Environments* 27(3): 1–14.

Telford, P.G., and M. Johnston. 1996. "Paleozoic geology of the Niagara Escarpment and the assessment of scientific values." In *Proceedings of the Leading Edge '95 Conference: A Conference Exploring the Connections and Interrelationships between Environment, Use and Culture in the Niagara Escarpment Biosphere Reserve,* ed. S. Carty et al., 175–181. Toronto: Ontario Ministry of Environment and Energy.

Tovell, W.M. 1992. *Guide to the Geology of the Niagara Escarpment.* Ecological Land Classification Series No. 26. Ottawa, ON: Sustainable Development Branch, Environment Canada.

16

1993

CONSERVATION AND USE OF THE MAI PO MARSHES, HONG KONG[1]

J.G. Nelson

INTRODUCTION

Rapid reconnaissance studies, or what elsewhere have been termed rapid rural surveys, are valuable ways of securing significant information and planning insights where motivation is high but time and resources are limited. The results of the studies are useful in their own right and can make the case for investment in more comprehensive studies and research. Rapid reconnaissance studies can be aided considerably by knowledge systems such as the ABC Resource Survey Method. The method can provide a framework for the researcher to organize an array of varied disciplinary, professional, and local knowledge and observations quickly into a coherent cross-disciplinary package. The significance and constraints steps in the method can also facilitate assessing and interpreting the relevance of the information for planning and decision-making purposes, including identification of knowledge gaps and research needs.

The following is an illustration of the use of the ABC method in a study of conservation and land-use planning challenges and opportunities in the Mai Po marshes, Hong Kong. Research on the ground was completed in about five days during trips to Hong Kong for other reasons. The background documents were mainly collected in the Hong Kong and Mai Po area, notably in a short visit to the site and the associated World Wildlife Fund facilities. The visit involved a field tour and intensive discussions with experienced staff and accompanying geographers from the University of Hong Kong. Assistance from knowledgeable local people is invaluable in reconnaissance research.

MAI PO MARSHES

The Mai Po marshes in Hong Kong (Figure 16.1) are a remnant wetland system that has changed substantially in area and natural character as a result of human activity. Most of this activity has occurred in the last three decades. Prior to the 1920s much of the Mai Po area consisted of extensive mangroves, marshes, tidal flats, and wetlands that had not been directly affected by agriculture or other human activity. Between the 1920s and the 1960s, much of the area was converted to *gei wais* – areas of intertidal marshland enclosed by an earthen dike fitted with a sluice gate to allow for alternating entry and drainage of tidal waters and the exploitation of shrimp and other fish. The *gei wais* included uneven patches and fringes of wetland favourable to varied bird and other life, including important migratory species. Since the 1960s the *gei wais* have steadily been converted to sites for rice production, new housing, aquaculture, and other uses associated with the rapid growth of Hong Kong.

The World Wild Fund for Nature, Hong Kong, is leading the attempt to conserve the *gei wais* and their important ecological functions through their purchase and continued operation as well as through environmental education activities and other programs. The Mai Po area and many of the *gei wais* are designated as a conservation reserve, but the pressures on the wetlands continue, especially with accelerating industrialization and urbanization in adjoining mainland China. Such modernization pressures are underway in many parts of Asia and require more vigorous and comprehensive conservation and sustainable development efforts. In the case of the Mai Po, for example, the creation of a Biosphere Reserve would likely be beneficial, especially if it were more strongly supported by the Hong Kong and Chinese governments.

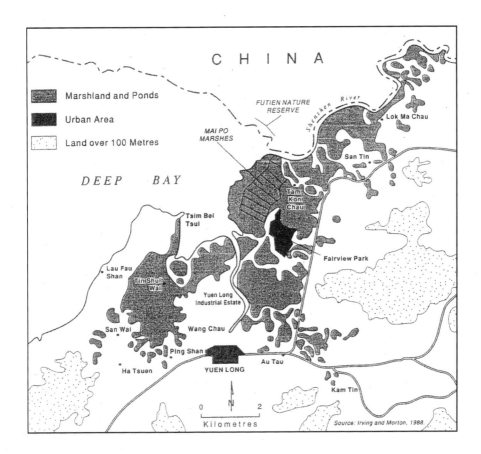

Figure 16.1　　　Mai Po Marshes, Hong Kong

Many small places have great ecological and natural heritage value. Their importance far transcends their size. Such a place is Mai Po, the site of about 380 ha of marshland adjoining Deep Bay in the northwest part of the New Territories of Hong Kong (Figure 16.1). At one time such marshland extended along much of the shore of Hong Kong. Today the Mai Po marshes are the largest surviving remnant.

Deep Bay itself straddles the border between Hong Kong and China, a relatively remote location that historically favoured protection of the outstanding natural qualities of the bay and the marsh. However, this location is now at a disadvantage because it is exposed to pollution and other pressures from the rapid industrialization underway in the Shenzhen River valley, the southern boundary of a special economic zone set up by China in 1980. Much of the border area is quite hilly so that new developments are concentrated in the low-lying valley and coastal lands.

Pressures on the Mai Po marshes and other parts of Deep Bay are also building up on the Hong Kong side. A large new residential area has been constructed adjacent to the marshes and christened Fairview Park. A new city is being built at nearby Tin Shui Wai. A large array of roads, sewer lines, and other infrastructure has been built to serve these new urban areas. Older agricultural residences are being converted to modern homes and apartments. Other land is being used for industrial or development purposes, for example to house shipping containers and other equipment connected with the high volume of traffic and shipping in the great port of Hong Kong.

In the face of this intense and wide-ranging development, it is proving to be very difficult to conserve the Mai Po marshes, as well as an adjoining mangrove area on the Chinese side known as the Futien Reserve. This is the case in spite of the fact that both Mai Po and Futien are official nature reserves, Mai Po having been established as a nature conservation area in 1975.

It is, however, very important to make every effort to protect and manage carefully the Mai Po marshes not only because of their outstanding natural qualities but also because of their land-use history and socio-economic and cultural importance. The marshes consist mainly of mangrove and mudflats as well as large areas that have been modified or reclaimed historically to produce rice, shrimps, fish, wood, and other produce valued by humans over the centuries. The natural and cultural characteristics of the Mai Po marshes can be organized and briefly described by use of the ABC Resource Survey method.

ABIOTIC RESOURCES

Bedrock lies an average of some 30 m below the surface and consists of largely metamorphosed sedimentary rocks of Carboniferous age. The rocks are buried beneath sediments laid down as a result of sea-level fluctuations during Quaternary glacial periods. These changes are portrayed in Figure 16.2 (Irving and Morton, 1988). Further details on the geologic character and history of the study area generally can be found in Chin and So (1986).

BIOTIC RESOURCES

The Mai Po marsh is an important nesting and staging area for birds. It is difficult to be precise about the number of species and individuals involved because of variations in such factors as the area included in the counts and irregular publication of systematic bird lists (Chalmers et al., 1990; Picken, 1991). The Mai Po marsh area is part of the Hong Kong territory where a systematic list of 380 species has been recorded in an apparently wild state within the last fifty years (Chalmers et al., 1990).

The checklist of birds of Mai Po Nature Reserve records 250 species representing some fifty families so that the area is said to be justly famous as an internationally recognized bird sanctuary. For most of the year, the patient bird watcher might see as many as seventy species in a day, thus attesting to the reserve's conservation importance (World Wide Fund for Nature, n.d.). Forty-two species are listed as residents. Another sixty-one species are listed as migrants, mainly in April/May and September/October. Ninety-four species are listed as winter visitors. Waterfowl are particularly important in Mai Po marsh, as can be shown by referring to a waterfowl count held in Deep Bay Hong Kong (Chalmers, 1990). This count included areas in the reserve as well as close by. From 1985 to 1990 the yearly total number of birds ranged from 36,454 to 38,947. (Table 16.1).

These bird populations are associated with a large and diverse flora. About 1,900 plant species are native to the Hong Kong area and many of these grow in the vicinity of the Mai Po marshes. The plants growing in the Mai Po reserve have been heavily influenced

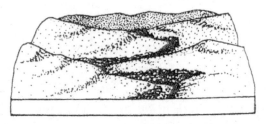

15,000 years ago: Upland with fast flowing streams.

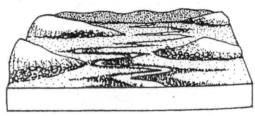

8,000 years ago: Estuarine flood plan.

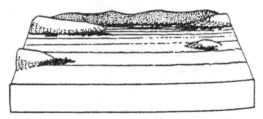

6,000 years ago: Flooded by the sea.

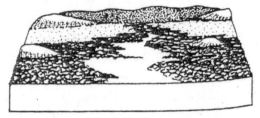

1,000 years ago: Mangrove swamp.

Figure 16.2   Evolution of the Mai Po landscape

Group	Number	Species
Cormorants	3407	1
Herons, egrets, etc.	6753	13
Ducks	5730	16
Rails, coots, moorhens, etc.	1136	8
Waders	5120	28
Gulls and terns	15745	7
TOTAL	37891	73

Source: Chalmers 1990:64.

Table 16.1   Deep Bay Bird Count, 1990

by agricultural, fishing, and other activities, including construction of berms and dikes to control water flow (World Wide Fund for Nature, n.d.). Invading plants on the disturbed areas include common reed grass *(Phragmites communis)*, sow thistle *(Sonchus oleraceus)*, hairy bur marigold *(Bidens pilosa)*, tassel-flower *(Emilia sonchifolid)*, and herbs such as *Achyranthes aspera*. The Mai Po marsh area is well known for its extensive mangrove community, which supports a rich variety of other life. The principal genera in the Mai Po mangrove include *Kandelia, Aegicents, Avicennia,* and *Acanthus,* with *Kandelia candel* dominant (World Wide Fund for Nature, n.d.[b]).

The Mai Po herpetofauna are inadequately studied but include a wide array of species (World Wide Fund for Nature, n.d.[c]). Four snakes have been recorded for the Mai Po reserve area that are dangerous to humans: king cobra *(Ophioplagus hannah)*, Chinese cobra *(Najanaja)*, and many–banded *(Bungarus multicinctus)* and banded *(B. fasciatus)* kraits (World Wide Fund for Nature, n.d.[c]). A total of 144 fish species have been recorded in the nearby Pearl River estuary, which extends to the west of Deep Bay, with 60 per cent having marine, 20 per cent freshwater, and 20 per cent estuarine origins (Irving and Morton, 1988).

The estuary, Deep Bay, and the marshes in the Mai Po area have long been important for fishing and oyster-farming. Today most of the economically valuable species are caught by bottom-trawling. Deep Bay is generally recognized as a fish nursery ground, and Chinese fishermen reportedly are forbidden to fish there, although about fifty Hong Kong fishermen worked these waters in the late 1980s (Irving and Morton, 1988). Oysters and other shellfish grow in the Mai Po area and have been cultivated since at least the nineteenth century. Grey *(Mugil cephatus)* and other mullets are fished in the Deep Bay area. The fry are especially numerous in December–March and are trapped near tidal creeks with fine mesh seine nets. The fry are then transferred to nearby fish ponds, where they are grown for a year and then marketed.

Shrimp are an especially important member of the fish community in the shallow waters of Deep Bay. They largely subsist on the litter and other organic debris copiously supplied by the mangrove. The shrimp in turn attract a number of predators, including humans who regard several species as nutritious food, notably the *Metapenaeus eusis* – the *gei wai ha* – which is especially enjoyed for its sweet taste (Irving and Morton, 1988: 27).

CULTURAL RESOURCES

Examination of the term *gei wai* reveals the historical and cultural background of the Mai Po area and the fundamental role that humans have played in the evolution and current state of the marshlands and adjoining waters (World Wildlife Fund, n.d.) (Figure 16.3). In essence, a *gei wai* is an area of intertidal marshland of up to ten hectares, which has been enclosed by an earthen dike. A sluice gate at the seaward side of the enclosure allows water to flood the *gei wai* at high tide, and for it to be drained at a subsequent low tide. Juvenile shrimps are washed into the pond with the incoming tide through a wide-meshed net, which keeps out predatory fish. By closing the sluice gate, the shrimps remain in the pond until they grow to a marketable size. The mature shrimps are harvested by placing a net across the sluice channel when the gates are opened to drain the pond. Harvesting takes place up to one hundred times each year (Irving and Morton, 1988).

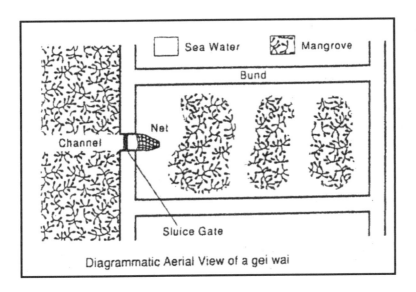

| Sea Water | Mangrove |

Bund

Channel — Net

Sluice Gate

Diagrammatic Aerial View of a gei wai

Figure 16.3   Gei Wais

Prior to the 1920s much of the Mai Po area consisted of extensive mangroves, marshes, tidal flats, and wetlands that had not been directly affected by human activity. Between the 1920s and the 1960s, much of the area was converted to *gei wais*, which occupied about 800 ha of the Deep Bay shoreline, including the Mai Po reserve area (Figure 16.4). Toward the end of the 1980s, only six of twenty-four ponds or about 60 ha in the reserve were operated as traditional *gei wais* (Irving and Morton, 1988). The loss of the *gei wais* is a major threat to birds, fish, and other valued aspects of the area. The current ecology of the area is a direct result of the construction of *gai wais*, principally after 1924. The *gei wais* reached their maximum extent in the 1960s and declined rapidly thereafter, so that most of them were abandoned or converted to fish ponds and urban and industrial uses by 1985.

This decline has occurred for many reasons. First, there has been a trend toward more intense economic use, for example commercial fish cultivation (aquaculture) in open, cleared ponds rather than in the *gei*

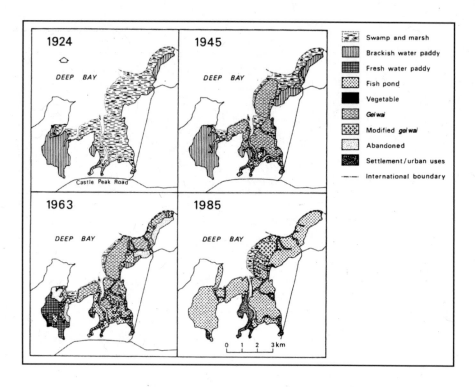

Figure 16.4   Land Use Change in the Deep Bay, 1924–1985

wais with their patches and fringes of mangrove vegetation and their irregular depth. Second, marsh and nearby land have been sold for urban development. A third factor is the multiplication of an exotic fecund fish, *Tilapiamossambica*, which competes intensely with the shrimp and local fish for food and habitat. A fourth factor is the natural tendency for shrimp ponds to silt up, reducing shrimp productivity. In addition there are increased levels of pollution introduced from streams such as the Shenzhen, especially in recent years. This pollution has had an adverse effect on oyster production as well, so that little of this historic activity occurs in the area today. Finally, more economic opportunities are available to *gei wai* cultivators than in the past. The cleared, open fish ponds lack the biotic variety of the *gei wais* and the new industrial and urban landscape is not conducive to much biodiversity.

PLACES

CONCLUSIONS

In an attempt to retain the *gei wais*, the Mai Po marshes, and the biodiversity associated with them, the World Wide Fund for Nature, Hong Kong (WWF Hong Kong) has purchased rights to ten *gei wais* within the nature reserve and is planning to acquire as many as possible in the future. WWF Hong Kong is also restoring the *gei wais* in the newly purchased areas as well as constructing paths, an educational centre, warden's facilities, and other infrastructure. WWF Hong Kong is also raising funds for the staff members now running the nature reserve. There is a growing emphasis on providing environmental education to urbanized students, thousands of whom visit the reserve annually. The education programs at the Mai Po reserve are very important to school children, who otherwise would have little understanding of the importance of traditional shrimp fishing activities to the creation and maintenance of the Mai Po habitat or, indeed, of the productivity, diversity, and overall value of the mangroves and other elements of the Mai Po ecosystem.

To a considerable extent, the Hong Kong government is co-operating with the WWF Hong Kong, as well as bird clubs, educators, and others interested in the Mai Po and its economic, conservation, education, and historic values. The Hong Kong government owns the land on which the reserve is situated and is working with the WWF Hong Kong to purchase the rights to use the *gei wais* from farmers and fishermen. The goal is for Mai Po reserve staff to arrange management that will sustain the traditional landscape and its ecological values. The Hong Kong government is also co-operating with WWF Hong Kong in its plans to replant trees and mangrove and restore parts of the Mai Po. The aim is to continue to provide for the array of habitats and functions needed to maintain and enhance the diverse plant and animal life of the Mai Po. There is also interest in maintaining the many natural services that the area offers, not only to the residents of the Hong Kong area, but to people in more distant lands who benefit from the migratory birds and other wildlife that feed here.

The future of the Mai Po is in the balance. On the one hand, WWF Hong Kong and the Hong Kong government – as well as the

Chinese government in the case of the Futien Nature Reserve – are working to protect the Mai Po in many ways. But the area is severely threatened by the growing amount of serious pollution from the Shenzhen and other rivers. Management measures are not adequate to prevent increasing organic and toxic pollution, which eventually will destroy the fish, shrimp, and other resources upon which birds and other life as well as much human economic activity depend. Another serious threat is the growing encroachment of mainland Chinese fishermen who move into the reserve to catch crabs and other animals and also take some waterfowl and other birds. Hong Kong government officials apparently are not adequately controlling these activities, at least in part because the perpetrators are mainland Chinese.

More co-operative activity is needed among the governments and private organizations involved in the future of the Mai Po, an area that exemplifies what is happening to many significant natural and cultural landscapes in rapidly industrializing and urbanizing Southeast Asia. In the case of the Mai Po and comparable areas, the establishment of a Biosphere Reserve may be a promising option. UNESCO Biosphere Reserves are intended to promote sound economic as well as educational, conservation, and research use of areas such as the Mai Po. Biosphere Reserve status could make the many values of the Mai Po more explicit and widely known and, thereby, attract more local and international visitors, as well as financial and other support.

POSTSCRIPT

The fate of the Mai Po Marshes is not known since the writing of this paper in the early 1990s. More research will be very worthwhile as the Mai Po could be a model for other small heritage areas if successful conservation approaches have been found.

NOTES

1   Adapted from J.G. Nelson, "Conservation and Use of the Mai Po Marshes, Hong Kong," *Natural Areas Journal* 13(3) (1993): 215–219.

REFERENCES

Chalmers, M.L. 1990. "International waterfowl count in Deep Bay, Hong Kong 1990." In *The Hong Kong Report 1990*, ed. Verity Picken, 64–69. Hong Kong: Hong Kong Bird Watching Society.

Chalmers, M.L., M. Turnbull, and G.J. Carey. 1990. "Report on the birds 1990." In *The Hong Kong Bird Report 1990*, ed. Verity Picken, 4–63. Hong Kong: Hong Kong Bird Watching Society.

Chin, T.N., and C.L. So, eds. 1986. *A Geography of Hong Kong*, 2nd ed. Hong Kong: Oxford University Press.

Irving, R., and B. Morton. 1988. *A Geography of the Mai Po Marshes*. Hong Kong: World Wide Fund for Nature, and Hong Kong: Hong Kong University Press.

Picken, V. 1991. *The Hong Kong Bird Report 1990*. Hong Kong: Hong Kong Bird Watching Society.

World Wide Fund for Nature, n.d.(a). Checklist of birds, Mai Po Nature Reserve. Hong Kong: World Wide Fund for Nature.

World Wide Fund for Nature, n.d.(b). Checklist of plants, Mai Po Nature Reserve. Hong Kong: World Wide Fund for Nature.

World Wide Fund for Nature, n.d.(c). Reptiles and amphibians, Mai Po Nature Reserve. Hong Kong: World Wide Fund for Nature.

World Wide Fund for Nature, n.d.(d). Gei wai utensils, Mai Po Nature Reserve. Hong Kong: World Wide Fund for Nature.

1993

THE NEW FOREST: ANALYSIS AND PLANNING OF A HISTORICAL LANDSCAPE IN ENGLAND[1]

J.G. Nelson

INTRODUCTION

A glance at a map of the New Forest region illuminates the many threats facing this special part of England (Figure 17.1) (Edwards, 1991). North and east of the New Forest is the rapidly expanding metropolis of London. Bournemouth, Southampton, and other nearby urban areas are expanding into the region. The associated pressures include residential and industrial development, oil exploration, aggregate mining, power plants, oil refineries, road construction, water diversions, campsites, bed and breakfast accommodation, information centres, amusement parks, and other manifestations of recreation and tourism. About 15 million people live within a few hours drive of the New Forest. Given their very large and diverse demands and those of hundreds of thousands of foreign tourists estimated to visit annually, it is remarkable that the New Forest has been able to retain so many special qualities amid a sea of change (Ecotech Research and Consulting Ltd., 1992).

What are the geological or Abiotic, plant or Biotic, and land-use, institutional, or other Cultural qualities of the New Forest landscape that have caused it to be so highly valued and conserved in England as to be recommended for a status equivalent to that of a national park by the Countyside Commission and other government bodies? With this question in mind, the ABC Resource Survey Method was used

Figure 17.1   New Forest Area

as a general organized framework for this study of the New Forest area. This study is based upon a review of previous writings, notably those listed in the references and general information in municipal and other government offices and the New Forest Interpretation Centre in Lyndhurst. Informal interviews also were conducted, notably with staff of the Forestry Commission. This study is an example of curiosity-driven research carried out on a rapid reconnaissance basis for a total of about two weeks during visits to England primarily for other purposes.

ABIOTIC RESOURCES

Geologically the New Forest occupies a central position on Eocene and Oligocene sediments, mainly soft sands and clays, laid down in a series of depositional cycles during early to mid-Tertiary times beginning about 60 million years ago (Tubbs, 1968). Over the millennia the original sediments have been weathered and eroded by stream and other processes so that only some of the original strata now are exposed or underlie the surface of the New Forest. The sediments form the basement of broad up to 400-foot plateaus descending to terraces near the coast, remnants of fluctuating high and low sea levels in glacial or Pleistocene times.

Much of the New Forest surface is covered with gravels left behind by ancient preglacial streams and by the enlarged rivers and spillways of glacial times. The New Forest area does not appear to have been covered by ice but shows soil and surface disturbance features arising from near ice or periglacial climatic conditions induced by cold weather, freeze-thaw, and unstable conditions resulting from New Forest's proximity to ice sheets lying not far to the north. Interspersed among the plateaus and terraces are a series of ridges and stream valleys, wide and relatively steep-sided to the north, grading into gentler slopes and extensive plains in the south. These landform patterns are associated with a complex of soil and site conditions ranging from gravel and sands through clays and clay loams to peat, muck, and mire in low-lying less-well-drained areas. These variations are reflected in vegetation patterns, for example heather moor on the leached plateau gravels and sands, acid grassland with bracken and gorse on the lower valley slopes, and bog and floodplain meadow on the valley floors.

Present-day vegetation patterns do not, however, necessarily reflect those of the past. For example, extensive tracts of woodland are located along main streams such as Lymington and Beaulieu (Figure 17.1). These valleys currently have relatively large amounts of oak and conifer, arising from enclosure and planting during the last two hundred years, mainly to satisfy demand for lumber. In earlier days these treed areas "could have been described as a mosaic of deciduous woodland, irregular glades and extensive lawns" (Tubbs, 1968).

Aside from their effects on vegetation patterns, the landforms and surface deposits of the New Forest area are significant for production of gravels and sands for use in road and other construction. Post-World War II mining in the 1960s and 1970s was frequently conducted without much aesthetic and environmental sensitivity. One result was "barbaric mutilation of open heathland scenery" and conflicts between industrial and amenity interests (Tubbs, 1968: 15). More effective land-use and other controls have reduced the extent and intensity of mining impacts, but road, residential, and other growth pressures continue, and considerable vigilance is necessary to conserve scenic landscapes.

BIOTIC RESOURCES

Over the centuries, humans have continued to put much pressure on animal and plant life (Tubbs, 1968, 1986; Drummond and Allison, 1979; Chapman, n.d.). Yet red, fallow, and other deer still roam the New Forest in the thousands. It is home to many species of pony and cattle as well as deer, birds, and other life highly valued in an increasingly industrial and urban landscape. The woods, heath, meadows, and wetlands are also outstanding for their insects: "for the presence of Britain's only cicada, the New Forest cicada, for a wide variety of moths and butterflies, and for a range of beetles, probably unique in the British Isles" (Bennett, 1989). More species of beetles have been identified in the New Forest than in any similar area in Britain. Overall the New Forest is highly significant in Britain as well as central and western Europe for its biodiversity.

As Tubbs' field mapping shows, the New Forest has many square miles of Ancient and Ornamental Woodland, dominated by old oak, beech, sycamore, and other species (Figure 17.2). This Woodland is,

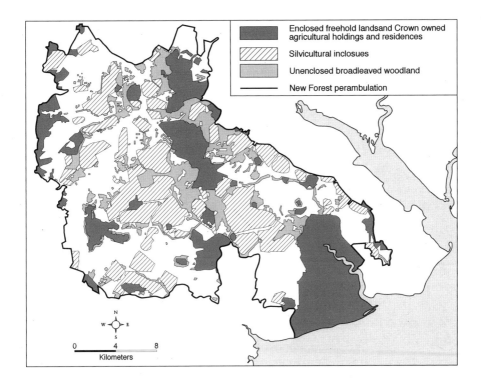

| | Enclosed freehold lands and Crown owned agricultural holdings and residences |
| Silvicultural inclosues |
| Unenclosed broadleaved woodland |
| New Forest perambulation |

0   4   8
Kilometers

Figure 17.2   The New Forest Landscape, 1986

however, frequently close to or mixed with coniferous growth, including native Scots pine as well as yellow cedar, Douglas fir, Norway spruce, and other exotics introduced from North America and Scandinavia and often in silvicultural enclosures. Much of the unclosed or open woodland is grazed and logged as well as being used for recreation and other purposes so that it cannot be considered wild, natural, or pristine in the North American sense. Many miles remain as moor or heath, covered with heather, grasses, various flowering plants, and scattered stands of yellow-flowered gorse or birch trees. The heaths and moors are often open and are frequently traversed by walkers and grazed by sheep, ponies, and some cattle.

CULTURAL RESOURCES

The New Forest is also remarkable for its signs of human history. Old pit houses and other artifacts remain from Neolithic times, five or six thousand years ago (Tubbs, 1986). New Stone-age folk appear to have cultivated what is now acidic heath land and forest between about 4000 and 1000 BC when the climate was warmer and wetter than now: the so-called post-glacial climatic optimum. Bronze and iron-age people succeeded the Neolithic folk and left tools and other artifacts behind them on land, which gave way more and more to heath and treeless upland as the climate became colder and the soils more acid and boggy in the centuries before and after the time of Christ.

The Romans came to England about AD 50, and it was not long until they had built roads and settlements in the New Forest area. Their successors, the Angles and Saxons, invaded the area from mainland Europe in the fifth to the eleventh centuries. It was Harold, a descendant of the great Danish King Canute, who was defeated and killed by the Norman, William the Conqueror. And William undertook a settlement survey (Domesday Book) and set the New Forest on its course to the present day.

William set aside the New Forest as a place to hunt for food, sport, and physical activity. The area was designated as a Forest in about 1086, not as a place for preservation of extensive stands of trees, but rather as a sometimes wooded, sometimes heathed landscape, rich in deer, wild boar, and other animals whose protection was the major purpose of the reserve. Hunting of the deer and other game animals by the people was prohibited by William and his successors, as were other activities likely to reduce the wildlife population. The breaking of the New Forest regulations was subject to severe penalties, including death. In return for the loss of hunting, snaring, and other activities, which had been important for their livelihood, the people of the New Forest were allowed certain rights by William and his successors. These rights – common rights on the crown land – included the grazing of ponies, sheep, and cattle, the cutting of peat, and the collecting of some wood for fuel, charcoal burning, and other activities.

A major challenge to deer and wildlife protection and to the subsistence and economic interests of the New Forest peoples grew steadily in the fifteenth to nineteenth centuries. This challenge was the increasing demand for wood for the British fleet as well as for houses and other uses for the increasing population of southern England. The port of Buckler's Hard, located on one of the small streams draining into an estuary on the shores of the English Channel within the New Forest area was, for example, a major ship-building centre in the eighteenth and nineteenth centuries. Ships were built to fight in wars against the Dutch and the French. Several ships that served in Nelson's fleet in the Napoleonic Wars were built at Buckler's Hard. These ships included the Agamemnon, a favourite of Nelson's, an approximately eighty-gun vessel, whose construction apparently required the cutting of about forty acres of Ancient and Monumental Forest, including oak, birch, and beech.

Increasing military activities and growing commerce overseas put much pressure on the New Forest and other woodland in Britain, leading to more and more influence by professional foresters and to the enclosure and planting of lands with the Scots Pine, Douglas fir, and other native and exotic species valued for construction. This change from a basically wildlife to a strong lumbering role for the New Forest led to vigorous protests from persons outside the forest as well as those living within the area. The outsiders included people who visited the New Forest from London and other urban centres. They extolled the oak and other deciduous forests as well as the heath and other qualities that attracted them to the place. They opposed the growing of fir and other exotics and continued enclosure for wood production because of its impact on these qualities and on the New Forest landscape generally.

In the final analysis, the overall landscape of the New Forest is its most striking special attribute. As a result of the interacting human and natural history described briefly here, the New Forest has retained a mix of land types unique in England. The mix consists of the relatively treeless heath, the largely deciduous Ancient and Monumental Forests, coniferous enclosures, considerable mixed growth, improved green swards, lawns or meads, especially near streams, and pastured and cultivated fields, notably in the southern part of the area.

Noteworthy also in the New Forest landscape are the often red-brick, low-lying houses, shops, and other buildings set singly, in small groups, or in numerous small villages and towns such as Lyndhurst, Beaulieu, Burley, and Ringwood, one of a number of sites recorded in the Domesday Census that William compiled in about 1079, more than nine hundred years ago. These settlements, set among the still-narrow and winding roads of the New Forest, often are the site for old inns and public houses that serve many visitors so well today.

So it is the interplay of the natural and the human history of the New Forest that has produced the landscape mosaic of the New Forest that is its greatest special quality today. The heath, with its ling, bell, and cross-leaved heather and other plants, as well as the deer, ponies, archaeological sites, and old inns, are all important in their own right. But nowhere else in England are they all put together in the mosaic that is unique to the New Forest.

It is important to note, however, that this mosaic has been and is a constantly changing one. It is not an artifact of a particular period in the past, such as the forest of William's time. For the New Forest would then not contain the old coniferous or mixed wood stands, nor the old mills, inns, villages, and roads introduced in the nineteenth and early twentieth centuries. But throughout the various economic, technical, social, and other changes the area has undergone, the basic character-istics of the landscape mosaic have been protected to a considerable degree. One thinks here of the Ancient and Monumental deciduous forests with their oaks and beeches, of the deer that are culled much below their former numbers today, of the ponies whose population has also fallen, and of the extensive heath upon which the animals graze and hikers walk in enjoyment.

INSTITUTIONS AND MANAGEMENT ARRANGEMENTS

Why have these special qualities and the unique landscape mosaic of the New Forest survived? Many agencies and forces are involved, including the

Forestry Commission, which holds and manages some 70 per cent of the area on behalf of the Crown, English Nature (formerly the Nature Conservancy), which offers statutory advice on nature conservation, especially for Sites of Scientific Interest, and the Countryside Commission, which has statutory responsibility for the provision of recreation and amenities for the people of England (Forestry Commission; Department of Environment, 1992). The Countryside Commission has publicly underscored the special qualities and the unique and outstanding character of the New Forest. The Commission also has stressed the fact that, like so many other special areas in the U.K. and other parts of the world today, the New Forest is not the responsibility of any single government agency at the central or local level.

The role and contributions of central agencies such as the Forestry Commission, the Nature Conservancy, and the Countryside Commission notwithstanding, the New Hampshire County Council and the New Forest District Council have both prepared management plans that recognize and attempt to maintain and enhance the special qualities of the New Forest (Land Use Consultants, 1986; New Forest District Council, 1986; 1991). Private groups have also been very important in maintaining the special qualities of the New Forest. Indeed, it was non-government groups and private individuals who worked to secure passage of the 1875 Enclosures Act, which limited the development of forestry in the area and was a major reason for the landscape mosaic that remains today. At the time of this research in the 1990s, the government was considering new ways of conserving the New Forest, including the creation of a national park, an idea welcomed by some but not others who see this arrangement as likely less favourable to the role of local people than historic institutions such as the Verderers.

The Verderers: A Heritage Institution

However, ultimately, the New Forest probably owes the continued existence of its unique landscape to an institution, which today is found in no other area in England. This institution is the group known as the Verderers. The group was set up by William the Conquerer at the time he created the New Forest. Its basic role is to protect the rights of the commoners, the rights to graze domestic animals and to collect wood and peat from the crown land. This the Verderers have been able to do up to now, with the assistance of the other agencies and groups noted previously.

The Verderers have been able to do this because they have the right to review land-use proposals that could affect commoners rights. Only about 350 people still hold the rights to the common. Their numbers reportedly are dropping because of lack of use of the rights or because the land to which the rights apply is being sold or leased to newcomers not interested in exercising them.

The arrangements for the Verderers are said to have changed over the years. However, a key element of the Verderers remains: five of the ten are elected by the people whose interests they represent, the people who hold the rights to the common. The other Verderers are appointed by the Crown to represent the major agencies involved in the management of the New Forest, i.e., the Ministry of Food, Fisheries and Agriculture, the Forestry Commission, English Nature, and the Countryside Commission. The Verderers work to maintain the land-use activities and interests of the holders of the common rights. This in turn works to maintain the sheep, cattle, and pony-grazing, the heath and other special qualities, which have come down through time in the New Forest landscape. An example of this role of the Verderers involves a proposal for a major road bypass around the town of Lyndhurst in the north central part of the New Forest. Many residents of Lyndhurst and many recreationists and commuters to the New Forest want this bypass in order to reduce the traffic congestion on the old road through town during weekends and other peak periods. Holders of the common rights have objected to the bypass on the grounds that it would block the movement of ponies and other stock. The Verderers interceded in the planning process for the bypass, objecting on behalf of the holders of the common rights. In the end, a bypass may go ahead, but, if so, its negative effects will likely be mitigated by burying parts of the road or by other remedial measures.

In sum, the Verderers appear to be an essential historic means of protecting the rights of commoners and indirectly the land uses and the heath and other land types that have been important to the special landscape qualities of the New Forest through the centuries. Such an institution is lacking in other areas with special qualities in England and other parts of the world.

CONCLUSION

In a modified form, a council like the Verderers might represent the common interest of the citizens in recreational, educational, and other access to the countryside in Canada and other countries as well as the public interest in the character of historic landscapes. In Canada, for example, control of access and of tree-cutting or other activities which could change landscape character is tied strongly to private ownership and to the associated matter of legal standing rather more than the public interest in decision-making. In this regard, in Canada, we do not have access to the United States doctrine of public trust as a basis for intervening in proposed changes in landscapes which are against the environmental, recreational, and other interests of the citizens at large. Nor do Canadian citizens hold common rights to certain uses in the strict historic and legal sense of the ancient English commoner. But the general idea of a common or public right – as well as councils or means by which it might be expressed – is a useful one as we search for a means of helping the public to protect its interest in common goods such as outstanding landscapes and other important legacies of the past.

POSTSCRIPT

The New Forest was recently designated as a national park; however, the management arrangements for the park and for other institutions of concern such as the Verderers require further research.

NOTES

1   Adapted from J.G. Nelson, "Sustaining the New Forest Landscape, U.K.: The Special Role and Planning Significance of the Verderers," *The Operational Geographer* 11(3) (1993): 18–21.

REFERENCES

Bennett, L. 1989. *A Guide to the Nature Reserves of Southern England*. London: Macmillan.

Chapman, J. n.d. *New Forest Today*. Lyndhurst, England: Forestry Commission, Queen's House.

Department of the Environment. 1992. *The New Forest, The Government's Proposals, A Consultation Paper*. Bristol, England: Department of the Environment.

Drummond, M., and P. Allison. 1979. *The New Forest, A Photographic Record of 100 years of Forest Life*. Beaulieu, Hampshire, England: Pioneer Publications.

Ecotech Research and Consulting Ltd. 1992. *Tourism in the New Forest*. A Report to the New Forest District Council, Birmingham, England.

Edwards, A.-M. 1991. *New Forest Walks*. Newbury, England: Countryside Books.

Forestry Commission. 1990. *The Future for the New Forest*. Edinburgh, Scotland: Forestry Commission.

Land Use Consultants. 1986. *The New Forest Landscape*. Manchester, England: Countryside Commission.

New Forest District Council. 1986. Forest and Downlands. Villages Local Plan, New Forest District, n.p.

New Forest District Council. 1991. New Forest District East Local Plan. New Forest District Council, n.p.

Pasmore, H. 1991. *A New Forest Commoner Remember*. New Forest Leaves, Burley, Ringwood, Hampshire, England.

Tubbs, C.R., 1968. *The New Forest, An Ecological History*. Newton Abbot Devon, England: David and Charles.

Tubbs, C.R., 1986. *The New Forest, A Natural History*. London: Collins.

18

2003

THE GREAT SAND DUNES: PLANNING FOR A NEW NATIONAL PARK IN THE SAN LUIS VALLEY, COLORADO[1]

J.G. Nelson

INTRODUCTION

Within the southern Rocky Mountains lies a large basin known as the San Luis Valley of Colorado (Figure 18.1). This basin forms the northern part of the Rio Grande that eventually flows through the states of New Mexico and Texas, as well as Mexico, into the Gulf of Mexico. On the eastern flank of the valley is a large complex of sand dunes managed by the U.S. National Park Service in a national monument created by President Hoover in 1932. In recent years, the professional and general view of the dunes has changed, from a focus on their unique geography and landforms, to recognition that the dunes are part of a diverse ecosystem that extends well beyond the boundaries of the monument. This recognition by the U.S. National Park Service, a private organization, the Nature Conservancy, and other agencies and organizations, as well as politicians and citizens, has led to the creation of innovative new conservation arrangements centring on a proposed national park. These arrangements and related planning approaches are the prime interest in this chapter that should be of value to relevant government agencies, non–governmental organizations, and participating individuals in Canada and other countries.

Figure 18.1   San Luis Valley, Colorado

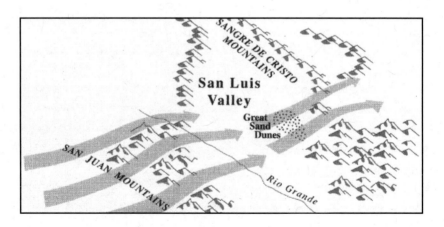

Figure 18.2   Dune Origins

The conservation arrangements and the natural and cultural features and patterns of the Great Sand Dunes National Monument are organized and discussed in this chapter in terms of a general application of the ABC Resource Survey Method. The research involved reviewing books and documents obtained in the Great Sand Dunes National Monument Interpretation Center, local bookstores, and libraries, including the collection of the Arizona University Library. Informal interviews were also conducted with staff of the National Monument and the Nature Conservancy.

ABIOTIC RESOURCES

The great sand dunes and the monument cover about 103.6 square kilometres (40 square miles) and in places attain a vertical relief of about 230 metres (750 feet). The dunes are a result of erosion and transport by prevailing winds blowing over glacial and postglacial silts and sands laid down centuries ago in the Rio Grande basin to the west. The winds have unloaded the silts and sands against the eastern barrier of the Sangre de Cristo Mountains before passing over the relatively low Medano Pass onto the foothills and plains of central and eastern Colorado (Figure 18.2). The dunes are stunning and remarkably beautiful landforms that are visited by approximately three hundred thousand people annually.

The major reason that concerned agencies, organizations, and citizens have taken a wider view of the dunes and the monument is water. The National Park Service recognizes that the sustainability of the dunes depends on the maintenance of water levels in the system. Decline in water levels could lead to desiccation and erosion of the dunes. In this respect, the upper watershed of the dunes system lies east of the monument on U.S. National Forest Service wilderness lands in the adjoining Sangre de Cristo Mountains. This federal agency has a different mission than the National Park Service, including industrial logging and other multiple-purpose uses. Any forest or other disturbances from such activities can affect water flow, erosion, and other processes that, ultimately, could affect the dunes. Potential threats also lie to the west, where water withdrawals for long-standing irrigation projects on ranch and settled lands are believed to be lowering the water table and stressing small lakes and wetlands in the dunes region. These wetlands provide prime habitat for sandhill crane, waterfowl, and other migratory birds, including the occasional whooping crane.

Of major concern have been proposals for the mining and export over the mountains – to Denver and other growing foothills urban areas – of large quantities of groundwater, deposited over the centuries in the deep deposits of the San Luis Valley. The Baca Ranch, located immediately west and north of the monument, is of particular interest. Private investors, interested in exploiting the groundwater supplies, purchased this ranch some years ago.

BIOTIC RESOURCES

In the 1990s, the Colorado Nature Conservancy, a major non-governmental conservation organization in the state, developed a strong interest in the sand dunes area for the foregoing reasons. The conservancy was also apprehensive because inventories and assessments led to the identification of the San Luis Valley as a significant target for its biodiversity protection programs in the state (Figure 18.3). At this time, about 40,469 hectares (one hundred thousand acres) of the Medano-Zapata Ranch, to the west and south of the monument, came up for sale and were purchased by the Nature Conservancy (Figure 18.4).

The valued features of the monument region include: alpine tundra; the Sangre de Cristo Mountains; extensive pine forests; alpine lakes; large stands of Aspen and Cottonwood; massive sand dunes and grasslands; as well as nearby lowland lakes and wetlands, which offer valuable habitat to migratory birds and other animals. Wildlife is diverse, including Rocky Mountain species such as elk, bighorn sheep, black bear, pika, and ptarmigan. Desert species embrace kangaroo rats, short-horned lizards, and six to eight thousand insects indigenous to the sand dunes. Grassland species consist of pronghorn antelope, prairie dogs, jack rabbits, and badgers. Wetland species include leopard frogs, beavers, avocets, pelicans, and white-faced ibis. Archeological remains

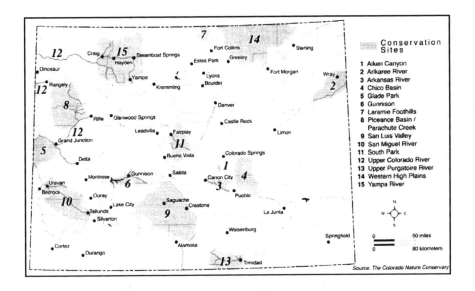

Figure 18.3   Colorado Priority Conservation Sites

also attest to the presence of early humans in this area thousands of years ago.

CULTURAL RESOURCES

The recognition of this wide-ranging ecological diversity, and especially the threat of water export and shortages for local ranchers and other land uses, caused numerous federal, state, and local organizations other than the conservancy and the U.S. National Park Service to take an increasing interest in the conservation of the sand dunes and adjoining lands in the 1990s. Local, state, and federal politicians and concerned citizens developed the idea of expanding the monument into the surrounding lands and waters and creating a national park. This designation would conserve the full range of biologic and hydrologic features of the region, as well as the geology and landforms protected by the national monument (Figure 18.4). Following various

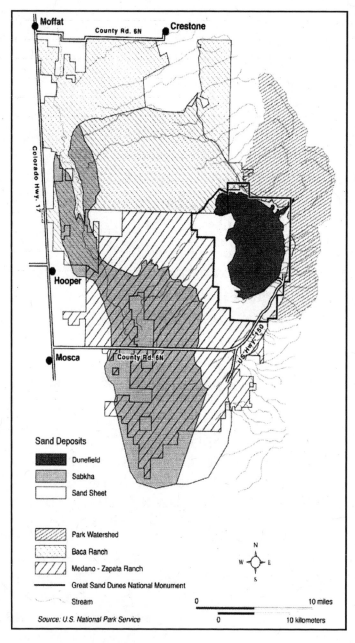

Figure 18.4   Landforms and Land Tenure

PLACES

Table 18.1   Great Sand Dunes National Park and Preserve Act of 2000

- Expands the boundary of the existing monument by about 28,300 hectares (70,000 acres), 26,700 hectares (66,000 acres) of which are privately and/or state owned. The secretary of the interior is authorized to designate the area as a "National Park" when sufficient area (generally considered to mean the Baca Ranch) is acquired.

- Authorizes government acquisition (from willing sellers) of all private and state lands, mineral interests, and water rights within this new boundary.

- Creates a new NPS unit called the "Great Sand Dunes National Preserve" where hunting would be allowed, by transferring about 17,000 hectares (42,000 acres) of USFS lands (dunes watershed) to the NPS.

- Authorizes the secretary of the interior to establish the 37,000 hectares (92,000 acres) "Baca National Wildlife Refuge" when sufficient lands have been acquired. The refuge is to be formed from the western 1/3 of the Baca Ranch and NW 1/4 of the Medano/Zapata Ranch.

- Expands the Rio Grande National Forest by about 5,600 hectares (14,000 acres) consisting of the northeast corner of Baca Ranch, which includes the 4,317 meter (14,165 foot) Kit Carson Peak.

- Authorizes the continuation of existing grazing leases by The Nature Conservancy on federal and acquired lands that are incorporated in the national monument/park.

- Preserves all existing federal water rights and wilderness designations.

- Does not create a "federal reserved water right" and requires the United States to follow procedures established by the state of Colorado in obtaining water rights for the protection of the new park.

- Requires the establishment of a 10 member advisory council to work with the NPS on development of a management plan for the park and preserve

Source: U.S. National Park Service (From Official Summary
of Great Sand Dunes National Park and Preserve Act, 2000.)

Table 18.1   The Great Sand Dunes, Colorado

political bipartisan meetings, a bill was passed by Congress in November 2000 and was proclaimed by the president, creating new conservation arrangements for the Sand Dunes National Monument area. These arrangements reflect numerous consultations, adaptations, and compromises made by concerned agencies, non-governmental organizations, and other groups and individuals to reach an agreement that was, so far as possible, in their own as well as the general interest.

The framework for the new arrangements is set forth in the Great Sand Dunes Monument and Preserve Act (U.S. 2000). It is not possible to discuss the Act in detail here; highlights are provided in Table 18.1, which summarizes the major features of the Act and associated interaction, planning, and adaptation among concerned agencies, organizations, and individuals. To this official summary should be added reference to an important section of the Act, which states that when:

> ... the Secretary (of the Interior) determines that sufficient land having a sufficient diversity of resources has been acquired to warrant designation of the land as a National Park, the Secretary shall establish the Great Sand Dunes National Park in the state of Colorado. (U.S. 2000, sec. 4)

Provision for continued interaction, planning, and adaptation among concerned parties is, therefore, built specifically into the legislation.

Figure 18.5 shows the proposed framework for the national park as seen primarily from a federal government perspective. This should be compared to Figure 18.4, which reveals the complex set of land-tenure arrangements from which the foregoing framework must be created (personal correspondence, Chaney, March 2001). One of the key adaptations that made the proposal possible was the inclusion of the Nature Conservancy's Medano-Zapata Ranch as a major private in-holding within the boundaries of the proposed national park. In this context, the conservation goals of the National Park Service and the Nature Conservancy were generally compatible, centring in both cases on protection of biodiversity and water.

The agreement also is somewhat unusual in that it not only provides for protection of elk and other wildlife but also allows for grazing

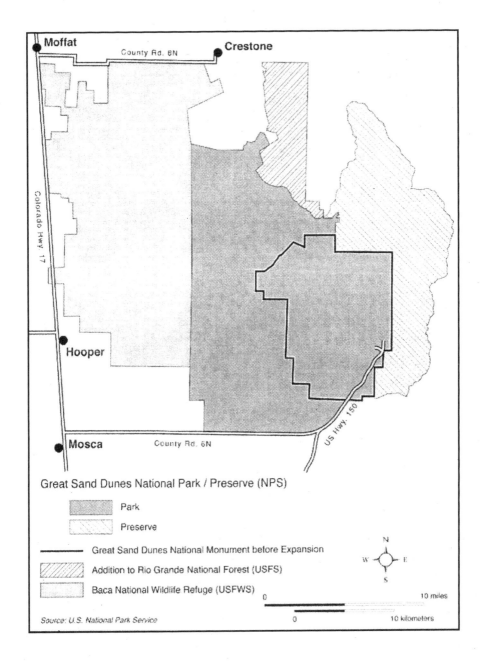

Figure 18.5   Proposed Land Management

by cattle and bison, which have been herded domestically for many years. Domestic stock is not normally considered consistent with the official preference for indigenous wildlife populations in U.S. national parks. The agreement recognizes that grazing has traditionally been a natural feature of this landscape. It is being used as a land management and conservation tool by the Nature Conservancy, as well as a potential source of income.

Another significant adaptation to the planning challenges posed by Great Sand Dunes Monument involved the creation of a national preserve in the headwaters in the Sangre de Cristo Mountains (Figure 18.5) (personal correspondence, Chaney, March 2001; Gibson, March 2001). The U.S. Forest Service, the owner of the lands, wished to protect the interests of hunters who have harvested mountain sheep and other animals in this area for many years. Hunting groups, tourism, and other agencies and concerned individuals also supported the continuation of a hunt. Hunting is, however, generally prohibited in national parks. The solution to this challenge was the establishment of a national preserve that allows for regulated hunting but can be used to prohibit logging and other activities that could disturb the water regime and the Great Sand Dunes area to a significant degree. The national preserve apparently was originally created as a U.S. protected area category in the late 1970s in Alaska. The need there, also, was for a high level of conservation while providing for long-standing hunting by local people, primarily for subsistence purposes.

Another adaptation to the planning challenges of the Great Sand Dunes Monument situation is the proposed purchase and resale by the Nature Conservancy of the Baca Ranch, west and north of the monument. As noted previously, the current owners are primarily interested in developing underlying groundwater resources for export to the eastern slope. They have, however, encountered major local, state, and national opposition and are considering a sale. The current asking price is about $30 million for approximately 40,469 hectares (100,000 acres) – a price that is beyond the immediate resources of the federal government (personal correspondence, Gibson, March 2001). The government has been able to appropriate about $8.5 million since the passage of the new legislation in the fall of 2000. The Nature Conservancy secured a credit of $22 million to cover the expected purchase price. The conservancy expects to resell the land to the federal government and recover its investment in the next few years.

The Baca Ranch land would be divided among three federal agencies: the U.S. National Park Service, the U.S. Forest Service, and the U.S. Fish and Wildlife Service. This agreement would result in strict conservation arrangements for the national park lands and more flexible conservation and land-use arrangements for the wildlife refuge and U.S. Forest Service lands. The completion of the purchase and re-sale would trigger the creation of the Great Sand Dunes National Park from the current monument and national preserve. The Nature Conservancy is also contributing to the completion of the new conservation arrangements through its proposed purchase of state lands, located to the west and south of the monument, that are within the Medano-Zapata Ranch. This block of land will become a major in-holding in the proposed new national park. An estimated $3–4 million are being raised by the conservancy for these purchases in the Medano-Zapata (personal correspondence, Gibson, March 2001).

CONCLUSIONS

Enough details have been given to make it possible to highlight the major innovative characteristics of the new conservation arrangements for the Great Sand Dunes Monument area. These include:

1. Bringing together an array of different types of pro-tected areas to meet the more specific objectives of the National Park Service, the Nature Conservancy, and other national, state, and local organizations. These ob-jectives could provide the protection of water resources needed to maintain the Great Sand Dunes landforms and plant and animal life as well as inhibiting proposals to export groundwater by local ranchers and other users. These arrangements also could satisfy the more general objectives required for conservation and sustainable use

of the ecosystem as a whole. The result is a more or less mutually supportive set of protected areas – a protected area mosaic of the kind recommended for parts of the Yukon in the early 1980s (Nelson and Theberge, 1986, also see Chapter 6, this volume), or as a multiple-use module (MUM) in the United States in recent years (Noss, 1987). The new arrangements for the Great Sand Dunes Monument can also be seen as an example of effective public and private stewardship, or comprehensive landscape planning (Brown and Mitchell, 1997).

2. Creating the new protected area mosaic in stages over time. The numerous interactions and adaptations involved are in line with such theoretical approaches as adaptive management (Gunderson et al., 1995; Lee, 1993), mixed scanning (Etzioni, 1967), and transactive or interactive and adaptive planning (Friedmann, 1973; Cardinal and Day, 1998; Nelson and Sportza, 1999).

3. Multidisciplinary and cross-sectoral planning, management, and decision-making that are broadly inclusive and civic in nature. Much of the interaction and adaptation is built on regular communication, monitoring, and assessment and is informal rather more than formal in character. To date, for example, no memorandum of understanding or other formal agreements have been made between the U.S. National Park Service and the Nature Conservancy for the Sand Dune National Monument region.

4. Planning, management, and decision-making that stress social and political processes and careful consideration of the different values, interests, and objectives of the various concerned parties.

5. The new arrangements involved negotiations and planning for a mix of different types of protected areas that, in many ways, reflect the values and interests of different user groups and government agencies. They are built upon scientific and scholarly ideas and methods, notably

ecosystem science. In this context, planning occurs at various overlapping and interacting scales. For example, the Conservancy has been, and is, planning for the Great Sand Dunes area: strategically at a broad ecoregional or state level; regionally at the San Luis Valley level; and also at the site level in the context of the Medano–Zapata Ranch. At each scale, targets are identified after inventory and analysis reveal biologic, hydrologic, and other significant areas vital to the diversity and integrity of the area of interest. Subsequently, conservation plans and management plans are developed as a framework that drives the conservancy's efforts (personal correspondence, Gibson, March 2001).

6. The taking up by private organizations, such as the Nature Conservancy, of increasingly strong roles in protected area and regional conservation planning. This arises, in part, because of the decline of government funding and involvement, and in part because extensive landscape-scale planning and management are often beyond the jurisdictions of government and traditional federal and state-protected area agencies. The efforts of NGOs can, in these situations, be facilitated through the regulatory and legislative frameworks of federal, state, and local government. This is evident in the Great Sand Dunes area where initiatives of the Nature Conservancy have been complemented by the U.S. National Park Service, the U.S. Forest Service, the federal Fish and Wildlife Service, and state agencies.

In conclusion, as the Great Sand Dunes case shows, the U.S. federal government agencies can bring an array of potentially complementary types of protected areas together to address and adapt to challenges, including national monuments, national parks, national preserves, fish and wildlife refuges, and Forest Service wilderness areas. Although this option is not so evident in the Great Sand Dunes case, the varied federal tool kit can also include federal Bureau of Reclamation lands. The interactive efforts of these federal and state agencies, and the various institutional arrangements available to them, can be increasingly applied to building corridors and connections among various natural areas and land uses involved in conserving and sustaining valued ecosystems.

POSTSCRIPT

In 2004 the Great Sand Dunes National Monument and associated lands were established as a national park by the U.S. Congress. The ensuing planning and management arrangements require more research.

NOTES

1   Adapted from J.G. Nelson, "Linking Public and Private Stewardship: Planning for the Great Sand Dunes National Monument Area, Colorado, and Its Implications for Canada." In *Protected Areas and the Regional Planning Imperative*, ed. J.G. Nelson, J.C. Day, L. Sportza, C. Vasquez, and J. Loucky, 133–146 (Calgary: University of Calgary Press, 2003).

REFERENCES

Anonymous. 2001. "Setting a wild example." In *Wilderness Activist*. Canadian Parks and Wilderness Society/CPAWS, National Newsletter, Ottawa: 1.

Brown, J., and B. Mitchell. 1997. "Extending the reach of national parks and protected areas: Local stewardship initiatives." In *National Parks and Protected Areas: Keystones to Conservation and Sustainable Development*, ed. J. G. Nelson and R. Serafin, 103–116. NATO ASI Series, vol. G 40. Berlin: Springer.

Cardinall, D., and J.C. Day. 1998. "Embracing value and uncertainty in environmental management and planning: A heuristic model." *Environments* 25(2–3): 110–125.

Etzioni, A. 1967. "Mixed scanning: A 'third' approach to decision-making." *Public Administration Review* 27: 385–392.

Forbes, G., S. Woodley, and B. Freedman. 1999. "Making ecosystem-based science into guidelines for ecosystem-based management: The Greater Fundy ecosystem experience." *Environments* 27(3): 15–23.

Friedmann, J. 1973. *Retracking America: A Theory of Transactive Planning*. Garden City, NJ: Anchor Press.

Gunderson, L. H., C. S. Holling, and S.S. Light, eds. 1995. *Barriers and Bridges to the Renewal of Ecosystems and Institutions*. New York: Columbia University Press.

Lee, K. 1993. *Compass and Gyroscope: Integrating Science and Politics for the Environment.* Washington, D.C.: Island Press.

Nelson, G. 2002. "Some perspectives on the human dimensions of park and protected area research and ecosystem-based planning, management and decision-making." In *Managing Protected Areas in a Changing World*, ed. S. Bondrup-Nielsen and N.W.P. Munro. Proceedings of the Fourth International Conference of Science and Management of Protected Areas, 14–19 May 2000. Canada: SAMPAA: 692–710.

Nelson, J.G., and L.M. Sportza, eds. 1999. "Special issue: Regional approaches to parks and protected areas in North America." *Environments* 27(3): 1–15.

Nelson, J.G., and J.B. Theberge. 1986. *Aishihik Lake Resource Survey: Institutional Aspects.* Environmentally Significant Area Series. Report 5, Committee on Northern Studies. Waterloo: University of Waterloo.

Noss, R.F. 1987. "Protecting natural areas in fragmented landscapes." *Natural Areas Journal* 7(1): 2–13.

Sportza, L.M. 1999. "Regional approaches to planning for protected areas and conservation." *Environments* 27(3): 1–14.

U.S. Congress. 2000. *Great Sand Dunes National Park and Preserve Act.* Washington, D.C.

PART V

PART V: COMMUNICATION AND EDUCATION

INTRODUCTION

Chapter 19 is intended to show how the ABC method can be used as an underlying framework to organize and communicate information leading to a sense of place among people of varied professional, educational, and civic backgrounds. The chapter is a summary of a Heritage Landscape Guide prepared for the Grand River Valley, Ontario.

In the Grand and other guides, the landscape or landscapes of study areas can readily be described in terms of leading geologic, landform, or Abiotic, plant, animal, or Biotic, and land-use, planning, or other Cultural characteristics. These can be listed to briefly define landscapes, as in this guide with Luther, Guelph, Conestogo, and other landscapes of the Grand River basin. The intent of the guide is to promote a broad professional, civic, and ultimately political understanding of the natural and cultural history and landscape of this watershed (see also Chapter 8, this volume). The watershed is diverse in natural, economic, and social terms and is faced with basin-wide planning and decision-making challenges that require better understanding of the region as a whole as well as greater and more informed participation of the people living within it. Several landscape guides of this kind have been prepared for awareness building and educational purposes in other urban and rural areas in Ontario. The ultimate aim is to build greater understanding of the environmental, land-use, and broad social and cultural characteristics of these places among residents and visitors alike and to encourage their interest and involvement in planning for the future. The Grand River watershed and other landscape guides have been used by universities and schools in the region as well as the general public.

Chapter 20, the final chapter in Part V and the book, is entitled "Retrospect and Prospect: Strengthening and Broadening the Approach." Here the general direction and contribution of the ABC method to understanding, planning, and making decisions about places are highlighted as they appear in this book. Some suggestions are also made for future use and development of the ABC method, notably in regard to cultural, aesthetic, and human dimensions.

19

2003

A HERITAGE LANDSCAPE GUIDE TO THE GRAND RIVER WATERSHED[1]

J.G. Nelson

GRAND RIVER LANDSCAPES

Figure 19.1 is a map of eight major landscapes – and related sites – in the Grand River watershed. These landscapes were identified on the basis of their different geologic, hydrologic, or Abiotic; vegetation, wildlife, or Biotic; and economic, social, and Cultural characteristics. The distinguishing features of these landscapes arise principally from differences in glacial history and landforms, ethnic history and settlement, types and levels of economic development, and land-use and land-cover patterns. In identifying these landscapes, they are not seen as having firm boundaries. Rather, they merge into one another.

The eight landscapes represent the broad landscape mosaic that makes up the Grand River watershed. Other smaller, more local landscapes occur within or among these major landscapes such as Kitchener's urban heritage districts, the Grand River forest, and the Dunnville marshes. Although we have not attempted to describe and map these local-scale landscapes in any detail, they definitely merit work in the future, as well as more careful consideration in planning, management, and decision-making.

We need to be especially concerned about significant landscapes that cross government boundaries and receive different treatment in different jurisdictions. An excellent example is the Grand River forest, which is divided between Waterloo Region, with its relatively

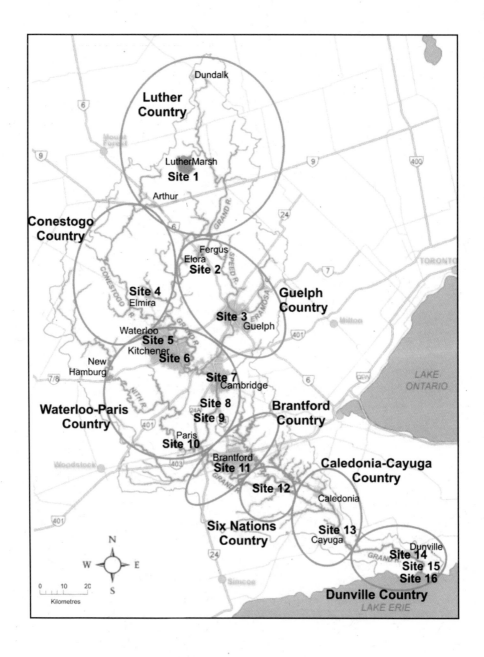

Figure 19.1   The Grand River Basin, Ontario, Canada

well-developed Environmentally Sensitive Area (ESA) and heritage conservation system and Brant County, which has a less well-developed one. In urban areas we have to be concerned about the traditional emphasis on protection of individual historic buildings or other structures to the neglect of the surrounding landscapes of which they are a part. Without concern and care, older heritage buildings can stand out amid a landscape of unsympathetic development and change. Each of the eight major landscapes will now be described in terms of its own noteworthy Abiotic, Biotic, and Cultural features. Some relevant sites within each of these landscapes will also be discussed briefly to provide for some detail on the natural and cultural history and current complex character of the watershed. Each of the eight landscapes is introduced by a checklist of key Abiotic, Biotic, and Cultural features. The guide is also organized so as to be useful for visits to the whole or part of the watershed or particular sites within it.

NORTHERN REGION

Landscape #1 – Luther Country

This landscape is located in the northern extremity of the watershed (Figure 19.1). It can be reached rather readily from Guelph or Kitchener. Along the way, the Grand diminishes in size. The river and the surrounding countryside have a pastoral rustic quality. The small pleasant town of Grand Valley is located on the winding river. From here rural roads can be taken to Luther Marsh, a scenic and highly significant site in the watershed.

Noteworthy features of Luther Country include:

- flat to undulating unbevelled till plains;
- soils relatively high in clay, often ill-drained by immature stream systems;
- relatively little evidence of ancient Paleo-Indian or Archaic First Nations culture, a hunting area in pre-European Woodland times;

- mixed needle-leaf evergreen and deciduous forest extensively logged and cleared by the end of the nineteenth century;
- Irish and Scots as major European settlers; and
- predominantly rural farming area with pasture, feed crops and beef, and a few small urban areas such as Grand Valley.

Site 1: Luther Marsh Wildlife Management Area

The Luther Marsh Wildlife Management Area comprises approximately 5,600 ha (13,832 acres) of gently undulating land, lake, and wetland. Early settlers in the area removed much of the original forest to make their living in the logging industry. Up until 1952 the marsh consisted of a small lake and associated wetlands that were imperfectly drained through Black Creek. The Luther Dam was built across Black Creek in 1952 as a part of the implementation of the Finlayson Report of 1932 that recommended engineering and other works to provide greater control of river flow. The intent of these efforts was twofold. One was to reduce the frequency of flooding in downstream towns and cities, such as Cambridge and Brantford. The other was to hold water to augment low summer flows that could lead to nearly dry river beds and poor water quality downstream at places such as Brantford and Paris. Today the Luther Marsh area is managed through the co-operation of the Grand River Conservation Authority, Ministry of Natural Resources, Ducks Unlimited, and other concerned organizations.

The Luther Marsh area is home to a diverse assemblage of indigenous and exotic plants and animals, including twelve that are either provincially or regionally rare. Pheasant, duck, and other small game, as well as fish, including carp and perch, are abundant in the area. They provide opportunities for controlled recreational hunting and fishing. Some species such as wild turkeys have been re-introduced to the region in recent years. The Luther Marsh area is also an ideal place for bird watching, canoeing, hiking, and other naturalist activities. The area is used as a research and monitoring station for birds and other vulnerable, threatened, and endangered plant and animal species.

Landscape #2 – Guelph Country

This landscape includes villages such as Erin and the Eramosa River Valley, as well as the towns of Elora and Fergus to which the City of Guelph is connected by roads originally built in early European settlement days.

Noteworthy features of Guelph Country include:

- flat to undulating bevelled or smoothed till plains with frequent spoon-shaped hills or drumlins;
- high clay soils with some prominent stream systems, such as the Speed, an east bank tributary of the Grand, which passes through the City of Guelph and enters the main river at the old Town of Preston;
- little evidence of ancient Paleo-Indian or Archaic First Nations cultures;
- Scots and other early settlers cleared and logged forests and built early stone-worked river towns such as Guelph, Fergus, and Elora;
- John Galt's radial design of downtown Guelph differed from the grid or haphazard development of many other Ontario towns and has been said to be reminiscent of the layout of Washington, D.C., on a small scale;
- the University of Guelph, one of the leaders in agricultural and rural planning programs in Canada, began as the Ontario Agricultural College (OAC) in 1882, with an early version of a master plan, and has a number of historic buildings including Creelman Hall (1924) and the Ontario Veterinary College (1922); and
- the Guelph landscape has been a stage for the evolution of various forms of transport, including railroads, which faded away with the growth of roads such as Highway 401. Canadian National Railway freight lines to Elora and Fergus were abandoned in 1989. Rail lines and facilities have frequently been removed, for example the Canadian Pacific (CP) passenger station lasted until 1983 when it was demolished for an apartment building.

Site 2: Elora

The deep Grand River Gorge begins in Elora and runs a highly scenic route for approximately two kilometres through the Elora Gorge Conservation Area to the village of Inverhaugh. Cedar, white birch, white pine, and upland shrub thickets line the Gorge, showing the ability of plants to colonize different areas. The forest of the Gorge seems to have been largely cut-over and cleared in the mid- to late nineteenth century to provide wood for construction and also for tanning and fuel for local mills. It has returned to forest, in part through the protection efforts of the Grand River Conservation Authority (GRCA). In its present state, it is hard to tell that it was ever disturbed. The Gorge serves as a prime recreational area for the upper Grand. The white-water areas attract many kayakers and "tubers." Within Elora a variety of arts and crafts shops and dining establishments are located in a historic milling centre.

Elora is located only about 10 km from Fergus, which is also a river town where hard rocks cross the channel and create falls and rapids. Like Elora, Fergus was an early industrial town. Many of the mills have been adapted to new uses and markets. Picturesque river trails and a Heritage District are signs of heritage planning interests in Fergus. In addition to its popular Scottish highland games, Fergus is conscious of its natural heritage and recently introduced major improvements to its sewage plant, in large part to protect trout and other fish in the Grand.

Site 3: Guelph Downtown Area

Guelph's downtown core is a site with a number of intriguing attributes. Not only does it provide dramatic examples of drumlins, it showcases a rich cultural and planning heritage begun by John Galt with his innovative radial street pattern (Figure 19.2). This was a dramatic departure from the grid pattern used by most British land surveyors. This pattern made the downtown a focal point for the city. The Church of Our Lady was built atop a nearby drumlin.

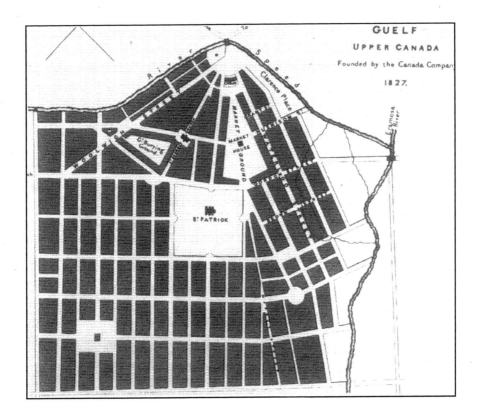

Figure 19.2   John Galt's Plan of Guelph, 1827

Downtown Guelph is an example of a downtown core strug-
gling to overcome the impact of 1970s and 1980s industrial decline,
new urban development projects, and a shift in retail trends. A number
of historic buildings have been lost to development in recent decades.
However, many still remain and the basic integrity of the old core has
been largely maintained. The city has been active in attempting to
promote the core as a centre of culture with the construction of the
River Run Centre for the performing arts.

Landscape #3 – Conestogo Country

This landscape lies west of Guelph Country and the Grand River, beginning approximately at Elmira. This town is quite different from nearby Elora and Fergus, especially in cultural terms. Elora and Fergus are Scottish in character. Elmira is a Mennonite village, which still has ties with the Pennsylvania Dutch in the United States. Elmira, St. Jacobs, and other parts of the Conestogo landscape can readily be reached from either Guelph or Waterloo. St. Jacobs is part of Waterloo Region and abuts the northern boundary of the City of Waterloo.

Noteworthy features of Conestogo Country include:

- the Conestogo River, a west bank tributary of the Grand River;
- extensive undulating till plains fringed on the south by rolling recessional and end moraines of the central Grand River watershed;
- numerous woodlots used by Mennonites for maple sugar, bees, timber, fuel, and other purposes as part of the farm enterprise;
- landscape is Mennonite in character, frequently with stone farm buildings and numerous surrounding barns and outbuildings. Old Order Mennonites have resisted use of electric power for their houses and farm operations except for situations where they have to pasteurize milk by provincial law for public sale;
- numerous Mennonites have shifted away from traditional values and do not use the horses and buggies nor closely follow the traditional values of the Old Order Mennonites;
- Mennonite families tend to be quite large, the amount of farmland remaining in the area is limited, and a lower limit of 36 ha (90 acres) is generally set for farm size; the result is difficulty for young Mennonites to find work in their home region. Many are involved in furniture making, house renovation and other enterprises on the farm or in nearby villages, towns, and cities;

- the Conestogo and Mennonite landscape can be thought of as lying on the transition from a relatively complex urban area in Waterloo Region to the essentially rural landscape, villages, and small towns of much of Wellington County;
- a farmer's market was moved from the site of the old Kitchener City Hall to an area just north of the Woolwich-Waterloo townline in the 1970s, following the sale of the original market land by the City of Kitchener to Eaton's stores. The new facility has grown into a major market and tourism facility in its own right, with a recent addition of a Best Western Hotel for bus tours and other visitors; and
- tourism has had a major effect on St. Jacobs, which has moved from being a declining rural village in the 1970s to a major touring centre for visitors today.

SITE 4: ST. JACOBS

Pennsylvania-German Mennonites began to settle in the area of St. Jacobs in the 1790s. Early Mennonites and Germans were attracted to the area's close proximity to the Conestogo River and the opportunities for water power and industrial development. In the 1970s, St. Jacobs rapidly grew mainly as a result of two events: (1) the adaptive re-use of old mills and other buildings, and (2) the introduction of local dining and other services for tourists keyed around the opportunity to observe traditional horse and buggies and other features of Old Order Mennonites.

The old Main Street with its mills, blacksmith shops, tannery, and other buildings is now lined with restaurants and other clothing and souvenir shops for tourists. St. Jacobs is also the place of origin and the headquarters of a local firm that became an international success story: Home Hardware. St. Jacobs is also the site of the Visitor Centre, which has videos, displays, and pamphlets on Mennonite and other comparable groups such as the Amish and the Hutterites.

From the northwest corner of St. Jacobs, a rural road runs west to the village of Hawkesville and on to Wallenstein and other small historic villages of Conestogo Country. Along the way, the road crosses the Conestogo floodplain, where cattle sometimes may be seen grazing to the verge of the stream banks, or even wading and drinking in the river itself. This makes for an attractive pastoral scene, more or less in the spirit of the art of well-known nineteenth-century Grand River artist Homer Watson. However, such practices contribute to increased bank erosion and to rising sedimentation as well as organic pollution in the rivers of the watershed. From the St. Jacobs–Hawkesville rural road, the higher rolling hills of the Waterloo Moraine can be seen, marking the northern border of the neighbouring Waterloo-Paris landscape.

Landscape #4 – The Waterloo-Paris Country

This uneven landscape arises from the ridges or moraines deposited at the edge of glaciers and the kames, kettles, spillways, and other land-forms created by meltwater from the retreating ice. Noteworthy features of Waterloo-Paris Country include:

- rolling gravelly and sandy recessional and end moraines laid down close to ancient ice;
- spillways and old channels formed by ancestral Grand and other meltwater streams;
- moraines and similar deposits serve as aquifers for large quantities of groundwater used for domestic and industrial purposes in Kitchener, Waterloo, Cambridge, and other nearby sites;
- hills, valleys, and scenic vistas valued for residential development in Waterloo, Kitchener, and Cambridge areas in the last two decades;
- much of this country is still covered in forests and woodlots, a transitional area between Carolinian and mixed needle-leaf evergreen and deciduous forest;

- site of the Grand River forest, a unique stretch of wooded terrain running between Cambridge and Paris on the Grand River, paralleling a stretch of the Grand River that is free of dams and weirs for about twenty-five kilometres;
- considerable influx of settlement after Napoleonic wars including German, Scots, Irish, and English;
- coming of the railroads in the mid-1850s boosted the industrial economy of the region, with Berlin, later Kitchener, becoming a major centre for manufacturing of furniture, buttons, leather and metal products, meat processing, and other industries;
- the construction of Highway 401 in the 1950s led to renewed growth in Waterloo-Kitchener-Cambridge, eventually including a large Toyota Plant in Cambridge; and
- over the years the towns and cities of Galt, Preston, Hespeler, Kitchener, and Waterloo have grown towards one another, with Kitchener and Waterloo now forming one continuous urban area; Galt, Preston, and Hespeler have been amalgamated into current-day Cambridge.

SITE 5: UNIVERSITIES AND HIGH-TECH PARKS

The post-World War II development of the University of Waterloo and Wilfrid Laurier University (formerly Waterloo Lutheran) has led, among other things, to Waterloo becoming a leader in the field of computing and high technology, which emerged in the 1980s and became fully developed through the 1990s. Within the City of Waterloo are several locations where "High Tech Parks" have been created since the early 1980s. These businesses can be seen along the Phillip St. corridor north of Columbia St., the North Waterloo Business Park around Weber and Northfield Roads, and the University of Waterloo Technology Park on the North Campus of the university. Wilfrid Laurier University has developed important business and social programs. The older manufacturing economy of cities such as Kitchener, Preston, and Galt has struggled to move into an advanced twenty-first-century economy with varying levels of success.

Site 6: Kitchener Heritage Districts

Kitchener has been an active city in terms of heritage planning. Since the designation of its first heritage district in Doon (1988), a second has been designated (Victoria Park Neighbourhood), another is nearing designation (St. Mary's Neighbourhood), and at least one heritage district study is being undertaken (Pioneer Tower Area).

The Victoria Park neighbourhood is an example of the type of area that can be protected as a Heritage Conservation District. The area includes fine residences from the late nineteenth and early twentieth century, many of which belonged to the business and civic leaders of Berlin at the turn of the twentieth century. Not only are these houses significant in terms of appearance, many of them help to tell the story of the early growth of the city. Contrary to many opinions, such districts also tend to maintain or have increased property values. The St. Mary's neighbourhood is a unique district in Ontario. It is perhaps the first effort in Ontario to designate a post–World War II veterans' housing development as a heritage district.

Site 7: The Former City of Galt in Present-Day Cambridge

Galt is home to many mills and historic sites dating from the early days of settlement in the region. The historic sites include Cruickston reserve (now know as "rare"), a rural site of high natural and cultural research value. The industrial sites formed the backbone of the community's early economy. These old buildings lined the river bank, notably on the east side of the river. Many were seriously damaged by the great 1974 flood. Initial plans were to tear them down and construct a solid rampart along the river. Discussions arose, a design competition was held, and the Living Levee was the result. The creation of the Living Levee from the remains of several old mills deemed to be too heavily damaged for restoration, but seen by residents as being too important to the heritage of the area to completely remove, is an example of the ability to find innovative ways of dealing with life along the floodplain of a river. The space now provides valuable parkland along the river's edge, allowing for people to rest and relax along the water while only being minutes away from the stores and offices of the city.

SITE 8: THE GRAND RIVER FOREST

The Grand River forest contains almost 800 ha (1,976 acres) of continuous deciduous or Carolinian forest, extending over eighteen kilometres from the south end of Cambridge to just above Paris. The Grand River forest is easily observed from many sites. Amongst the best is the Cambridge–Paris Rail Trail located between Cambridge and the Glen Morris Bridge, about half-way between Cambridge and Paris (Figure 19.3). The Cambridge–Paris Trail is part of a much larger network throughout the watershed. It provides an excellent opportunity to explore the forest and observe the remnants of early settlement along with diverse plant, animal, and bird species. The Grand River forest contains relatively little undisturbed primary or old growth forest as a result of extensive logging and clearing for settlement, fuel, and other purposes in early European days.

SITE 9: GLEN MORRIS

Glen Morris is an entry point to the Cambridge to Paris Rail Trail. The trail was the site of an historic heavy duty, as well as an electric, rail line, which carried goods and people from beyond Brantford to Kitchener as late as the 1950s. A sign at the ford briefly indicates the history of the railroad. A small way station was located nearby. Just to the southeast is the Pinehurst Conservation Area. It has been extensively reforested and is a major camping and day use recreational area both summer and winter. The area includes a large kettle lake and some rolling hills or kames of the Paris Moraine.

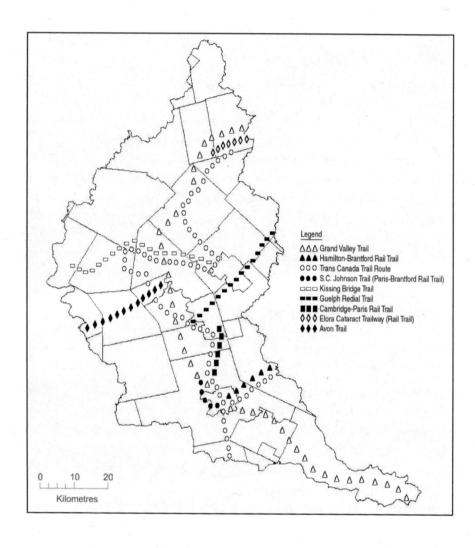

Figure 19.3   Trails of the Grand River Basin

Site 10: Paris

The small town of Paris roughly marks the southern border of the Waterloo-Paris morainal country. This town is located at the forks of the Grand and a major west bank tributary, the Nith. Paris originated in the 1820s and 1830s. Hiram Capron was an early entrepreneur and Loyalist who developed the local gypsum deposits and a plaster of Paris industry. The Grand River at Paris is the site of an old weir and is an endpoint for much of the canoe traffic that has developed since the designation of the Grand River as a Canadian Heritage River in 1994. This canoe traffic often begins well upstream in Cambridge or north of Waterloo. The stretch of river from Cambridge to Paris is almost twenty-five kilometres long and free of dams and weirs.

SOUTHERN REGION

Landscape #5 – Brantford Country

The City of Brantford marks the gateway to the sand plains landscape located on the southern fringe of the Waterloo-Paris Country.

Noteworthy features of Brantford Country include:

- ancient shorelines, beach and sand plain deposits laid down in ancient glacial lakes;
- the Grand River floodplain, which is extensive along this meandering reach of the river;
- location in the Carolinian Zone with several species of concern, including the grey fox, wood turtle, green snake, American badger, Henslow's sparrow, Acadian flycatcher, northern bobwhite, least bittern, hooded warbler, short-eared owl, Louisiana waterthrush, red-headed woodpecker, and fish, such as the black redhorse and silver shiner;
- Paleo-Indian sites located near Fairchild Creek and remains of longhouses and other Woodland Indian activity have been found in the general area;

- Loyalist settlers after the 1776 U.S. Revolutionary War and later European migrants developed industries in the City of Brantford from the early 1800s, a national leader in manufacturing until the decline of the 1970s and 1980s; and
- much of the floodplain was settled prior to the development of new zoning and building regulations following the great flood of 1974. The city is, therefore, a special planning area in terms of the flood policies.

SITE 11: BRANTFORD CITY

The history of Brantford dates back to 1784 when Chief Joseph Brant, or Thayendanega, and the Six Nations were granted land along the Grand River in recognition of their loyalty to the British during the American Revolutionary War (1776–83). Early industrial development was focused on the Grand in the early 1830s. Brantford was the end-point of the new navigation canal. At one time, the Grand River Navigation Company operated numerous steamers, schooners, and paddle-wheelers to transport goods and people along the Grand. The "Age of Railways," from about 1850 to 1900, led to the decline of the canal. The railroads contributed strongly to the growth of Brantford as an early manufacturing centre dealing in agricultural equipment, machine tools, and, later, trucks and other heavy-duty goods. Since the 1960s, Brantford has struggled with the decline of both the past industrial activity and the downtown core of the city. Attempts to revitalize its economy include a recently established casino. In addition, Wilfrid Laurier University opened a Brantford campus in the downtown centre. Brantford's population of 87,000 people continues to experience great economic challenge, as is evident in numerous run-down buildings in the downtown area. Brantford contains several National Historic Sites, including the Alexander Graham Bell Homestead, the Royal Chapel of the Mohawks, and the Woodland Cultural Centre, which preserves and enhances First Nations Heritage and provides interpretation from a First Nations Perspective.

Landscape #6 – Six Nations Country

The Six Nations landscape is a remnant of the large block of land granted to the Mohawks along the Grand River after the U.S. Revolutionary War. South of the City of Brantford, Highway 54 leads to the Mohawk-New Credit Reserve, the core of the Six Nations landscape.

The reserve has a population of about 9,500 people, three quarters of whom either work outside or in one of the three hundred small businesses on the reserve (Woodland Cultural Centre, website). The Native people claim that they are historically entitled to land along the river as well as the river bed of the Grand. The west bank, or reserve side, of the river, is readily distinguished by its almost continuous forest. While the First Nations are in the best position to tell the story of this area, we will offer some general information about the reserve and the Six Nations area, remaining as sensitive as possible to First Nation's views.

Noteworthy features of Six Nations Country include:

- underlying bedrock is Salina Formation, capped by deposits of glacial till overlain, in turn, by sediments deposited by ancient glacial lakes;
- the 9,200 ha (22,734 acres) of Carolinian forest and less intrusive pasture and other land uses distinguishes this landscape from any other in the watershed;
- a wide diversity of animals with southern affinity has been recorded, including the American badger, grey fox, eastern hog-nosed snake, wood turtle, Acadian flycatcher, northern bobwhite, least bittern, hooded warbler, peregrine falcon, silver shiner, American ginseng, and bird's foot violet;
- the former house of E. Pauline Johnson, the poetess, is on the reserve. It has been refurbished and declared a National Historic Site. Other notables from the area include Tom Longboat, the famous long-distance runner, and the men renowned throughout North America for their skills in building skyscrapers in places such as New York; and
- tourism is of growing importance economically; a spring Pow

Wow and Fall Fair are held on the reserve and the people run the Woodland Cultural Museum on the former site of their school in Brantford.

SITE 12: OHSWEKEN

Ohsweken, a town located within the Six Nations Reserve, is home to Veteran's Park, which contains a Six Nations Memorial, a community picnic area, and one of the reserve's last remaining pre-Confederation buildings: the Six Nations Council House. Built in 1863, the Council House is no longer in use but was used as the headquarters for the Confederacy Council of Chiefs until 1924 when the Elected Council was mandated. The House remains an important part of Six Nations history, being visited by Sir John A. MacDonald as well as many other leaders.

The Chiefswood National Historic Site near Ohsweken was known as the capital of 'Upper Native Canada' during the mid- to late nineteenth century and is associated with several historically important people and events, including E. Pauline Johnson, a renowned Six Nations poet; Alexander Graham Bell, inventor of the telephone; and Homer Watson, famed Grand River artist. In 1997, Chiefswood was restored to its 1880 glory and remains one of the four remaining pre-Confederation buildings on the Six Nations Reserve.

Landscape #7 – Caledonia-Cayuga Country

The Caledonia-Cayuga landscape is extremely flat to undulating country, predominantly rural. Caledonia and Cayuga are small towns, with often modest brick and frame houses quite different from the more elaborate Victorian and historic houses in the cities in the northern part of the watershed.

Noteworthy features of the Caledonia-Cayuga Country include:

- flat-lying glacial till and lake deposits, which drain late in spring;
- little remaining forest, much is now in hay, pasture, scrub, and successional forest stands;

- marshes and wetlands located along the large, wide river, in part resulting from damming or back-up behind weirs;
- Cayuga Slough forest, north of the town of Cayuga, with well-developed stands of red oak, sugar maple, red maple, and white ash. It is home to a wide variety of Carolinian Canada plant and animal species (Eagles and Beechey, 1985);
- historic and "ghost" towns, which developed along the Grand in the mid-nineteenth century to serve the Grand River Navigation Company and the other ship traffic along the river; numerous mills and other industrial activities were located along the Grand at that time; and
- the introduction of railways in the 1850s and later led to the decline of the canal and towns such as York, Mount Healey, and Indiana. A small settlement remains at York today but the other two have largely disappeared. Remnants of the old canal can be found en route from Brantford to Caledonia, Cayuga, and Dunnville.

SITE 13: RUTHVEN

Ruthven Park dates back to 1845 when David Thompson (1793–1851) constructed a mansion there for his family after accumulating wealth working as a contractor on the Welland Canal and as a leading promoter of the Grand River Navigation Company. Ruthven Park was in the Thompson family from 1845 to 1993. It was obtained through the generosity of a sole surviving Thompson heir by the Lower Grand River Land Trust Inc. The mansion is a Classical Greek Revival architectural style, reflecting the Victorian Era. It has three floors with thirty-six rooms, plus the Barracks, Coach House, and several outbuildings. The mansion and its contents have remained in their original form. The 648 ha (1,600 acre) Park consists of 364 ha (900 acres) of Carolinian forest, and an additional 243 ha (600 acres), which are being actively cultivated by local farmers. Ruthven Park contains over four hundred different species of plants, with ten of them being provincially endangered. The Ruthven is a provincially and naturally recognized historic site, which is attracting more visitors each year.

Landscape #8 – Dunnville Country

The Dunnville landscape encompasses the area around the mouth of the Grand, stretching west and east along the Lake Erie coast. Much of the area is rural and agricultural. However, the river and nearby lake have led to a strong historic interest in commercial and sport fishing and water-based recreation. The Dunnville landscape has a different flavour or feel than other landscapes in the valley. The extensive river marshes, the wetlands, the big river, and the lake make this a landscape of the water as much or more than the land.

Noteworthy features of the Dunnville landscape include:

- a clay-rich plain, sandy delta, and coast, mostly laid down by ancient lakes and rivers of glacial times;
- susceptibility to flooding. Devastating floods occurred in 1913, 1916, 1930, and 1974;
- marshes stretching north of Dunnville behind the weir and south of it towards Lake Erie, about 364 ha (900 acres) have been designated as a National Wildlife Area;
- important habitat for nesting and migratory ducks and other waterfowl as well as songbirds and a breeding and nursery area for fish;
- arrival of United Empire Loyalists in the 1780s; other people of diverse backgrounds, such as Scots, Irish, English, and German, moved in later with the development of river traffic and the canal;
- rapid growth of Dunnville town after completion of the Feeder Canal in 1829 and, with subsequent development of the canal system to Brantford, Dunnville became a gateway for transport of goods along the Grand, the Welland Canal system, and to Buffalo and U.S. ports;
- railways were built to serve industries in Dunnville, but their effect on river traffic undermined the town's development;
- Port Maitland and other small centres in the delta became cottage and tourism centres serviced from Hamilton and other cities in the late nineteenth and early twentieth centuries;

- large historic homes and buildings remain in Dunnville, but much of the heritage has been lost to 1960s downtown redevelopment, glass storefronts, and glossy signage;
- the Feeder Canal, which can be followed by foot, bike, or car to the Welland Canal. The paths trodden in the early days by mules, horses, and men pulling barges can be seen along this route; and
- parts of the old canal are now overgrown with algae and scrub, offering habitat for amphibians and birds.

SITE 14: TOWN OF DUNNVILLE

The historic town of Dunnville is located where the Grand River enters Lake Erie. Perhaps as a result of its distance away from a major urban centre and transportation routes, Dunnville is overlooked by many residents and visitors to the Grand River watershed. Yet the wide and slow Grand River at Dunnville provides excellent opportunities for fishing and boating. Visitors can also enjoy a variety of town services, including the mudcat festival, carnivals, and boat races.

SITE 15: DUNNVILLE MARSHES

The marshes are excellent waterfowl and fish habitat. Boat rental and other facilities are available at Byng and other places near Dunnville and the weir. Groves of deciduous trees have established themselves along the river shores and terraces. Major species in the groves include white willow, silver maple, white elm, green ash, and American basswood. In addition, the wetland vegetation supports a large and diverse community of fish species. The diversity of provincially rare plant, animal, and fish species has resulted in the marshes being designated as a Life Sciences Area of Natural and Scientific Interest (ANSI-LS). The marshes are generally divided into five areas: shoreline grove and basin marsh, delta marsh and scrub/grove islands, alluvial island forb and grove, river bend levee forb, and alluvial island forb and drowned floodplain mosaic.

SITE 16: ROCK POINT PROVINCIAL PARK

Rock Point Provincial Park is the only provincial park within the Grand River watershed. It is a 187 ha park located on a set of limestone shelves, sand beaches, and dunes along the shore of Lake Erie near the Grand River. It supports an important area of Carolinian forest along the shore and provides habitat for a diverse mix of plant and animal life, including migrating birds, monarch butterflies, mammals, and fish. Classified as a "Recreation" zone park under the Ontario Parks' guidelines, its purpose is to offer recreational activities, including hiking, boating, canoeing, fishing, swimming, bird watching, environmental education, and some hunting, in a scenic landscape.

PLANNING

The major forces for change in the Grand River watershed seem to be urbanization and associated processes such as sprawl, proliferating roads, and communication infrastructure. The pressures seem to be greatest on the Waterloo area or on the Waterloo-Paris landscape. However, these processes are changing all the landscapes of the Grand in various ways, as are other processes such as the intensification of agriculture. A big challenge for planning for the Grand watershed is the virtual absence of law, policy, and responsibility for planning at the regional landscape scale. Smaller landscapes can be addressed through the official plans of the municipalities, although not much of this has actively occurred. It appears that the Grand River Conservation Authority or some other body or combination of bodies should address the future of the larger-scale landscapes in the Grand, but this is a challenge yet to be addressed.

NOTES

1   Adapted from J.G. Nelson, ed.,*The Grand River Watershed: A Heritage Landscape Guide*. Heritage Landscape Guide #2. An Environments Publication. University of Waterloo, Waterloo, Ontario, 2003.

REFERENCES

Nelson, J.G., J. Porter, C. Lemieux, C. Farassoglou, S. Gardiner, C. Guthrie, and C. Beck. 2003. *The Grand River Watershed: A Heritage Landscape Guide.* Waterloo: Heritage Resources Centre, University of Waterloo.

20

RETROSPECT AND PROSPECT: STRENGTHENING AND BROADENING THE APPROACH

J.G. Nelson

The ABC method arose in the academic and professional milieu of the 1970s and 1980s. At that time, the increasing pace and magnitude of economic and technical growth and development had brought rising challenges to land use, environment, and quality of life in Canada and many other parts of the world. Pressures were of a kind and scale seldom experienced before. The accelerating use of chemicals in many phases of economic activity is an outstanding case in point, manifesting itself, for example, in more widespread use of and demand for feedstock, notably petroleum. The academic and professional communities were challenged to find ways of addressing these issues and especially to provide the information needed by planners, managers, politicians, and the wider society to make efficient, effective, and equitable decisions about them.

In response, many disciplines, professions, and industrial and technical sectors produced increasingly specialized information on bedrock, minerals, landforms, permafrost, hydrology, plants, animals, soils, drilling and exploration systems, First Nations land tenure, hunting and fishing, land-claims, economic costs and benefits, and a stream of other relevant topics. This new information also included innovative methods of planning and making decisions, for example, environmental and social impact assessments of project proposals and broader methods of public consultation. One challenge that was insufficiently addressed, and remains so today, is methods of bringing such diverse information together and organizing, evaluating, and interpreting it in ways conducive to broader cross-disciplinary, cross-sectoral, and civic understanding, planning, and decision-making. The ABC method was developed in response to this challenge.

The origins of the ABC method lie in the 1960s and 1970s with the collection, organization, and use of diverse geologic, soils, biologic, land-use, and other information for urban and regional planning in highly settled southern Ontario, notably the Golden Horseshoe between the cities of Toronto and Buffalo. In the 1970s and early 1980s, a group of ecologists, geographers, and planners at the University of Waterloo applied this ABC system to understanding and planning for change in Canada's North, where there was growing concern about ongoing and emerging large-scale impacts of oil exploration, pipeline proposals, and related development on environment and indigenous people. Subsequently, the ABC method was refined and elaborated upon in applications in other parts of Canada, the United States, Europe, and Asia.

One refinement has been to make the method more systematic, consistent, and replicable through the use of academic and professional criteria acceptable in public planning and decision-making situations. The chapters in Part I illustrate this reasonably well. Another line of development has been to refine and elaborate the Cultural or human dimensions of the method, particularly the institutional dimensions. Criteria and procedures for identifying, organizing, analyzing, evaluating, and interpreting laws, policies, agencies, protected areas, and other forms of land management have been developed in ways that make it possible to link or "match" them with significant land-use and environmental issues in planning and decision-making. These refinements are illustrated in the chapters in Parts I and II.

Another important line of development has been to use the method in a less technical and more generally civic way. Here the focus is as much or more on understanding a place in terms of its natural and cultural history and its distinctive Abiotic, Biotic, and Cultural characteristics than on addressing more specific planning and decision-making challenges. When applied in this focused (Part II) yet comprehensive (Part III) way, the method can include a review of the history of institutions and planning and their implications for researchers, professionals, and the public as demonstrated, for example, in Chapter 12 on the San Pedro Valley.

In these respects, the ABC method can be seen as a fundamental way of thinking about places. It can be valuable in greater understanding of home areas as well as those visited elsewhere. The chapters in Parts II and III illustrate this. Chapter 19 in Part IV shows how the method can be used for educational purposes as an underlying organizational framework for preparing landscape guides for places.

Another line of development has been the use of the ABC in situations where satellite images, air photos, and related geographical information systems are a major source of information. In such circumstances, the imagery can be used to collect, organize, and interpret information thematically, for example, in producing a map or maps of forests, wetlands, or urban or other land cover changes. The studies of Fairy-Peninsula Lakes or Segara Anakan in Chapters 13 and 9 are examples.

The imagery can also be used more holistically to map, analyze, evaluate, and integrate land cover changes in a place and interpret them for planning and decision-making. The study of the Segara Anakan, Java, is the main example in this book (Chapter 9). The potential for greater use of the ABC with satellite imagery and geographical information systems represents an important research challenge in the further development of the ABC method.

All of the foregoing examples show the ABC method is flexible to theory, context, scale, technology, available resources, and time. One major challenge in the further development of the method is to attempt to push it beyond the technical, professional, and planning context in which it has been developed so far. Much of the thinking about the ABC has been shaped by its utility in bringing diverse scientific, scholarly, and technical information together so that it can be understood and applied in multidisciplinary, multisectoral, and civic situations for planning and decision-making purposes. This perspective has put a kind of envelope around the method, which has constrained incorporation of information of a more aesthetic or humanistic kind.

For example, the work with the method has attempted to represent First Nations interests primarily from the perspective of equity and social justice. This perspective or concern is part of a broad scientific, scholarly, and ethical perspective taken in Canada, the United States, and many other places.

But little attempt has been made to try and build such a cultural perspective into any application of the method in a fundamental way. For example, in some of our work, historical research often led to peoples and cultures other than those of a more "western" affinity. We see this, for example, in Chapters 6 and 7 on the First Nations in Yukon and Northwest Territories and in Chapter 12 on the San Pedro Valley. In doing the last study, considerable information was encountered on the knowledge systems of the Native people who occupied or had occupied part or all of the valley and surrounding region. Among these people were those of the Pueblo culture. In a rather detailed and provocative study, Hamilton A. Tyler (1991) showed that these people thought completely differently about birds and the animal world than people of a more western persuasion. The Pueblo people did not classify and think about birds in terms of the genera and species system that is standard in scientific, professional, and naturalist groups in western society.

Without going into the details of Tyler, who spent years "bird watching over the Pueblo's shoulder," they classify or group birds according to classes such as Birds of the Sun (macaws, parrots, and parokeets), Birds of the Sky (eagles, ospreys, and large hawks), Rain Birds (swallows, swifts, hummingbirds, and doves), Water Birds (ducks, snipes, killdeer, and sandhill cranes), and so forth. They apparently do not see species as distinctly as western society does. Rather they build them into assemblages such as the general set of birds of a season (Tyler, 1991).

So how is such a system to be built into the ABC? Perhaps this is not a major problem from the point of view of an attempt to describe and understand the Pueblo system. But it poses considerable challenges in planning because Pueblo indigenous knowledge of birds does not correspond with the scientific and professional system used by the wider society in making decisions about birds in the context of project proposals.

Another similar challenge is how to incorporate art, notably art in the western tradition, into the ABC for purposes of understanding, planning, and making decisions about places. Here we can use the example of painting, notably landscape painting. Styles, or schools, exist in this respect. Think of the Impressionists (Art Gallery of Ontario, 1998). Within this school, many artists developed their own style; for places in France we have paintings or images seen and prepared by a number of them such as Degas, Van Gogh, and Cezanne.

How can we incorporate these into the ABC? Can they be built into an artistic category within the Cultural component and be valued, for example, as an expression of the capacity of a place to evoke or be associated with artistic endeavours? They certainly can be explicitly used to show how an artistic school or an individual artist views a landscape or place at some point in time. Such painting also can tell us, to some extent, what was present and what was not. For example, historic paintings, like historic photographs, can show the state of individual buildings, squares, villages, or rural fields or the condition of the forest or other vegetation at some time in the past.

And this has been done, at least implicitly, for some of the studies in this book, for example through Bartlett and other portrayals of the nineteenth-century San Pedro Valley and the U.S. southwest (Wilson, 1995; Skolnick, 1994), Constable, Turner, and landscape artists of the New Forest area in southern England (Wilton and Lyles, 1993), and early Canadian Pacific Railroad (CPR) artists in the Banff area of western Canada (Render, 1974). Yet the knowledge and preferences of such artists leads them to stress certain things and downplay or leave others out. For example, the railroad artists sometimes painted in such a way as to obscure the stunted and burnt forests typical of much of the southern Canadian Rockies in the nineteenth century. This could, of course, have been a response to the interests of their sponsors, the CPR, in producing scenery likely to attract tourists. This point can also be illustrated by reference to the Group of Seven, a school of early-twentieth-century Canadian artists who painted in the Georgian

Bay area, highlighted in Chapter 3 (Hill, 1995). These artists often painted landscapes in a broadly representative way, with an orientation to a wilderness perspective, not forgetting exceptions such as the bold abstract art of Lauren Harris.

So the rugged, glaciated bedrock of the Canadian Shield is often vividly portrayed along with the pine, poplar, and other trees of the forest, often in bright fall colours. But artifacts and traces of humans are much less evident, perhaps because they were not there, perhaps because they did not fit the wild perspective well. Such passing over of scenes not wanted is not uncommon and is part of artistic licence to highlight and accent what the painter sees as significant and indicative of his style. Clarence Gagnon, the great French Canadian painter of early-twentieth-century Quebec landscapes, such as Charlevoix east of Quebec City, is said to have deliberately left out telegraph poles and other signs of the modern in portraying the land and people in what he saw as their traditional self-sustaining style (Newlands, 2005).

But perhaps too much has been said for some readers who may find it difficult and perhaps unnecessary to grapple too much with the humanistic dimension of places. Yet without some conscious effort to do this, the ABC method will fall short in its attempt to incorporate all that is meaningful in understanding and planning for places. It will also fail to meet the ways of knowing and preferences of many people and may indeed be inequitable in that regard.

In closing we can return to the basic theme set forth in the Preface – understanding the extent and intensity of change in places around the globe in the last forty years, the development era. The effects of the commitment to development worked for growth in some places, notably urban areas, and less so for others, notably smaller rural communities, the countryside, and wilderness. The extent and intensity of development is seen as having been moderated by new approaches and theory such as environmental planning, sustainable development, and green tourism. But details on the extent to which moderation has actually occurred in places on the ground is not well understood and the underlying commitment to growth has continued. Indeed, growth and the stock market are now so ingrained in the global system that slowing is perceived as catastrophic and deserving of every antidote by governments.

The tracking system that we have usually used to measure the extent, intensity, and effects of post-1950s development has been highly specialized in accordance with the world view of western and increasingly of global society. Changes in the gross domestic product (GDP), interest rates, employment, housing, investment, air and water quality indices, number of species at risk, and other specialized measures are employed to monitor changes. But very little attention has been paid to how all development changes and effects come together to modify and transform places on the ground. The big contribution of a comprehensive mapping survey and assessment system such as the ABC method is in showing how all the specialties come together to track the extent and intensity of change at various scales on the ground.

Part I of this book shows how the rising demand for oil and gas and other resources needed to drive the growing urban engine has reached out to convert Yukon and Northwest Territories in Canada into industrial hinterlands. The patterns of change in the North take the form of competition for land, First Nations land-claim settlements, oil and gas leases, and parks and wildlife reserves to replace undivided wildlands. The chapters in Part I show similar forces at work in the mid-north of Canada as well as more highly settled southern lands. The Bruce Peninsula, its forests, and fish, after having been heavily exploited in the late nineteenth and early twentieth century, were left to rural folk. Afforestation and natural recovery in the 1940s and 1950s made it a magnet for parks and recreational and tourism development in 1980s and 1990s, mainly because of urban population growth in Toronto and the cities of the south. The chapters on Fairy and Peninsula Lakes show similar forces at work there. And the recreational and nature conservation arms of the growth and development model reach out to organize Banff, Long Point, the Huron Coast, and Frenchman's Bay in the more heavily settled south. The chapters on Java, Hong Kong, the New Forest, the Carpathians, and the Sand Dunes of Colorado show the same pattern of change internationally.

The aim here is not necessarily to identify or advocate for solutions to the effects of the growth and development model, although numerous proposals for response are discussed in the various chapters of this book. Rather, the principal purpose is to show how comprehensive methods of mapping, analysis, assessment, and reporting can illustrate much better how places are being modified and transformed by growth. The ABC method brings out all the dimensions of change – the geologic, hydrologic, and Abiotic, the plants, animals, and Biotic, and the land-use, land tenure, institutional, and Cultural – as well as how they interact over time to consume space and change landscape character and ways of life. In doing this, the ABC approach provides professionals, decision-makers, and citizens with the food for thought they need to understand development-driven change and be in a better position to deal with it than when supplied only with specialized and fragmented economic, biological, earth science, or other measures. These more specialized systems are valuable in their own right but do not give the big picture of interaction among Abiotic, Biotic, and Cultural dimensions that people need to put all the effects into place. With this greater understanding, the ability of people generally to have greater access to and involvement in future planning should come much closer to achievement.

In closing then, the ABC method is a valuable tool for understanding and planning places at a variety of scales and in a range of different natural and human circumstances. As the chapters in this book demonstrate, the method can be applied to areas ranging from thousands to a few square kilometres. It can be used in wildlands, agricultural landscapes, river valleys, lake basins, and urban regions. It can be used for detailed analysis, assessment, reconnaissance, and educational and research purposes. Its maps can be presented in a relatively simple schematic fashion or in a complex technical way. It can work across and link scientific and scholarly specialities, professions, businesses, and the citizenry.

The ABC method seems especially useful in strategic planning because it more or less simultaneously maps and describes the natural and human domains and the ways in which they interact to give character to places. The method does not deal first with the natural or the human and then try to fit the one with the other. This process has often been seen as divisive because "the first from the gate" seems to set the agenda for others to follow. In linking the natural and the human, the method comes closer to telling the whole story, allowing all to see their roles, interdependencies, and effects on the world around them. In this sense, the ABC is an interactive technical, professional, and civic tool of great potential value to people everywhere.

REFERENCES

Art Gallery of Ontario. 1998. *The Courtauld Collection Masterpieces of Impressionism and Post-Impressionism.* Toronto: Art Gallery of Ontario.

Hill, C.C. 1995. *The Group of Seven Art for a Nation.* Ottawa: National Gallery of Canada.

Newlands, A. 2005. *Clarence Gagnon: An Introduction to His Work and Art.* Richmond Hill, ON: Firefly Books.

Render, L.E. 1974. *The Mountains and the Sky.* Calgary: Glenbow Alberta Institute.

Skolnick, A. 1994. *Paintings of the Southwest.* New York: Charles Potter.

Trenton, P., and P.H. Hassrick. 1983. *The Rocky Mountains: A Vision for Artists in the Nineteenth Century.* Norman: University of Oklahoma Press.

Tyler, H.A. 1991. *Pueblo Birds and Myths.* Flagstaff, AZ: Northland Press.

Wilson, J.P. 1995. *Islands in the Desert.* Albuquerque: University of New Mexico Press.

Wilton, A., and A. Lyles, 1993. *The Great Age of British Watercolours.* Munich: Prestel.

INDEX

A

ABC Method, 35, 56–57, 158
    Abiotic information, 3, 6, 8–9, 41, 55
    academic and professional criteria, 464
    aesthetic or humanistic information, 465, 467
    application to private zone, 11
    archaeology (*See* archaeological remains)
    Biotic information, 3, 6, 8–9, 41, 55
    conflict-resolution maps, 8–9
    cross-disciplinary approach, 19, 42, 464
    Cultural information, 3–9, 36, 55, 464
    in detailed analytical studies, 31–33
    educational purposes, 465
    in establishing new park, 99, 145
    flexibility, 42, 51, 465
    framework for sustainable development, 247 (*See also* conservation and development)
    in institutional analysis, 10–11, 156, 173–74, 464
    integration maps, 9
    for land-use and conservation planning, 43–48
    linked with planning theory, 275
    linking the natural and the human, 16, 41, 471
    mapping of human ecology, 20
    modified for citizen understanding, 258–59
    origins of, 15–21, 464
    rapid reconnaissance studies, 393
    and remotely sensed data, 245, 248, 464
    retrospect and prospect, 463–69
    significance and constraints maps, 7–9, 42, 44
    in strategic planning, 470
    structural and functional maps, 6–7

    theme maps, 6, 42–44
    using satellite images, 245, 248, 465
Aboriginal communities. *See* Native people
Acadian flycatcher, 453, 455
Acanthus, 399
Achyranthes aspera, 399
acid grassland, 409
acid rain, 356
adaptive management, 50, 365, 428
    Great Sand Dunes of Colorado, 426, 430
    for San Pedro National Conservation Areas (NCAs), 321
    water policies, 327
adaptive planning, 11, 36, 364–65
adder's mouth, 68
advocacy planning, 50
Aegicents, 399
aerial photography, 9
agreement forests, 227
agriculture, 129, 314–15, 399. See also grazing
    abandoned farm lands, 335, 338
    Fairy and Peninsula Lakes, 338
    maize, squash, beans agriculture, 221, 314–15
    pollution from (Grand River), 226
    rice fields *(sawah),* 240
    run-off and soil erosion, 346
Aishihik ESA, Yukon, 10, 33, 185, 187
    ABC method, 162
    Biosphere Reserve category, 172
    First Nations lands, 171
    institutional arrangements, 151–74
    mining, 170
    physical and cultural setting, 160–69
    recommended as IBP, 160
    unsettled land-claims, 170
    village, 160
    wildlife map, 162–63

Aishihik Lake
 national landmark, 170–71
 national wildlife area, 170
Aishihik Lake hydroelectric facility, 160, 170
Alaska, 428
Algonquin to Adirondack corridor, 379
All Terrain Vehicles (ATVs), 304
Allegheny Mountains, 386
Alpine glaciation, 355
alpine lakes, 422
alpine tundra, 160, 422
alvars, 289, 293, 383
American ginseng, 455
American Southwest, 301, 307, 310, 315, 317
 arrival of Spanish, 313
 geological history, 309–10
 hunting and gathering lifestyle, 314
American War of Independence, 221, 454–55
Angles and Saxons, 412
animal migration routes. *See* migratory routes
antelope, 319
anthropology, 16, 19
Apache, 316, 318
Appalachians, 388
applied ecology, 15
applied human ecology, 41
aquatic wildlife habitat. *See* habitat
aquifers, 216–17
archaeological remains, 8, 36
 Bat Cave site, 314
 in the Carpathians, 360–61
 Chiricahua stage artifacts, 314
 Grand River, 221
 Great Sand Dunes area, Colorado, 422
 Lehner Mammoth Kill site, 311–13
 Murray Spring site, 311, 313
 Naco site, 311
 Neolithic agricultural and mining remains, 360
 New Forest, 412, 414
 Paleo-Indian sites, 311–15, 323, 385, 453
 Paleolithic discoveries, 360

San Pedro Riparian National Conservation Area (NCA), 311, 323
 Woodland sites, 221, 385, 453
Archaic or Desert cultures, 314
Area Development Ordinance, 170, 203
Areas of Natural and Scientific Interest (ANSIs), 125, 293–94
Arizona, 301, 303, 309, 315, 317, 319
Arizona Department of Water Resources, 326–27
Arizona University Library, 421
arroyos, 321
ash, 68
aspen, 68, 422
Association of Canadian Universities for Northern Studies, 368
Association of Universities for Research on the Carpathians (proposed), 368
Austria, 274
Austro-Hungarian Empire, 361
Avicennia, 399
avocets, 422

B

Babocomari Creek, 318
Baca Ranch, 422, 428–29
badgers, 422, 453, 455
Bahre, Conrad, *A Legacy of Change,* 318
balsam fir, 335
Banff National Park, 31, 467, 469
 historical mapping, 31, 39
 human/nature interaction, 18
 landscape change, 31
 recreational land use changes, 39–40
BAPPEDA, 245
barrel cactus, 311
Barrows, Harlan, 17
Bartlett, William, 467
basswood, 68, 459
Bastedo, Jamie, 19
Bat Cave site, 314
bats, 354
Battie, James, 317, 320

Bruce Peninsula National Park (1987 to 2006)
  evolution of ecosystem planning, 277–99
  State of the Park report, 297
Bruce Peninsula Park Reserve (near Cabot Head), 100, 146
Bruce Snowmobiling Association Trail, 133, 136, 139
Bruce Trail, 133, 146, 282, 388
  conflict zone, 139
  cultural significance, 136
  recreational role, 139
Brunel Lock and Dam, 344
Bruntland Commission, 36
Buckler's Head, 413
buckthorn, 311
Buffalo, 458
Bukk National Park, Hungary, 354
bullhead, 68, 337
bulrushes, 68
Bureau of Land Management (BLM), 325–27
Burley, 414
burning. See fire
burreed, 68
butterflies, 410, 460

C

Cabot Head, 111, 125
  managed as wildlife reserve, 100, 146
  "sheep backs" at, 103
  significance of, 145
  wave-cut stack at, 108
cacti, 311
Caledonia, 223, 456–57
Caledonia-Cayuga Country, 456–57
  Carolinian Canada plant and animal species, 457
  historic and "ghost" towns, 457
Calf Pasture Point, 60, 93
California Gold Rush, 317
Cambridge, 442, 449
Cambridge-Paris Rail Trail, 451
camels, 313
Cameron Lake, 131, 133

Cameron Lake/Dorcas Bay dune complex, 111–12
Canada Land Company, 221
Canada Land Inventory (CLI), 335
Canada Wildlife Act, 171
Canadian Arctic Resources Committee (CARC), 31
Canadian Donner Foundation, 31
Canadian Heritage River status
  values of, 213–14
  water quality and, 228
Canadian Heritage Rivers, 180, 210
Canadian Heritage Rivers Board, 210–11, 214, 231
Canadian Heritage Rivers Program (CHRP), 210
Canadian International Development Agency (CIDA), 180, 235
Canadian Landmark, 170, 202. See also national landmark
Canadian Landmark designation
  Native people's interests and, 171
Canadian National Railway, 443
Canadian Pacific Railway (CPR), 443
  landscape artists, 467
Canadian Parks and Wilderness Society, 298
Canadian Parks Service, 227. See also Environment Canada, Parks; Parks Canada
Canadian Wildlife Service (CWS), 153, 172
  budget cuts, 204
  co-operative management with private owners, 171
canals, 454
  Erie Canal, 388
  Fairy and Peninsula Lakes, 338, 344
  Grand River, 223
  Welland canal, 459
  Welland feeder canal, 223, 458–59
cane, 311
canoeing, 442, 453
Cape Croker and Saugeen Indian Reserves (Native hunting lands), 129, 131, 139, 280
Cape Croker Indian Reserve, 129
Capercaillee, 360
Capron, Hiram, 453

H

habitat, 8, 110, 117–18, 120, 335–36, 342, 383, 385
   breeding and nursery for fish, 125, 141, 458
   breeding area for waterfowl and terrestrial bird, 356
   breeding habitat for Henslow's sparrow, 125
   cormorant, 70
   critical habitat for birds, 75, 400, 458
   deer, 100, 117, 121, 127, 141, 145, 335, 344
   faunal and floral habitat dependence, 123
   feeding habitat for shorebirds, 70, 75, 92
   fish habitat, 337, 344, 459
   fisher habitat, 123
   grizzly bear, 160
   herptile habitat, 123
   mangroves as, 240
   for migrating birds, 422, 458, 460
   monarch butterflies, 460
   moose, 160
   pike habitat, 123
   staging areas, 36, 263, 460
   trout habitats, 160
   waterfowl, 356, 459
habitat fragmentation, 286
habitat loss, 267
hairy bur marigold, 399
Hamilton, 458
Harp Lake, 346
Hawkesville, 448
hay meadows, 356
heath, 411, 414, 416
heather moor, 409
heavy metals, 356
hemlock, 68
Henslow's sparrow, 125, 453
herring gulls, 70
Hespeler, 449
Hiawatha National Forest (Michigan), 386
hickory, 218
Hidden Valley, 344, 346
Hidden Valley Resort hotel, 339–40

High Bluff Island, 58, 85
   Biotic constraint, 75
   Biotic significance, 71
   critical habitat for birds, 75
   designated Wilderness Area, 89
   double-crested cormorant colony, 70
   faunal diversity, 71
   mature forest on, 75
   recreational and educational potential, 80
   significant (for Abiotic, Biotic, and Cultural), 85
   songbirds, 70
   structural features, 76
   vegetation, 69
Highway 6, 145
   commercial development corridor, 143, 280, 288
   major transportation corridor, 133
Highway 11, 339
Highway 60, 340
Highway 401, 443
   renewed growth in Waterloo-Kitchener-Cambridge, 449
hiking, 78, 82, 133, 288, 304
   Bruce Trail, 133, 136, 139, 146, 282, 388
   Grand River area, 225
   Grand River Basin trails, 452
   Luther Marsh, 442
Hillsdale, 344
hinterland areas, 7, 79, 133, 186, 469
historic sites, 8, 216, 227, 450, 454–55
Historical zones, 91
Hohokam agriculture and irrigation, 315
holokarst, 106, 111
Home Hardware, 447
Hong Kong, 395–96, 469
   government co-operation with WWF, 403
   rapid growth, 394
hooded warbler, 453, 455
Hooker Ranch, 318
Hoover, Herbert, 410
Horican Marsh Natural Wildlife Refuge (Wisconsin), 386
horses, 313
Huachuca Mountains, 325
Hudson River, 388

human ecological approach, 51, 252
human ecology, 16–19
human heritage resources
    interest in protecting, 210
    rivers, 212
human or cultural ecology. *See* human
        ecology
human role in changing the earth, 15, 17,
        283, 297
Hungary, 274, 352, 354–55, 359
Huns, 361
hunting, 139, 152, 160
    Carpathians, 361
    effects on local and migratory bird
            populations, 95
    Government hunting in San Pedro,
            319
    Luther Marsh area, 442
    national park objectives and, 143
    Native people, 129, 131, 171, 280
    Presqu'ile Provincial Park, 78, 80, 82,
            92, 95–96
    Sangre de Cristo Mountains, 428
    territorial parks, 170
    traditional hunting areas, 133
hunting and gathering lifestyle, 314
Huntsville, 338, 340, 344
Hurons, 129
hydroelectric development, 160, 170, 301

I

Illinois, 375, 377, 380
Imperial Eagle, 360
incremental planning, 50
Indian and Northern Affairs Canada, 210
Indiana, 457
indigenous people. *See also* Native people
    land uses and ways of life, 152
Indonesia, 10–11, 237. *See also* Segara
        Anakan area
industrial hinterlands, 469
information systems, 3, 11–12
institutional mosaic, 158–60, 170, 172
institutional types
    matching with ESAs (*See* management
            types)

interactive planning, 51, 364
International Biological Programme
        (IBP), 160, 172, 186, 202
International Migratory Birds
        Convention, 89
International Union for the Conservation
        of Nature (IUCN), 153–54
Inuit, 188
Inuvialuit Land Administration, 188
Inuvialuit settlement (1984), 188
    national parks and, 203
Iowa, 377
Irish, 442, 449, 458
iron, 356
Iron Gate (Danube River), 355
iron wood, 311
Iroquois
    awarded land along Grand for loyalty
            to Britain, 221
    Bruce Peninsula, 129
irrigation, 301, 315

J

jack rabbits, 422
jaguar, 319
Java. *See* Segara Anakan area
Jobe's Woods, 78, 85
    aesthetic values, 82
    Biotic constraint, 73
    Biotic significance, 71
    faunal diversity, 71
    recreational and educational potential,
            82
    terrain sensitivity, 63
    undisturbed mature forest, 71
Johnson, E. Pauline, 455–56
Johnston's Harbour, 117, 125, 127, 143
joint planning or management
        committees, 182
jumping cholla, 311
juniper, 66

P

W

Walker Lake, 346
Wallenstein, 448
warblers, 70
water, 319
    adaptive management approach, 327
    Great Sand Dunes, 421–23, 429
    groundwater, 322, 422
    pollution from sewage, 339, 346
    proposals for mining and export,
        422–23, 428
    submerged streambeds, 105, 380
water conservation, 4, 26, 421–23, 429
    linking with wildlife conservation,
        327
    San Pedro area, 326–27
water diversions, 407
water lily, 68
water purification plants, 338
water quality, 298, 337–38, 340
    binational and federal-provincial
        agreements, 89
    Grand River, 217, 227–28
    lack of information, 346
    San Pedro Riparian National
        Conservation Area (NCA),
        304
Water Resources Plan. *See* Upper San
    Pedro Partnership
waterfowl, 70, 120–21, 141, 335
    hunting, 75, 263, 404
    Mai Po marsh, 397
waterfowl and terrestrial bird breeding
    areas, 92, 125, 356
waterfowl habitat, 31, 335, 459. *See also*
    habitat
waterfowl staging-areas, 36, 160, 263, 400
Waterloo, 449
Waterloo Moraine, 448
Waterloo–Paris Country, 448–49
    forests and woodlots, 448
    moraines, 448
    noteworthy features, 448–49
    settlement, 449
    universities and hi-tech parks, 449
Watson, Homer, 448
wave-cut platforms and stacks, 103, 106,
    108, 111

weasel, 69
weirs, 453, 458
Welland feeder canal, 223, 458–59
Western Carpathians, 354
wetlands, 114, 127, 141, 143, 293, 337,
    342, 346, 422, 457–58
    around Emmett Lake, 125
    Carpathians, 356
    'cienegas,' 320–21
    classification, 120
    Dunnville and Grand River, 218, 225,
        246
    fragmentation, 254
    Long Point, 263
    loss of, 251–52, 254, 286, 320, 324
    Mai Po, 394, 401
    New Forest, 410
    provincially significant, 294
    regionally significant wetlands, 294
    residential development in, 252
    Segara Anakan, 237
White, Gilbert, 17–18
white ash, 457
white-backed woodpecker, 360
white birch, 444
White Carpathians, 354
white cedar, 66, 68
white elm, 459
white-faced ibis, 422
white pine, 68, 444
white spruce, 68, 335
white sucker, 337
white-tailed deer habitat, 335, 344
white willow, 459
whitefish, 120, 160, 287
Whitehorse, 33, 160
whooping crane, 422
Wilcox Playa, 309
Wild and Scenic Rivers Program (U.S.),
    210
wild fires, 320
wild grape, 66
wild turkeys, 442
wilderness, 18, 158, 282
Wilderness Areas Act, 89
wilderness zoning
    Bruce Peninsula National Park, 146
wildlife habitat. *See* habitat